Law FOR THE Psychotherapist

Robert G. Meyer, PH.D.

E. Rhett Landis, M.A.

J. Ray Hays, J.D., PH.D.

W. W. NORTON & COMPANY • *NEW YORK* • *LONDON*

A NORTON PROFESSIONAL BOOK

Published simultaneously in Canada by Penguin Books Canada Ltd.,
2801 John Street, Markham, Ontario L3R 1B4
Printed in the United States of America
First edition

Library of Congress Cataloging-in-Publication Data

Meyer, Robert G.
  Law for the psychotherapist.

  "A Norton professional book."
  Bibliography: p.
  Includes index.
  1. Psychotherapists—Legal status, laws,
etc.—United States. 2. Forensic psychiatry
—United States. 3. Psychotherapy—United
States. I. Landis, E. Rhett, 1959–
II. Hays, J. Ray, 1942–   . III. Title.
[DNLM: 1. Forensic Psychiatry—United States.
2. Jurisprudence—United States. 3. Psycho-
therapy—United States—legislation.
WM 33 AA1 M58L]

ISBN 0-393-70033-X

W. W. Norton & Company, Inc., 500 Fifth Avenue, New York, NY 100110
W. W. Norton & Company Ltd., 37 Great Russell Street, London WC1B 3NU

1 2 3 4 5 6 7 8 9 0

Acknowledgments

I AM INDEBTED to many students and colleagues who helped in the evolution of this book, especially those who directly contributed to my knowledge in the forensic and professional areas: first and foremost, Steven R. Smith, but also Norman Abeles, Curtis Barrett, Philip Johnson, Paul Lipsitt, Fred Pesetsky, Harvey Tilker, Patricia Carpenter, and Peter Mayfield.

—RGM

I gratefully acknowledge the contributions of the staff and residents of the Mental Health Division of the Federal Correctional Institution-Butner, North Carolina, whose varied insights into forensic issues are only feebly articulated here. I am also indebted to my clients "on the streets," whose interactions with various aspects of civil law have been alternately rewarding and exasperating but which they have always faced courageously. Finally, without the tireless support and encouragement of my wife, Dawn, my contribution to this project would have been impossible.

—ERL

We are indebted to Susan E. Barrows of W. W. Norton, whose boundless patience and continuing direction salvaged this project on more than one occasion. We would also like to thank the many colleagues, students, and friends whose support enabled us to persevere. Special thanks are owed to Sandy Hartz and Suzanne Paris for their invaluable logistical assistance.

Contents

Preface

IN SOME SENSE this book may be seen as a survival guide for practicing psychotherapists. Therapists cannot avoid contact with the legal system. Our purpose here is to help them interact with the law in ways that preserve their professional integrity and autonomy and ultimately serve the needs of their clients. The book is structured to provide specific recommendations and guidance where possible, along with examples to illustrate important points.

This book is obviously written *for* psychotherapists, but it is *about* the law and legal issues. Consequently, the organization of Section I corresponds with a number of important legal topics. Historical information and details of legal theory and practice are discussed to the degree necessary to help therapists understand the current state of affairs and to grasp how these issues will affect them. Because the primary audience is psychotherapists there is also a focus on clinical issues that dovetail with the legal topics addressed. That is, each chapter includes information derived from literature in the therapeutic professions that will inform clinicians responding to specific legal challenges or concerns.

Chapter 1 deals with malpractice and professional liability. It differs from the other chapters in this section in that it addresses legal efforts to regulate the practice of psychotherapy directly. Chapter 2 focuses on the legal concept of "insanity" and the question of responsibility, the most consistent interface between criminal law and psychotherapy. Chapter 3 deals with matters of competence to participate in various legal matters, both criminal and civil. As such, it serves as a bridge to the following chapters, which address topics primarily in civil law.

Chapter 4 deals with involuntary civil commitment, a topic which brings into question the ways that therapists have traditionally conceptualized the basis for efforts to help impaired individuals who may not want such intervention. The doctrine of *parens patriae* is a key concept here and may represent the thinking of most therapists. By contrast, the law now favors other rationales for intervening with those who may be seriously disordered. Chapter 5 discusses the problems associated with predictions of dangerousness, a topic closely identified with commitment, but which is becoming important in many other areas of law.

Child custody is the major focus of Chapter 6, though related family law issues such as divorce and adoption are also addressed. Perhaps more than any other area, child custody illustrates the need for close cooperation between lawyers and therapists with a joint dedication to protecting the welfare of clients, in this case children of divorce as well as abused and neglected children. Chapter 7 focuses on civil liability actions for personal injury, an area where therapists increasingly serve as expert witnesses to help courts understand the impact of harmful events.

Chapter 8, the last in this section, is quite different from the others. It provides specific guidance on participating in legal proceedings as an expert witness. This information is aimed not only at forensic specialists and others who frequently testify in court, but also at practicing therapists who must venture into the legal arena only infrequently.

Section II deals with the interface of law and psychotherapy from a different perspective. Rather than conforming to legal topics, these four chapters address broad clinical concerns and then consider the diverse legal issues that may come into play. This section may be viewed as a cross-reference of legal implications of therapeutic and clinical issues, and serves as a counterpoint to Section I. Chapter 9 deals with disorders which may impair reality contact, such as schizophrenia, amnesia, and dissociative disorders. Chapter 10 examines conditions in which a lack of impulse control plays a central role, for example, kleptomania, suicide, and personality disorders. Chapter 11 focuses on biological dysfunctions such as organic brain syndromes, mental retardation, and chronic pain. Finally, Chapter 12 deals with child-related issues such as incest, delinquency, and abuse.

The above comments help to indicate what this book is not. It is not a comprehensive guide to mental health law for lawyers, although many attorneys would find it a helpful starting point in exploring these topics. This also is not a comprehensive guide for therapists. The implications of law for therapists are now so far-reaching and complex that they are beyond the scope of any one book. Our purpose here is to deal with the most pressing and widely applicable concerns in a sensible and pragmatic way. The treatment is eclectic and some selection of information was necessary. What is offered here is only one set of perspectives, while many others could be identified.

A Note About Case Examples

Cases are included to illustrate important clinical or legal themes. The majority of these examples are "real" in the sense that they are derived from actual experiences of the authors. In order to preserve the anonymity of those involved, identifying information has been omitted or altered and many unessential details have been changed. Great care has been taken to protect the confidentiality of clients. Every effort has been made, however, to present the cases as realistically as possible, and to capture the flavor of the therapeutic and legal challenges involved.

Some of the cases are fictional. Although based on clinical experience, they represent a composite of several specific cases and serve to illustrate prototypic problems. Still other cases are borrowed from other published sources. In these instances, full bibliographic references are given. Finally, some of the cases described here do not disguise the identity of those involved. These examples are derived from legal cases which make all relevant information a matter of public record. Because important legal cases are widely reviewed and discussed, the anonymity of the principals is quickly lost; any attempt to disguise these cases would be superfluous and would obscure the ongoing legal process in these areas.

Terminology and Notations

Consistent with the audience for this book, the term "psychotherapist" is used rather broadly, and for our purposes is functionally defined. It is used here to refer to anyone who provides therapy, counseling, assessment, and related services in applied clinical settings, and includes clinical psychologists and psychiatrists, as well as practitioners in psychiatric nursing, clinical social work, educational counseling, and other fields. Often the more convenient "therapist" will suffice, with terms such as "clinician," "mental health professional," and "practitioner" offering some variety but still referring to the same groups. Those with whom psychotherapists work are sometimes referred to as "clients," particularly in psychology and social work. Psychiatrists and nurses are more familiar with "patients." These terms are freely intermixed here. A concerted effort has been made to avoid sexist language.

The text includes numerous legal case citations and references to legal journals, as well as literature in psychology, psychiatry, nursing, and social work. To maintain some uniformity, all references and citations employ the style established by the American Psychological Association. Citations in text include the author's last name followed by the year of publication, and in some cases (extended quotes) the relevant page number. References to law journals are handled in the same way, though this is not the usual practice in legal writings, where footnotes are used for all references. Case citations are given a modified version of this treatment, for example: *Rouse v. Cameron* (1966). For some cases dates are not included in the text, particularly those involving prolonged appeals, countersuits, or other maneuvering, making the filing date or appeal decision seem misleading in relation to the final outcome. Complete bibliographic references are given at the end of the book. In the reference section, cases are listed in their usual legal style (i.e. *Rouse v. Cameron*, 373 F.2d 451 (D.C. Cir., 1966)), since anyone wishing to retrieve original opinions would have to utilize this format.

Incidentally, legal case citations convey a bit of information directly. The name of the plaintiff is given first, the defendant or respondent last. In instances involving appeals, the appellant is usually listed first, even though he or she may have been the defendant in the initial action. The citation above refers to a civil suit, as evidenced by the name of the plaintiff, an individual named Rouse. If the case had involved a criminal proceeding, it might read *People v. Poddar* or *Minnesota v. Andring*. The citation may be read as follows: "The case of Rouse against Cameron, which is documented in the *Federal Reporter*, volume 373, beginning at page 451. This documentation includes the opinion of the District of Columbia Circa Court of Appeals promulgated in 1966."

Lawyers have journals much like those in the therapeutic professions. These include scholarly writings, mostly theoretical, as well as commentary on recent trends and legal decisions. The other major sources of literature in the law are "reporters," publications which simply reproduce the decisions or "opinions" of the many courts in this country. Major reporters include the U.S. (Supreme Court decisions), Federal (U.S. Courts of Appeal), Federal Supplement (U.S. District Courts), and a series of regional reporters subsuming state jurisdictions, including the Atlantic, North Eastern, North Western, Pacific, South Eastern, South Western, and Southern. Some states have their own reporters, though these are not as widely available in law libraries. Specialty reporters focus on decisions throughout the country that deal with specific topics. For example, the *Mental Disability Law Reporter* focuses on issues that are often of interest to psychotherapists, and covers state and federal, civil and criminal law.

INTRODUCTION

Psychotherapy and Justice in America

> In a healthy democracy the majority and the non-conformist depend upon each other, and each supplies a vital component to the whole. Stability is provided by the majority, while vitality flows from the non-conformist. Consequently, the democrat protects the rights of the non-conformist not merely as an act of decency, but more significantly as an imperative for himself and the whole society.
>
> —J. P. Roche, 1956

ULTIMATELY, LAW EXISTS to promote social order and to limit the actions of individuals that might be destructive to that order. While most vertebrate species have a rudimentary social order "built in" in the form of instinctive behaviors, man alone depends so heavily upon a rationally developed system for controlling and organizing behavior. The virtues of rule of law may seem obvious—persons and property must be protected, disputes settled in an orderly and reasonable fashion, institutions for the public good maintained, and so forth. But as the epigraph above indicates, it is also for the collective good that a broad range of individual liberty is maintained. Certainly in American political culture the maxim that "he who governs best governs least" receives at least superficial deference. Any system of laws must strive to balance the wishes of society against the liberty of individuals. Some thinkers outside the law have even suggested that the need for expression of individual differences is a biological imperative (Ardrey, 1970).

For at least three reasons, this balancing act is probably most difficult in areas that involve mental disorder or incapacity. First, persons so affected

1

are likely to engage in behavior beyond the usual bounds set by society — and in very striking and unsettling ways. Second, those who are "impaired" to some degree may be most easily deprived of their liberty or lack the ability to assert their own valid interests against the motives of society. Finally, as practices in totalitarian regimes demonstrate, being different in socially disapproved ways may be wrongly equated with mental disorder, a syllogism that leads to political oppression and demagoguery. In response to these types of problems, the American legal community has developed a complex of statutes and procedures which ideally should reflect both society's political and ethical interests and the burgeoning knowledge and methods of psychotherapy and mental health. Unfortunately, a rapprochement between law and mental health is impeded by a number of fundamental differences in the ways these professionals view the world and their role in society.

When attorneys describe the fundamental source of law, they frequently speak of the Magna Charta, Richard the Lion-Hearted, or Charlemagne — in short, the actions and ideas of politicians. This heritage insures that legal practices tend to focus on issues with important *political* implications. For example, as will be discussed in Chapter 1, legal theorizing about whether confidentiality in psychotherapy should be legally protected has been based upon a cost/benefit analysis as a matter of public policy, rather than on whether the individuals in therapy deserve such protection.

The law is also primarily *procedural*. Fairness is thought to inhere in a set of relatively stable and uniform procedures which afford diverse individuals a nominal degree of equality under the law. To the extent that every person receives the same protections and obligations, the law will be fair, at least over the long run. Consistent with the notion that there are two sides to every story, our legal system is explicitly *adversarial*, meaning that most procedures are required to have two opposing sides with the explicit purpose of defeating one another. It is assumed that each side, acting out of self-interest, will do the best possible job of elucidating different facets of the case, and that courts can extract some meaningful middle ground from the controversy. Although the procedural and adversarial nature of American law sometimes produces results which seem unjust, the system generally sees failures in specific cases as less important than preserving these two overarching principles. In this vein, Justice Oliver Wendell Holmes, Jr., once observed that " . . . this is a court of Law, young man, not a court of justice."

Finally, the law generally is based upon an assumption, from the broad Judeo-Christian tradition, that human behavior is guided by *free will*. With few exceptions, behavior is seen as a voluntary product of the moral reasoning of the actor. This concept is central to the idea of responsibility, without which law tends to become meaningless.

By contrast, psychotherapy (used here in the broad sense to include all disciplines that study human behavior, including psychology, psychiatry, and some branches of nursing and social work) tends to view behavior as a product of causal relationships rather than a wholly voluntary production of the individual. Understanding of the processes that *determine* behavior is sought to promote changes in behavior, particularly the actions of people who may experience difficulty with legal and other social institutions.

Therapy also tends to be *conciliatory* and to focus on resolving conflicts and problems while identifying ways to smooth interpersonal relationships through mutual aid or even sacrifice. Psychotherapy is marked by tremendous diversity in theories and procedures, such that different therapists hold very different ideas and clients are dealt with in many different ways. In part this reflects psychotherapy's focus on the *qualitative* nature of the therapy process as opposed to specific procedures. It is widely believed that "nonspecific" factors inherent in the personal relationship between patient and therapist may be as important as the actual methods employed.

Psychotherapy tends to be conceptually *idiographic*. Although as a field psychotherapy is informed by social psychology, sociology, and other disciplines that emphasize social and political behavior, most therapists view their commitment to their clients as so imperative that attention to issues in these broader contexts may receive little attention. The agenda in classical therapy is usually determined by the values and interests of the client, not by public policies or interests.

Because of the clash of perspectives between psychotherapy and the law, mental health professionals often find their interactions with legal systems confusing, frustrating, or even frightening. Given the broad range of conditions that are now addressed by the law, such interactions are inevitable for practicing professionals, particularly psychotherapists. This book aims to summarize and explain mental health law and the legal system in general so as to reduce confusion, alleviate frustration, and allay fear on the part of psychotherapists, regardless of their professional training. A basic goal is to promote effective responses to the most frequent and significant legal challenges and pitfalls that confront the therapist. A second purpose is to point out areas where legal practice could be better informed by psychology and psychiatry and perhaps to motivate members of these disciplines to work for changes in policy that would reflect what is now known about human behavior and aberrance.

There are other reasons for therapists to understand key legal concepts

and procedures. Perhaps the most important is that, despite their differences, law and psychotherapy have something important in common: they
both aim to change behavior in beneficial ways. In fact, the differences cited
above in the stereotypic, and therefore partly inaccurate, characterizations
of these two orientations may be less significant than supposed. Further,
psychotherapy must inevitably take place within a broader social, political,
and legal context. While many therapists are philosophically inclined to
resist these pressures, they do exist. Some thinkers have argued for more
explicit recognition of the role of social factors in the outcome of psychotherapy (see, for example, Strupp and Hadley, 1977). More cynical views
have even suggested that traditional therapy is a procedure explicitly used to
maintain the status quo and enforce political conventionality in areas that
the law has difficulty penetrating (see Szasz, 1977; Lazarus, 1984).

Whether their purposes are viewed as working for good or ill, it is likely
that law and psychotherapy will need to work more closely in the future. It is
our belief that closer cooperation will lead to improvements in the thinking
and practice of both fields, and will aid those whom these professions are
supposed to serve.

A Brief Introduction to the American Legal System

While it is impossible to summarize the myriad procedures and subsys-
tems that make up the American legal community, there are a few important
points which may be new to many therapists.

Most will remember from high school civics the concept of division of
powers among the legislative, judicial, and executive branches of the federal
government. Most states follow this general plan, so that law may be described or differentiated according to how it is promulgated. *Statutory* law
refers to provisions written by legislatures or the Congress. Any statute
passed by a legislative body is generally binding upon everyone in that
jurisdiction. For example, a state legislature may pass a law governing licensure of a professional group; members of that profession in the given state
are then regulated as described in the state law.

The other important branch of law is *case law*. Returning to civics, it is
the job of courts to interpret laws written by legislatures or the Congress. As
the process of clarifying the statutes proceeds, court decisions effectively
become part of the law. If a court determines that the state licensing law was
not meant to allow licensure by reciprocity, then that determination has the
same effect as if the legislature had specifically included it. Of course, the
legislature could then choose to modify the law to allow reciprocity, and that
would be within its purview.

Throughout this book we will refer to both statutes and cases as establishing a variety of legal limits and responsibilities for therapists. While the distinction is not always important, it may be in some cases. Statutory law is made by large groups of elected representatives; case law is made by individual judges or small judicial panels. In some respects case law may be less stable over the short term; when cases are appealed they may well be reversed. Over the long haul, case law may actually be more stable. While political fads and elected officials change, courts strongly value the concept of *precedent*. In order to minimize the adverse effects of changing legal standards, courts try to rely on the reasoning of earlier decisions when possible and to leave well-settled ideas undisturbed, a doctrine known as *stare decisis*.

For this reason important conflicts between law and psychotherapy may be better resolved by acting at the legislative level where political pressure may be used to motivate appropriate change. Once made, case law is changed primarily by appeals and the appeals process is unpredictable. Legislatures may always pass new laws which limit the impact of case law by explicitly resolving relevant issues.

Constitutional law will occasionally be of interest here. Remember that the Constitution stands above all legislated laws. Courts are sometimes asked to decide if statutory or case law conflicts with the higher authority of the Constitution; if so, then those provisions must give way. This type of law is primarily the province of the United States Supreme Court. Because language in the Constitution, particularly the Bill of Rights, is so broad and abstract a great many issues can be argued in this way. For example, state commitment laws in Florida were challenged on the basis that they conflicted with the first and eighth amendment rights of patients (*O'Connor v. Donaldson,* see Chapter 4).

This case also brings up the distinction between federal and state laws. Many issues of interest to psychotherapists are governed by state law, such as professional licensing, civil commitment, and most criminal matters. One side effect of these state provisions is a lack of uniformity. Some areas of law are a crazy quilt of imcompatible legislation, while others, influenced by broader, nationwide trends, may be quite consistent. Federal laws are less frequently important for therapists, except for federal criminal law (which governs acts on federal property) and some federal attempts to bridge gaps in state laws governing child custody and other issues. Obviously, these apply to everyone in the United States.

Criminal codes and courts deal with the prosecution of persons accused of violations of the law. Criminal acts are those that are specifically prohibited, and in general behavior which is not specifically mentioned in criminal code is not prohibited. Many people believe that the term "criminal" means serious; it does not. Misdemeanors are nonserious criminal acts, while felonies are those that can lead to more extreme penalties. Criminal law can be conceptualized as prohibiting acts that are so problematic that they represent an affront or threat to society.

By comparison, civil law deals with private rights and remedies. The conflicts are among citizens rather than between the state and one or more persons. Major areas of civil law include torts (civil liability), contract law, and family law. Most of the topics addressed in this book pertain to civil law. It is important to note that the distinctions between statutory and case law, and between federal and state law, cut across the criminal/civil distinction. These classifications occur in all possible combinations.

American Courts and Jurisdiction

The American legal system is very complex, composed of many different types of courts in the 50 states and at the federal level. Any given legal transaction may be governed solely by state law, or solely by federal law, or perhaps by both. The federal and state court systems are composed of various trial and appellate courts.

Jurisdiction, a term which describes a court's power to hear and decide a case, is defined by statute or Constitutional provision. There are several types of jurisdiction, the most important of which include original jurisdiction, appellate jurisdiction, and subject matter jurisdiction. Original jurisdiction implies that a court has authority to hear and decide a case, usually when first filed. Appellate jurisdiction means that a court has authority to review, and possibly second guess, a case already decided in an inferior court. Appellate review is generally discretionary; while one may always appeal lower court decisions, the appellate court may refuse review. Subject matter jurisdiction means that the court is qualified by statute or the Constitution to hear a particular type of case. For example, state family courts have jurisdiction in divorces, delinquency matters, and probate proceedings, while the criminal courts do not.

When therapists will be involved in legal proceedings, understanding jurisdictional matters may be very helpful in gaining insight into the nature of the proceeding and how to cope with it. Unfortunately, state court systems differ greatly. Generally, there are justice and trial courts, courts of appeal, and one highest court. Justice courts have limited original jurisdiction and usually process minor civil and criminal cases, such as routine traffic violations or small personal claims. Trial courts are a state's general court of original jurisdiction. Most serious matters are heard here. Many states find it useful to have specialized trial courts to hear only civil or criminal matters. Some go further to establish subject matter jurisdiction for courts that will serve highly specialized roles. Appellate courts primarily serve as discretionary courts of review with very limited original jurisdiction, while all appeals would ultimately be channeled to a state supreme court of some type.

The general courts of original jurisdiction in the federal system are district courts. Each state may have one or more districts, and large districts even have more than one division. Each district is administered by a federal magistrate and a federal district court judge. Appeals from federal courts are handled by 14 circuit courts of appeal, plus one for the District of Columbia. These courts may review decisions by district courts within their jurisdiction, review orders of many administrative agencies, and issue some original writs in appropriate cases. The United States Supreme Court has limited original jurisdiction and may exercise appellate jurisdiction over district and circuit courts and the highest courts in each state. That is, the course of appeal from a state supreme court would be directly to the U.S. Supreme Court. Appellate jurisdiction may be activated either by appeal or by a *writ of certiorari*.

The effect of appeals may seem to be straightforward: if dissatisfied with a lower court ruling, appeal to a higher one. In practice, the legal maneuvering is much more complicated. Often appeals merely lead to orders that a court of original jurisdiction hold a new trial, reconsider some matter under new guidelines, or refrain from some action. Also, when appeals under one rationale no longer seem likely to succeed, it is sometimes possible to start with new appeals at a lower level. An example would be asserting that new evidence had come to light that had not been available in an earlier proceeding. Thus, many cases weave a tangled web through a torturous process of appeals. Very important, precedent-setting cases often have a rich history all their own.

While the preceding discussion of legal matters and systems is vastly oversimplified, it does provide a toehold for understanding some of the issues that will be addressed throughout this book. Many of these issues present important challenges for psychotherapists from various disciplines. We hope that the material to come will help therapists to respond to these challenges as opportunities to interact productively with the legal system.

The Psychotherapist in the Office and in Court

CHAPTER 1

Malpractice and Professional Liability

> If one day you are served with a summons and complaint alleging professional misconduct or substandard service, expect to read a laundry list of horrible things about yourself since lawyers will frequently cite every possible cause of action they can scare up.
>
> —Cohen, 1987, p. 261

WHILE CRIMINAL LAW deals with wrongs done to society at large, civil law serves to redress injuries and wrongs done to individuals. In a sense, the potential for civil liability protects individual members of society from reckless, negligent, and sometimes even intentional misconduct of others. It does so by demonstrating that bad behavior will lead to aversive judgments. Psychotherapists, of course, believe that their role is to help others and do not perceive that anyone in society should need to be protected from them. From this perspective, the possibility of civil law suits in the course of psychotherapeutic practice seems difficult to fathom, if not outright unfair. From the perspective of the legal system and disgruntled consumers, however, therapists, like any other identifiable group, sometimes behave badly and should be held accountable.

Malpractice suits, the largest class of legal actions against all of the helping professions, have increased exponentially since the mid-1960s. It has been widely reported that 90 percent of all malpractice suits ever filed in the U.S. have taken place in the last 20 years. Physicians in medical specialties have been hardest hit, with the number of suits and large monetary awards making professional liability insurance almost impossible to obtain in cer-

11

tain high-risk specialties. By comparison, psychotherapists are at relatively low risk for malpractice litigation. The American Psychological Association's malpractice insurance program, clearly one of largest providers for clinical psychologists, processed an average of less than 100 claims per year in the 10-year period ending in 1986 (Fulero, 1987). Psychiatrists account for as little as three-tenths of one percent of all claims filed against physicians (Slawson & Guggenheim, 1984), and in 1980 less than one percent of all psychiatrists covered by the American Psychiatric Association's Professional Liability Program were sued. It is generally believed that rates are even lower for psychiatric social workers, nurses, and other psychotherapeutic professionals.

While the major therapeutic professions as a whole are rarely affected by malpractice or other professional liability actions, there is a clear trend toward increasing litigation. Also, the effect of lawsuits on the practice of the unfortunate professionals who are affected cannot be measured in probabilities or dollars. Even suits with no merit may have catastrophic effects on a therapist's professional esteem and standing, not to mention personal life and financial stability. Practicing therapists are understandably concerned about what they may be sued for, under what conditions, and what methods they might reasonably employ to prevent these happenings. This chapter aims to explain briefly the legal theories that underlie professional liability and then to review a number of areas where therapists have been sued in the past. There will be a greater focus on areas which affect the large majority of working psychotherapists, with lesser emphasis on matters of interest only to those in administrative, teaching, or other special roles. Each area of potential liability will be accompanied by pragmatic suggestions that should help therapists practice so as to avoid legal entanglements.

This area of mental health law is particularly problematic for several reasons. Psychotherapists often react to the very concept of professional liability as if the legal system were mounting a systematic, *ad hominem* attack on the motives or qualifications of their professions. In reality, as noted above, the practices of very few therapists are actually "attacked" in this way, and in a substantial proportion of cases the censure may be deserved. To the extent that unscrupulous individuals are discovered and punished for bad practice, the civil lawsuit may help protect the public and bolster the integrity of psychotherapeutic professions. Still, there are key areas where the actions of civil courts seem to be at odds with professional practice, contrary to the welfare of clients/patients, or counterproductive for society. It is important that therapists understand these areas of liability so that they can advocate for effective changes through legislation.

THE LAW OF TORTS

A tort is a wrongful action which harms another in some legally recognized way, such as physical injury, monetary loss, emotional trauma, or damage to reputation, to name a few. The law requires that all citizens behave in a responsible fashion that will prevent these kinds of harm to others; behavior which falls short of this acceptable minimum creates a tort if it leads to harm. The injured party may ask the courts to impose liability to recompense the injury. As an example, someone who stores flammable liquids in unsafe containers leading to a fire or explosion could be held responsible for loss of property, physical injuries, or emotional trauma if the blaze were to extend to a neighbor's home. The test is generally whether a reasonable and prudent person would take similar action. There would generally be no liability if the fire did not affect anyone else's property or person, if other factors actually produced the injuries, or if the behavior was within the bounds of common sense and conduct.

There are two broad categories of torts—unintentional and intentional. Unintentional torts arise out of the concept of *negligence*, which refers to reckless or careless failure to take reasonable and prudent measures to ensure that others are not harmed by one's actions. In the example above, storing gasoline in unsafe containers would reflect a degree of carelessness and lack of regard for safety that would lead to liability. Intentional torts obviously refer to voluntary actions that aim to produce injury. Battery is a clear example; striking another person is intended to do some harm.

Malpractice is a special case of negligence. While we all have a basic duty to exercise reasonable care to safeguard others, professionals have a special obligation to adhere to a higher standard in the course of their work. That standard is determined by the usual or basic levels of knowledge, skill, and expertise utilized by others in the same profession. Malpractice is the formal term applied to professional actions that do not comport with the conduct of reasonable and prudent practitioners in a given field. If malpractice results in harm, then the negligent practitioner may be held liable for damages.

While most professional liability claims arise under the law of unintentional torts (malpractice), there are suits argued under the theory of intentional torts, and a small minority of cases involve theories other than tort liability. These other theories of liability will be addressed later with reference to specific causes of action. It is often important to draw a distinction between malpractice proper and novel theories of litigation that may expand therapist liability in unforseen ways.

LITIGATION IN CIVIL SUITS

In civil law the complaining party is called the plaintiff, while the person responding to the lawsuit is called the defendant. It is important to remember that civil actions are controversies among individuals; the plaintiff is merely an individual or group, not the government. It is the plaintiff's responsibility to demonstrate a valid cause of action or basis for the lawsuit when it is filed; otherwise the court will refuse to hear the case. Even if a trial is set, the plaintiff initially carries the *persuasion burden*. This means that at the outset the plaintiff must make a *prima facie* showing that malpractice has taken place; otherwise the case will be dismissed with no defense necessary. If the persuasion burden is met, then the defendant presents his or her side of the case, hoping to rebut the allegations. The judge or jury must then weigh all the evidence. The case is decided by preponderance of the evidence, meaning that whichever side has the slightly stronger case will win.

As with most types of lawsuits, the majority — 85 to 90 percent — of malpractice and other professional liability claims are settled out of court (Slawson & Guggenheim, 1984). Settlement does not in any formal way imply culpability on the part of the defendant. If there is no settlement and the case is dismissed in hearings or after the plaintiff's presentations at trial, then the defendant "wins" from the legal point of view. In reality there are many hidden costs in being sued for malpractice, and it is unlikely that any successful defendants feel that they have really won anything. If the court finds for the plaintiff, then there is the issue of *relief* from injuries. The simplest type of relief is the *injunction*, which is an order from the court demanding that the practitioner cease a harmful action. For example, a patient who sues for wrongful commitment might win an injunction barring a therapist from keeping him confined to a hospital.

The term "damages" is used to denote financial awards made by the court for relief from injuries. Similar in effect to an injunction, *nominal damages* merely affirm the plaintiff's complaint but with essentially no monetary compensation. These outcomes usually indicate that any injury to the plaintiff was minimal or that the therapist's conduct was only technically inappropriate. *Compensatory damages* refer to an effort to place a monetary value on injuries done to the plaintiff and then to require the defendant to pay this amount. Traditionally, compensation focused on areas where documentation was relatively easy, such as lost earnings, but courts are increasingly willing to place a value on "pain and suffering" and other intangibles. *Punitive damages* are rarely awarded. Only when the professional's conduct is especially reprehensible do the courts impose these additional penalties above compensation. Punitive damages are intended to deter similar conduct in the future, both by the defendant and by other practitioners.

ELEMENTS OF MALPRACTICE

What must the plaintiff prove to carry his burden? There are four basic elements to the legal test of malpractice. First, the injured party must demonstrate that the professional owed a *duty* of care to the plaintiff. This is usually a matter of showing that a professional relationship existed, with the duty arising automatically out of that relationship. The duty is often discussed in terms of standards of care, and is usually defined by the courts as reasonable professional practices followed by others in the same discipline and either considered standard practice or at least accepted by a significant minority of other professionals.

The second element concerns a *breach* of the duty defined above. The practitioner must have failed in some way to live up to the demands of acceptable practice. The breach of duty may involve overt actions, such as giving the wrong treatment, or may arise from omissions, such as failure to take precautions against suicide. In any event, the court will look to other practitioners or to codes of professional conduct to see if the therapist breached responsibility to the patient. Professional ethical guidelines, though not part of statutory law, may become legally binding on therapists for two reasons: (1) They may be directly relevant to determining professional duty, since they are readily introduced as standards against which clinical practice can be measured. (2) They are indirectly influential because they guide the thinking of others in the same field who will be called to testify regarding customary practices.

It is important to note that simply making incorrect decisions is not a breach of duty. The courts recognize that people make mistakes; even highly competent and dedicated professionals make errors that work ill for those in their care. Individual therapists are not required to exercise consummate skill or to possess total knowledge of their field, only to have and utilize the skills and knowledge common to average practitioners in that specialty. Malpractice arises when therapists lack expertise or knowledge widely held in their profession or when they possess these assets but failed to exercise them.

In malpractice, this departure from professional conduct must lead to a demonstrable *injury* to the plaintiff, the third element. It is not sufficient to show that the practitioner simply made a mistake or practiced in a way that could have led to harm; the specific injuries that resulted must be fully desribed and substantiated for the court. Any injuries not specifically presented at trial cannot be considered. In areas such as medical malpractice the injuries may be quite tangible; however, in the practice of psychotherapy injuries are often "psychic" and involve real but less tangible emotional distress.

Finally, the fourth component of malpractice involves a showing that the practitioner's negligence was the *cause* of the injury. If the plaintiff's problems would have arisen even without the negligence, then there is generally no liability. For example, a patient with Alzheimer's disease will definitely suffer progressive brain damage and psychological impairment. It is unlikely that incorrect diagnosis or treatment would make much difference in the course of the illness, so it might not be possible to demonstrate that malpractice was the "cause" of any injuries.

MALPRACTICE AND PSYCHOTHERAPISTS

The preceding discussion on the elements of malpractice suggests a variety of reasons why claims against therapists are relatively rare. The most obvious is that it may be difficult to establish a standard of care. Though ethical codes describe abstract principles of responsibility, these are often difficult to translate into concrete actions that should or should not be taken. By nature, the issues that bring people into therapy are somewhat idiosyncratic and require that individual differences be taken into account. Hence, there are rarely established, recognized practices for dealing with all clients, or even for all those with similar difficulties. This makes it difficult to establish that a therapist failed to act reasonably. The difficulty is increased by the broad range of theories regarding psychological problems. Courts recognize that practices employed by a minority of therapists may be accepted as "standard" practice within a particular school of thought. In the absence of a clear mainstream perspective on mental health issues, the courts cannot equate nonstandard care with substandard care.

Individuals who are dissatisfied with their therapists may be reluctant to bring a suit against them because of the public nature of the proceedings. Suing the therapist will inevitably make all of the very private and sensitive issues involved public knowledge, an experience which may be more distasteful than simply accepting bad professional conduct. A related issue arises from the nature of the therapy relationship. Since most people are emotionally attached to their therapists, they may not recognize that they are being badly treated or may rationalize poor practice as an attempt to help them.

If a case is brought, the plaintiff may have difficulty persuading a jury that he was injured. Though "psychic" injuries and distress may be quite legitimate, they are difficult to demonstrate to a jury. Broken bones may be documented by x-rays, but often the only evidence of emotional pain may be the word of the plaintiff, who may or may not seem credible. Also, clients usually have experienced some significant difficulty—perhaps the difficulty which led them to seek therapy in the first place. It may be easy for the defense to align any current problems with the preexisting condition, rather than with the professional conduct of the therapist. This possibility is enhanced by the fact that causal models for psychological problems are quite variable.

Due to the prevalence and potential costliness of malpractice and other professional liability litigation, most therapists carry professional liability insurance, provided through major sanctioning bodies, such as the American Psychological and American Psychiatric Associations, as well as through private insurers. This coverage often provides several important services to the practitioner. First, the liability carrier usually assumes responsibility for legal services; it is in the interest of the carrier to avoid major liability by employing well-qualified and experienced attorneys to represent their clients. Second, if the case proceeds to trial and the plaintiff wins, the insurance company normally pays the damages. There are limitations to this scheme, however. If the carrier wishes to settle out of court, the therapist is usually required to abide by this decision. Also, suits alleging sexual improprieties may not be covered, though the majority of carriers will provide legal expenses if the therapist denies the allegations. Admission of the allegations relieves the insurance company of any responsibility.

Most therapists who receive notification that they are being sued are probably quite shocked, and a degree of disequilibrium is not surprising. Most respond in one of three ways. These response styles illustrate a number of important points about malpractice and related litigation.

The first group manifests the "lawsuit denial syndrome." These are practitioners who are so entrenched in psychodynamic formulations that they cannot respond in a pragmatic way to the real problem at hand. In lawsuit denial, the complaint is rationalized as a fascinating clinical phenomenon. The therapist becomes mired in endless (and unproductive) speculation about unresolved, transference-related explanations for the client's "aggressive" behavior, and is unable to accept the anxiety associated with recognizing the suit as anything more than a derivative of the client's unresolved primal conflicts and fixations. Prone to act out the denial by contacting the client/patient to insist that he recognize the immature and neurotic reasons for such hostility and to "work through" these issues, the therapist usually compromises her own legal position. Also, the protracted denial prevents prompt consultation with an attorney, who could see the matter more clearly. In extreme cases, the therapist may even rationalize earnest efforts to resolve the complaint as a sign of the civil law's systemic neurosis.

A very different group promptly forgets anything they knew about the subtleties of human behavior and adopts an "aversive de-allegation procedure." Predominantly behaviorist in orientation, these therapists attempt to eliminate undesirable suit-filing behavior by exposing the client to as many aversive stimuli as possible. Consistent with the conditioning principle of temporal contiguity, prompt filing of countersuits for defamation of character or barratry is common. The result is that the client's behavior is shaped such that he retains ever larger law firms, who effectively expand the grounds for liability. This escalation is also promoted by the therapist's refusal to reinforce "bad" client behavior by considering a modest out-of-court settlement to be paid by the insurance carrier. When the carrier's attorneys subsequently insist that the therapist go along or go it alone, the affected therapist may generalize the aversive conditioning by complaining to the local bar association or suing the lawyers for malpractice (symptom substitution?). These therapists are generally successful in making things aversive for all concerned (including themselves), but may be less effective in preserving their reputations as the accusations and counteraccusations fly.

Some more existentially oriented clinicians adopt an approach which might be described as "fatalistic pseudo-realism." Believing that therapists are exploited and persecuted for a variety of social problems not of their making, these clinicians view themselves as tragic heroes trapped in Kafkaesque circumstances beyond their control. Since they expect to be crushed under the heels of the bourgeois legal system no matter what they have or have not done, efforts at mounting a defense are deemed futile. They merely go through the motions of working with their attorneys while wondering what it all means.

While the above descriptions are obviously caricatures, they point out a number of important misconceptions and self-defeating reactions that can plague therapists confronted with allegations of professional misconduct. They also include a number of grains of truth. First, the truths:

(1) Clients do sometimes bring lawsuits for highly idiosyncratic, if not pathological, reasons.
(2) Some clients may simply be litigious and will back down when firm limits are set by the therapist-attorney team.
(3) Bad things sometimes happen to good people. Even very skilled and dedicated therapists can and have been sued. Sometimes they are even found negligent.

Now, for the misconceptions:

(1) Most lawsuits are brought for pathological motives and are not to be taken seriously. The reality: While it is impossible to know how many therapy-related suits are justified, it is clear that many are, as will be discussed below. Also, unless the complaint is patently false, the courts will take it seriously and so should the therapist.

(2) Most cases will be resolved by quick, aggressive action. The reality: Hostile responses in the form of countersuits are usually self-defeating, since they make the therapist look desperate. They also increase legal fees. As for taking quick action, timely consultation with counsel is wise, but plan to be in for the long haul. Cases that go to trial take between three and four years, longer in groundbreaking areas.

(3) Getting sued is a fact of life, and if one is sued it will be disastrous. The reality: There are strategies to reduce the likelihood of being sued, suits against therapists are relatively rare anyway, and even when suits are filed they are often settled discreetly without a trial. Studies indicate that even cases that proceed to trial are generally won by therapists (Slawson & Guggenheim, 1984).

Following are a list of generic suggestions to cope with the threat or reality of malpractice litigation. Issues tied to specific areas of practice and liability will be addressed later in relation to detailed discussion of those types of malpractice and professional misconduct.

(1) Keep accurate, up-to-date records in straightforward language. When problems or conflicts arise with a given client, describe these forthrightly, along with your reasons for the actions taken. Civil actions often turn on intricacies of timing and behavior that are difficult or impossible to recall accurately without notes. Good documentation will enable you to show what you did when, and why.

(2) Maintain professional liability insurance. Pay the premiums, keep all paperwork up-to-date, and know how to contact your carrier in an emergency. Periodically review the nature of your coverage and note any limitations.

(3) If you receive notification that you are being sued, contact the carrier immediately so that its legal advisors can assist you in responding to the initial round of legal maneuvering.

(4) In almost all cases the insurance company will provide an attorney. Evaluate this person's experience and knowledge in the area of professional liability to be certain that she can effectively represent you. Insurance companies do not like to lose money through suits, so they normally employ well-qualified counsel. If not, you must be prepared to hire additional representation.

(5) Discuss your situation with no one unless instructed to do so by counsel. This injunction includes the client and his or her family, any and all acquaintances, and coworkers not involved in the case. It is appropriate to seek support from colleagues, but be certain to confine the consultation to support, without identifying the patient in any way or sharing specifics of the case that could come back to haunt you.

(6) Expect to settle out of court, even if you feel strongly that your actions have been exemplary. Because insurance companies want to minimize legal expenses and therapists want to avoid damage to professional reputation, it is often worthwhile to settle complaints for modest sums, even if they have little merit. While this practice may seem like extortion, it is the rule in all areas of civil liability.

(7) If no settlement is reached within a reasonable period, engage in constructive self-criticism. While it is difficult to admit to shortcomings or outright failures, it is more costly to have these revealed in a public forum such as a civil court.

(8) If settlement still seems out of the question, be prepared for a long seige. As mentioned earlier, litigation may take years, even without appeals.

(9) Keep a low profile. Any actions which draw attention to your practice or practices may be turned against you at trial. Maintain strict silence on the complaints against you. Never respond to the client's attorney in speech or writing without the aid of counsel, and keep informed of the status of the case.

CAUSES OF MALPRACTICE ACTIONS

Psychotherapists generally share a certain sense of identity, take pride in their work, and view themselves as making an important contribution to society. Because most would never consider practicing in a less than conscientious manner, it is difficult to see that a lawsuit is sometimes a valid course of action for an aggrieved client. Rather, there may be an unspoken consensus that suits are usually unfair efforts to second-guess dedicated practitioners or are at best ineffective ways to resolve unfortunate situations where no one was really at fault. Against this understandable bias it is important to remember that a respectable number of cases involve conduct which is clearly unethical and which draws censure from professional boards as well as the civil courts. Some of the precedent-setting cases discussed later in this chapter will illustrate reprehensible actions on the part of licensed practitioners.

A recent analysis of malpractice claims filed with the American Psychological Association's Insurance Trust makes this point clearly. Table 1.1 summarizes these data, collected from 1976 to 1986, on a nationwide basis. Causes of action can be loosely ordered along a continuum from most to least overt forms of malpractice. Grounds such as sexual impropriety and improper fee collection procedures seem to involve more active, even willful misconduct, while other causes such as failure to warn or inadequate diagnosis seem to involve mitigating factors such as irresolvable value conflicts and difficult clinical challenges.

Scrutiny of Table 1.1 reveals that sexual impropriety, perhaps the most overt type of misconduct, is also the most frequent cause of action. Countersuits due to improper fee collection are just as prevalent as suits for inadequate diagnosis. Finally, the establishment of a "duty to warn" ten years ago (see "failure to warn" and *Tarasoff* Liability section later in this chapter) was viewed as a catastrophe for therapists, but has been the source of a miniscule number of claims. While "clinical" sources of liability, includ-

TABLE 1.1
Causes of Professional Liability Actions
Against Psychologists, 1976–1986

Rank	Cause	% *
1.	Sexual impropriety	22.5
2.	Incorrect treatment	18.5
3.	Loss from evaluation	11.8
4.	Death of client	10.5
5.	Breach of confidence/privacy	8.5
6.	Failure/incorrect diagnosis	7.2
7.	Countersuits from fee collection	7.2
8.	Defamation, libel, slander	5.3
9.	Violation of civil rights	3.6
10.	Bodily injury	3.0
11.	Assault and battery	1.3
12.	"Failure to warn"	0.6
		100.0

*Corrected for missing values. Adapted from Fulero, 1987.

ing incorrect treatment, loss from evaluation, and inadequate supervision (of suicidal clients), are well-represented, there are also many causes that are easily avoided.

These results properly apply only to licensed psychologists covered by the APA policy, but they are probably representative of claims in general. Reports of liability patterns for psychiatrists are quite similar (*Psychiatric News*, 1983), with sexual misconduct accounting for a disproportionate number of claims (Gartrell et al., 1986) and issues such as inadequate diagnosis and client suicide representing secondary, but significant, areas of liability.

Although it has been assumed that psychiatrists' dual role as psychotherapist and physician would greatly expand their liability, results of nationwide claims analysis indicate otherwise (Slawson & Guggenheim, 1984). These data are difficult to interpret due to peculiarities in classification; nevertheless, it appears that liability for injuries due to physician-specific functions, such as inadequate physical exams and complications from medical and surgical procedures, account for as little as 8.1 percent of the injuries which occurred. Use of medications was an issue in 16.1% of cases, although the majority of these were subsumed under inadequate supervision (suicides with prescribed medications), rather than under medical complications due to side effects. It has been speculated that ECT represents a high-risk procedure in terms of liability, but it accounted for only 6% of all claims and was associated with the smallest settlements (averaging less than $4,000).

In the following section, we will review a number of specific causes of malpractice and other liability actions. It is important to note that a given type of negligence could be argued under one of several different theories or under several at once. For example, a negligently conducted evaluation could be argued as loss from evaluation or as defamation. For the sake of clarity, closely related issues will be lumped together and addressed within a broader context. Each specific issue will, where possible, contain specific recommendations to avoid liability. Though "*Tarasoff*" cases account for a very small number of claims, this topic will be discussed in detail due to the inordinate interest the area has received.

Sexual Impropriety

> . . . . the defendant, a psychiatrist, treated the lady for an "anxiety state." The evidence states "transference" took place and she fell deeply in love with him. He took up a social contact with her and took her out to tea and dinner. This, the judge was told, further aroused . . . her feelings toward the doctor,

and her condition deteriorated. The evidence given was that social contact between [therapist] and patient was contrary to normal and approved practice. Mr. Justice Barry held that the doctor, although acting in good faith, was negligent. (Judd, Judd, & Burrows, 1986)

Would that tea and dinner were all the extracurricular contact taking place between therapists and their clients! Unfortunately, research indicates that over 2,000 practicing therapists have engaged in sexual intimacies with their patients, and that the vast majority of these are repeat offenders (see Bouhoutsos, 1984; Gartrell et al., 1986; Holroyd & Brodsky, 1977). This behavior persists despite clear proscriptions by the major therapeutic professions. The American Psychological Association's *Ethical Standards for Psychologists*, principle 6 (a), states flatly: "Sexual intimacies with clients are unethical." Similar wording is found in codes for psychiatrists and social workers (APA, 1985; NASW, 1980).

Recently, Gartrell et al. (1986) conducted a nationwide survey of psychiatrists and reported that 6.4 percent of their respondents acknowledged sexual contact with their own patients. Ninety percent of the offenders were male, and 95 percent of the contacts involved heterosexual activities. Most of the contacts began during therapy or within six months of termination. These findings are consistent with large-scale surveys of psychologists. For example, Holroyd and Brodsky (1977) reported that 5.5 percent of male and 0.6 percent of female psychologists acknowledged sexual intercourse with clients, while an additional 2.6 percent and 0.3 percent, respectively, began sexual relationships with former clients within three months of termination. Bouhoutsos et al. (1983) reported that 4.8 percent of male and 0.8 percent of female psychologists in California had engaged in sexual misconduct, and Pope, Levenson, and Schover (1979) found that 7 percent of their sample made similar admissions.

What motivates professionals to engage in sexual liaisons forbidden by ethical guidelines? In the Gartrell et al. study, three-quarters of the offenders reported that the encounters were motivated by "love" or "pleasure," while one-fifth said that they were intended to "enhance the patient's self-esteem and/or to provide a restitutive emotional experience." The majority believed that the clients came away with good feelings about the intimate relationship.

These rationalizations contrast sharply with other data from the same study. Of psychiatrists who had been in therapy themselves and had become sexually involved with their therapists, 80 percent felt that the contacts had been exploitive. Outcome research of clients who have been sexually involved with therapists indicates that 90 percent sustain significant damage as a result, with 11 percent requiring hospitalization and 1 percent committing suicide (Bouhoutsos et al., 1983). Typical outcomes for female clients include difficulty developing trust, poor self-image, depression, and difficulty expressing anger appropriately (Feldman-Summers & Jones, 1984; Sonne et al., 1985). No reports indicate positive outcomes.

Because therapist-client sexual contact is explicitly disapproved by all major professions and because it is demonstrably harmful to clients, it is also fertile ground for malpractice litigation, as borne out by data cited earlier indicating that it is the leading cause of malpractice actions. While many therapists may fear false allegations of sexual impropriety, the data suggest that many claims are in fact true, and that a great many real incidents are not reported. Despite their adverse experiences, as little as 4 percent of those affected make a complaint to licensing boards or file civil suits (Bouhoutsos et al., 1983).

The most widely cited precedent for tort action in this area is *Zipkin v. Freeman* (1968). Dr. Freeman, a licensed psychiatrist, accepted Mrs. Zipkin on referral from her general physician. She complained of recurrent headaches and gastric upset that could have been attributed to anxiety. At the psychiatrist's instigation this patient left her husband, filed lawsuits against both her husband and brother, and subsequently burglarized their homes. The major efforts at "treatment" consisted of nude swimming parties and overnight trips with the doctor for the purpose of sexual trysts. Mrs. Zipkin was also persuaded to move into an apartment above the doctor's office and to supply him with financial capital for speculative business ventures. At trial Dr. Freeman's behavior was found unprofessional; the Zipkins eventually received a total indemnity of $5,000.

The Zipkin case obviously involved outrageous conduct by the therapist and is unusual in that the perpetrator was a guru-type who set out to exploit his patient. It is far more common for therapists to report that they became sexually involved with a patient due to feelings of depression, loneliness, need, or vulnerability, and most are separated, divorced, or experiencing marital problems at the time (Bouhoutsos, 1985). An overwhelming majority express remorse and recognize their conduct as unacceptable. Thus, while some offenders act unprofessionally due to psychopathy or other pathology, the majority claim to have acted against their better judgment in a time of deep personal need and compromised functioning.

Patients who become involved with their therapists are predominantly female and younger than their therapists by more than a decade. They are described as depressed, lonely, passive, lacking self-esteem, and searching for acceptance and emotional closeness (Bouhoutsos, 1985). The stereotypic case involves a male therapist striving to adjust to middle age and personal problems who, despite his training, misinterprets the client's overtures for purely emotional support and acceptance as efforts to establish a romantic or erotic connection. The confused client accepts the therapist's advances as a substitute for the type of caring or love she is really seeking.

A second major pattern involves mutual sexual or romantic attraction (Keith-Spiegel & Koocher, 1985). The two parties may signal their interest in a variety of ways, such as small gifts from the client, special meeting arrangements or considerations from the therapist, or an overly social style of interacting. "The tendency to repress, deny, or rationalize the implications of these overtures is strong during the early phases of the developing relationship when it is still possible to deny them" (Muehleisen, 1987). Typically, the client makes the hidden agenda explicit. No matter how the therapist responds at that point, problems are likely to ensue.

While the personal problems and impairments of offenders do not excuse their conduct, these factors do at least suggest ways to approach the problem. To avoid liability for true allegations of sexual misconduct, therapists must be sensitive to their own vulnerabilities. Muehleisen (1987) suggests that therapists ask themselves the following questions if inappropriate feelings or attractions toward a client develop:

(1) Does my attraction for or fantasy about this client cause me to adjust my routine? Do I find myself preoccupied or frequently fantasizing? Do I arrange appointment times and places to permit the possibility of developing a liaison? Do I find reasons to increase the frequency of contacts?

(2) Why am I attracted to this client? Do I fantasize being a hero, enjoying power and control or my client's admiration of me?

(3) What are my own vulnerabilities at this time? What is the quality of my own intimate relationships? Do I feel alone and need someone to feel close to?

(4) What will be the consequences to other important relationships, my client's or my own? Would this attraction be present in a nontherapeutic setting? To what extent will this relationship ultimately produce a greater sense of disappointment or failure in my client?

(5) To what degree do I find that I can check my own impulses? How readily can I talk with colleagues about my attraction to this client?

Any indication that matters could get out of hand requires immediate action. Consultation with a trusted colleague should be the first course of action, and the therapist should consider entering treatment himself. Research indicates that those who seek consultation *after* a sexual liaison with clients have lower rates of recidivism than those who do not (Gartrell et al., 1986). Those who seek assistance *before* may be helped to avoid actions that are detrimental to themselves and their patients.

More problematic issues arise if termination is considered as a fail-safe option against misconduct. It is generally unfair to punish a client for the therapist's inability to manage transference or countertransference phenomena, and unanticipated termination is likely to precipitate feelings of rejection, failure, or victimization. On the other hand, consideration must be given to the potential for more severe consequences that could result from allowing the relationship to become eroticized, and in some cases termination might be required. If so, the therapist must not abandon the client, but should assume responsibility for making appropriate arrangements for future care. The therapist must also accept full responsibility for the termination on the grounds of personal problems. Revealing the reasons for termination in full detail has the effect of blaming the client for being seductive or manipulative.

Thus far, we have dealt with preventing true allegations of sexual misconduct; clearly, there are false allegations as well, although it is difficult to judge how many. Keith-Spiegel and Koocher (1985) note that even implausible false claims may have devastating effects on a therapist's practice, professional relationships, and private life. Preventing such allegations requires sensitive management of clients prone to feeling victimized or rejected and to using manipulative means to act out their anger. The following suggestions can be made:

(1) Consult professional literature on the problems of therapist sexuality and relations with clients (e.g., Edelwich & Brodsky, 1982) and structure your practice accordingly. Maintain a professional relationship with all clients and conduct your practice in a businesslike fashion.

(2) Be cautious in handling client requests for special considerations (meeting times, payment arrangements, etc.), which, if granted, could be interpreted as signals of more than professional caring.

(3) Discuss limits of ethical therapist behavior during initial meetings with all clients, or make copies of your profession's ethical standards available and encourage discussion (Brenner, 1982).

(4) Be sensitive to the potential interactions of each client's psychological style with therapist behavior such as hugging or praising that could possibly be perceived as inappropriate.

(5) If a patient seems even subtly provocative, seek advice from another professional and make clear plans for confronting this behavior.

(6) If a client seems to be "testing the waters," confront this in a sensitive way. "What is not spoken in therapy often is what leads to trouble" (Reed, 1984).

(7) If a client does express a desire for a romantic or sexual relationship, do not respond in an offensive way. Express flattery, but identify the client's feelings with more appropriate commitment to the closeness of the therapy relationship. Be clear in indicating that a sexual liaison is not in the client's interests, and will therefore definitely not take place.

Improper Treatment

Suits for improper treatment do not refer to applying the wrong type of procedure. They actually refer to negligence during the course of interventions that might otherwise be proper and helpful to the patient. Because many procedures are subsumed under the rubric of "psychotherapy," it is difficult to generalize about causes of liability. It is actually extremely rare for treatments without at least some kind of physical or somatic component to lead to such claims.

One of the leading cases in this area is *Abraham v. Zaslow* (1972). Like many novel therapeutic ideas, Dr. Zaslow's "Z therapy" was developed in California and aimed to reduce "primal rage." Zaslow claimed to break down resistance by applying "tactile stimuli" whenever the patient was not being fully open and honest. The tactile stimuli actually included tickling, poking, and beating administered while the client was forcibly held. One patient who received over 10 hours of this procedure suffered such severe bruising of the upper half of her body that kidney failure ensued. Although the procedures employed might arguably have been proper for an adherent of "Z therapy," they did not comport with the proper conduct of psychotherapy as a general treatment. The client recovered $170,000 in damages.

Allegations of improper treatment may also be raised in the use of medication or such specific procedures as ECT. As an example, a psychiatrist who failed to give appropriate muscle-relaxing medications before ECT was held liable when a compression fracture occurred during the ensuing seizure (*Stone v. Proctor*, 1963). Liability connected with prescription medications appears more likely to result from unnecessary prescription than from mismanagement, though there has been considerable litigation regarding tardive dyskinesia, a permanent neurologic complication from excessive use of neuroleptics (see *Faigenbaum v. Cohen,* 1979). Surprisingly, psychiatrists are about as likely to be sued for problems with *non*-psychotropic medications as for poor management of postsurgical and other medical complications for clearly psychiatric interventions (Slawson & Guggenheim, 1984). This pattern suggests that more effective referral and consultation with medical specialists would be helpful. Special problems may arise with patients who have significant medical problems requiring treatments that may conflict or interact with other somatic therapies. If psychotherapists implement treatments that compromise these health-maintaining efforts, they are likely to be held liable.

In talking therapies liability for improper treatment is unlikely unless interventions are clearly inappropriate (Hogan, 1979). Examples would include suggesting that clients act out hostilities toward others, giving business advice to clients, or demanding that clients change jobs, move, get divorced, or change their circumstances as a condition for continuing the therapy. Obvious mismanagement of transference phenomena may also lead to liability. An example would be the therapist who is overtly angry and critical, causing the client undue distress or anxiety in addition to whatever factors brought them into therapy. In all of the above examples, the behavior of the therapist would be clearly at odds with the mainstream of clinical practice.

Treatments that are not helpful or are even botched do not necessarily lead to liability. The impropriety of the procedure must be the result of negligence on the part of the therapist. While inadequate training may lead some therapists to lack necessary technical skills, it appears that lack of care by competent professionals is a more common source of error. Given that many mental health settings are short of staff, many therapists have excessive responsibilities and the quality of their work inevitably suffers. It is always the responsibility of professional therapists to set a reasonable limit on their practice so that they can apply their knowledge and expertise properly.

Obviously, the adequacy of any psychotherapeutic intervention depends on many factors. The major professions require a minimum of five years of postgraduate study to develop sufficient expertise in the methods and procedures of each discipline. The best way to avoid liability for improper treatment is to ensure that all of the therapist's training and expertise are brought to bear on each case. The following points deserve consideration:

(1) Develop coherent, detailed treatment plans in writing. This applies whether doing "talk therapy" or using psychoactive drugs. Vague descriptions such as "dynamic therapy" or "trial on TCA's" (tricyclic antidepressants) are inadequate. Note important procedures and potential pitfalls in advance and make plans to address these. Not only will such preparation help to prevent problems, but it will also help demonstrate that the therapist was not careless or un-

skilled in planning and administering the treatment if a suit does arise.

(2) If an esoteric or complex treatment is anticipated, review relevant literature. Consult with other professionals who are experienced with those procedures. Under no circumstances undertake an unfamiliar mode of treatment until fully understanding it. Be prepared to accept peer supervision when appropriate.

(3) If others will be involved in the treatment process, supervise or coordinate appropriately.

(4) Periodically review treatment plans to ensure that proper procedures are being followed.

(5) When psychotherapeutic treatments may interact with medical or other problems, consult with proper specialists. (This point will be addressed in detail later.)

(6) Most importantly, do not try to provide care for more clients than is feasible. When this principle is unheeded, the quality of your work will inevitably suffer.

Loss from Evaluation

Although a frequent cause of action, liability for evaluative failures has not been widely discussed in the literature. This may be due in part to the wide range of situations where these cases arise. It is difficult to summarize in a systematic way all of the issues relevant to loss from evaluations.

Loss from evaluation is generally a different cause of action from negligent diagnosis, in that the conclusions or opinions are often not about diagnostic issues per se. In fact, they often involve issues outside mainstream mental health practice. Therapists are involved in a broad range of nonmental health settings where their assessments play important roles in decisions affecting those assessed. Professional evaluations "may result in denial of employment, denial of promotion or transfer, denial of child custody, denial of probation, or the diagnosis of, or failure to diagnose, suicidal or homicidal potential" (Cohen, 1987). If the subject of an evaluation disagrees with the results and is aware that these findings have had a negative impact on him, he may institute a suit for loss from evaluation. As in other types of litigation, it is necessary to prove that the evaluation was negligently conducted. Therapists are not liable for reaching unflattering but true conclusions, and even inaccurate conclusions do not give rise to liability unless they were the product of negligent practice and result in some identifiable harm.

While it is difficult to give specific guidelines for avoiding malpractice suits in this area, the following suggestions should give a general orientation.

(1) Do not accept referrals for evaluation that require judgments outside your expertise.

(2) When performing evaluations for courts, employers, disability boards, etc., clearly explain the nature of the evaluation to the examinee. Describe the purpose of the assessment, the procedures that will be used, and the nature of the feedback to any third party. Get signed permission from the examinee to proceed under these conditions.

(3) Develop and adopt specific procedures for evaluations and be able to justify these by appealing to research, standard clinical practices, or diagnostic systems. Departures from standard procedure should be documented along with rationale.

(4) Use tests and other procedures according to standard methods. Do not use any technique for purposes that have not been validated.

(5) Note all sources of information that contributed to the evaluation, particularly outside sources. Recognize that this information may not be accurate. If outside data play a key role in the outcome of the assessment, note that the validity of the conclusions rests on the accuracy of those data, and that other conclusions are possible.

(6) Spend and be able to document sufficient time to collect data, consider it carefully, and develop conclusions.

(7) When formulating conclusions, stay close to the data. Do not engage in fanciful speculation, but rely on clearly documentable conclusions tied to the data at hand.

(8) In writing reports, do not use pejorative language or vague, jargonistic phrases that can be misconstrued. Assume that your report will definitely be read by the examinee and his attorney.

(9) State conclusions as opinions, not rigid pronouncements.

The bottom line in these cases is that each evaluation should be conducted as if it will need to be defended in court. Be thorough, meticulous, and professional, and convey results in a way that is accurate but minimizes negative impact on the examinee.

Improper Diagnosis

While many of the issues that underlie liability for negligent evaluation are also related to improper diagnosis, the latter is more often seen in mainstream mental health settings. Improper diagnosis is also closely tied to actions for improper treatment, largely because legal conceptions view diagnosis as prescriptive. That is, a given diagnosis is thought to automatically mandate a specific treatment. This area of liability borrows heavily from medical malpractice.

Incorrect diagnoses are seen as leading to injury in several ways. If an existing condition is not diagnosed at all, then generally no treatment is offered, and so injury may result if the disorder becomes progressively worse or if the patient suffers unnecessarily with a treatable problem. For example, Tourette's syndrome causes numerous social and interpersonal problems for the small number of patients who suffer with it, and it normally responds very well to the neuroleptic medication, haloperidol. Negligent failure to identify the syndrome could be cause for liability simply because this prevented the patient from receiving appropriate treatment. On the other hand, if an incorrect diagnosis is made, ineffective, unnecessary, or even harmful procedures might be employed. Even unnecessary treatments with no lasting consequences may lead to liability if the treatments were painful, costly, or unpleasant for the patient.

Not all incorrect or missed diagnoses result in liability, only those that result from negligence. The complainant must demonstrate that the therapist did not possess basic skills or knowledge which others in the same discipline normally do possess. Alternatively, if the diagnosis was arrived at through carelessness, it could be deemed negligent even if the practitioner were well-trained and knowledgeable.

Although the effects of treatments are often important in documenting injury in improper diagnosis cases, improper treatment is a completely different cause of action. Improper diagnosis usually involves treatments that were properly performed but badly chosen. The procedures employed may have been perfectly executed and appropriate for the diagnosis, assuming it were correct. Of course, in improper diagnosis the assumption is false. Improper treatment, to be discussed below, refers to improper execution of the treatment itself, whether properly chosen or not.

Trying to specify methods to avoid liability for improper diagnosis is difficult because these cases may involve many complex clinical issues. Various aspects of a professional's broad training and experience may be relevant. The following points warrant consideration:

(1) Be familiar with current developments in your field. What is common knowledge for a whole professional group necessarily changes with new discoveries and developments.

(2) Adhere to standard diagnostic conventions. Be concrete in connecting specific client behaviors, symptoms, and characteristics to formal criteria.

(3) Always consider alternative diagnostic hypotheses. If considerable uncertainty remains, it is better to continue with evaluative procedures than to become committed to one "shaky" diagnosis.

(4) In difficult cases adopt temporary intervention strategies that are appropriate to all alternatives, and delay procedures that may have negative outcomes.

(5) If a diagnostic problem is very challenging, document the efforts spent in trying to resolve it. Consult with colleagues, review recent literature, and if necessary ask for formal review of the case by a qualified professional group. These steps help to demonstrate that thorough professional knowledge was brought to bear, and that the therapist was diligent in discharging her duty to the patient.

Breach of Confidentiality, Breach of Privacy

> Neither laws nor ethical codes can protect a client's confidences. Only you can. (Brenner, 1982, p. 90)

The confidential relationship between practitioners and their clients is a tradition within all of the helping professions. The notion that confidentiality is fundamental to a caring relationship originated with the Greeks. The oath of Hippocrates states in part:

> Whatever I see or hear, in the life of men, which ought not to be spoken of abroad, I will not divulge, as reckoning that all such should be kept secret. (as cited in Smith, 1979)

This commitment to confidentiality has been maintained through the current ethical guidelines and codes of the major psychotherapeutic professions, but with some qualifications. These limitations arise due to changing legal conceptions and policies which try to balance the privacy rights of individuals against the wishes of society.

Individuals in psychotherapy overwhelmingly assume that confidentiality is absolute, that the therapist must not disclose information about them even in a court of law (Meyer & Willage, 1980; Miller & Thelan, 1986). An even higher proportion believe that confidentiality *should be* absolute, even if they know otherwise. The primary source of a clinician's duty to maintain confidentiality arises out of professional ethical guidelines, but these recognize a number of exceptions. In addition, the law may actually require breach of confidentiality under certain circumstances, principally when the client represents a threat to third parties or reveals past behavior involving child abuse. These issues will be addressed later in this chapter.

From a pragmatic point of view, maintaining confidentiality is crucial to the trust that psychotherapy requires. Clients have a right to expect that their secrets will not be revealed without extraordinary justification, and when confidences are revealed this is manifestly harmful to the client. Therapists are generally held liable for breaches of confidentiality because these are so clearly a preventable way to harm one's clients. Breach of confidence refers to active revelation by the therapist without the expressed consent of the client. That is, the therapist communicates the confidential information to some third party through speech, writing, or some other medium. Breach of privacy is closely related and refers to unintentional disclosures, such as leaving confidential records in an unsecure location so that they fall into the wrong hands.

What recourse is open to the client if a private therapist does unethically divulge confidential information? One avenue is to ask that professional's peers to review the matter and to discipline the therapist. If a state licensing board or professional organization finds that the therapist acted unethically, various measures may be taken to rectify the situation. In the most extreme case, the therapist may lose his or her right to practice.

A second alternative is to file a civil lawsuit alleging breach of confidentiality or negligent breach of privacy. The latter theory is especially applicable when the therapist failed to take reasonable steps to comply with a duty to maintain confidentiality. Under these theories the plaintiff must show that he was harmed in some way by the disclosure. A recent Supreme Court case (*Roe v. Doe*, 1974) is illustrative. A woman who had been involved in therapy some 10 years earlier sued her former psychiatrist over distribution of a book which inadequately disguised her identity. The text included transcripts of therapy sessions, details of her childhood and family, and intimate and allegedly humiliating descriptions of her divorce and sexual experiences. Because the information provided made the plaintiff readily identifiable, the court issued an injunction against distribution.

Litigation may also arise under contract theories, alleging that assurances of confidentiality are so intrinsic to the therapy relationship that courts should enforce this expectation. The therapist who reveals confidential information (without legally recognized cause) violates the therapeutic "contract." Whether the suit will be successful depends on a variety of factors, including whether or not the expectation of confidence was reasonable, whether potential exceptions were discussed with the patient, the extent and reasonableness of the disclosure, and whether the client held up his end of the contract by attending sessions, paying fees, etc.

Therapists who want to avoid liability connected with revealing information about their patients should recognize the conditions that justify breach of confidence. These can be briefly summarized as follows:

(1) The client gives written consent to the release. The authorization should be as specific as possible, with a predetermined expiration date. Only release that information which is explicitly covered, and attempt to safeguard any information which may be damaging to the patient.

(2) All states require that therapists with knowledge of current or past child abuse or neglect report this information to the relevant agencies, even without the consent of the client whether the child, the abuser, or a collateral (see Chapter 6). It is unclear whether any additional information other than the fact that an allegation has been made must be revealed (Weisberg & Wald, 1987). While the initial report must usually be made "immediately," the therapist should consult an attorney before providing any further information.

(3) Therapists who choose to pursue involuntary civil commitment are normally exempt from liability for breach of confidence as long as they are acting in good faith. Obviously, the therapist must share some information with police, magistrates, or judges to pursue the commitment. When the patient poses a risk of suicide, revelations to family members may also be allowed to aid in prevention.

(4) In the last decade courts have imposed a duty on therapists to protect third parties who might be harmed by their clients. When a therapist determines that a patient poses a threat to an identifiable person or persons, they may breach confidentiality to warn them, at least in states which have addressed this issue. Note that other actions may be more appropriate (see later section on *Tarasoff* liability).

(5) Client information may generally be used without specific permission in teaching and research where there is a reasonable expectation that those involved will adhere to professional standards in maintaining confidentiality. This is a technical exception and usually works only because clients are not aware of it. It is recommended that therapists obtain full consent for such uses rather than exploit this allowance.

Beyond these specific issues there are several general guidelines to aid the therapist. First, a general point which will be made throughout this text: Keep records that will not be damaging to clients. Do not record potentially harmful information that is not relevant to the therapy and do not use pejorative terms. Keep records that you would be willing to share with the client at any time. If records are not suitable for review by the client, what does that say about the quality of the therapy relationship?

(1) Discuss the limits and exceptions to confidentiality with all clients as they enter treatment. If there will be no confidentiality (such as with court-ordered therapy), make this explicit.

(2) Discuss the ramifications of voluntary releases, including the adverse effects these may have in the event of unforeseen legal efforts to gain access to therapy materials.

(3) When the client requests a release of information, it is helpful to discuss the material required, prepare the information in written form, and allow the client to approve it before it is released. Never release any information in verbal form unless the client is present.

(4) Hire responsible office personnel and explain the importance of confidentiality. Minimize the number of persons who have even passing access to sensitive materials. For example, if you employ a bookkeeper, do not keep billing information in the same location with progress notes.

(5) Develop a system for both maintaining and disposing of records. After a reasonable period (on the order of five to seven years after the client is no longer receiving services), records should be shredded. Records must be secured at all times; try to forsee problems arising from such unlikely causes as burglary or fire. (Remember that the Watergate affair began with the burglary of a therapist's office for the sole purpose of stealing confidential information.)

(6) In scholarly writings that refer to specific clients clear the work with them to ensure that they are adequately disguised. Get written permission to proceed. If any one detail that a client himself would recognize is to be used in any form of publication, get permission. When drawing upon broad clinical experience and recollections to write composite case studies or similar works, a reasonable rule is that if any client would conclude that he is being discussed specifically, the work is not sufficiently vague.

(7) If information regarding any client will be used for teaching or research, explain these procedures in advance and secure written approval.

Defamation, Libel, and Slander

The *Roe v. Doe* case cited above brings up the issue of libel and slander. In that case there was no allegation that the information given about the former patient was false, merely that the therapist was obligated to keep it secret (in fact, the potential for damage was great because it was all true with no real attempt to alter identifying information). Defamation refers to various acts which spread false or misleading information that harms another person's reputation. If the therapist has maliciously spread damaging lies, it is likely that he will be held liable, and there is essentially no defense unless the therapist claims not to have made the statements at all.

Negligently spreading false information may also lead to liability. Libel cases arise when a therapist carelessly makes false statements about patients in some lasting form, such as in writings or films, while slander usually involves falsehoods which are merely spoken. These actions both require that false information be communicated to someone and that harm results. If the therapist merely notes incorrect information in his own records without revealing it to others, there is no cause for action. Similarly, unless damage to reputation or community standing is shown, there may be no liability.

Consider, for example, an individual referred for evaluation. If the person evaluated disagrees with the conclusions reached, he may allege that the examination was conducted improperly and that communicating incorrect conclusions (falsehoods) to others has damaged him. These actions are obviously quite similar to cases categorized under "loss from evaluation." Similar problems arise when collateral sources of information are uncritically accepted. If the therapist could reasonably expect the information to be true, then reporting it as part of the individual's history or basing conclusions on those data would not be negligent. For example, it is common practice to rely upon information obtained from other professionals, so that using such data without efforts at verification would not generally be negligent. On the other hand, a report which repeats as fact unfounded allegations made by an estranged spouse would reflect careless disregard for the impact of those statements on the subject. The therapist should label the allegations as such and note their source or perhaps seek independent documentation.

There are a limited number of *privileges* (not to be confused with testimonial privilege) that protect therapists from liability for libel and slander. Absolute privileges apply in various legal proceedings such as courtroom testimony, reports, and depositions, and reports to legislative bodies. In such proceedings all parties give information which they believe to be true on pain of being cited for perjury. In essence, the threat of a libel suit is unnecessary and is suspended in those situations. Qualified privileges apply when information is revealed to other professionals, agencies such as hospitals or insurance companies, and family members and some significant others. Qualified privilege requires some demonstration of a good faith belief that the information conveyed was true.

Consistent with the earlier discussion on confidentiality, the best way to avoid liability for defamation is to reveal as little information as possible about clients, and then to do so only with their permission. Whenever information is sought from outside sources, exercise care in making the request. Be sure to identify the client fully and accurately. When derogatory or potentially damaging information is reported to you, be sure to note the source of this information and do not assume it is factual. Any communication that could have a negative impact on the subject should be well-documented and demonstrably true.

Suits and Countersuits Related to Fee Collection

Psychotherapists are highly trained professionals who have every right to receive good compensation for their services, and there is no reason to believe that clients should have any lesser obligation to pay their therapist than to pay their plumber. However, no amount of money a client may owe is worth incurring a countersuit connected with overaggressive fee collection procedures. Despite the large number of practitioners in non-fee settings, a fair number of such suits are filed every year.

This is difficult to fathom. Research on fee payment problems in psychotherapy has generally shown that refusal to pay may be a form of resistance paralleling important problems in the therapy proper. Inability to confront payment problems has been correlated with therapist inexperience and difficulty establishing appropriate boundaries (see, for example, Brenner, 1982). When individuals or families in conventionally scheduled therapy become delinquent in paying bills, it is the responsibility of the therapist to address this problem. One solution may be to offer a reduced fee which the client can meet. It is more difficult to generalize about collecting fees for various assessment and consultative services.

Most of these suits related to fee collection are argued along lines similar to breach of confidence or libel. It is usually alleged that communications to collection agencies, lawyers, or others amount to unapproved release of confidential information (the fact that the person was in therapy). Alternatively, the countersuit may assert that the therapist's claims for payment are false or unreasonable. If any of the allegations are substantiated, the therapist not only will be denied the fees he sought, but will also be liable to pay damages to the client.

Though there is no excuse for incurring such liability, the following points may be helpful in averting any difficulties:

(1) Have a set policy for fees, including billing and due dates, procedures for handling delinquent fees, whether missed appointments are charged, etc. Compose a brief written description of these

policies, be sure that each client receives a copy and understands it, and stick to it. It may be wise to ask an attorney to review these procedures.

(2) Be sure that fees are reasonable.

(3) When clients become delinquent, confront the problem early, while it can be addressed in a flexible way. Don't wait until a large bill has accumulated, when mentioning it is likely to intimidate, embarrass, or anger the client.

(4) Where applicable, collect fees in advance. Some types of work, such as child custody evaluations, are notoriously likely to lead to payment problems. It is fair and reasonable to require payment for such services in advance, perhaps into an escrow account.

(5) Do not use collection agencies. In extreme cases an attorney may be consulted to aid in collection, but do not sue.

(6) Both the American Psychological and the American Psychiatric Associations require that members engage in some *pro bono* (for the good of the community) services with no expectation of financial gain. If a client simply refuses to pay for services rendered, adopt this spirit and consider this part of your contribution.

Client Suicide

While the law generally does not hold anyone responsible for the acts of another, there are exceptions. One of these is the responsibility of therapists to prevent suicide and other self-destructive behavior by their clients. The duty of therapists to exercise adequate care and skill in diagnosing suicidality is well-established (see *Meier v. Ross General Hospital*, 1968). When the risk of self-injurious behavior is identified an additional duty to take adequate precautions arises (*Abille v. United States*, 1980; *Pisel v. Stamford Hospital*, 1980). When psychotherapists fail to meet these responsibilities, they may be held liable for injuries that result.

Not every completed suicide or gesture is cause for liability—only those which could reasonably have been prevented. Demonstrating negligence requires proof that the patient should have been identified as suicidal based on widely recognized criteria used by most other therapists of the same training. Given that prediction of suicide is not well standardized, it is rare for therapists to be held liable for failing to guess at suicidal intent when the patient denied it or did not appear depressed. If evidence of suicidality is missed due to inadequate examination, the therapist may be held liable. For example, patients who present significant depressive symptoms, among others, should generally be questioned about suicidal ideation and any history of past gestures. Failure to do so amounts to negligent examination, since most therapists would explore these issues.

Obviously, if a patient makes any overt statement indicative of self-destructive tendencies, the therapist could not claim that the harm was unforseeable. This is merely one of the reasons that all "threats" should be taken seriously. While a review of literature on suicide is not possible here, it is worth noting that factors such as formulation of a plan, availability of method, and number of past gestures are associated with increased probability (see Chapter 10).

Once suicidality is noted, the therapist must take reasonably prudent steps to prevent harm. Of course, a variety of factors influences the likelihood that any given patient will act out, so what steps are reasonable will depend on the circumstances of the case. The response must be in proportion to the risk.

Hospitalization is considered the safest option, but confinement alone is not adequate. Specific measures to prevent suicide must be ordered. Also, the patient may not be willing to enter the hospital voluntarily. In all states danger to self is a valid basis for civil commitment, as will be discussed in Chapter 4. Once the patient is hospitalized, a new problem develops: deciding when the crisis has passed sufficiently to allow release. Occasionally a recently released patient commits suicide, leading to suits which have been characterized as "wrongful release" actions. These suits have lead many inpatient facilities to adopt the maxim, "When in doubt, don't let 'em out" (Halleck, 1987).

Less restrictive methods may be appropriate in some circumstances. For example, a client with a supportive and responsible family might be managed at home with frequent care and monitoring by the therapist. This arrangement obviously requires the consent of all involved and may take on aspects of substituted judgment, since the patient is not able to see to his own welfare. Formal informed consent procedures (see later section) should be employed when nonhospital alternatives are employed. An even less restrictive but widely used measure is to make a "contract" with the patient that he or she will not suicide, at least until the next meeting with the therapist. It is not clear under what conditions this would amount to adequate supervision.

Choosing among various alternatives in dealing with the suicidal patient may be difficult and requires balancing the benefits to the patient in being free from unnecessary restraint against the risk to the patient from his own impulses. The courts have recognized that "calculated risks of necessity must be taken if the modern and enlightened treatment of the mentally ill is to be pursued intelligently and rationally" (*Baker v. United States*, 1964). It is important that therapists make explicit the risks and benefits associated with their actions in managing the suicidal patient, and make clear that the choices made reflect deliberate and skilled professional decisions. Special issues or concerns in this process include:

(1) Be sensitive to suicidal indications in therapy, particularly in depressed patients or those with significant impulse control problems or self-punitive motives. Be ready to discuss suicide at any time and assume that you must initiate this dialogue.

(2) Consider a range of options to deal with suicidal impulses. Describe the risks and benefits associated with each and document the reasons for your choice. The deliberateness of the decision could be crucial in averting liability in the event of a tragic suicide.

(3) Be prepared to reconsider management issues as clinical and other factors change.

(4) Know civil commitment procedures for your state, especially how to obtain emergency commitment. If necessary, be ready to use this knowledge to act quickly.

Violation of Civil Rights

This category of liability may include many different types of actions. Prominent areas of litigation at present include patients' rights to treatment (as opposed to mere custodial care) and, more recently, patients' rights to refuse treatments they find objectionable. Since these cases generally pertain to involuntarily committed residents in public hospitals, the rights to treatment and to refuse treatment are discussed in Chapter 4 on civil commitment. Related information can be found in Chapter 3 where we discuss incompetency and guardianship. It is sufficient here to note that therapists may not impose treatments on competent patients, and civil commitment is not the same as incompetence to take part in treatment decisions. These suits normally are directed only at therapists and administrators in large institutions.

Suits for wrongful commitment may also be subsumed under this category. When patients feel that they were unnecessarily confined against their will as a result of a civil commitment action, they may attempt to sue any psychotherapists involved in the process. Since a judge or magistrate must formally approve involuntary commitments, it is rare for therapists to be sued successfully on these grounds. Also, in most states commitment statutes offer immunity from liability as long as the therapist acted in good faith. A smaller number of jurisdictions allow suits which claim that the therapist was negligent in performing an examination which in turn led to the confinement. In practice, unless there is an outright conspiracy with family or others to obtain the commitment, liability is highly unlikely.

Bodily Injury, Battery, and Assault

Webster's defines battery as the "unlawful beating or use of force on a person without his consent." While this does not sound like any activity common to psychotherapy, suits for battery or assault have been brought against various practitioners. The most notable to date is *Hammer v. Rosen* (1960). Dr. Rosen, a proponent of "direct analysis," believed that regressed and psychotic patients require aggressive means to establish contact. In the case of at least one client this involved punching, slapping, and hitting to the face and upper body. The client successfully sued. Note that this case did not involve malpractice per se; the actions and injuries sustained had nothing to do with professional conduct. Dr. Rosen's attack was unlawful under any circumstances and was litigated as an intentional tort.

Even normal, widely used therapeutic procedures may lead to liability for battery if the client has not consented to the procedures. Generally this is only true for methods that employ touching or application of some physical procedure, such as giving injections or using biofeedback equipment. It is normally unlawful to touch another person's body without their consent, and this is no less true in psychotherapy. In addition to physical procedures, it is possible that other therapy methods could lead to liability when proper consent is not obtained. An example would be flooding or implosion techniques that are quite aversive and intentionally create very high levels of anxiety. If the client does not understand and agree to the procedure in advance they might successfully sue for assault, which does not require actual bodily injury. The importance of informed consent is addressed in the next section.

"Failure to Warn" and *Tarasoff* Liability

Therapist liability for the violent actions of their patients has created considerable controversy among both the legal and therapeutic communities. This area of litigation overlays a number of important issues of mental health practice, including the confidentiality of therapy relationships, problems in the prediction of dangerousness, and patient's rights to treatment. While many clinicians were concerned by early rulings in this area, recent attempts to expand liability in radical ways overshadow the significance of earlier case law. Despite troubling legal precedents, litigation in this area remains quite rare, as noted earlier.

As with many areas of mental health law, California courts had led the

way in establishing therapist liability to third parties. The frequently cited
case of *Tarasoff v. Regents of the University of California* (1976) provided
the name under which this category of litigation is known. Because this case
is so widely discussed in both the legal and psychotherapeutic communities,
a thorough analysis here is not warranted. It is sufficient to note that a
college student, Prosenjit Poddar, was receiving outpatient therapy through
the university's student counseling service. Though seen for only a few
sessions, he impressed his therapist as potentially violent, and made specific
references to his anger at a young woman named Tatiana (later identified as
Tatiana Tarasoff) who spurned his romantic advances. The therapist concluded that he was likely to harm this woman.

Because the patient refused voluntary hospitalization the therapist contacted the police and attempted to have him taken to a state mental health
system triage center for involuntary commitment. The police spoke to Poddar, then refused to detain him. On the advice of his supervisor, who feared
a lawsuit for breach of confidence, the therapist did not pursue the matter
further. Not surprisingly, Poddar did not return to treatment after his
confidence was breached, and just over two months later he killed Ms.
Tarasoff.

Ms. Tarasoff's parents sued the therapist, the university, and the campus
police, claiming that Tatiana's wrongful death was brought about by the
negligence of the defendants. They specifically claimed that the therapist
should have warned Ms. Tarasoff that Poddar presented a danger to her, and
that they should have confined Poddar to a hospital. The latter cause of
action was dismissed due to provisions of the Lanterman-Petris-Short Act,
the state law which governed civil commitment. Eventually, the California
Supreme Court held that the claim of a "duty to warn" was a sufficient cause
of action. This merely means that the Tarasoffs were allowed to file a suit on
those grounds; the court's opinion noted that they would be hard-pressed to
win such a suit. The case was, predictably, settled out of court.

The defense in *Tarasoff* argued, among other things, that therapists are
obligated to protect the confidentiality of their clients and that warnings
would compromise the practice of therapy. The court disagreed, holding
that " . . . the protective privilege (to not disclose confidences) ends where
the public peril begins." In this case the therapist had accurately determined
that Ms. Tarasoff was in peril, so the therapist was obligated to take some
action to protect her. Though a warning might have been a reasonable way
to discharge this duty, the court went on to state that in other cases therapists would have to take "whatever other steps are reasonably necessary
under the circumstances." This language makes it erroneous to summarize
Tarasoff as a "duty to warn" case, a point which will become important in

discussing later cases. It is notable that the only other specific action mentioned in the opinion is warning the police, which the therapist did.

A second major concern for therapists was the court's holding that the duty to protect arises whenever a therapist " . . . determines, or pursuant to the standards of his profession should determine, that his patient presents a serious danger. . . ." This opinion was announced during the same period that a variety of naturalistic studies indicated that qualified therapists had no expertise in predicting dangerousness (see Chapter 5), a factor which was addressed in detail by an *amicus curiae* brief submitted by the American Psychiatric Association. These arguments were ignored by the court, leading some authorities to wonder what it would mean to " . . . apply standards to skills that do not exist" (Stone, 1976b).

Criticism of the *Tarasoff* decision (actually decision*s*, since the court agreed to a rehearing after numerous professional organizations submitted friend of the court briefs) was widespread and vociferous even from the legal community. A survey of therapists attempted to assess the impact of the ruling on practitioners (*Stanford Law Review*, 1978). Results indicated that therapists would attempt to protect themselves from Tarasoff liability in several ways, including falsifying records, refusing to work with potentially dangerous patients or groups, intentionally not discussing issues related to aggression, and other measures. Although the methods of this study have been criticized (Goodman, 1985), results did reflect the perception that the Tarasoff ruling would be catastrophic for psychotherapy.

A series of subsequent California cases further refined the duty to protect. In *Bellah v. Greenson* (1978) the court considered a case in which a therapist's patient committed suicide and the family alleged that they should have been warned of this potential. Apparently sticking to the "public peril" justification for breaching confidence, the court held that the therapist had no duty to warn unless there was a risk of "violent assault to others." The possibility of suicide did not *require* the therapist to violate confidentiality. This ruling does not imply that therapists cannot give such warnings if they view them as advantageous to the patient in the long run.

Language from the decision in *Mavroudis v. Superior Court* (1980) further specified that the danger of violence to others must be "an imminent threat of serious danger to a readily identifiable victim" in order to trigger a duty to warn. In *Thompson v. County of Alameda* (1980) the court further narrowed the duty to protect others by saying that a duty arises only when there are "specific threats to identifiable victims." It is noteworthy that in this case an incorrigible juvenile sex offender revealed to authorities that he intended to murder whatever child he next accosted. Nonetheless, on the recommendations of a juvenile counselor, a licensed therapist, he was released from custody and carried out his threat. When the parents of the murdered youngster sued the county authorities, the court determined that since they could not have been identified and warned, the county had no duty to protect their child.

Incidentally, this reasoning was followed closely when the Colorado courts dismissed *Brady v. Hopper* (1983), a suit brought by those injured in John Hinckley's attack on President Reagen. Because Hinckley did not make explicit threats against these specific victims, his therapist, Dr. Hopper, was not held to a duty to protect them.

The *Thompson* case produced considerable dissent, which has led to a radical shift in arguments for therapist liability. In all of the cases above, the court focused on warnings as a method of discharging a duty to threatened third parties, and generally attempted to balance the utility of warnings against the costs to the individual therapy patient whose confidence would be breached. When there is no readily identifiable victim, warnings are either impossible or of limited value if aimed at an amorphous group of potential victims; the scales would tip in favor of maintaining confidentiality. But the facts in *Thompson* beg for other types of protective action. Although there was no specific victim named (probably even the patient did not know at that time whom he would kill), there was a very specific threat. Two dissenting justices noted that the original opinion in *Tarasoff* spoke of "other reasonable steps," and noted that in the instant case merely keeping the perpetrator confined would have been a reasonable way to protect the children who were collectively threatened. The importance of this reasoning will become clear shortly.

Though the early cases cited above tended to confine therapist liability to narrow circumstances, "since 1976, 14 [other] states have either adopted or indicated strong acceptance for the *Tarasoff* rationale, all but two of these coming since 1980" (Goodman, 1985, p. 219). Many of these cases actually expand bases for liability in several ways. These include requiring therapists to accurately predict dangerousness even in the absence of overt threats, as well as requiring various active efforts to intervene so as to prevent violence.

The New Jersey courts, in *McIntosh v. Milano* (1979), held that therapists could be sued for failing to protect even when there were no threats communicated. The plaintiff alleged that the therapist should have inferred both dangerousness and the identity of the potential victim from other information available. Similar reasoning was applied in *Jablonski v. United States* (1983), a suit against several therapists at a Veterans Administration hospital. Their patient had been convicted of rape many years earlier and had recently threatened the mother of his girlfriend, but their assessment indicated that he did not meet civil commitment criteria. The primary therapist and his supervisor each warned the girlfriend that she might not be safe in the apartment she shared with the patient and that she should move out, which she eventually did with additional encouragement from her minister and others (Winslade, 1987). However, she subsequently visited the apartment, where the patient killed her.

The victim's estate sued for negligence on several grounds. The court ruled, in part, that the therapists were negligent because they did not forecast the homicide based on the "psychological profile" of the patient. Apparently the court was confident of its own diagnostic prowess and believed that average practitioners using common skill and knowledge would have come to the same conclusion without the benefit of hindsight. The California Supreme Court similarly referred to "negligent failure to diagnose dangerousness" in allowing proceedings in *Hedlund v. Superior Court of Orange County* (1983), which is still in litigation. These holdings reinstate crucial questions as to how courts will retrospectively decide that therapists were or were not negligent in predicting dangerousness.

Perhaps more troubling in the *Jablonski* decision was the court's holding that the therapists were negligent even though they had warned the victim. The court found that the warnings were inadequate because they were not effective, perhaps equating effectiveness with whether warnings are heeded. It appears that the therapists were held negligent for merely inferring that the victim might not be safe, rather than predicting that she would definitely be murdered. Thus, the language of *Thompson* takes on a new twist: Therapists can be held liable unless they accurately infer a specific type of harm to a specific identifiable victim, even when no threat is made toward anyone.

Most recently, in *Currie v. United States* (1986), a Federal District Court has ruled that therapists have a "duty to commit" potentially dangerous patients in an attempt to protect any potential victims. In this case, a patient at a VA outpatient clinic, diagnosed as suffering post-traumatic stress syndrome, threatened to blow up a building owned by IBM, his former employer. His therapist concluded that he did present some danger and contacted IBM (which was already receiving threats directly), the FBI, the local police, and the U.S. attorney's office. The therapist also concluded that the patient did not qualify for involuntary commitment under North Carolina's state law. The patient later took homemade explosives and a gun to an IBM office and killed an employee.

The victim's estate sued the VA, alleging that they were negligent in failing to warn *all* potential victims of the patient's hostility and in failing to confine the patient to prevent the attack. The defense argued that there was no duty to protect the defendant, who, by virtue of being only one of numerous employees, could not be identified. They also argued that no duty to commit had been recognized, and that the therapists could not be subjected to liability for failing to commit a patient who was not "commitable" in the first place. Noting the inequity in early rulings that a duty to protect arises only when a specific victim is known, the District Court accepted the argument that patients who will act out in random or only broadly predictable ways do create a duty for therapists. The court went on to hold that the therapist wrongly interpreted the state's civil commitment law, that the patient was commitable, and that it could speculate on whether North Carolina law would recognize a duty to commit. The ruling asserted that such a duty exists.

The court noted that creating an unrestricted cause of action for use whenever uncommitted patients acted out could create an excessive burden on therapists and lead to overcommitment. The court also recognized that "good faith" decisions not to pursue commitment made with proper professional diligence should not lead to liability. Consequently, the court propounded the "Psychotherapist Judgment Rule" (or P.J.R.) as a test to determine when failure to commit is negligent. The elements of the test include:

(1) "The competence and training of the reviewing psychotherapists,
(2) whether the relevant documents and evidence were adequately, promptly and independently reviewed,
(3) whether the advice or opinion of another therapist was obtained,
(4) whether the evaluation was made in light of the proper legal standards for commitment, and
(5) whether other evidence of good faith exists."

Ironically, though the *Currie* case breaks new ground in imposing a harsh burden on therapists in general, the defendant therapists won the most recent appeal. When the court applied the test above it noted that the therapists were well qualified and highly experienced, that adequate documentation and review were extant, that on two separate occasions panels of board-certified therapists had discussed the case, and that the therapists must have acted in good faith since they too had been threatened by the patient and would have confined him if they thought it possible. Although this case is now on appeal in the Fourth Circuit and although the test described is exceptionally vague, therapists should recognize this decision as the current state-of-the-art in defining duty to protect third parties.

Avoiding *Tarasoff* Liability

Following California's lead, 14 states have adopted Tarasoff theories of liability, while only two have rejected this logic (Goodman, 1985). Therapists now correctly assume that to avoid liability they must warn third parties who are specifically threatened by their clients. These warnings must often be given in spite of licensing laws which require confidentiality, although at least one state (Maryland in *Shaw v. Glickman*, 1980) has held that statutory protection of confidentiality is a bar against suits for failure to warn. Obviously, states whose laws explicitly mention exceptions for dangerousness expect warnings to be given, and usually the therapist is protected from suits by disgruntled patients for breach of confidence. Therapists in states that have not addressed the issue may be in a real bind, because it is not known whether they could be sued for failure to warn or for breach of confidence if they give "unnecessary" warnings. Whenever warnings are given they should be as discreet as possible and include only information directly relevant to the threatened party's safety. Moreover, the rationale for the disclosure should be discussed with the client (Beck, 1982).

Regarding the newly recognized duty to commit, it is unclear whether other jurisdictions will accept this theory. Certainly, the logic for requiring therapists to do more than simply warn has been written into numerous decisions, including *Tarasoff* itself. Less clear is whether commitment could be used as an alternative to warning, although this would seem more than reasonable. To the extent that revelation of therapy confidences to impartial authorities is less intrusive to clients than revealing their passions toward significant figures in their lives, commitment could be seen as a more viable therapeutic option. Of course, such judgments are hard to make.

Numerous questions can be raised regarding any adaptation of the "Psychotherapist Judgment Rule." Does a valid license to practice demonstrate adequate "competence and training"? What kinds of documents are relevant and what qualifies as a prompt and independent review? If the advice or opinion of other therapists is sought, must it be followed, or may the consultants merely aid in exploring the relevant issues? Can the consultants then be held liable for their part in the decision?

Most therapists probably already pursue the general guidelines described in the P.J.R. when patients make overt threats or appear to pose a significant danger to a third party. Careful documentation and consultation with qualified colleagues serve as a first step in meeting this challenge. If the decision to commit or warn remains unclear, it is safest to leave the ultimate responsibility to a judge or magistrate by initiating civil commitment proceedings (see Chapter 4), even if there is some doubt as to whether the client meets the appropriate criteria. If the court refuses to commit, it is unlikely that civil suit could be effectively brought against the therapist.

OTHER LIMITS ON PSYCHOTHERAPEUTIC PRACTICE

Informed Consent and Related Liability

The concept of informed consent can be conceptually seen as a way of protecting basic individual liberties. To the extent that consumers of psychotherapy and related activities are not informed about what these services entail, they are not free to make basic choices in their own interests. Their privacy is violated when they are treated in ways to which they did not fully accede. Conversely, competent adults who receive adequate information about the options available to them are free to exercise their own judgment in determining what service is best for them. Because of this linkage between informed consent and infringement of personal liberty, a variety of issues related to informed consent can lead to liability for therapists. Some of these specific issues will be addressed below.

The broad goal in informed consent is to provide consumers with sufficient information to make a reasoned decision about the services offered them. Much thinking in this area is derived from medical practice and tends to focus on cost-benefit analyses. For example, it is suggested that key information includes the risks inherent in receiving no intervention, the various alternative treatments, and the costs, advantages, and disadvantages of each alternative. This reasoning may be best suited to areas of treatment with the potential for severe and permanent negative outcomes. Some types of therapy, such as ECT and psychosurgery, fit this model well, as do some types of pharmacological therapies. In some situations, behavioral interventions may also require special attention to informed consent issues. This is particularly true when aversive methods or deprivation are to be used (see *Knetch v. Gillman*, 1973).

A key problem in informed consent arises from the possibility of "overinforming" the patient. If the intent is to empower clients to make their own decisions, excessive information, particularly regarding highly unlikely negative outcomes, may actually decrease their ability to come to a reasonable decision. For example, minor medical diagnostic procedures that require use of intravenous lines carry an exceedingly small risk of severe complications due to blood-born infections. It is unclear whether giving this information would help patients make a decision, or make them overly cautious about a service that they might really need. Unfortunately, withholding potentially negative information may expose therapists to liability if one of the unspecified treatment failures results. One attempt to resolve this dilemma has been to ask clients to choose whether they wish to be informed of all forseeable outcomes or only those with a reasonable probability.

A problem arises when the client is unable to give informed consent. Children, for example, are viewed as unable to weigh the complex choices involved in mental health care, though it is assumed that parents may substitute in giving consent to most procedures. In addition many of the potential recipients of psychotherapeutic services experience difficulties which may compromise their decision-making in subtle ways (Gutheil & Bursztajn, 1986). Still, as discussed in Chapter 4, even persons who are committed to hospitals against their will may retain the legal capacity to make treatment decisions, regardless of therapists' views of their actual capacity in this area. Only through establishing guardianship (see Chapter 3) does the law address the need for substituted consent and decision-making for seriously impaired individuals. Failure to obtain informed consent from an appropriate substitute decision-maker can lead to liability if the procedures lead to any harm (see *Clites v. Iowa*, 1980 for an example involving tardive dyskinesia in a mentally retarded youth).

For very complex decisions or those which involve irreversible procedures, such as psychosurgery, even the patient's consent may be inadequate. Experimental or highly controversial methods typically require review by special panels of other professionals and sanctioning bodies such as patient advocacy groups. Many institutions establish review boards to address particularly difficult questions. When treatment involves esoteric procedures, information to the patient should generally include a direct statement that the treatment proposed is experimental and that many potential outcomes are not well-known or understood.

Abandonment

Once therapists establish a working relationship with clients, they assume a duty to provide ongoing care. This duty may be more significant in psychotherapy than in any other professional service because continuity and trust are so essential. The therapist may not abandon the patient by refusing to provide services when needed (emergencies) or by unexpectedly terminating the relationship with the client. Breaching this duty can lead to liability.

On the other hand, the therapist is not obligated to accept or keep any and all clients who present themselves. If reasonable efforts are made to find adequate care from other sources, the therapist may discontinue seeing a client. The therapist can neither be in the office every hour of every day nor devote all of his or her time to one individual. Reasonable provisions for emergency services and timely consultations are sufficient to discharge this duty.

(1) Make provisions for clients to contact you by phone if they have an emergency. Also provide the number of a colleague who has agreed to serve as "backup" in emergencies, and possibly the number of a local hospital or crisis service.

(2) When you cannot be contacted (for vacation or other reasons), make provisions for a responsible and well-qualified colleague to accept emergency calls. Reciprocate this favor.

(3) If you choose not to provide care to a given client, making arrangements for a new caretaker is your responsibility. At least three potential therapists should be identified and arrangements made for the client to consult with one or more of these. If none works out, additional referrals must be made. Only when another licensed professional has accepted the patient (and vice versa) does the original therapist's responsibility end.

Negligence Connected with Referral

While therapists may not abandon their clients, neither should they hold on to them when referral to other practitioners would be beneficial. Failure to refer is a type of negligence if it leads to some injury to the client. For example, a client consulting a psychologist who describes a recent blow to the head followed by recurrent headaches, personality changes, and difficulty with memory and concentration, may have sustained a neurologic injury. Alternatively, he may be displaying a conversion syndrome. The psychologist would be expected to ascertain whether a neurologist or other physician was involved in the case, and either consult with that person or make an appropriate referral to help in the diagnostic process. If the psychologist proceeded on the assumption that no organic damage was present, he could be held liable for negligently failing to refer the patient to a practitioner capable of treating his problem.

Referrals are generally made in order to obtain the services of a professional with greater expertise in a given area. For this reason it is sometimes difficult to decide when a therapist should have known that a referral was warranted. If, by definition, a psychotherapist is not an expert in neurology, say, then what level of expertise should be expected in screening for the referral? As in other areas, the standard has generally been that others in the same discipline would seek the help of a specialist in the same circumstances.

Because malpractice litigation is so common in medical settings, doctors often resort to "defensive medicine" to cover all potential causes of liability. While overuse of consultants *may* help prevent liability for negligent diagnosis or failure to refer, it is costly and frustrating for clients. Therapists should refer when they believe there is a reasonable possibility that the patient will benefit, not as a reflex to avert a very unlikely cause for liability. There have also been recent cases in which a referring professional was held to share liability vicariously when a consultant engaged in negligent practices. That is, referring to an "expert" made the original caretaker liable for the expert's errors.

SPECIAL LEGAL ISSUES IN CONFIDENTIALITY AND PRIVILEGE

The legal background of the right to privacy began as an integral part of ancient Jewish law (the Talmud) over 1500 years ago (Margulis, 1977). Early English common law recognized a broad right of privacy which has been associated with the concept of "honor among gentlemen." Ironically, it was actually established as a legal precedent when Lady Henrietta Berkley asserted a privilege not to testify in the 1689 trial of her lover, Lord Grey (Baldwin, 1962).

In the United States, the first formal description of the legal boundaries of privacy was written by Samuel Warren and Louis Brandeis. In 1890 these two Boston lawyers published "The Right to Privacy," a journal article which became the basis for many subsequent judicial decisions and legislation. They defined privacy as the right to be left alone or elect not to share information about private matters, habits, and relationships. Important Supreme Court decisions have affirmed this reasoning (see *Griswold v. Connecticut*, 1965).

Confidentiality and Privilege

The terms confidentiality and privilege, though often confused, actually refer to different legal concepts. Confidentiality refers to the broad expectation that what is revealed in a private or "special" relationship based upon trust will not be shared with third parties. Obviously, the kind of information revealed by individuals in therapy fits into this category. Privilege is a narrower concept that concerns the admissibility of information in a court of law, though in practice it really refers to whether courts may legitimately compel revelation of confidential information for the purposes of legal proceedings. Changes in legal conceptions of privilege and confidentiality obviously set limits on the degree of privacy which therapists and clients can maintain, regardless of tradition and professional interests. While the current trend is toward the erosion of both confidentiality and privilege, there have been persuasive calls for limiting legal interference with the strict privacy that should be maintained in psychotherapy (see Meyer & Willage, 1980).

The most obvious situation in which a therapist may ethically breach confidentiality is with the approval of the client. The most common breach of confidence is created by the client's own signature on an insurance company claim form or an application for services from a state welfare agency. Third-party payers assert that they have a right to substantiate the basis for claims, and clients usually accept this reasoning, perhaps due to financial pressures. A typical authorization to release information might read as follows:

> I hereby authorize any physician, medical practitioner, hospital, clinic or other medical or medically-related facility, insurance company, or other organization, institution or person, that has any records or knowledge of the health, observation, diagnosis or treatment of either myself or any member of my family to give to [the] insurance company any and all information it requests with respect to such records or knowledge. A photocopy of this authorization shall be as valid as the original. (Smith, 1979, p. 108)

The message disguised within the convoluted language is frightening: "I hereby authorize any . . . person . . . that has knowledge of . . . myself or any member of my family . . . to give . . . any and all information." Smith characterizes this blanket release as an unlimited search warrant with no time limit or expiration date.

It is extremely unlikely that clients understand the ramifications of such a release. Once the form is signed, all the information collected may be placed in archives or computer databanks and kept indefinitely. Clients may never know where that information eventually ends up, or who will see it, or how it will be used. Because it is rare for clients to review this information after it is collected, there is potential for inaccurate or misleading data to be stored and perpetuated.

Why do those in therapy (and other types of treatment for that matter) agree to sign away their right to privacy? As mentioned above, they probably do not realize that they are doing so, and may expect insurance carriers to obey professional standards of confidentiality. They may also agree because they simply need the benefits of third-party reimbursement, which they will otherwise be denied. Therapists probably participate in this system for similar reasons.

Psychotherapists may be caught in an ethical bind. Releasing information about the therapy under these conditions may be legal and technically ethical, but is it really in the client's interests? Many practitioners attempt to limit the amount of sensitive information provided, which may be workable in some circumstances, particularly for outpatient therapy. Most carriers, however, require considerable documentation before they will reimburse for inpatient care. Should the therapist "help" the patient by revealing enough to justify the payments or should he maintain confidentiality even though it may be financially disastrous for the client?

In response to these sorts of issues, some 40 states have adopted nondisclosure laws aimed at limiting the release of sensitive information by therapists and institutions such as state agencies, and to a lesser extent by private insurance carriers (Weisberg & Wald, 1987). These laws try to redress the problems of information leakage in large agencies where not only professionals but also support personnel such as secretaries and data-processing specialists may obtain access to information on the health, mental status, financial and social background of their clientele. While bureaucracies invariably compile records, at least the sensitive records can be confined within the agency or group that developed them. Statutes often employ very broad language intended to protect all information from release without the explicit consent of the affected party, and attempt to enforce confidentiality on state-employed therapists as well as their coworkers. Therapists employed by state agencies and community mental health centers should be particularly attuned to the prohibitions of nondisclosure laws likely to be binding upon them. Failure to comply can lead to a variety of sanctions, as specified in the statute. Private practitioners are rarely affected by these provisions.

Privilege

Testimonial privilege is a special case of confidentiality. It refers to a valid basis for refusal to testify in legal proceedings, and is granted to protect important relationships based on trust. Because privilege, the right to refuse to testify, sometimes interferes with legal proceedings, courts are reluctant to recognize it. Common law concepts of privilege have been narrowed to include only spousal and attorney-client privileges, though there have been legal treatises suggesting a basis for broader privileges. On the other hand, legislatures recognize the need for confidentiality in certain important circumstances, even over and above the wishes of the court. Statutes may establish additional privileges, such as physician-patient and psychotherapist-client, which the courts in that jurisdiction must respect (note that a clergy-parishioner privilege is mentioned in the first amendment).

In the late 1950s and early '60s, there was a movement to extend privilege specifically to psychotherapists. Because the potential information lost to the courts may be significant, important public policy reasons are required to grant an extension of privilege to a new group. It has to be shown that the professional's work (and therefore society) would be greatly harmed by allowing the courts to compel breaches of confidentiality.

How is this to be assessed? The most widely recognized test of the appropriateness of testimonial privilege derives from the thinking of the eminent legal scholar, Wigmore (1970). Wigmore proposed a cost-benefit analysis from society's perspective as follows:

(1) The communications must originate in a confidence that they will not be disclosed.
(2) This element of confidentiality must be essential to the full and satisfactory maintenance of the relation between the parties.
(3) The relation must be one which in the opinion of the community ought to be sedulously fostered (actively encouraged).
(4) The injury that would inure (occur) to the relation by the disclosure of the communications must be greater than the benefit thereby gained from the correct disposal of the litigation.

While Wigmore's criteria can be seen as a test to be employed in any given case, these standards have been broadly applied to the practice of psychotherapy to justify the creation of a formal privilege. As noted earlier, nearly all therapy clients expect confidentiality; successful therapy generally requires both a relationship based on trust and full sharing of information, much of it sensitive, between client and therapist; the therapeutic professions are recognized as important contributors to the quality of life in society; and compromising the practice of psychotherapy by denying privilege is unlikely to aid courts in an appreciable way. Most states have recognized the validity of this reasoning and have enacted legislation to create a formal psychotherapist privilege.

It is important to note that Wigmore's test addresses only social utility as a basis for privileges. Other thinkers have suggested that therapists should be able to assert testimonial privilege simply based upon the privacy rights of patients. While there is currently no recognized common law privilege for therapists, at least one state and one federal district have elucidated such reasoning (Alaska in *Allred v. State* and the 6th circuit in *In re Zuniga*), and favorable readings of these cases may lead to greater recognition.

A central concern in establishing privileges is defining who will be covered. Most states include only psychiatrists and clinical psychologists. Other groups, such as psychiatric social workers, school psychologists, and pastoral counselors are often excluded, although each of these groups provides important services and may receive sensitive and important information in the course of their work. A key issue is the legal recognition of the profession. These latter groups are generally not controlled by licensing boards, and most privilege statutes utilize state licensure as part of their definitions. These groups may also lack the political clout to gain consideration by legislative bodies.

Privilege itself is not the absolute shield it appears to be. Even if the professional has a statutory right to privilege, the interpretation of when it applies is left to the court. Also, with rare exceptions (Everstine et al., 1980), the right to claim the privilege belongs to the patient, not the therapist. If the client waives the right to privilege, the therapist must testify.

Why would the client waive privilege? The usual reason is called the patient/litigant exception. When individuals file lawsuits alleging that they have suffered emotional pain or psychological trauma, then the court has an interest in exploring information surrounding these claims. Obviously, information from past or current therapy would seem material and relevant. Courts have generally held that once the issue of mental or emotional state is raised by the plaintiff, then information that would otherwise be privileged becomes discoverable. After all, it would hardly be fair to allow the plaintiff to allege psychic damages, then forbid the defendant from exploring these issues fully.

The patient/litigant exception creates a Pandora's Box effect; once any privileged information is released, all privilege is destroyed, although some courts have reasoned that if the plaintiff can show that some confidential information is clearly irrelevant, then it will not be admitted. Even if the therapist believes that revealing confidences will be harmful to the patient, he cannot assert privilege. It belongs to the patient and is his to waive (see *In re Lifschutz*, 1970, and *Caesar v. Mountanos*, 1976). By the same token, the therapist cannot choose to waive the privilege if it exists and the patient wants to assert it.

Although therapists usually wish to assert testimonial privilege, they sometimes do not. If a disgruntled client sues for malpractice, the therapist will generally be allowed to give testimony about the details of therapy as part of their defense. The same is true if therapists sue to obtain fees owed them. The court usually tries to minimize the amount of information revealed, and it is common for material to be explored in chambers or with the jury absent before deciding what can be admitted.

Additional failures of privilege arise due to the presence of third parties. Courts have interpreted the Wigmore criteria to mean that if information is given to a third party there is no expectation of confidence and hence no privilege. While it makes sense to assume that someone who discusses his therapy with a neighbor cannot assert that his secrets must be protected from the court, what of people who give information to an insurance carrier or participate in group therapy? A recent Minnesota case (*Minnesota v. Andring*, 1984) has recognized that group therapy does involve an expectation of privacy, and that privilege should apply. Similar reasoning should apply to third-party reimbursement.

Other exceptions to privilege arise in civil commitment procedures and during court-ordered evaluations. Finally, the Supreme Court has decided that criminal defendants may assert their sixth amendment rights to compel testimony in their defense, even over common law exclusions, such as a psychotherapist-patient testimonial privilege (*Pennsylvania v. Ritchie*, 107 S.Ct. 989, 1987).

CHAPTER 2

Criminal Responsibility and the Insanity Defense

The character of every act depends on the circumstances in which it is done.

— Oliver Wendell Holmes, Jr.

Free Will is but an illusion.

— Anatole France

MR. WILLIS WAS charged with disorderly conduct and two counts of assault. At the time of the alleged offenses he was a patient in a psychiatric hospital near his home town; he was accused of assaulting members of the nursing and security staff.

For a number of years Mr. Willis had harbored delusional beliefs that agents of a foreign government meant to harm him in some way. He had been admitted to other hospitals on three previous occasions. Given this history of mental disorder, his attorney raised a question regarding criminal responsibility at the time of the alleged offenses. That is, he asked the court to order an examination by a forensic psychologist or psychiatrist to determine if his client may have suffered from a mental illness sufficient to compromise his ability to know right from wrong. The court would hear testimony regarding the accused's mental status at the time of the offenses and then decide if Mr. Willis should be held responsible for his actions under those conditions. In addition, the judge directed the examiners to gather data regarding the accused's current mental status and functioning.

The judge would hear this evidence and decide if the accused was able to participate effectively in the legal proceedings that would ensue.

Following Mr. Willis's arrest, he was released into the custody of his family, who sought the assistance of a local mental health center where Mr. Willis was placed on antipsychotic medication and seen three times per week for intensive therapy and supervision. Consequently, by the time the court ordered a forensic evaluation his mental status had greatly improved. He was able to recognize that his fears had been delusional and that his legal situation could have serious consequences. He presented as bright and articulate and was motivated to aid his attorney in his own defense. He was diagnosed as paranoid schizophrenic, in remission. While many signs of mental illness remained, he was viewed as stable and functional at that time. Relevant information was relayed to the court, which reviewed these findings in an open hearing and determined that Mr. Willis was mentally competent to stand trial if the State wished to pursue the charges against him.

The findings regarding his mental status at the time of the alleged offenses were less benign. The accused had become quite psychotic during the weeks preceding his hospital admission, claiming that "hit men" had been sent from totalitarian countries to kill him. His behavior was so bizarre that he was stopped by police, who transported him to the local hospital for possible commitment. At that point he agreed to become a patient voluntarily. Although he was initially cooperative, the following day he became agitated and suspicious and asked to be discharged. Staff members felt his condition required inpatient care and sought involuntary commitment. In a subsequent attempt to flee the hospital grounds he struggled briefly with a nurse's aide and later struck a security guard who tackled him near the gates — hence the assault charges.

The examiners collected data from a variety of sources, including Mr. Willis, staff at the hospital, records from previous hospitalizations, family members, and the police officers who had detained him. He was also given a battery of medical and psychological tests. The examiners concluded that at the time of the alleged offenses he had been acutely paranoid and likely to respond to even innocuous behavior from others as if his safety were threatened. When hospital staff detained him it confirmed in his mind that they were part of the plot to kill him. His attorney intended to argue that the "assaults" were attempts on his part to escape this fate and that, given his intense and unshakable belief that he was about to be killed, his actions were justifiable attempts at self-defense. The attorney believed that the examiner's findings would be interpreted by the jury as evidence that Mr. Willis did not understand that what he was doing was wrong, or that his desperation would have prompted him to act despite such knowledge.

The results of the psychological evaluation suggested that Mr. Willis may have been legally "insane" at the time of his criminal acts, but that his condition had improved sufficiently since that time to render him mentally competent to stand trial. The district attorney felt that it would be pointless to continue prosecution when it appeared that a jury would find the accused not responsible. The case was resolved when Mr. Willis agreed to continue care through the local mental health center under the supervision of the court in exchange for dismissal of the charges against him.

The example given above is a real one, though certain details have been changed to maintain the confidentiality of those involved. It suggests a number of important ideas. First, "insanity" or criminal responsibility and competence to stand trial are completely distinct. The former refers to judgments about an offender's mental status at the time of a crime, while the latter refers to his condition at the time of the ensuing hearings and trial, which may be very much later. Questions concerning insanity and competence may be raised independently, and the determination of one issue has no strict implications for the other. It is also important to note that insanity is not a defense only to charges of murder, as many people believe, but may be raised against lesser charges. The ultimate decisions on these questions are not made by psychologists or psychiatrists. The experts who examine the accused provide a broad range of clinical data to the court, data which require special training and experience to gather and interpret. The court receives this evidence and makes the formal determination regarding the defendant's legal culpability at the time of the offense.

In the following pages we examine the insanity defense in detail. Incompetency to stand trial is considered in Chapter 3, along with other questions of legal capacity.

THE INSANITY DEFENSE

The whole notion of the insanity defense makes professionals in both law and psychotherapy uneasy. Lawyers are uncomfortable with the idea that persons may not be held accountable for their actions, although the rationale for such exemption has existed in legal lore for at least a thousand years (Smith & Meyer, 1987). Clinicians find it disquieting to view the behavior of some individuals as blameworthy and morally culpable when those actions may be the product of ingrained processes largely shaped by experience or genetics. Of course, even such insight does not make it any easier to exonerate someone for serious and frightening crimes. Despite this uneasiness and decades of criticism, the insanity defense remains a part of our legal system because it serves an important purpose: It assures that punishment for criminal acts will not be exacted from those who cannot profitably be viewed as guilty in the usual sense of the word.

Put simply, the rationale for the insanity defense is that some persons, due to mental illness or incapacity, do not have powers of decision-making or behavioral control that we normally expect from those whom the law will govern. Anglo-American law, partly due to its connection with the Judeo-Christian religious tradition, places strong emphasis upon individual free will and "the consequent ability and duty of the normal individual to choose between good and evil" (*Morissette v. U.S.*, 1950). From this perspective, guilt arises when one chooses to ignore what is required by law for the social good, and voluntarily does wrong. The law speaks of the *mens rea* (evil intent) and the *actus reus* (evil act) which ensues. Both of these elements must be present to make a "complete crime" (*Blackstone's Commentaries*, 1898). Even when criminal offenses have the same outcome, such as the death of another person, there may be varying degrees of criminal responsibility, depending on the state of mind of the offender. The accused could face charges ranging from reckless homicide to first degree murder, as willful involvement in the crime ranges from negligence or carelessness to malice aforethought.

Generally, adults are presumed to have the capacity for free choice between good, lawful behavior and unlawful conduct, and are therefore held responsible when they commit criminal actions. But what of persons who, because of significant mental illness or disability, appear to have little ability to know what is lawful or to manage their own behavior accordingly? Our legal tradition holds that "guilt is necessarily based upon a free mind voluntarily choosing evil rather than good; there can be no criminality in the sense of moral shortcoming if there is no freedom of choice or normality of will capable of exercising a free choice" (Sayre, 1932). That is, persons who are deprived of their free choice by mental incapacity are not blameworthy; they are not to be held responsible for bad behaviors over which they had little control. Although they may clearly have committed a criminal act, because they could not voluntarily embrace evil intent they have not committed a complete crime and must be dealt with differently from other offenders.

Criminal responsibility normally carries several justifications for levying punishment against an offender. At the most basic level, it incapacitates the offender, making it impossible, by virtue of incarceration or similar mechanism, for him to repeat the unacceptable behavior. It may also be a deterrent, helping to assure that the criminal will not choose a similar course in the future. To the extent that others in society observe the negative consequences of unlawful behavior it may serve to deter them from similar acts.

More recently, criminal responsibility has been viewed as justification for rehabilitation efforts, though these may be undertaken as much for the long-term benefit of society as for the good of the offender. Finally, punishment "may express a formal social retribution" (Smith & Meyer, 1987). Put more simply, it may be a way for society to act out its repugnance at criminality and maintain the illusion that the world is a just place because those who do harm to others are punished.

Since punishment is viewed as inappropriate for those who are found "insane" or not criminally responsible, they receive different disposition from the courts. If they are so severely impaired, they are not likely to learn the error of their ways through simple punishment, nor are they suitable examples to others. Incapacitation and rehabilitation may be served in other, more humane ways, such as confinement for mandatory treatment. Although the law recognizes these differences, society at large may have a difficult time accepting them. What often remains, particularly in cases of bizarre and sensational behavior, is society's nagging fear, anger, and frustration when retribution is not forthcoming. These impulses prompt intermittent calls for abolition of the insanity defense.

The first insanity defense to attract widespread attention in America was the 1800 case of James Hadfield, which was actually tried in Britain but widely publicized in the United States. A jury found Mr. Hadfield "not guilty, he being under the influence of insanity at the time the act was committed" (Slovenko, 1973). American satirist Mark Twain (Samuel Clemens) helped crystalize a short-lived backlash against the finding through his essay *A New Crime: Legislation Needed*, which alleged that numerous criminals were encouraged to act out with the assumption that they could fake insanity and win acquittal for their crimes. In his view it was the insanity defense that was the real crime. Mr. Hadfield himself faded from public view, largely because he was locked away in an asylum until his death 40 years later.

Public fascination with insanity adjudications probably stems from a few highly publicized cases, such as those involving shocking crimes followed by unpopular acquittals. Ultimately, the decision to punish or exculpate a disordered offender is not a psychological or medical one, but involves ethical and moral considerations. Public dissatisfaction with the choices made reflects the continuing tension between the values of individual accountability versus mercy for those who are tragically afflicted. Often these ethical imperatives are in direct opposition, and choosing between them remains difficult and problematic. In an attempt to reconcile these conflicting motives, the law has evolved a series of tests or descriptions to define those whose mental illness is so severe that they should not be held responsible for their criminal conduct. We will briefly review these before discussing the pragmatic challenges that face a clinician who may become involved in an insanity case.

INSANITY TESTS

The M'Naughten Rule

A delusional misfit aims to assassinate a popular political figure, but the intended target survives and continues as the nation's leader. In a dramatic and highly publicized trial the would-be assassin is found insane and acquitted of the charges against him. A storm of protest follows as the outraged public, the press, and other political leaders push for restriction of the "insanity defense."

While this may sound like a synopsis of John Hinckley's attempt on the life of Ronald Reagan, it is actually a brief account of events in 1843. The first and certainly most influential formal legal test of insanity used in this country is derived from English law. As early as the 1500s, common law had recognized that "lunatics and idiots" whose mentality approached that of a "wild beast" could not be held responsible for otherwise illegal conduct (see Brooks, 1974). Still, these issues were largely ignored until the trial of one Daniel M'Naughten, who held delusional beliefs that Britain's Tory party was responsible for his difficult lot in life. He saw Sir Robert Peel, prime minister and the head of the party, as his chief persecutor and resolved to kill him. He fired a pistol into the prime minister's carriage, which unfortunately was occupied by the minister's secretary, who died of his wounds. The judge at M'Naughten's trial instructed the jury that he should be acquitted if they believed that he was insane at the time of the crime, and he was indeed found not responsible.

The reaction from Queen Victoria and the House of Lords, who feared politically motivated violence, was swift. The judges of England's highest court were assembled and directed to determine a strict rule defining when an insanity acquittal would be justified. They settled on the following test:

> That the jurors ought to be told in all cases that every man is to be presumed to be sane, and to possess a sufficient degree of reason to be responsible for his crimes, until the contrary be proved to their satisfaction; and that to establish a defense on the ground of insanity, it must be clearly proved that, at the time of the committing of the act, the party accused was labouring under such a defect of reason, from disease of the mind, as to not know the nature and quality of the act he was doing; or if he did know it that he did not know he was doing what was wrong. (*Daniel M'Naughten's Case*, 1843).

Although the instructions to the jury in the M'Naughten trial were somewhat less restrictive, the test given above is generally associated with his name. This rule was adopted by American courts and was the basic legal test of insanity in this country until the 1950s. It continues to be used today in many state jurisdictions, and forms the basis for the recently enacted rule for federal courts described in more detail below.

The M'Naughten test has been widely criticized for a variety of reasons. Most of these complaints center on its narrow focus on "knowing," apparently confining the database for insanity decisions to cognitive functions. One commentator provided a hypothetical illustration of the rule's application: If the accused believed that he were squeezing a lemon when, in fact, he was strangling someone, then he "did not know the nature and quality" of the act (Shapiro, 1984). From a pragmatic point of view very few persons, even those who are profoundly disturbed, are this out of touch with reality.

In some sense the M'Naughten rule asks that crazy behavior be explainable in very logical and straightfoward terms in order to meet criteria for insanity. If a crime is committed simply because the accused did not understand what he was doing, then society will understand and excuse it. If it is prompted by more complex factors that seem obscure to nonclinicians, then it will not be excused. Yet, there appear to be many factors which contribute to criminal behavior which do not fit well into the simplistic model offered by the M'Naughten rule. Recognition of the rule's limitations prompted one scholar to observe that it made it "impossible to convey to the judge and jury the full range of information material to an assessment of defendant's responsibility" (*United States v. Brawner*, 1972).

Irresistible Impulse

Partly due to dissatisfaction with the M'Naughten rule, many jurisdictions adopted a complementary test that would take into account the degree of volitional control a defendant could reasonably exercise. As early as 1872 courts recognized that some impulses could not be resisted by will or reason. A person overwhelmed by rage, fear, or other "heat of passion" could "avoid criminal responsibility even though he is capable of distinguishing between right and wrong, and is fully aware of the nature and quality of his act provided he establishes he was unable to refrain from acting" (*Pennsylvania v. Walzack*, 1976). The intense impulse need not be the result of a mental illness to meet this criterion. In fact, it may be easier to persuade a jury that an impulse was irresistible if it is the result of emotions with which they can empathize. For example, a man who catches his wife in an illicit sexual encounter and immediately kills her may have an easier time convincing a jury that he was overcome by rage, jealousy, and betrayal than one who is equally distraught because of delusional beliefs related to a mental disorder.

Most jurisdictions have attempted to limit irresistible impulse defenses to instances of extreme provocation. The "cop at the elbow" test is a common guide. The reasoning is that if an individual were so overwrought that he would be oblivious to the possible consequences of a criminal act even with an officer of the law at hand to see the crime and make an arrest, then that impulse clearly would be irresistible. A case summarized by Shapiro (1984) illustrates the resistance to extending this defense to the mentally ill. The defendant, who had a history of antisocial conduct and repeated arrests, experienced delusional commands to "get a body." He subsequently approached four police officers sitting together in a restaurant and shot one of them dead. He killed with not one, but four, officers literally at his elbow. The state argued that this was not an irresistible impulse, but one not resisted. In practice discriminating between irresistible and unresisted impulses is quite difficult, and such guides as the cop at the elbow test are of little help.

At a practical level, irresistible impulse acquittals are rare, except when the crime quickly follows some clear provocation and is motivated by strong, easily recognized motives. These crimes generally entail vengeful acts directed at another person, although sometimes indirect revenge through damaging property may also be covered. Most state jurisdictions recognize an irresistible impulse defense, often in combination with the M'Naughten rule; further, the Supreme Court has applied it to criminal law by way of dictum.

The Durham Rule

As noted earlier, the M'Naughten rule has been generally regarded as too restrictive by clinicians and more progressive legal scholars. In an attempt to open up the lines of communication between experts and the courts, Judge David Bazelon of the District of Columbia Circuit Court of Appeals formulated a new rule in *Durham v. United States*, (1954).

> Unless [the jury believes] beyond a reasonable doubt either that [the accused] was not suffering from a disease or defective mental condition, or that the act was not the product of such abnormality, you must find the accused not guilty by reason of insanity. . . . He would still be responsible if there was [sic] no causal connection between such mental abnormality and the act.

This test requires the jury to determine if a criminal act was causally connected to a mental disease or defect. It can be viewed as similar to questions of proximate cause in tort law, where the court tries to determine if some harm would not have occurred "but for" a major contributory act. The Durham rule may be interpreted as saying that if a criminal act would not have happened but for the accused's mental impairment, then there is no criminal responsibility. Ultimately, all tests of insanity aim to answer this question.

The Durham rule was originally viewed as a significant advance because it would allow experts to testify in their own terms. However, courts found it difficult to interpret the data offered, and attorneys often introduced an extremely broad (and often irrelevant) range of information in an attempt to explain criminal acts as the result of mental illness. As mentioned above, the Durham rule was more a statement of the court's intent than a formal test or guide for experts and jurors. In fact, research on insanity verdicts demonstrated that jurors reached similar conclusions when given the Durham rule and when no specific instructions were given at all (Simon, 1967). In practice, it produced such freewheeling testimony that juries were frequently confused and overwhelmed, and the D.C. Circuit dropped it in 1972. The Durham rule is not currently used in the United States.

The ALI Standard

In 1962 the American Law Institute concluded an extensive study of criminal responsibility by proposing a Model Penal Code complete with a rule that combined concepts from the existing tests of insanity and was somewhat more flexible than M'Naughten. Ten years later this standard was embraced by the D.C. Circuit court as a replacement for its Durham rule in *United States v. Brawner*, (1972); it was subsequently adopted by several states and the majority of federal jurisdictions. The Model Penal Code rule is:

> A person is not responsible for criminal conduct if at the time of such conduct, as a result of mental disease or defect, he lacks substantial capacity either to appreciate the criminality [wrongfulness] of his conduct or to conform his conduct to the requirements of the law. (American Law Institute, 1962)

The ALI standard seems to provide a number of improvements over earlier tests. It embraces issues related both to cognition and to volition, essentially bridging the traditional gap between M'Naughten and irresistible impulse. Note, also, that the traditional and narrow "know" is replaced by the term "appreciate." This is consistent with the interpretation of some American courts, which sought to broaden the M'Naughten criteria to cover those who may have the abstract knowledge that society views a given act as wrong, but who are unable to internalize and accept this knowledge due to incapacity. Perhaps most importantly, the concept of insanity per se is eliminated in the ALI standard. There are no all or none judgments, and clinicians may testify more effectively to the nature of the accused's mental status and the possible implications for decision-making and behavioral control. Under traditional instructions, juries may have been overly influenced by expert opinions regarding "insanity," believing it to be a matter for professionals. Under the ALI rule it is clear that the judgment to be made concerns legal and ethical responsibility, thus placing it squarely within the jury's discretion.

In recognition of the difficulty that may arise with the volitional prong of the test, namely deciding which acts could not be versus were not resisted, the ALI standard typically carries a caveat:

> The terms "mental disease or defect" do not include an abnormality manifested only by repeated criminal or otherwise antisocial conduct.

This exception appears to make the defense inaccessible to the psychopath, sociopath, or antisocial personality. Though chronic antisocial conduct may lead to a formal *DSM-III-R* diagnosis, the ALI standard would view this as a description of bad character rather than a discrete impairment compromising the conduct of an otherwise law-abiding individual. There are some difficulties with this caveat, which has not been fully accepted in all jurisdictions using the basic rule. It is unclear why a psychopath who is truly unable to conform to the law should be barred from the defense. Also, few persons diagnosed as antisocial personality exhibit *only* criminal or antisocial signs of disorder. There are few "pure" psychopaths.

The majority of American courts adopted the ALI rule or a similar combined cognitive and volitional test. Federal jurisdictions, in particular, embraced this standard over more traditional language. This situation continued until 1984 and the insanity acquittal of John Hinckley.

Insanity Defense Reform Act of 1984: The Hinckley Rule or M'Naughten II?

John Hinckley's attempt to assassinate President Ronald Reagan riveted public attention on the insanity defense. Videotapes of the attack, which gravely wounded four people including the president, were replayed countless times by the television networks, allowing people around the world to witness the offense in slow motion. Mr. Hinckley's extensive history of maladjustment served more to aggravate public outrage than to mitigate his responsibility, yet insanity could be his only defense to the charges.

The trial which followed, a news event itself, featured conflicting testimony from a variety of experts, including forensic psychiatrists and psychologists. Data presented to the jury ranged from notes taken by Hinckley's ex-therapist, through documentation of an extensive inpatient evaluation at a federal forensic hospital, to CAT scans of his brain. The jury confronted with this mass of data concluded that Hinckley was not responsible under the ALI rule, and he was acquitted.

The outrage that originally focused on Hinckley himself was soon directed at "liberals soft on crime [and] corrupt psychiatrists" (Rubenstein, 1986). Policymakers and journalists described the ALI standard as an invitation for social misfits to engage in serious crimes with the expectation that they could "get off." Among forensic clinicians it became fashionable to suggest that only a guilty verdict could have been correct, and that those who testified for the defense were either unscrupulous or ignorant. This hindsight was undoubtedly sharpened by absence of any direct knowledge of the case and by the certainty that such opinions would be well-received by the lay public. Against this background, the Congress eventually passed a statute that established a "reformed" test for insanity in all federal jurisdictions:

> It is an affirmative defense to a prosecution under any federal statute that, at the time of the commission of the acts constituting the offense, the defendant, as a result of a severe mental disease or defect, was unable to appreciate the nature and quality or the wrongfulness of his acts. Mental disease or defect does not otherwise constitute a defense. (United States Code, 1984)

This test has been used in federal courts since 1984. Under the statute the burden of proof is on the defendant to demonstrate insanity by clear and convincing evidence, indicating that the jury is to have a strong presumption of sanity. The similarity of this rule to the M'Naughten standard is clear (Rubenstein, 1986). There is no consideration given to volitional factors, only to cognitive issues, although the more expansive "appreciate" terminology has been retained from the ALI standard. As an affirmative defense, the insanity issue must be raised in the initial pleading of the case, at hearings well before the trial proper.

CURRENT STATUS OF THE INSANITY DEFENSE

What the Hinckley trial illustrated most clearly was that decisions about criminal responsibility remain very difficult and problematic. There was no question that Hinckley committed the acts alleged, nor was there any doubt that he was a severely disturbed individual. While the nature of his crimes warranted punishment, his disorder called for treatment. A jury deliberated carefully and came to what it believed was a just decision; nevertheless, many in our society disagreed. Even the subsequent legislation, which fundamentally reinstated the legal standards of 150 years ago, illustrates that little has changed in the attempt to balance social impulses toward retribution with more humane and moral impulses toward rehabilitation of the mentally ill.

There is widespread criticism of the insanity defense on many fronts, ranging from conservative, "law and order" politicians who advocate strict accountability to liberal attorneys who claim that insanity adjudications are merely a way of denying parole, judicial review, and other benefits to mentally ill offenders. Most complaints center on inaccurate perceptions of how widely it is misused, the very concept of insanity or mental illness, problems in obtaining expert testimony useful to the courts, the absence of clear legal and moral understanding of its implications, and the practical effects of insanity verdicts on defendants.

The persistent public belief that insanity acquittals are frequent and inappropriately applied to hard core criminals must be confronted. Surveys of legislators, college students, and the public at large show that it is commonly believed that one-third of all persons indicted for felonies plead insanity, with nearly half of those successful, yielding an overall estimate that about 15 out of 100 persons accused of crimes successfully avoid responsibility (Jeffrey & Pasewark, 1983; Pasewark & Seidenzahl, 1979). In reality, of all Americans tried for misdemeanors and felonies in 1978, only 1625—less than one-tenth of one percent—were acquitted due to insanity (Pasewark, Pantle, & Steadman, 1978). More recent estimates place the success rate for insanity pleas near the one per thousand level. Given that many offenders have some diagnosable mental illness, it is surprising that the rates are not higher. But, of course, the presence of mental illness does not automatically alleviate the criminal of responsibility; the disorder must have a significant role in producing the criminal acts.

Clearly, the amount of public attention directed at the insanity defense is inappropriate given its rarity. One reason for sparing use of the insanity plea is that it essentially amounts to an admission that the specific allegations are true. Many attorneys feel they have a much better chance of success with a conventional defense, possibly winning acquittal on a technicality or simply raising some "reasonable doubt" regarding the allegations. Unfortunately, cases involving sensational crimes and excessive press coverage tend to perpetuate the stereotype that many heinous crimes lead to insanity adjudications. Though insanity is not even raised as an issue in 98 percent of criminal cases, and is rarely successful then, it remains the focus of intense discussion among lawyers, therapists, and the public.

Aside from the belief that the insanity defense is frequently used, many are suspicious that it is attempted mainly by "'homicidal maniacs' and non-psychotic criminals who manipulate the criminal justice system" (Maloney, 1985). Research indicates that less than 10 percent of insanity verdicts involve homicides (Pasewark et al., 1978), with the majority involving property offenses or "victimless" crimes. When homicides are excused due to insanity, they generally involve family members or close acquaintances who become significant in the offender's pathological impulses or ideas, not randomly selected members of the public. As for the notion that well adjusted persons feign disorder, nearly three-fourths of insanity acquittees are diagnosed as psychotic (Petrila, 1982; Rogers, Dolmetsch, & Cavanaugh, 1981). These patients generally have histories of prior psychotic episodes, marginal adjustment, and previous hospitalizations, which are inconsistent with malingered or "faked" disorder. Other research indicates that those who plead insanity but have histories and clinical presentations consistent with antisocial personality disorder or other nonpsychotic conditions are almost always found responsible, at least in federal courts (Poss & Johnson, 1987).

The long-term effect of insanity judgment on the defendant is not perceived by most people. Lay people seem to imagine that an insanity verdict allows the defendant to walk out of the courtroom unencumbered. In reality, all jurisdictions provide for automatic initiation of commitment hearings along the lines of civil commitment, which will be discussed in Chapter 4. If the acquittee is found to present a current danger to society, he or she is confined to a secure institution for treatment. Though statutes vary in regard to the procedures for terminating this confinement, in practice the defendant/patient is likely to spend as much time involuntarily committed to a hospital as he or she would have spent in prison if simply convicted (Pogrebin et al., 1986). In fact, the Supreme Court has ruled that it may be justifiable to confine such patients longer than the maximum sentence they might otherwise have received. There is also wide variability in who retains control over the patient's fate. Convicted criminals generally enjoy periodic review of their status by parole boards, while patients typically are supervised only by hospital administrators, who are understandably reluctant to release them when there is any doubt as to their safety. Ultimately, being judged insane may be considerably more costly to a defendant than being convicted.

Much of the criticism ostensibly directed at the concept of the insanity defense is actually aimed at psychologists and psychiatrists who provide expert testimony. Many legal scholars suggest that expert opinions in this realm are of little value to the court. These claims are generally based on the belief that most insanity cases involve a "battle of experts" who give contradictory testimony. In reality, there is general agreement among experts around clinical issues (Petrila, 1982; Weiner, 1982). Most cases involving an insanity plea are resolved through plea bargains, as are the vast majority of criminal cases in general. Some difficult cases, such as the Hinckley trial, do involve contradictory testimony, and these promote the view that mental health experts are inconsistent, unreliable, and of little use to the courts. In practice, attorneys for each side in a major insanity case may interview and consult with dozens of experts in order to find a few whose testimony will be favorable to their case. Thus, cases that are "close calls" are biased to include conflicting testimony, both by the selection of the case and by the selection of the experts.

Halleck (1969) has argued that most discrepant expert opinions arise from disagreements about the ethical and legal implications of mental disorder, rather than about the nature and significance of the disorder itself. At Hinckley's trial, for instance, one expert endeavored to lecture the court on his (the expert's, not the defendant's) sense of justice. If experts properly confined themselves to clinical topics, the possibility for conflicting and unhelpful testimony would be reduced. More stringent qualification of witnesses would probably be beneficial, as practitioners with no specific familiarity with forensic and legal matters often provide less than satisfactory testimony.

Aside from the question of reliability or agreement among experts, some legal scholars argue that expert testimony is not helpful to the courts and merely confuses the jurors. Asserting correctly that the question of responsibility or sanity is a legal and ethical one, these critics claim that experts have no place expressing their opinions on such issues, as they are no more qualified than the jury to make such determinations. Some courts have aimed to prevent expert witnesses from offering opinions on the "ultimate issue" of insanity, confining them instead to reviewing and interpreting the subject's history, present symptoms, diagnosis, prognosis, etc. (see *Washington v. United States*, 1967). Often, these findings do not lead to a clear choice between the alternatives before the jury members, who remain faced with a difficult moral dilemma. It is wrong to view this as a lack of usefulness, however. The fact that clinical data do not foreclose the jurors' decision-making merely illustrates that such choices remain complex and fraught with philosophical conflicts, and that experts can testify without encroaching on the legal questions to be resolved. In one sense it may actually be the appropriate role of the expert to make the jury's decision *more* difficult by providing more data for it to consider.

Despite the widespread suggestion that clinicians should not offer conclusory opinions regarding sanity, courts typically ask for and expect one. Court orders mandating sanity evaluations generally require the examiner to prepare a written report containing, among other things, an opinion as to "... whether the person was insane at the time of the offense charged." Failing to comply with these orders as written may entail little risk of sanctions for contempt of court, but most experts are not inclined to test the waters. They give the courts what they order but say they do not want. Some forensic clinicians have interpreted the law's ambivalence about conclusory opinions as "talking out of both sides of its mouth" (Shapiro, 1984).

A PRAGMATIC APPROACH TO INSANITY EVALUATIONS

> At bottom, the determination whether a man is or is not held responsible for his conduct is not a [scientific], but a legal, social, or moral judgment. Ideally, [psychotherapists] — much like experts in other fields — should provide grist for the legal mill, should furnish raw data upon which the legal judgment is based . . . but once this information is disclosed, it is society as a whole, represented by a judge or jury, which decides whether a man with the characteristics described should or should not be held accountable.
>
> — *U.S. v. Freeman*, 1964

The court in *Freeman* succinctly stated an appropriate role for clinicians in insanity proceedings. Here we will review some of the pragmatic issues involved in generating "raw data" that will be informative to courts in their determinations of responsibility. It is important to remember that insanity is not a psychological or medical concept, and that clinical data must be structured in such a way that judges and juries may reasonably translate it into legal formulations.

A common difficulty encountered in an insanity evaluation is the fact that the time of the offense may be quite remote. In some cases the examiner may be asked to determine the mental status of the accused many months earlier. While some clinicians feel that retrospective judgments such as these are beyond the training and expertise of psychologists and psychiatrists, there are a number of reasons to believe that they can be made effectively. In fact, retrospective diagnoses and interpretations of behavior are not only possible but also common. Outside of forensic settings clinicians routinely collect historical data and draw inferences about diagnosis, treatment needs, and the like. For example, a middle-aged woman who presents with acute agoraphobia and panic attacks may describe an episode many years earlier during which she became very lethargic, lost interest in usual activities, and noted disturbances in sleep, appetite and libido. It takes little clinical acumen to retrospectively "diagnose" this as a major depressive episode, a common finding in persons who present with panic symptoms.

Further, many *DSM-III-R* diagnoses require interpretation of past history in order to assign specific labels. Consider antisocial personality disorder, which requires onset prior to age 15 as defined by specific criteria presented in the manual. When the subject to be diagnosed is an adult, the data required pertain to several years earlier. A formal diagnosis of schizophrenia requires at least six months' duration of symptoms comprising prodomal, active and residual phases in some combination. Again, attention must be paid to retrospective accounts of behavior to establish the diagnosis.

Similar reasoning can be applied to forensic issues, such as insanity evaluations, if two conditions are met. First, the clinician must stick to clinical data. If it is difficult to determine how "responsible" someone was in the past, it is largely because this is a legal and moral judgment outside the clinical realm. Second, many more sources of data must be considered in forensic than in routine clinical questions. Various processes may tend to bias the self-report of the subject, so that potentially more objective sources of information should also be used. In most settings investigation to establish the validity of a client's report is inappropriate, signaling a lack of trust or rapport with the clinician. In insanity evaluations there is every expectation that the subject's reports will be validated by other sources, and that attempts to actively gather information from many sources will be necessary. While some clinicians resist this process, feeling that it is a way of helping the courts convict the defendant, it is important to remember that if the information discovered indicates a severe mental illness compromising the defendant's functioning at the time of the offense, then documentation of this condition may help the defendant by demonstrating his appropriateness for treatment rather than punishment.

In most cases the issue of criminal responsibility is raised by an attorney hoping to mount an insanity defense, but the referral may also come from a prosecutor hoping to rebut one, or even from the judge seeking a neutral opinion. In any event, the first step in conducting the evaluation should always be to get a clear picture of what service is required, as well as the specific legal issues that pertain to the given jurisdiction. During the initial arrangements it is advisable to get a written request or order stating conditions of the clinician's involvement. If necessary, the referring attorney or the court clerk may be helpful in providing information on the specific legal standard for insanity in that jurisdiction. Often, attorneys may be in the process of "expert shopping" and will request only a limited evaluation with some feedback regarding initial impressions. Ethical clinicians will take care to insure that this process does not bias their perception of the case.

Obviously, the accused is the focus of the evaluation, but before the first interview at least two important issues need to be resolved. First, the clinician must decide how much background data to review prior the initial clinical interview. While allowing the referring party to provide some social history may expedite matters, this introduces the possibility that the expert's opinion will be challenged as biased. When the opinion is given in court, cross-examination may focus on the prejudicing effects of this information: "Doctor, can you say for certain that the information you reviewed about Mr. X's family background and social history prior to interviewing him did not influence your diagnosis?" For a variety of reasons (see Chapter 8), it is unwise to answer "yes" to such a question. To avoid this situation, many clinicians prefer to meet the accused one or more times prior to reviewing background data. A competing motive arises out of the clinician's need to look out for malingering. A complete knowledge of the case, including collateral information, before an interview enables the examiner to ask specific, detailed questions in a manner that makes deception difficult. Reconciling these two approaches to interviewing obviously requires several meetings with the subject. Initial interviews should serve to establish clinical impressions and to gather the subject's history in his own words. Later sessions may be devoted to clarification and confrontation of inconsistencies. At least three to four separate interviews should be conducted, preferably in different settings.

A second important concern prior to meeting the accused involves confidentiality, privilege, and Miranda-type warnings. The case law surrounding these issues is complex and not well standardized across jurisdictions, but some general trends are evident. First, if an expert is retained by the defense but comes to conclusions unfavorable to the defendant and is not called to testify, then he or she may be immune from subpoena to testify for the prosecution. The court in *Houston v. Alaska* (1979) found that the defendant must be free to explore the possibility of an insanity defense without the fear that his consultations might be used by the state, and likened this to the privilege in communicating with an attorney regarding defense strategies. There may be limits to this privilege, however, as other states have held that the prosecution may gain access to adverse preliminary reports under some circumstances (*State v. Carter*, Mo. 1982). Also, if the defendant calls a mental health expert to testify in court, privilege is waived altogether. That is, on cross-examination they may be asked to disclose any information revealed by the defendant during the evaluation. There may also be no privilege if the accused is incarcerated for purposes of a court-ordered evaluation at the request of the prosecution or the judge, on the reasoning that there is no expectation of confidentiality in such settings (*Pierce v. Georgia*, 1979).

There has been some question as to the accused's rights against self-incrimination in insanity evaluations. A key problem centers on the need to reconstruct the events leading up to the offense, as well as the defendant's behavior during the time in question and shortly after. If the defendant discusses these issues openly, an unscrupulous prosecutor may try to force the examiner to testify what the accused confessed to him. Some legal scholars suggest that a statement similar to the familiar Miranda warning should be given to alert the defendant not to reveal potentially incriminating details. This practice would undoubtedly hamper the collection of crucial data for the evaluation, implying a degree of partisan commitment to the prosecution's case that is inconsistent with a fair and unbiased evaluation.

Many clinicians refuse to place themselves in such a role. A straight-forward alternative may be to simply describe the purpose and conditions of the evaluation in layman's terms. In fact, ethical practice in clinical psychology and psychiatry probably requires this level of disclosure, regardless of legal standards. If the accused knows who requested the examination, its purpose, and that the results will be shared with the court, then he or she may make an informed choice as to what to reveal. If the examiner is forced, by threat of contempt citation, to say that the defendant recounted committing the offense, then the defense attorney may be able to capitalize on the lack of a formal warning to have the information extracted from the trial record or to form the basis for appeal.

Clinical Evaluation and Criminal Responsibility

As discussed above, initial meetings with the defendant should focus on establishing a working diagnosis and collecting clinical data. While it is not appropriate to review basic clinical interviewing skills here, several suggestions can be made. A thorough mental status exam should be conducted (Detre & Kupfer, 1975), including efforts to assess:

(1) physical appearance
(2) motor activities
(3) speech activity and patterns
(4) mood and affect
(5) alertness and attention
(6) content and organization of thoughts
(7) perception
(8) memory, abstract reasoning, and fund of knowledge
(9) attitude during exam and toward own condition

It is helpful to maintain a distinction between subjective data, reported by the subject, and more objective signs of psychological functioning observed by the examiner. This distinction may come to play a crucial role if malingering appears likely.

History-taking requires attention to conventional clinical content as well as issues specific to forensic evaluations. Questions regarding family background should include the possibility of domestic violence in the family of origin, drug and alcohol use, and criminal activity. When evaluating educational history, attention to matters such as disciplinary problems, truancy, and other signs of antisocial background should be noted, as well as the possibility of learning disability. A careful account of all marriages and divorces, children, and significant friendships should also be developed. Work history may help shed light on previous levels of adjustment. Particular attention should be paid to long periods of unemployment, particularly if the subject's financial condition was not significantly affected, as this may indicate a criminal vocation. A very thorough medical history should be gathered, even if the examiner is not a physician. Significant findings, particularly those related to head trauma or neurological signs may require consultation with a neurologist, neuropsychologist, or both.

Three key areas of history-taking are *psychological adjustment*, *drug and alcohol use*, and *criminal activity*. All prior contacts with mental health professionals, whether for treatment or evaluation, should be noted. If the history is positive for inpatient treatment, careful documentation of the dates and locations of confinement, medications received, follow-up care, and disposition is required.

Very detailed accounting of drug and alcohol use is advised. Many subjects initially describe themselves as moderate drinkers, but closer questioning reveals considerable variability, from intermittent, light drinkers to those who imbibe heavily every day. Given that well over half of all criminal offenses involve some type of intoxication, specifics of substance use must be established, including age of first use, amounts consumed, pattern of use (steady, intermittent extreme consumption with periods of abstinence, gradual increase over time, etc.), combinations of substances, and the subjective effects of all substances used on the patient. In those with a history of prescription drug use it is especially important to explore the possible interaction of prescribed and illicit drugs. The examiner should also probe for signs of dependence or withdrawal, and evaluate any prior involvement in detoxification or self-help programs.

Finally, the subject's history of criminal involvement should be explored, including arrests and convictions as well as their own reports of activity not detected by law enforcement authorities. The focus here is not on aiding the police but on describing the subject's behavior over time. Perhaps the most crucial information derived in the interview relates to the offense itself. The examiner must try to establish the parameters of the accused's mental status just before, during, and just after the offense. The defendant's own account plays a key role in this process. Questioning in this area may be difficult if the defendant believes that he is being pushed to confess or otherwise implicate himself.

Other work with the accused will involve testing (Grisso, 1986). A broad battery of psychological tests may be used to aid in diagnostic decisions, with a particular emphasis on objective, standardized measures. Care should be taken to select tests that allow some measure of response bias or "faking." A minimal battery might include the WAIS-R or a similar measure of intelligence, the MMPI or MCMI or a similar personality inventory, and one or more tests to screen for organic impairment. The Rorschach technique, while often helpful in identifying subtle signs of latent psychosis, is problematic because of its "fakability" and susceptibility to criticism in court. Examiners who use the Rorschach are advised to utilize the systematic approach of Exner (1983) and to integrate this data with other findings to strengthen their conclusions.

If specific questions arise in the course of clinical interviews, then testing aimed at certain issues may also be used. For example, a history of head trauma and suggestions of neurologic impairment might warrant administration of the Halstead-Reitan or Luria-Nebraska neuropsychological battery. If the examiner's expertise does not extend to the specific areas in question, then he should seek consultation with appropriate professionals.

Rogers et al. (1981) have developed a clinical tool specifically designed for insanity evaluations. The Rogers Criminal Responsibility Assessment Scale (RCRAS) is based on a model of the factors which should enter into translation of clinical data into the ALI standard for responsibility. It systematically measures five areas: the client's reliability, evidence of organic brain disturbances, evidence of psychopathology, cognitive control, and behavioral control. Objective decision rules enable the examiner to convert the specific data collected into an opinion under the ALI standard. Interrater agreement for the overall opinion appears quite good, indicating that when using such systematic methods professionals do often reach the same conclusion. Unfortunately, the utility of the RCRAS may have been reduced by the elimination of the ALI rule in federal jurisdictions.

Additional Data

While the clinical evaluation is under way, arrangements to gather collateral information can begin. At least five types of data should be considered. First, any documentation from the court, including orders and transcripts of hearings, should be examined, with an eye toward clarifying what data need to be provided. These documents help the examiner understand the current status of the accused within the legal system.

Second, a broad range of information related to the offense may be collected. Sources include arrest and investigative reports, statements from witnesses or victims, and records from jails or other holding facilities where the accused has been held. The examiner may even wish to interview these persons again. The arresting officers and witnesses can often provide a reasonable account of the defendant's actions during the offense, including observations of any unusual or bizarre behavior. These accounts can be compared with the defendant's own recollections. Law enforcement authorities can also provide "rap sheets" and other documentation of prior arrests and criminal investigations; these are invaluable in establishing the accuracy of the defendant's self-report.

Other professionals are another important source of information. Reports of fingerprint experts, forensic chemists, pathologists, document examiners and others are often crucial in establishing the physical facts of the case. While these details may not always be relevant, in some cases the defendant's account of his mental state may be inconsistent with the physical parameters of the offense (Shapiro, 1984). Of course, previous evaluations by other psychotherapists may also be available and should be considered after other sources of data have been studied.

Family and friends of the accused form a fourth source of information. The data they provide can serve to substantiate the history provided by the defendant in interviews, particularly in reference to previous episodes of disorder and treatment. The examiner must consider the possibility that these people may attempt to withhold information or fabricate information that they believe will exculpate the defendant. A candid discussion of the need for accurate information may or may not help overcome this bias.

Finally, records from previous hospitalizations, notes from outpatient treatment, documentation of participation in detoxification programs, and similar records may also be obtained. Often this type of information cannot be disclosed, however, without the consent of the defendant. That is, these agencies are likely to recognize a duty to maintain confidentiality unless this is waived in writing. Since the process of obtaining consent, requesting information, and waiting for its arrival may be time-consuming, it should be initiated early in the evaluation process.

Collateral information can be conceptualized as relating to the defendant's current status (court records), condition during and following the offense (arrest and incarceration data, reports on the offense by other experts), and history (family interviews, records of prior treatment, etc.). Taken together, these data can often effectively corroborate or undermine the account of the offense presented by the defendant. In some cases one or more sources may be unavailable to the examiner, as when there are no witnesses or surviving victims or when the defendant refuses disclosure by his family or previous caretakers. Still, given the variety of collateral sources, useful information can almost always be developed. The examiner who relies solely on the subject's self-report is not doing a complete evaluation. To the extent that key facts are unavailable, the examiner may be forced to qualify or equivocate in his opinion to the court. Since in some cases the court itself may be instrumental in dealings with collateral sources, the examiner may wish to inform the clerk of court, magistrate, or judge of difficulty in obtaining crucial information.

FORMULATING THE OPINION

We have emphasized the importance of collecting a broad database from which to develop an expert opinion. If these are not effectively integrated, however, these efforts will be to no avail. Shapiro (1986) has presented six criteria for completeness in a criminal responsibility evaluation:

(1) Evaluate the patient's ability to reconstruct his or her experience.
(2) Evaluate the extent of retrospective falsification and the reasons for it.
(3) Observe the consistency, or lack of consistency, of disturbed behavior in different settings.
(4) If available, consider inferences from psychological testing and whether or not they coherently "fit" the events of the offense.
(5) Gather and integrate all secondary sources of information.
(6) Gather and integrate the physical evidence with the inferred behavior and its relationship to the diagnosis made and behavior typical of that diagnostic grouping.

To the extent that all of these criteria can be fulfilled, the psychologist or psychiatrist should be able to develop a well-founded opinion as to responsibility, even when the offense took place some time past. Missing information may necessitate qualification of the opinion or alternative methods of data collection. For example, if an offense took place in a remote area, there may be no collateral information to substantiate the subject's account. The examiner may be reduced to explaining to the court that the accused provided a plausible explanation of behavior produced by a mental disorder, but that the probability that this explanation is correct cannot be assessed. As another example, consider the patient who describes a long history of mental health treatment and consents to release of this information to help document the progression of his disorder leading up to the offense. It is not unusual for hospitals or mental health centers to lag in complying with requests for records. If the absence of these records would compromise the evaluation, the examiner may find it helpful to convey this to the court clerk, magistrate, or judge, whose intervention may greatly speed the release of the needed information. In some cases, unusual sources may help to fill in other gaps, as in a recent case where the accused kept a diary for several months leading up to and including his offense. The diary was invaluable, given that there were no witnesses to his crime.

The basis for most tests of insanity is the presence of a diagnosable mental disorder. Consequently, the first step in formulating an opinion to be presented to counsel or to the court must be a carefully considered diagnosis. The examiner must avoid static thinking on this issue, refraining from viewing the diagnosis as a snapshot of the accused's past condition or of his present mental status. Rather, it is best to assume that the diagnosis must be consistent with the defendant's functioning over a long period of time, beginning before the offense and continuing up until the trial proper. This may be a period of months or years, and many defendants exhibit changes in adaptation over the course of arrest, incarceration, and prosecution.

If the examiner focuses on only one of these periods, the possibility of incorrect diagnosis is heightened. For example, defendants in federal courts must be transported to one of three federal Bureau of Prisons forensic centers. This process may take days or weeks, and can involve transit over hundreds of miles with temporary stays in an assortment of jails and prisons along the way. It is not uncommon for chronically disordered individuals to decompensate under these conditions and present as overtly psychotic when first examined. Their mental status at the time of the offense may actually have been much better. Alternatively, some subjects may actually improve when provided with basic necessities and a clearly structured institutional environment; they may present as well compensated when they had been acutely psychotic during the commission of the offense.

The relevance of these variations in clinical status to the final diagnosis must be documented and articulated to the court. Since laypeople rarely have an accurate understanding of the waxing and waning of many psychological disorders, they expect the examiner's diagnosis to translate into a thumbnail description of the accused's functioning at trial. If the subject's history and observed behavior at the time of the crime require a diagnosis of schizophrenia and suggest an acute psychotic episode leading to the criminal behavior, but he appears lucid when sitting in the courtroom, the court may be inclined to disregard the expert's opinion—after all, the defendant "doesn't look crazy." The clinician should anticipate this and explain the course of the disorder over time, factors that would lead to remission while waiting for trial, signs of latent psychosis on current psychological testing, and other factors that will allow the jury to gain an understanding of the appropriateness of a given diagnosis despite a changing clinical picture.

SPECIAL PROBLEMS IN RESPONSIBILITY EVALUATIONS

As mentioned earlier, there are many situations in which the jury will be faced with an extremely close call between holding an accused individual responsible for a criminal act or acquitting him. These cases are also difficult for the examiner, as they often involve conflicting indications of pathology versus planful, volitional acting-out. Some of the key areas of difficulty are discussed below, along with case examples.

Multiple Motivations for the Offense

Consistent with the wording of the Durham rule, most responsibility decisions boil down to determining whether or not an illegal act was produced by a mental disorder or was prompted by a rational choice to do wrong. In some instances, such as sharply defined paranoid delusions, it may be clear that the motivation for an offense is a direct outgrowth of disorder. Other offenses appear to be motivated by simple greed, avarice, or hatred—impulses which affect everyone but which the law cannot condone. Persons who commit offenses for these "sane" but less than noble reasons are held responsible and are punished. Unfortunately, many cases may appear to entail both pathological and immoral motives. Drawing a distinction between them is difficult in practice.

Shapiro (1984) describes a case in which a disordered individual was charged with bank robbery. He clearly considered the robbery a way to enrich himself financially, but was also prompted to follow through with the offense because he believed that he would indirectly help out the bank employees. He believed that they could steal money for themselves amid the confusion that would result. The subject also believed that the bank's female employees would be sexually stimulated by the anxiety they would feel during the holdup. Though this individual clearly knew that bank robbery was an illegal way to obtain money, he may not have acted out his plans without these delusional beliefs. In a very real sense his crime was motivated by both delusional and realistic motives.

The Disordered Offender Who Malingers Another Disorder

The finding that a person accused of a crime is mentally disordered is not sufficient to warrant acquittal. The disorder must bear some significant relationship to the offense, within the parameters of the legal test for insanity in that jurisdiction. Developing information to help the judge or jury determine the relationship between disorder and offense may be difficult under many circumstances, certainly when the accused malingers or "fakes" mental illness. This situation is even more problematic when a seriously disturbed individual attempts to fake symptoms other than those of the "real" disorder.

A recent case fits this description. The accused was an intelligent, attractive, successful young man who took out a contract to murder his business partner. When evaluated in a forensic hospital, the defendant described symptoms consistent with schizophrenia, including command hallucinations which he said had directed him to dispose of the partner, who was ostensibly an agent of the devil. During interviews he reported that he heard voices demanding that he kill himself and that he saw the intended victim flying about the room "on demon's wings." He also displayed behavior that could be construed as thought-blocking, clang associations, and flight of ideas. Still, he was able to follow his legal situation in detail, related well to staff when he wanted to obtain privileges, and retained an appropriate range of affect, all inconsistent with an acute psychotic episode.

Collateral information was crucial to resolving the uncertain clinical picture. The accused had worked as an aide in a state hospital and had received special training in mental health services. This background helped him not only malinger gross hallucinations, but also do a passable job of mimicking less widely known symptoms of psychosis. Further information indicated that, despite malingering, the accused also suffered from a significant disorder. The intended victim reported considerable friction in the weeks before the attempted murder, with the defendant making delusional accusations of fraud and conspiracy. After threatening the partner for his imagined transgressions, the defendant contacted a bouncer at a local lounge to discuss "taking out a contract." The would-be killer corroborated the delusional quality of the defendant's motivations. Family members and others described severely impaired functioning.

The examiner's final diagnosis was that, at the time of the offense, the defendant had been acutely paranoid and that a diagnosis of paranoid schizophrenia was appropriate. It was believed that this condition continued unremitted through the evaluation. The subject's other symptoms were attributed to malingering. Despite the severity of his disorder, it was clear the defendant knew that, even if his suspicions toward the partner were true, having him killed was wrong. His caution in hiring someone else to commit the murder, as well as arrangements to provide himself with an alibi, indicated that he was well aware of both the criminality and the potential ramifications of his actions. Under the test of insanity in that jurisdiction, the jury found the defendant guilty of conspiracy to commit murder, despite the presence of both a real and a faked mental disorder.

Amnesia for the Offense

In forensic settings it is common for subjects in competency or responsibility evaluations to report that they "blacked out" shortly before the alleged offense and only recall being arrested at some later time. The majority of these claims are false and are subsequently dropped in the face of overwhelming evidence. Still, some of these assertions appear genuine and persist even after the legal situation is resolved. Amnesia for an offense would not automatically alleviate one of responsibility, but it would indicate some acute disturbance of psychological functioning that should be evaluated. This evaluation is made more difficult precisely because the defendant cannot provide an account of the experience in question.

A middle aged single male was evaluated following his arrest for attempted rape. He reported that he had no memory for any of the alleged offense, but remembered waking up with a hangover in the county jail. His last recollection prior to the offense was of playing a drinking game at a friend's home. Witnesses' statements indicated that he had become severely intoxicated, walked next door, and entered the home of a single woman. The victim indicated that the defendant entered her room and said, "Love me." She was able to elude him and call for help.

The accused had an extensive history of alcohol abuse and dependence, including mild hallucinations, withdrawal symptoms on abstinence, and several prior episodes of lost time. He was also diagnosed as manifesting a significant personality disorder with avoidant and schizoid features. The examiner's report to the court noted that the defendant's prior sexual experience was severely limited, but that psychological testing and interview indicated extreme preoccupation with sexual content and impulses. It was noted that his usual interpersonal anxiety and reticence, resulting from the personality disorder, would militate against actualizing his sexual impulses in conventional ways. Alcohol intoxication may have reduced his inhibitions and precipitated more overt acting-out than the subject would normally exhibit. Collateral information did not indicate symptoms indicative of acute mental disorder, and there was no prior history of more severe dysfunction. The examiner concluded that the accused did not have a major mental illness at the time of the alleged offense.

The defendant subsequently pleaded guilty to a lesser charge. His attorney recognized that amnesia for the offense, while genuine, was not likely to alleviate him of responsibility in the eyes of a jury; neither was the potential relationship of the offense to intoxication. The courts have generally held that self-induced intoxication does not constitute a defense under the guise of insanity. In some cases an existing disorder which is inadvertently exacerbated by drug or alcohol use may serve as the basis for a successful insanity defense. Involuntary intoxication, as with poisonous chemicals or accidental overdoses, generally does lead to acquittal. The defense attorney in this case reasoned that because the accused had a long history of drinking and was familiar with the effects of alcohol on his behavior, even including alcohol hallucinosis and blackouts, the jury would interpret his behavior as voluntary. Incidentally, the defendant was given a long suspended sentence and successfully completed a residential detoxification program.

Esoteric Disorders or Combinations of Pathological Conditions

Cases that involve rare types of psychopathology or those that entail complex interaction of several psychological dysfunctions may present their own set of problems for the forensic clinician. This is particularly true when the criminal offense represents a sharp break from the individual's usual level of functioning. In patients with a discrete, identifiable disorder, the examiner may formulate an opinion that explains both mental status at the time of the offense and changes in the clinical picture over time. When several processes coexist, the implications of changes in clinical status may be less clear, making it more difficult to draw inferences about mental status during the offense. These are the cases most likely to lead to conflicting expert opinions about diagnosis and other clinical issues.

The accused described his early life as difficult. He was an only child whose father abandoned the family. His mother was an alcoholic who frequently entertained men at home. He described himself as a withdrawn and fearful young man, particularly around the opposite sex. Despite his inhibitions, he moved out of his mother's home at an early age and put himself through college and some technical training. He later served in the military during the Viet Nam war and saw extensive combat action, for which he won several citations for heroism. Significant difficulties followed his return to the states. First, he married an older woman who was extremely exploitive and sadistic towards him; he later believed that she was being unfaithful as well. He also developed intermittent delusions that coworkers were talking about him, plotting to cause him problems, and so forth. These persisted through several job changes. In middle age he developed intense panic attacks and symptoms of generalized anxiety. There was no evidence that these involved "flashbacks" to his combat experience, however. In an attempt to self-medicate his chronic anxiety, the accused began to drink daily, often to excess. Following the development of some minor health problems, his need for medical attention increased exponentially, and he presented with numerous vague conversion symptoms. Unfortunately, he received multiple medications, including antidepressant and anxiolytic drugs intended to reduce his demands on physicians.

Eventually, the defendant's wife left him and filed for divorce. Following this episode his behavior became increasingly strange. He would not accept the demise of his marriage and insisted that his ex-wife "remain faithful" to him. He began renting cars to follow her or watch her home to insure that she did not date other men. During this period he also began to double up on prescription medications, getting several physicians to write prescriptions which he had filled at different drugstores. His suspicions toward coworkers heightened to overt paranoia, and he was fired for threatening to "get even" with a supervisor. He began to carry a gun at all times. No longer employed, the defendant began to observe his ex-wife 24 hours a day. His children, acquaintances, and former employers were able to corroborate this account.

The offense took place in a grocery parking lot in broad daylight. The defendant observed his estranged wife return to her car along with a youth helping her with her groceries. He became enraged that she was "cheating on him" and intentionally flaunting this before him. He approached and shot them both repeatedly. Several hours later he turned himself in to the police and was charged with murdering his ex-wife and the assistant manager of the store.

When presented for evaluation, the defendant had been drug-free for almost six weeks. He was cooperative, remorseful, and situationally depressed. Still, signs of incipient disorder were clear, and psychological testing indicated potential for intermittent psychotic episodes during periods of high stress or intense negative emotions. The complexity of the clinical issues in this case made formulating responses to the referring attorney extremely difficult. The examiner felt that the accused had exhibited a personality disorder since early adulthood. Though he did not appear to warrant a formal diagnosis of post-traumatic stress disorder, his combat experience was clearly important in destabilizing his previously adequate personality functioning. In the years prior to the offense he evidenced a variety of anxiety-related symptoms, and later polysubstance abuse. Finally, he progressed from chronic suspiciousness to overt paranoia.

In all this individual may have qualified for a total of five discrete *DSM-III-R* diagnoses, including (1) somatization disorder, (2) agoraphobia with panic attacks, (3) paranoid disorder, (4) polysubstance abuse, and (5) mixed personality disorder with histrionic, compulsive, and dependent features. Of course, these are not discrete entities, but interrelated. For example, the instability of personality functions had clear implications for increasing anxiety symptoms, which could be seen as a motivation to abuse alcohol, pain medications, and anxiolytics. These drugs clearly compromised the subject's ability to control his behavior, and may have contributed to his decline into overt paranoia. Unlike the case of bad behavior attributed to intoxication alone, here existing pathology was antagonized by drug use.

The examiner explained these findings to the defense attorney in detail, including the implications of this complex clinical picture in view of that state's test of insanity. The attorney chose to seek another evaluation. The second clinician concluded that the defendant in fact suffered from post-traumatic stress disorder, and the attorney attempted a defense based on the assertion that the crime was a result of this condition. The defendant was convicted of two counts of second degree murder.

ALTERNATIVES TO THE CURRENT INSANITY DEFENSE

Criticisms of the insanity defense have been sufficiently forceful to spur experimentation with legal alternatives to the present system. Some of the most extreme proposals have included the claim that the whole issue of responsibility should be ignored altogether, with the law assuming strict personal accountability for all behavior (Szasz, 1986; Teplin, 1985). This proposal is unlikely to gain momentum, however, as the law as we know it is laid upon a foundation of free will. In fact, the Supreme Court has generally held that state laws abolishing the insanity defense violated constitutional rights to due process (*Sinclair v. State*, 1931).

Another radical proposal has been to exclude expert testimony on the assumption that responsibility decisions are not scientific, but morally and ethically based (Herman, 1983). Of course, even the philosophical decision facing the jury must be made within the context of the facts of the case. Mental health professionals are trained to gather and organize information about the defendant that the court would not otherwise have, and the primary result of excluding experts would be to reduce the quality of the information available to the jury (Hoffman & Browning, 1980). A less extreme suggestion is that courts retain impartial experts as a relacement for competing witnesses for each side. In practice, however, the parties cannot be prevented from calling their own experts, as this would violate the defendant's right to call witnesses (Smith & Meyer, 1987). In many areas the law already allows courts to retain independent experts, and it is likely that juries would accord more weight to the apparently impartial expert. The court-appointed expert might be particularly useful in helping each side in the case identify potential flaws or inaccuracies on the part of opposing experts. It could also help to provide the jury with more pragmatic, less doctrinaire information in cases where hired guns are at work.

Several states have adopted changes in the basic system of the insanity defense. These adaptations provide an indication of the directions the law may take over the next decade. One of the first major changes took place in Michigan. State law there had held that those acquitted of crimes due to insanity were automatically committed without further legal procedures. The state Supreme Court held in *People v. McQuillan* (1974), that acquittees had the right to a hearing to determine if they should be hospitalized under the state's civil commitment laws. Following a large number of such hearings to determine the status of the persons already committed, several were released and committed further offenses. The state legislature passed a law establishing a new type of verdict, "guilty but mentally ill" (GBMI) to circumvent the court's ruling. Under this statute, a defendant could be found guilty of the charge and mentally ill but not insane at the time of the offense. These individuals would be sentenced in the same way as other convicts. However, they would begin serving time in a hospital, with transfer to the prison system when or if treatment was completed. It is unclear whether this alternative was intended to provide treatment to mentally ill offenders or to discourage insanity verdicts. Data from Michigan indicate that it has accomplished the latter, with the number of insanity verdicts reduced (Slobogin, 1985). Other states have adopted similar laws.

Two related alternatives to the traditional insanity defense attempt to escape the all-or-none dichotomy of insanity versus responsibility. The first of these involves "diminished capacity." As noted earlier in this chapter, the law traditionally holds that a crime is comprised of both an act and an intent to commit the act. Serious crimes often require very specific intent to do wrong, while lesser offenses may only require carelessness or recklessness to lead to conviction. The notion behind diminished capacity is that some persons may not have been totally incapacitated by their mental condition, but neither did they possess a sufficient degree of free will to have the *mens rea* required to convict them for a serious crime. For example, a schizophrenic individual may not have had the degree of mental control necessary to justify conviction for first degree murder, being unable to coldly choose to do evil by killing someone. At the same time, the court may find that he was aware, at the time of the crime, that his actions would lead to the death of another person. While the acts comprising the offense may correspond to first degree murder, the jury may convict this individual of a lesser charge commensurate with his impaired free will. Diminished capacity defenses are generally associated with the ALI standard for responsibility, which speaks of degrees of capacity to conform to the law, rather than totally dichotomous decisions. Several states have taken measures to restrict diminished capacity defenses, beginning with California in 1982 (Maloney, 1985).

A related proposal for altering the insanity defense would require the state to prove *mens rea* as a part of the crime, just as it must prove the facts of the case (American Bar Association, 1983). At present most jurisdictions require the defendant to prove insanity in order to win acquittal. Shifting the burden of proof might actually lead to more acquittals, since criminal convictions require proof beyond a reasonable doubt. If this burden were placed on the prosecution, it is possible that many persons with some history of mental disorder could raise at least some doubt about their mental status at the time of the offense. This might even be true of defendants with intermittent disorders who were relatively free of impairment at the time of their crime. As a remedy, some proposals would require a lesser standard of proof for *mens rea* than for *actus reus*, although this distinction is hard to justify. In practice, it is likely that eliminating the insanity defense in its current form would lead to clearer thinking in the guise of *mens rea* issues at trial.

Finally, several states have experimented with bifurcated trials, with the issue of guilt or innocence for the facts of the case separated from mental status. Many states attempted to hold a preliminary trial with guilty intent presumed. If the defendant is convicted on the facts, a second trial is held if he wishes to plead insanity. This option appears to have little merit, as the Supreme Court has held many of these procedures unconstitutional because they alleviate the state of proving *mens rea* in the initial trial. Even when the first trial does not prejudice the second, the thorny philosophical problems regarding insanity, free will, and responsibility remain unchanged. These laws may do more to save time by disposing of cases the state cannot prove in the first place than to clarify the complex issues inherent in criminal responsibility questions.

SUMMARY

Despite extensive criticism and disagreement, the insanity defense is likely to endure in some form. Our legal tradition holds that free will is the moral basis for law, and that persons freely choosing to do wrong warrant punishment. Though it remains difficult to define the precise rationale, it is clear that individuals who are seriously impaired cannot exercise the same degree of volition as others in conforming to the law and social values. Society recognizes that it would be unfair, unproductive, and immoral to extract punishment from these individuals. Still, it is difficult to draw the line between those who choose to do wrong and those whose choice is limited by their mental disability.

The courts have traditionally called upon psychiatrists and psychologists to provide data on which these difficult decisions may be based. Even with their input, judgments regarding criminal responsibility remain problematic. One criticism by legal scholars is that biological and psychological data are irrelevant to the philosophical issues a jury must confront. A former Supreme Court Justice indicated that expert testimony regarding the psychological condition of the defendant was of little use because the "terms mean in any given case whatever the expert witness says they mean . . . no rule of law can possibly be sound or workable which is dependent upon the terms of another discipline whose members are in profound disagreement about what those terms mean" (*Blocker v. United States*, D.C. Circuit, 1961).

An alternative view would hold that the legal meaning of "insanity" is less established than terms in psychology or psychiatry. After all, there have been a plethora of standards developed, with some jurisdictions changing as often as each decade. While psychology and psychiatry have made significant advances in the last 150 years, the struggle of American courts with the very concept of criminal responsibility has gone nowhere. After a century and a half of criticism and experimentation, our courts have come full circle, with the most recently enacted standard a *de facto* replication of the M'Naughten test (Norris, 1987). This stagnation is probably due less to the failure of jurisprudence than to the slow change in society as a whole.

At present the proper role for psychotherapists in responsibility evaluations is to provide "grist for the legal mill." While this contribution requires some adjustment in the usual methods of clinical practice, it is clinical expertise itself which qualifies the expert to aid the court in these judgments. Foregoing the standards of professional practice to serve as a simple adjunct to legal machinery would obviate the basis for expert contribution. Ultimately, progress in this area will come only as more serviceable criteria for responsibility are established. It is clear that such innovation will require the cooperation of thinkers in both law and mental health.

CHAPTER 3

Legal Capacity and Incompetency

[Lawyers and judges have] a peculiar cant and jargon of their own, that no other mortal can understand, and wherein all their laws are written, which they take special care to multiply . . .

— Jonathan Swift, *Gulliver's Travels*

LEGAL SCHOLARS AND LAY PEOPLE agree that the most important concepts underlying American law involve guarantees of individual freedom. Consequently, any law that involves abridging personal freedoms is among the most problematic and difficult to administer. Philosophically, persons who suffer from a mental disorder or disability have the same guarantees of rights and privileges as others in society, but pragmatically the law has found it necessary to define circumstances under which key decision-making options may be taken away from impaired individuals, ostensibly for their own welfare. Incompetency is a legal term that describes persons who are found unable properly to exercise certain individual rights and legal prerogatives due to mental incapacity. These provisions are usually justified by the assertion that the incompetent cannot act effectively in their own best interest, and so society must altruistically intervene.

Individuals labeled incompetent rarely perceive the situation in this way. Findings of incompetency may be applied to a broad range of individuals who do not want such intervention. These persons may be "subjected to unwanted institutionalization, involuntary treatment, loss of control of their property, and loss of the ability to exercise many other important legal rights" (Smith & Meyer, 1987). In many cases declarations of incompetency may be more intrusive and liberty-depriving than criminal convictions, yet until recently there has been little emphasis on protecting the potentially incompetent from either exploitation or well-meaning but misdirected intervention. This lack of sensitivity may be changing, however.

Like insanity, there is no analogous concept for incompetency within either psychology or psychiatry. In fact, competency may refer to at least 30 different kinds of legal questions, each with its own tests, standards, and special issues (Mezer & Rheingold, 1962). This chapter will deal with only three issues: competency to stand trial, to make a will, and to manage one's own affairs, also known as guardianship. These three areas are representative of the range of legal issues involved, and are also most likely to involve the practicing psychotherapist.

COMPETENCY TO STAND TRIAL

Mr. French was a 31-year-old, divorced, white male charged with trafficking in cocaine. He was referred by the court for a 30-day inpatient evaluation for competency to stand trial following the recommendation of a local psychiatrist who examined him on the day of his arraignment. Approximately one year earlier, Mr. French had learned that authorities held a warrant for his arrest and he fled the country, traveling to Europe, where he "went underground" and lived in several bohemian communities. This secretive life-style did not agree with Mr. French, who became increasingly convinced that he was being pursued by groups ranging from the CIA to the Mafia to his ex-wife and her "stable of paramours." He believed that someone was trying to "gaslight" him or to have him declared incompetent, even though, in his words, "There's nothing wrong with me; Hey, I could bring peace to the whole world if these people would just stop the games." He became overwhelmed by fears about the imagined plots against him, and turned himself in at an American Embassy. He was escorted home by U.S. officials.

During the evaluation, Mr. French was overtly psychotic. He became convinced that radio receivers had been planted within his neck and that the strange words and thoughts that raced through his mind were "injected by these micro receivers." He had difficulty following conversations due to the frequency (no pun intended) of these hallucinated radio messages. Still, he admitted to some prior contacts with the courts and evidenced considerable sophisticated knowledge of criminal proceedings. It was felt that despite his distractibility he would be capable of understanding and following the proceedings against him. Cooperation with his court-appointed attorney was another matter. Mr. French held the delusional belief that his attorney was somehow connected to the plots against him and refused to cooperate in any way. He intended to proceed *pro se* (as his own lawyer). When this information was presented to the court, the judge determined that due to his mental disorder (paranoid schizophrenia) he could not enjoy the benefits of repre-sentation by counsel. He was found not competent for trial and, on the recommendation of the examiner, placed in a secure hospital for 90 days of observation and treatment aimed at restoring competency.

Competency to stand trial is an issue distinct from the insanity defense (see Chapter 2). Competency refers to the accused's ability to participate effectively in his own trial, independent of his functioning in the past. While questions of sanity are rarely raised, questions of competency are far more frequent. Studies indicate that between 50 and 75 percent of patients con-fined to security hospitals are there in connection with incompetency to stand trial; of these less than one percent will ever be found not guilty by reason of insanity (Schwitzgebel & Schwitzgebel, 1980). On a nationwide basis there are more than 25,000 incompetency evaluations each year, but less than one in ten leads to the conclusion that the defendant cannot stand trial (Gobert, 1973; Wulach, 1980). There are several possible reasons for the excessive number of referrals, which will be discussed later.

The Legal Perspective

Some of the most important features of Anglo-American law involve the rights of the accused in a criminal proceeding. Defendants have the right to a speedy and public trial, to be represented by counsel, to call and confront witnesses, to testify on their own behalf, and so forth. Without these rights, the prosecution would generally have an overwhelming advantage. These and other procedural protections are often referred to as *due process* of law, and collectively serve to insure the fairness of legal proceedings. As early as 1746, British courts recognized that mentally ill persons might be so incapa-citated that they would be effectively deprived of due process (see Lipsitt, 1986). The proceedings could not be fair and just if disorder compromised the defendant's ability to formulate a defense, consult with an attorney, or present his side of the case. Some scholars have drawn an analogy to trying the accused *in absentia*.

In American courts, incompetency findings may have served more to divert troublesome individuals from the legal system into mental health treatment than to assure due process. Traditionally, most jurisdictions lacked specific standards for incompetency until the case of *Dusky v. United States*, when the Supreme Court attempted to define the constitutional limits of competency for trial (Rosenburg & McGarry, 1972). The Court held that:

> The test must be whether [the accused] has sufficient present ability to consult with a lawyer with a reasonable degree of rational understanding, and

whether he has a rational as well as factual understanding of the proceedings taken against him. (*Dusky v. United States*, 1960)

Of course, this test could hardly be described as specific, but it has provided a degree of uniformity in legal thinking about competency to stand trial. Two broad areas of competency can be defined. The first centers on the ability to know and understand the charges and legal processes taken against the defendant. The phrase "rational as well as factual" has been widely interpreted to mean that the accused must understand not only the specifics of the allegation, but also the potential consequences of trial (i.e., sentences), the relative merits of basic legal strategies, and so forth. The second broad requirement is that the accused be able to consult with an attorney. Given that the large majority of laypeople do not understand legal procedures or the advice of their attorneys, "reasonable" understanding may be considerably less than perfect (Slovenko, 1987).

Questions of competency to stand trial may be raised at any time during the criminal process by any participant. While logic would suggest that the defense would commonly raise the issue, recent statistics indicate that the prosecution is actually more likely to seek competency evaluations (Slovenko, 1987). When neither side raises the issue of competency, but the trial judge believes there are reasons to doubt the defendant's capacity, then the court must order the evaluation on its own (see, for example *Pate v. Robinson*, 1966). Generally once any legitimate question is raised, all proceedings must stop until the question is resolved. The defendant cannot refuse an incompetency evaluation.

When an evaluation has been ordered, the defendant is usually sent to a secure mental institution for a predetermined period of time. This period may be as long as three months. Mental health experts subsequently present their findings in a formal hearing, with the judge making the final determination of competency. Though the burden of proof varies from one jurisdiction to the next, in practice the court nearly always follows the recommendations of the examining psychotherapist. If the defendant is determined to be competent, then the legal proceedings are carried to their logical conclusion. If found incompetent, the defendant may be released if the charges against him are minor. More often, he is returned to a mental institution for a period of treatment to restore competency or held pending civil commitment proceedings.

Being subjected to an incompetency evaluation may create a number of problems for the criminal defendant. In most cases, bail is denied and the accused must enter a secure hospital. That is, he or she is effectively incarcerated despite not having been convicted of any charges. Given that the process may take many months, the defendant's right to a speedy trial may be compromised. Also, the right to avoid self-incrimination may be affected by information disclosed to therapists during the examination. This information may not be privileged, so that the professionals involved could be called to testify in the trial. Finally, if the individual is found incompetent, he may be committed for an extended period of treatment aimed at restoring competence. The rules for these commitments are usually less stringent than for civil commitment, and may actually allow for longer confinement than conviction for the crime charged.

The Basis for Incompetency

Incompetency may be caused by a variety of problems, including emotional, mental, or physical. Research indicates that over 80 percent of the findings of incompetency for trial are related to the presence of an acute psychotic disorder or mental retardation (Roesch & Golding, 1980). It is important to note that while many incompetents are psychotic, the converse is not true. Many psychotic defendants are found competent for trial (Shapiro, 1984). Mental retardation must generally be moderate to severe before general intellectual functions are sufficiently impaired to lead to incompetency (Maloney, 1985). Of course, the co-presence of multiple disorders may be considerably more incapacitating than the individual conditions in isolation. Defendants may also be found incompetent based upon physical handicaps. In the well-publicized case of Donald Lang, accused of killing a Chicago prostitute, the defendant was found to be free of mental disorder or disability, but due to congenital defects was deaf and mute. His conviction was overturned because a state appeals court ruled that his handicaps prevented him from enjoying the benefits of effective counsel (*People v. Lang,* 1975). The court went on to say that special trial procedures might sometimes be adopted to compensate for the idiosyncratic needs of specific defendants, and that these measures could lead to a fair trial for otherwise incompetent individuals.

While the issue of competency is generally raised regarding only the trial proper, the legal tradition requires that the defendant be competent throughout the entire process of criminal adjudication, from initial contact with authorities through execution of the sentence. Recent case law has focused on issues ranging from competency to waive *Miranda* rights (see Maloney, 1985) through competency to be executed. The recent Supreme Court ruling in *Ford v. Wainright* (1986) reaffirmed the position of many state courts that the Eighth amendment prohibition of cruel and unusual punishment is violated when severely disturbed individuals are subjected to capital punishment. This is part of a more general principle that offenders must be competent at all stages of their involvement in the criminal justice system.

A more recent, and seemingly inconsistent, Supreme Court opinion indicates that there may be limits to this thinking. In *Colorado v. Connelly* (1986), the Court held that individuals can be convicted of crimes on the basis of confessions prompted by severe mental illness (in this case command hallucinations representing the voice of God). This opinion seems to suggest that there are no competency requirements prior to initiation of formal legal proceedings in criminal cases.

Assessment of Competency

The assessment of competency requires the examiner to evaluate the defendant along two dimensions. The first involves conducting a thorough clinical examination and coming to a conclusion as to diagnosis. The second pertains to the specific questions posed by the court. While therapists often do good clinical evaluations, both experience and research suggest that most evaluations do not reflect the criteria for competency, but merely give a summary conclusion (Roesch & Golding, 1980). This is hardly surprising, since other data indicate that lawyers and judges are often unclear about the specific legal questions involved (Rosenburg & McGarry, 1972). The crucial part of the evaluator's job is to draw the connection between diagnosis and the specific areas of competency relevant to a given case or jurisdiction. While the defendant's adjustment has obvious implications for his ability to participate in the legal arena, there is no one-to-one relationship between diagnosis and competency, and any causal relationship must be spelled out for the court.

The foundation for the competency evaluation is a thorough clinical interview. Particular emphasis should be placed on mental health history and related information to help focus the current diagnostic question. Often psychological testing may be helpful in clarifying diagnosis or in specifying the subject's general level of intellectual functioning. This may be particularly true when interview and historical data indicate the possibility of neurologic impairment.

Several specialized instruments have been developed to aid in assessing components of competency, but do not necessarily simplify the process of deriving a final opinion. In some cases only limited validation of these techniques has been accomplished, so they should be used advisedly (Grisso, 1986).

Perhaps the most widely used and accepted methods were developed by the Laboratory of Community Psychiatry (Laboratory of Community Psychiatry, 1973; Lipsitt, Lelos, & McGarry, 1971). The Competency Screening Test (CST) was designed as a screening device intended to identify those who are clearly competent before commitment for evaluation. It consists of 22 sentence stems such as "When I go to court the lawyer will _____"; "If Jack has to try his own case, he _____"; "If the jury finds me guilty I _____." Answers are scored 0, 1 or 2, with higher scores indicating greater certainty of competency.

The Competency Assessment Instrument (CAI) (Laboratory of Community Psychiatry, 1973) is an attempt to structure and standardize a formal competency interview. It is based upon a group of 13 separate facets of criminal competency, with the subject rated on each dimension. There is no established decision rule, so the resulting information must be integrated by the examiner according to his or her own logic or according to the preferences of the court. This instrument may provide the most comprehensive set of information about competency. The domains assessed are listed in Table 3.1. Each is rated on a scale from one to five, with five indicating severe incapacity.

TABLE 3.1
Components of Competency Assessment Instrument

1. Appraisal of available legal defenses.
2. Unmanageable behavior.
3. Quality of relating to attorney.
4. Planning of legal strategy, including guilty plea to lesser charges where pertinent.
5. Appraisal of role of:
    Defense counsel
    Prosecuting attorney
    Judge
    Jury
    Defendant
    Witnesses
6. Understanding of court procedure.
7. Appreciation of charges.
8. Appreciation of range and nature of possible penalties.
9. Appraisal of likely outcome.
10. Capacity to disclose to attorney available pertinent facts surrounding the offense, including the defendant's movements, timing, mental state, and actions at the time of the offense.
11. Capacity to realistically challenge prosecution witnesses.
12. Capacity to testify relevantly.
13. Self-defeating versus self-serving motivation.

From McGarry et al., 1983

There are continuing efforts to refine assessment instruments such as these. For example, the Fitness Interview Test (FIT) is a revision and expansion of the CAI which aims to give a broader assessment of all possible grounds for a finding of incompetency to stand trial (Roesch et al., 1984). The Interdisciplinary Fitness Interview is a promising methodology that involves both mental health and legal professionals in the evaluation process (Golding, Roesch, & Schrieber, 1984). This approach also takes into account the specifics of a given defendant's legal situation, endeavoring to tailor the decision-making process to the exact competencies required. Finally, Burling and Saylor (1984) have developed the Court Competency Inventory, a series of 15 role-played situations to assess both legal and social competence. These items were chosen by examining characteristics of persons previously determined to be incompetent. While the ongoing research is likely to be of benefit in the long run, as yet these new instruments have not been widely accepted.

Recent Changes in Incompetency Procedures

As mentioned above, defendants found incompetent are usually not released. Most jurisdictions have provided for confinement until competency can be restored, and until the 1970s this provision was widely abused. Although most persons referred for competency evaluations were charged with only minor offenses, such as disturbing the peace, a study of defendants committed following an incompetency determination showed that they spent an average of 4.3 years in confinement, far longer than the average sentence they could have expected if they had simply been convicted (Geller & Lister, 1978; Steadman & Braff, 1974). Other research revealed that fully half of these unconvicted defendants spent the rest of their lives in confinement (Ennis, 1972).

In 1972 the plight of individuals found incompetent for trial was considered by the Supreme Court, which ruled that this practice was unconstitutional in *Jackson v. Indiana* (1972). Mr. Jackson was a mentally retarded individual who was also deaf and mute. An Indiana court found that he was incompetent to stand trial for two counts of robbery totalling nine dollars, and ordered him sent to a state hospital where he spent the next four years. Because of the intractibility of his problems, it was likely that he would have remained incarcerated for the rest of his life. Not only was Jackson never convicted of a crime, but he also was never given an opportunity to challenge the allegations against him. The Supreme Court found that his confinement violated his fourteenth amendment rights to due process, since he had not in fact been convicted of any crime but was forceably incarcerated by the state. In fact, his confinement could be likened to a presumption of

guilt on the charges. The Supreme Court decided that confinement following an incompetency determination must "bear some reasonable relation to
the purpose for which the individual is committed." That is, it must be
aimed at restoring competency, not just warehousing the mentally disordered defendant. If competency cannot be expected within a reasonable
period of time, "then the State must either institute the customary civil
commitment proceeding that would be required to commit indefinitely any
other citizen or release the defendant."

The Supreme Court failed to define a "reasonable" period of time, and
since the *Jackson* decision various criminal jurisdictions have adopted a
range of procedures. States typically allow from one to five years of treatment to restore competency (Gobert, 1973), with many computing the time
allowed as a function of the maximum sentence for the crime charged. The
reasoning here is that more serious offenses call for greater efforts on the
part of the state to pursue criminal charges by treating the accused until he
becomes competent. Minor offenses with potentially very short sentences do
not justify these extreme efforts to obtain a conviction. The State's right to
pursue more serious charges is used to justify the longer confinement. Some
states still have not established clear limits on length of confinement (Roesch
& Golding, 1980). Many proposals for reform would sharply limit treatment
to a period of three to six months. Currently, in federal criminal proceedings
the initial competency evaluation may be followed by a four-month period
of "treatment and observation" (U.S. Code, Title 18, 4241(d)). If the defendant is likely to be restored to competency in the foreseeable future, an
extension beyond the four months may be granted by the court. In practice,
if this four-month confinement does not lead to restoration of competency,
the charges are generally dismissed, with either release from custody or
initiation of federal commitment procedures if the defendant is considered
dangerous and mentally ill. The viability of this system indicates that state
statutes allowing much longer treatment periods are not justified.

Mr. Zapata, a recent immigrant to the United States, was arrested with
several other hispanic individuals in connection with an undercover drug
"sting." During questioning he became tearful and asked that the officers
execute him immediately, as he could not stand torture. When arraigned in
court he became extremely overwrought, sobbing openly, wailing aloud in
Spanish, and wetting his pants. The court immediately ordered an examination by a Spanish-speaking psychologist and by a board certified forensic
psychiatrist. Both examiners reported that, in their opinions, Mr. Zapata
suffered from mental incapacities that would make him incompetent to
stand trial, although they cited different reasons. The first examiner noted
that the accused spoke virtually no English and in addition was mildly

mentally retarded. She believed that his ability to comprehend and participate in legal proceedings was severely compromised. The second examiner
emphasized the importance of depressive symptoms, noting that the defendant was so overwhelmed by situational depression that he was unmotivated
to defend himself against the charges. The judge determined that Mr. Zapata was incompetent to stand trial at that time and ordered him sent to a
forensic hospital for a set period of treatment.

On arrival at the hospital, Mr. Zapata was extremely fearful and agitated,
fearing that staff would force him to take shock treatments and heavy doses
of tranquilizing drugs. Over the course of several days he was able to develop rapport with a bilingual psychologist. It became clear that his fears were
based on experiences as a political prisoner in his native country. There,
torture by authorities was common in both criminal proceedings and mental
hospitals where political dissidents were sent. Through the combined effects
of a therapeutic milieu and antidepressant medication, his mental status
gradually improved. Testing, conducted in Spanish, indicated that after his
acute depression had lifted his intellectual functioning improved to the borderline to low-average range. He gave a history of school failure and marginal adjustment, and was perceived as a fairly inadequate individual who
would be easily overwhelmed by stress.

Not surprisingly, this patient had little understanding of American legal
proceedings and rights, so hospital staff explained these to him in a variety
of ways. Once he realized that he really did have an opportunity to defend
himself against the charges, he became interested in returning to court. His
court-appointed attorney was invited to the hospital to confer with Mr.
Zapata and found him able to comprehend the issues they discussed.

The therapist composed a report to the court noting that Mr. Zapata's
acute depression had lifted, and that he was less cognitively impaired and
more motivated to defend himself. During the course of his hospitalization
he had evidenced an ability to learn about American legal proceedings. He
held no irrational beliefs about his attorney and could cooperate in formulating a defense. However, his ability to speak and understand English was
still sharply limited, certainly too limited to follow testimony and arguments
in court. The examiner believed that with some modifications of courtroom
procedure Mr. Zapata would be competent to stand trial. These conditions
included: (1) availability of an interpreter throughout all proceedings; (2)
continuation of prescribed medication; (3) in the event of signs of decom-
pensation due to the stress of trial, employment of measures such as frequent recesses or shorter trial days; and (4) availability of a local mental
health expert fluent in Spanish to consult with Mr. Zapata. The court accepted the therapist's opinion and adopted all of the conditions specified.

This case illustrates a number of interesting points. First, many therapists might empathize with the plight of an intellectually limited political refugee, frightened and intimidated by authorities, and then be reluctant to "help the police" by treating the individual to restore competency. In the case at hand, the therapist was careful to explain the purpose of the hospitalization and always dealt with the defendant in a forthright manner. It is also important to note that once Mr. Zapata was returned for trial his lawyer found that the state had a weak, entirely circumstantial case. The defendant's testimony was very persuasive and led to dismissal of the charges against him. Restoration to competency did not allow the state to "railroad" him; it helped him to resolve his legal problems. Note also that treatment went somewhat beyond the bounds of usual clinical practice to include instructing the patient regarding the basics of legal procedure and philosophy. Under these circumstances this is an appropriate service both to the court and to the patient. The case also illustrates that relatively brief hospitalization may be effective in restoring competency, without resort to the lengthy periods often provided by state law.

A number of current issues in competency for trial could have complicated this case. For example, the therapist felt that Mr. Zapata may not have retained competency without medication, and there is some current debate as to whether defendants can be required to take drugs under similar conditions. Because he voluntarily took the medication offered, this did not become an issue, though a minority of courts will not accept medicated defendants even on a voluntary basis. Another factor which could have come into play was the lack of strong evidence against the defendant. In one sense his four-month confinement was needless, since there was little chance that he would be convicted. There have been proposals to "short-circuit" incompetency evaluations when the defendant can be found not guilty without the formality of a full trial.

Current Issues in Competency to Stand Trial

As is clear from the position taken by the Supreme Court in *Jackson*, legal scholars consider confinement for treatment of incompetency to serve a totally different purpose from civil commitment. In day-to-day practice this distinction may be blurred, however. As will be discussed in Chapter 4, there has been a clear trend toward requiring extreme justification for civil commitment. Many distinctly disordered individuals do not qualify for involuntary hospitalization, because current statutes require that they be imminently dangerous as well. By contrast, the same individuals, if charged with a crime, may be found not competent for trial and hospitalized for that reason. This situation—the relatively liberal hospitalization criteria for incompetency in combination with very restrictive commitment laws—is prone to abuse. The long periods of treatment allowed by state laws clearly exacerbate this trend.

Consider these issues from the perspective of police officers. Their job leads to frequent contact with disordered individuals, ranging from very dangerous violent offenders to relatively harmless but eccentric folks whose weird behavior attracts public attention. Obviously, the serious offenders require intervention, but what of the persons who merely make other people anxious? Often there is public pressure to keep "weirdos" off the street, and many officers may feel that for humanitarian reasons these persons should receive treatment, even against their will. Until the last decade these individuals could be taken to a public hospital for commitment, but increasingly commitment laws based on the doctrine of "police power" (see Chapter 4, p. 116) lead to the immediate release of these would-be patients, who return to the streets only to become involved in more contacts with police. "It is now more difficult than at any time in living memory to confine an unequivocally mentally ill person to a mental hospital against that person's will" (Meyers, 1986). Due to continuing public pressure, officers often resort to criminal charges as a way to get these troublesome individuals involved in treatment. Recent statistics indicate that the majority of persons found incompetent are charged with misdemeanors, while about a third are charged only with disturbing the peace (Geller & Lister, 1978). In a real sense many of these may be persons whose only offense is the fact that they are visibly disordered.

Prosecutors may also be motivated to utilize incompetency evaluations and confinements for inappropriate reasons. In states that allow long confinements, treatment for incompetency may actually serve to replace criminal prosecution and punishment. In a study of people found incompetent, it was found that charges against nearly three-quarters were dropped following release from treatment, as if the time served in the hospital satisfied the prosecutor's prerogative to pursue incarceration (Geller & Lister, 1978). Prosecutors may also use incompetency proceedings to deny bail, avoid speedy trial regulations, obtain special information about the defendant, or get a preliminary opinion on criminal responsibility while circumventing guarantees against self-incrimination (Smith & Meyer, 1987).

The defense is unlikely to benefit from a competency evaluation unless serious charges are lodged, and for their part defense attorneys are reluctant to raise the issue in minor cases, as the client may actually spend more time being evaluated than he might receive following a plea-bargained conviction

(Steadman & Braff, 1975). Defendants may sometimes broach the issue of incompetency as a way of obtaining an initial examination by mental health experts, with an eye toward gathering information for use in an insanity plea. It may also serve simply to delay the trial while a defense is prepared.

One of the most interesting areas of current debate concerns the use of psychotropic medications to enhance competency by moderating acute disorders. While courts have generally held that enhancing competency through the use of medication may be justified, academic legal scholars tend to criticize "artificial competency," possibly due to uncertainty about the actual role of competency proceedings. A small but respectable minority of courts do not allow the use of medication even with the defendant's consent, although it has been suggested that these refusals may themselves violate constitutional protections (Winick, 1977). Slovenko (1987) has suggested that discomfort with medicated defendants probably reflects confusion with civil commitment and the defendant's behavior in the community, rather than pragmatic concerns about participation in criminal proceedings.

At least two concerns about drug-induced competency are well-founded. First is whether a defendant should be required to take medicines aimed at restoring his or her competency. The legal debate is similar to the one currently raging in regard to patient's rights to refuse treatment despite civil commitment. While this debate will be reviewed in the Chapter 4, there are issues specifically relevant to the incompetent defendant. Most important is the potential for abuse if merely being charged with a crime and found incompetent were to become sufficient cause to impose invasive treatments. As discussed earlier, competency confinement and treatment provisions may already be misused as a replacement for the more stringent civil commitment procedures. Allowing forced medication of those found incompetent would invite circumvention of the whole right-to-refuse-treatment movement in civil matters.

In many cases a defendant who is incompetent for trial will also be incompetent to make choices about treatment. It has been suggested that those who are civilly committed should have guardians appointed to make treatment decisions and that a similar provision might be used in deciding to medicate incompetent defendants. Unfortunately, this would likely pit the individual's best interests as a criminal defendant hoping to avoid prosecution against his needs for treatment as a patient — an unsound arrangement from the start.

The other problematic issue involved in drug-maintained competency is the effect of the defendant's presentation on the jury. Case law requires that jurors be informed about the effects of any medication used to maintain the functioning of a criminal defendant, especially if his mental status is an issue in the case, as with insanity and diminished capacity pleas. If the defendant appears calm and well-adjusted in the courtroom, he may be unable to effectively present to the jury his claim to have been seriously compromised at the time of the offense (George, 1976). In fact, if he pleads insanity, research indicates that success is unlikely unless he appears overtly psychotic at the time of the trial (see, for example, Steadman, Keitner, Braff, & Arvanites, 1983). Aside from the insanity issue, it is unclear what bias may be introduced into the jury members' deliberation by informing them that the defendant could not stand trial without medication. Are they likely to feel that the defendant needs to be incarcerated whether or not he has clearly been proven guilty?

One of the most troubling issues centers on the defendant's rights against self-incrimination and the nature of examinations for competency. Courts have held that the defendant cannot object to a motion by the prosecution or the judge to initiate competency hearings. Because the information discussed with the examiner is usually not privileged, and because it may be useful to the prosecution in the event of an insanity plea or in the penalty phase of the trial, the defendant may unavoidably aid in his own prosecution. This possibility was vividly illustrated in the case of *Smith v. Estelle* (1979).

Ernest Benjamin Smith and a friend, Howie Ray Robinson, robbed a Dallas convenience store. Robinson shot a clerk during the course of the offense, and both men were indicted for capital murder. While they were awaiting trial, a judge asked Dr. James P. Grigson, a psychiatrist, to assess Smith's competence to stand for trial. Dr. Grigson spoke to Smith for about 90 minutes and concluded that he was competent. He filed no report with the court, but forwarded a letter stating his conclusions. Smith's attorneys were not informed that their client had been examined by a psychiatrist.

Smith was found guilty on the evidence, and at the sentencing hearing Dr. Grigson was called to testify and admitted over the objections of Smith's attorney. He offered the opinion that Smith was "a sociopathic personality . . . on the far end of the sociopathic scale." He went on to state that "We don't have anything in medicine or psychiatry that in any way at all modifies or changes this behavior. . . . There is no treatment. . . . Mr. Smith is going to go ahead and commit other similar or same criminal acts if given the opportunity to do so." The jury promptly sentenced Smith to death.

Smith's attorneys filed an appeal that was subsequently heard in a federal appeals court. The court found that failure of the prosecutor to notify the defense that Smith would be evaluated by an expert who could be called to testify against him violated his rights against self-incrimination and to effective counsel, as provided by the fifth and sixth amendments. Although the court held that Smith could not be compelled to undergo examination and have the results used against him, it did not specify how the results of incompetency evaluations could be used. Dr. Grigson's conduct would raise serious ethical concerns for most practitioners. But what of responsible clinicians who try to aid the court in competency determinations? Can they be compelled to reveal any or all of the information they obtain, even though they did not intend to participate beyond the competency hearing?

Possible Reforms

For reasons already presented, incompetency to stand trial is prone to a variety of abuses. Not only is this problematic because of the extreme infringement of individual rights that may result, but it is also particularly distasteful since a number of relatively simple reforms could provide an effective remedy.

The clearest need at this juncture is for improved and more specific legal standards defining incompetency. Research indicates that a large percentage of psychotherapists involved in competency evaluations do not address appropriate issues in their reports to court, probably because they are unclear about what factors are relevant. The most common problems are that a summary opinion is given with no justification and that the examiner confuses competency with absence of psychosis or retardation. This failure is hardly surprising since other studies show that lawyers and judges are equally vague as to the issues involved (Pfeiffer, Eisenstein, & Dabbs, 1967; Roesch & Golding, 1980; Rosenburg & McGarry, 1972).

Some states have attempted to overcome these problems by establishing their own criteria for competency, which provide greater detail and differentiation than the *Dusky* standard. For example, the Nebraska Supreme Court, in *State v. Guatney* (1980), enumerated 20 different considerations in determining competency, although the process of integrating these into a final decision was not addressed. It is interesting to note that many of these factors correspond to elements of the CAI (McGarry et al., 1983) and other instruments. Other states, including New Jersey, Florida, and Arizona, have adopted their own criteria. Many lawyers have pointed out that such standards may be overly specific and often include factors that are not relevant to typical cases (American Bar Association, 1983). They probably are most useful as guides to help clinicians conduct a thorough evaluation rather than as rules for legal application.

Perhaps greater progress could be made through interdisciplinary cooperation to establish clear criteria that adequately define the legal concept of criminal competency in terms that psychotherapists can effectively use in conducting evaluations. Continued development and validation of testing instruments could provide important raw material for this dialogue. Ultimately, the adoption of more uniform standards that are persuasive across jurisdictions will signal significant advances in this area.

From a procedural point of view, competency evaluations should be conducted outside an institutional setting whenever possible. Recent estimates suggest that at present over 185 million dollars are spent annually on inpatient competency studies (Winick, 1985). There is evidence that only a small portion of the time that a defendant spends in a hospital is actually used for evaluation, and given that less than 10 percent of those referred are found incompetent, many cases may require only basic screening on an outpatient basis (Wulach, 1980). Potential benefits include allowing the defendant to be released on bail, eliminating the high costs of institutional placement, and reducing the incentive to misuse incompetency proceedings as a substitute for civil commitment.

This latter purpose can also be served well by limiting the time allotted to restore competency. Statutory limits not to exceed three months should be established, with requirements for interim progress reports on a monthly basis. While these reports need not be extremely detailed, they should serve to ensure that psychotherapists are actively working to return the accused to court as expeditiously as possible. Under no circumstances should the accused be held longer than the maximum sentence for the offense charged. The doctrine of least restrictive treatment should be observed, with defendants in community rather than institutional placements whenever possible. In fact, some states have already established procedures for bail or release on recognizance while criminal proceedings are suspended for treatment (Slovenko, 1987, note 32).

The possibility that the accused may be innocent of the offense charged has prompted a number of suggestions to save time and expense by providing a preliminary finding on the facts of the case. A common scenario would have those found incompetent undergo a "provisional trial." If the defendant were found not guilty, then there would be no point in proceeding with treatment to restore competency. If the defendant were found guilty while still incompetent, then the verdict of the provisional trial would be set aside until the defendant could be retried. While these proposals would help ensure that innocent individuals are not needlessly confined, they have important political and social flaws. In cases involving serious offenses, public outrage would likely follow verdicts vacated due to incompetency, especially if the defendant does not regain competency within the allotted time, and therefore is not held accountable for acts already established in the provisional trial. A less extreme proposal might require the judge to rule on the strength of the prosecution's case, with the option of dismissing the charges if there is not clear and convincing evidence of guilt. If the state were to prove a prima facie case, then the judge could determine a likely sentence and the incompetent defendant would be held for treatment for either the length of sentence or the three-month limit, whichever was less.

Courts should unequivocally recognize the fifth amendment rights of potentially incompetent defendants by restricting use of the information developed by examiners to the incompetency hearings. To ensure due process, defendants need to be able to raise the issue of competency without fear of self-incrimination. Also, it is unfair to place therapists in the position of receiving unsolicited confessions which are then used by the prosecution against marginally competent individuals.

The type and amount of information provided to the courts may need to be adjusted in other ways as well. At present, some judges specifically request information as to how courtroom procedures might be adapted to the needs of a given defendant. This practice could be profitably expanded. The more specific the requests of the court, the more focused the examiner's responses. Also, marginal cases that must now be forced into all-or-none decisions of competency could be resolved through the accommodation of the trial judge in using more flexible courtroom procedures.

Competency to stand trial, affecting as many as 25,000 defendants per year (Wulach, 1980), may be the most crucial issue involving psychotherapists in criminal matters. Because of the minimal attention this area has received, numerous procedural and theoretical problems await resolution, thereby inviting abuse. Although findings of incompetency effectively abridge the rights of criminal defendants, in general neither legal nor psychotherapeutic practitioners adequately understand the issues involved.

TESTAMENTARY CAPACITY

Testamentary capacity refers to the mental faculties required to make an enforceable will. Wills are legal instruments designed to establish an orderly disposition of property after death and have been employed in Anglo-American law since the sixteenth century (Keeton & Gower, 1935). Since that time the law has recognized that adults have the right to express their preferences or "will" about how their estates should be managed. But the law also recognizes that severe mental incapacity compromising a person's ability to exercise will or to express himself also obviates the legal documents he composes. If a written will does not appear to express the person's "true" wishes, then it will not be enforced. When the courts find that the deceased did not possess testamentary capacity, the will is ignored and property is distributed according to legal conventions or according to earlier wills made during periods of lucidity.

The law of testamentary capacity is fairly straightforward, at least in its statement. The testator must be able to do the following (Epstein, 1962):

1. Understand the nature and extent of his or her property.
2. Realize the persons who are the natural objects of his bounty (relatives and friends).
3. Understand the distribution of the property contained in the will.
4. Understand the nature of a will and be able to form an intent to make a disposition of property that will be carried out after death.
5. Generally know how these elements relate to each other and form an orderly scheme for the distribution of property.

"Neither eccentricities, mistaken beliefs, old age, nor unreasonable provisions in the will establish incompetence" (Smith & Meyer, 1987). The cognitive abilities described above generally require only limited understanding of basic information. Because a will is a single-party instrument, there is limited possibility for fraud in its formulation. Consequently, it is usually held that less capacity is needed to make a will than to enter into contracts or conduct complex business matters.

Challenging a Will

Generally wills are private documents which are discussed only by the testator, a close relative (usually a spouse), and an attorney. They become public after the testator's death, when they are opened and offered for probate. If one or more potential heirs are displeased by the distribution of property, they may choose to contest the will or try to have it set aside in favor of what they perceive as a distribution more in keeping with the "real" desires of the deceased. Once it is demonstrated that the will was properly executed, signed, and witnessed, then those attacking the will have the burden of proving incompetency.

There are three basic grounds for contesting a will which commonly involve psychotherapists. The first of these would simply hold that the testator lacked the cognitive abilities to formulate a meaningful will. As mentioned above, the capacity required is generally not very great, but in the case of persons who have extensive holdings or envision a very complex division of properties, it is possible that a probate court might determine that they were lacking. Obviously, a trained psychologist or psychiatrist would have no difficulty establishing the level of intellectual functioning pertinent to making a will if the testator were available for examination. Such determinations are far more difficult when the testator is deceased, leading to suggestions that special competency examinations could be performed at the time the will is formulated, with a therapist's report filed along with the will itself. There are limitations to this approach, which will be discussed in more detail later.

The second major source of incompetency to make a will arises if the testator was afflicted by an "insane delusion." Broadly defined as "a belief in things which do not exist and which a rational mind would not believe to exist," the delusion may invalidate all or part of a will if it directly affects the provisions made (see *In re Hemingway's Estate*, 1900). For example, if a testator believed that he had been visited by aliens from Mars, he might still be able to formulate a reasonable will, unless he also believed that he had been commanded to leave a fund to build them a landing base. From a legal perspective, an idea becomes delusional only if there cannot be evidence or reasoning to support it (*Steinkuehler v. Wempner*, 1907). Prejudices, incorrect beliefs, and socially disapproved motives toward family and acquaintances are not considered delusional, no matter how poorly rationalized or baseless. Only thinking which is so extreme as to be impossible in principle is sufficient evidence of insane delusions.

The third major involvement of psychotherapists in will contests centers on "undue influence." Undue influence was defined by one court as:

> . . . such control was exercised over the mind of the testatrix as to overcome her free agency and free will and substitute the will of another so as to cause the testatrix to do what she would not otherwise have done but for such control. (*Lipper v. Weston*, 1963)

In the usual case, a beneficiary under the will is accused of undue influence by other heirs who are slighted or excluded from the division of property. Most such allegations arise when the favored party has been in a close relationship with the deceased, such as when one child cares for a dying parent and is then "rewarded" with a larger proportion of the estate. Factors which can make an individual susceptible to undue influence include mental or physical conditions which require extreme dependence upon another for care and emotional nurturance, such that caregivers may exert some subtle or overt coercion. Evaluating the possibility of undue influence requires an

understanding of the relationships between the testator, the party benefit-
ting from the disposition of property, and those in a position to be coercive
(Grisso, 1986).

Therapists and Evidence in Testamentary Capacity

A wide variety of evidence can be introduced to indicate or rebut incompetency to make a will. This evidence may be very directly related to the will
and its execution, as when the wording, style, and provisions of the will itself
are used as evidence of an insane delusion. Documentable information pertaining to the testator's physical condition, health, behavior, and habits are
admissible, but not conclusive. For example, the presence of a serious physical illness requiring extensive personal care does not automatically establish
undue influence. Circumstantial or inferential data relating to substance
use, intellectual limitations, or intermittent psychotic disorders may also be
introduced.

Psychotherapists called to testify regarding any of these issues are faced
with a number of significant problems. In the vast majority of cases the
expert will never have met the individual in question, who is now unavailable
for examination. Often, the will was signed many years earlier, and data on
the subject's behavior and mental status at just that time may be difficult to
obtain. Further, those persons who were closest to the testator may be
motivated, consciously or not, to give biased accounts of the circumstances
surrounding the formulation of the will. "An ethical question facing experts
asked to testify is whether it is professionally appropriate to render an
opinion concerning the mental state of someone whom the expert never met
and who is now dead" (Smith & Meyer, 1987). The answer to this question is
likely to vary with the quality of the historical data available, the clarity of
clinical and diagnostic issues involved, and the closeness of the relationship
between psychological disorder or disability and the legal premises for incapacity.

A number of legal commentators have pointed out that courts often seize
upon will contests as a means to enforce social mores regarding fairness and
equity in property division, rather than to actualize the wishes of the deceased (Epstein, 1962; Spaulding, 1985). The imprecise definition of incompetency to make a will and the lack of clarity regarding the level of incapacity that should invalidate a will contribute to this process. Against this
background, therapists must use restraint when becoming involved in will
contests. Otherwise. the clinicians' testimony may be used to circumvent the
last wishes of an individual with whom they had no personal contact. Obviously, the potential for ethical conflicts in this area is considerable.

A potentially more constructive response focuses on determining the mental status of the testator at the time the will is signed. As attorneys prepare a will they may make arrangements for an evaluation by a therapist who then files a report to be notarized along with the will itself. This practice may be especially effective in forestalling challenges if videotapes are made of the evaluation interview and testing, as well as of the reading and signing of the will. If questions regarding testamentary capacity are raised later, the therapist has a reasonable basis for testimony, relying on his own expert findings at the specific time in question. Of course, it is possible that the evaluation will provide evidence that the testator does lack capacity. In those cases the attorney would at least know in advance about these difficulties, opening up the possibility of executing the will later, under better conditions, or of taking special steps to overcome the incapacity.

GUARDIANSHIP

Ms. Street was a 57-year-old single woman from a tiny community in the midwest. She had attracted the attention of members of the community because she lived alone on the outskirts of town, had numerous pets, dressed a little strangely, and sometimes seemed confused. The judge in her community sought an evaluation regarding her mental status and potential for dangerousness. He indicated that the court would consider involuntary commitment to the state hospital if this were indicated.

While cooperative, Ms. Street was aware that the examination had to do with "putting [her] in a home," a possibility which she did not relish. She gave a history which indicated that she had always been intellectually impaired, and that her parents, both school teachers, had kept her out of public view. Consequently, she did not have the benefit of basic schooling or socialization. Testing yielded an I.Q. of 61.

Ms. Street's parents had died about ten years earlier, and she had lived alone since that time. She had a sum of money from life insurance settlements in the only bank in town, and also received some type of disability benefits. She could not specify how the bulk of the money was handled and did not understand concepts such as interest, principal and investment. Whenever she needed money she would just walk into town and ask for some. The examiner learned that tellers at the bank would guess at the amount she would need for a given purpose, and supply her appropriately. Questioning about other daily needs revealed that she understood where and how to get medical care, how to purchase food, what to do if her home caught fire, and other basic survival skills. In fact, she had been caring for herself adequately for a full decade.

In a report to the court the examiner noted that results of formal testing indicated mild mental retardation, though this was probably an underestimate given that she had not received any appropriate instruction as a young person. There were no indications of other psychological impairment or disorder, and no reason to believe that she would be dangerous to herself or others. She appeared intellectually able to manage most demands of daily life, with the possible exception of finances. Finally, the examiner reported Ms. Street's sincere desire to remain in her home where she could care for animals and pursue a variety of simple hobbies.

The examiner advocated that the court appoint limited guardians to assist and support Ms. Street. First, since tellers at the local bank already served as *de facto* guardians for her money, the court could formalize this arrangement. The head teller subsequently agreed to take on this responsibility, including productive investment of the bulk of Ms. Street's funds so that her financial position would be more secure. They met on a weekly basis to discuss simple budgeting, pay bills, and withdraw cash for the next few days. It was also noted that retarded adults may be more prone to illness and injury than others, and that at least weekly home visitation by a concerned adult could serve to monitor her health over time. A local minister assumed this role at the request of the court. Finally, annual written evaluations by the nearest mental health center were suggested. These reports, along with communication from the two appointed guardians, would be reviewed by the court to ensure that Ms. Street's needs were being met.

Ms. Street herself did not find anything objectionable in these proposals. They did little to alter her lifestyle, and served more as a safety net to protect her health and welfare. In fact, she felt it would be pleasant to have regular contact with "such nice folks." The recommendations were adopted with little modification by the court.

In many respects Ms. Street's case represents the ideal of guardianship, a complex and poorly standardized area of the law which may promote greater abuse than any other. Only a limited discussion of issues relevant to guardianship can be presented here, along with a brief review of the role that therapists may play in these matters. From a theoretical point of view guardianship is important because it represents a transitional concept between legal incompetency and civil commitment, the topic of Chapter 4.

Guardianship is a system which strives to protect incompetent individuals from personal and financial harm. Broadly conceived, it refers to determinations that a person is or is not competent to manage important affairs and make personal-care decisions. For those found incompetent in these areas, a guardian is appointed to exercise the legal rights of the incompetent person. The guardian assumes control and management of personal property and financial assets, and may also be entrusted with decisions about where the incompetent will live, whether he or she should be placed in an institution, and what kinds of medical or mental treatments he or she should receive. Guardianship has the potential both for protecting and caring for those who cannot care for themselves and for great abuse (Jordan, 1985).

Traditionally, the legal emphasis in guardianship has been on protecting the property and finances of the incompetent, rather than looking out for other types of personal welfare. Ancient Rome provided for protecting the property of incompetents, and this practice continued through the English tradition and was adopted in America. Several of the colonies established legal protections for the property of incompetents, long before measures were taken to assure the personal welfare of the mentally disabled generally (Smith & Meyer, 1987). The traditional focus on financial rather than personal welfare may help explain why experts on guardianship generally believe that it does little to protect or serve the humanitarian and personal needs of wards, often doing more to benefit or enrich the appointed guardians or to perpetuate social conformity (Alexander, 1977; Mitchell, 1978; Pleak & Applebaum, 1985).

Determinations of Incompetency

As with other areas of incompetency, statutory definitions of those who require guardianship are quite vague. Jurisdictions clinging to traditional standards may emphasize the subject's lack of "sufficient understanding or capacity to make, communicate or implement responsible decisions concerning his personal property" (Brakel, Parry, & Weiner, 1986). More modern statutes adopt a broader functional view, defining as incompetent anyone who substantially risks personal harm due to inability to manage financial affairs or to obtain food, shelter, or health care. The latter view necessarily assumes functions similar to older civil commitment statutes based on the doctrine of *parens patriae*. Psychological impairment is the most common basis for incompetency, but drug or alcohol addiction, serious illness, old age, and even character disorder may also apply.

Incompetency is established through a judicial hearing. This is generally instituted at the request of family, friends, business partners, or others ostensibly interested in the welfare of the subject. Testimony is taken from those who know the person well and from experts who can describe the person's mental status. Therapists may be asked to participate under conditions similar to those in will contests, but at least here the subject is alive and available for examination. Experts are usually retained by the court and are considered impartial, acting in the best interest of the potential incompetent.

If the court rules that the individual is in fact incompetent and in need of a guardian, one is appointed. Generally this is the person who initiated the proceeding, but it can also be an employee of state social service agencies. Findings of incompetency may lead to extreme restriction of personal liberty or property rights, so that at least some constitutional due process guarantees should apply. In practice, however, these are often one-sided affairs and the alleged incompetent is rarely present. In as many as 80 to 85 percent of cases only a judge, the petitioner, and the petitioner's attorney are present (Schmidt, 1984). Even when the subject of the proceeding is invited to participate, he is not guaranteed an attorney, as in criminal proceedings (Gutheil & Applebaum, 1982). In theory, if the individual is restored to competence, then a guardian will no longer be required and full rights will be restored, but for a variety of reasons restoration of legal rights is very rare.

A recent trend involves the concept of limited guardianship or partial incompetence. Most individuals retain the ability to make at least some effective decisions for themselves, so they should not be subjected to total deprivation of legal rights and status. Under some conditions, a person could be declared incompetent in only limited areas, as in the case of Ms. Street. She was found incompetent to make informed investment decisions, but retained the right to spend money as she wished with informal advice. Though limited guardianship can help to preserve the autonomy and dignity of wards, courts prefer to see incompetence as an all-or-nothing proposition (American Bar Association, 1979). This perspective may have some merit, as a psychotherapist asked to state precisely which areas of functioning are so impaired as to require intervention and to differentiate these from less impaired skills is faced with a difficult task. Limited guardianships probably work best when an individual has a well-defined deficit in an important area of functioning.

Therapists have an important interest in guardianship aside from their role as experts aiding the court. As civil commitment standards have changed, guardianship arrangements remain one of the only areas of *parens patriae* justification for involuntary hospitalization. Given the very restrictive law surrounding civil commitment, having a difficult individual declared incompetent may be a far easier way to compel him or her into treatment (Kapp & Bigot, 1985). Therapists obviously bear a heavy ethical responsibility to ensure that treatment rendered to an involuntary patient under guardianship is truly in his best interests. Thorny moral questions surround the issue of instigating guardianship proceedings with family or other interested parties. Even when the need for treatment appears extreme, the costs to the potential patient may be high. Still, because other methods of compelling involuntary hospitalization are so restrictive, family and care-takers may be moved to consider this possibility.

Perhaps because of its historical emphasis on fiduciary matters, guardianship as a legal process has not adapted well to broader issues of personal welfare. Criticism from the legal arena has been strident. Based on the assumption that guardians will act in the best interests of their wards, these procedures allow for even greater deprivation of personal freedoms than conviction for serious criminal offenses. Convicts, for example, can decide what medical and mental treatments they will accept. The incompetent generally cannot. Because of the very vague standards and loose procedures employed, guardianship arrangements often fall far short of expectations. One scholar has suggested that we:

> . . . recognize guardianship for what it really is: the most intrusive, non inter-est-serving, impersonal device known and available to us and, as such, one which minimizes personal autonomy and respect for the individual, has a high potential for doing harm and raises at best a questionable benefit/burden ratio. (Cohen, 1978)

Within this milieu, therapists are advised to participate with caution. Perhaps here more than in any other area of interface between psychotherapy and the law, there is both the potential for important benefit to those in need and the possibility of exploitation and abuse.

CHAPTER 4

Involuntary Civil Commitment

I know as much about the dictionary, I presume, as the average person. I say to you that the words 'antisocial acts' is [sic] so general that it does not help anybody. You have got to tell us concretely what specific things he says and does that differentiate him from a normal person. . . . I am not going to keep anybody deprived of his liberty on adjectives and generalities, it has got to be verbs and nouns, something that a person does or says that differentiates him from normal people and makes him dangerous. . . . Liberty is too precious to leave it merely with the opinions of [psychotherapists].

—Cited in Katz, 1967

THIS COMMENT IS TAKEN from the transcript of a civil commitment hearing that later led to a landmark decision regarding the rights of involuntary mental patients (*Rouse v. Cameron*, 1966). It hints at a number of problems and challenges inherent in this area of mental health law, most significantly that lawmakers, judges, and attorneys approach these matters with motivations different from those of psychotherapists. Here we describe the current status of civil commitment as a legal process and the role that therapists are called upon to play. Since the concept of dangerousness is now firmly entrenched in state commitment statutes, we will briefly review the effects of this concept and the difficulties of clinical predictions in the process of commitment. Prediction of dangerousness is a complicated issue that involves several areas of mental health law; it is considered in more detail in Chapter 5.

Currently, legal opinions about the rights of involuntary patients to refuse or receive certain types of care are variable, and some recent case law

114

throws these issues into confusion. Nevertheless, we will discuss some general trends. Finally, though the major focus of this book is on pragmatic questions confronting the practicing therapist, we will advocate potential reforms and discuss theoretical and philosophical issues that may motivate therapists to influence policy decisions in the future.

Stated simply, civil commitment is a process for involuntarily hospitalizing persons who are both mentally ill *and* dangerous. The dual rationales for commitment are a source of considerable conflict among lawyers and therapists, and may be related to differences in the purposes for which the confinement is undertaken. Therapists obviously value the caring relationship toward their clients, and so view commitment as a means to a humanitarian end, the treatment of persons who cannot seek or accept it on their own. Because they see themselves as helpers, therapists rarely focus on the adverse consequences that may result from civil commitment. For their part, attorneys tend to adopt a very cynical view of any legal maneuvers that may deprive someone of his or her rights. Clearly, confining someone in a hospital against his will is liberty-depriving, perhaps more liberty-depriving than any other common legal function. Lawyers may discount the care and concern of therapists as irrelevant and assume that commitment is actually against the best interests of the patient. These opposing viewpoints clash in the operation of contemporary commitment procedures.

The first articulation of the basis for civil commitment in America took place in the 1845 case of *In re Oakes* (1845). Mr. Oakes was an elderly Cambridge, Massachusetts man, whose family, over his objections, delivered him to the McLean Asylum in Belmont. His behavior was somewhat unusual, but in retrospect it is difficult to know whether it was pathological or just socially unacceptable. Oakes was held at the asylum against his will and with no prior trial or judicial action, so he petitioned for release. His request was eventually heard by the Massachusetts Supreme Court, which deliberated two full days before issuing its opinion and ordering that Oakes remain confined. Scholars have noted at least five important precedents established by *Oakes*, including: (1) that the state has a right to confine disordered persons if they are somehow dangerous; (2) that "insane" persons lack free will; (3) that caretakers should have the major role in decision-making for the mentally disordered, including length of treatment; (4) that civil proceedings do not require the same due process considerations as criminal matters; and (5) that involuntary treatment is justified not only by the detainee's dangerousness, but also for his or her own welfare (Bartol, 1983).

Though the opinion noted the issues both of dangerousness and of humanitarian concern for the afflicted, *Oakes* has been widely regarded as a precedent for *parens patriae* justification for commitment. *Parens patriae*, which essentially means "the state as parent," is a doctrine which can be traced from ancient Roman law through the Anglo-Saxon tradition until its adoption by the American legal system. It refers to a duty of authorities to function as benevolent guardians for those who cannot fend for themselves, particularly if their incapacity is due to mental disorder. Psychotherapists usually see this as the basis for their participation in civil commitment.

As courts and statutes began to follow the reasoning of *Oakes*, "the diagnosis 'mental illness' alone was sufficient to justify confinement and involuntary treatment" (Bartol, 1983, p. 99). Several precedents established by this case served to short-circuit the rights of those who were considered for commitment. The notion that mentally disordered individuals lack free will provided a rationale for not giving due consideration to their wishes. After all, why pursue elaborate legal protections of someone's free will if mental disorder has deprived them of it? The court's opinion also established a precedent for "paternalism," the idea that family and professional caretakers will make decisions for an impaired individual based only on that person's best interests. The combined effect of these factors was that many jurisdictions were extremely receptive to commitment petitions, on the assumption that they would benefit the patient.

Unfortunately, the effects of involuntary commitment rarely matched expectations. As has been well chronicled (see Burgdorf, 1980; Deutsch, 1949), conditions in mental institutions across the country were deplorable, and staff greatly exaggerated the potential for treating severe mental disorders. Courts supported liberal commitment criteria on the grounds of potential benefit, but the benefits that were expected to accrue to detainees when sent to an asylum "for their own good" simply did not exist. As a mark of the political impotence of the mentally disordered, it took over one hundred years for substantive reforms to be adopted.

Largely as a reaction to these failings, recent statutory and case law governing mental health commitments have become much more stringent, and now focus closely on the issue of dangerousness as justification for commitment. *Police power* is a term for the general authority of the state to protect the public from harm and regulate behavior for the social good. Actions taken under police power deprive an individual of freedom or rights, as when someone convicted of a criminal offense is incarcerated to protect the public. Police power should be limited to cases where a compelling state interest outweighs the costs to an individual, and should not be used against the nondangerous mentally disordered. That is, disordered persons are thought to have the right to be "different" and remain at liberty.

Current legal standards do not recognize mental disorder alone as justification to exercise police power; individuals must also be dangerous to justify depriving them of liberty. Consequently, current law seems to meld both *parens patriae* and police power rationale in civil commitment proceedings, although in many respects police power issues such as dangerousness may be given disproportionate weight. "So appealing to the legal mind was the libertarian logic of the dangerousness model that by the mid-1970s virtually every state had, if not entirely thrown over need for treatment in favor of dangerousness, at least grafted dangerousness onto its existing standards for commitment" (Monahan, 1982).

CRITERIA FOR COMMITMENT

Following the Supreme Court's decision in *Addington v. Texas* (1979), the burden of proof is on the petitioner and the state, who must demonstrate by "clear and convincing evidence" that the detainee meets the statutory criteria for commitment. This level of proof is a compromise between mere "preponderance" of the evidence, used in other civil matters, and "beyond a reasonable doubt," the standard in criminal proceedings, and reflects a balance of the need to protect individual rights against the presumably well-intentioned intervention by the state. The court determined that language in the Constitution requires significant due process protections, but not as much as in criminal matters. It is noteworthy that states can adopt a more stringent level of proof if they wish. Kentucky, for example, requires proof of commitment criteria beyond a reasonable doubt, largely because courts there view commitment as a "quasi-criminal" proceeding.

The general standards for commitment require that the individual be both mentally ill and dangerous, either to himself or to others. In addition, most states describe other factors that may influence the decision, such as the requirement that there be some treatment available for the patient's disorder. Also, as laws have become more stringent, there has been increasing attention to the idea of "least restrictive alternative." If the treatment needed can be offered without involuntary confinement, then commitment is not justified. These latter provisions make little sense unless dangerousness arises *because of* the mental disorder, and this appears to be a tacit assumption of contemporary statutes (Chodoff, 1984). After all, what would be the purpose of confining someone because he is dangerous, treating an unrelated mental disorder, and then releasing him while still dangerous? This confusion of dangerousness with disorder may reflect the popular misconception that disturbed persons are frequently dangerous, or it may indicate that the real purpose of commitment is to confine frightening individuals under the guise of treatment.

There are a number of other problems with statutory criteria for commit-ment. While there appears to be a tendency to view dangerousness as a fairly serious, physical, imminent threat of harm to self or others, most laws do not define the term at all. Therapists may wonder if harm must be physical, or could it be emotional? What frequency and severity of harm equate to "dangerousness"? In some states criteria such as "need for treatment" or "gravely disabled" may substitute for dangerous to self, again with little clarification. "Mental illness" is similarly vague, usually defined so broadly as to include almost any psychological state. Would this include any diag-nosable condition, even personality disorders? Must the patient be overtly psychotic? While the intent may be to only consider "serious" disorders, the vagueness of statutory definitions allows for freewheeling interpretation by both judges and therapists.

The failure of states and courts to adequately define the key concepts underlying commitment leaves psychotherapists at a loss when serving as expert witnesses. Consequently, there is considerable latitude in the applica-tion of these standards, depending on the idiosyncratic views of the partici-pants. It is clear that changes in statutory criteria can lead to sweeping changes in hospital populations (McGarry, Schwitzgebel, Lipsitt, & Lelos, 1981; Miller & Fiddleman, 1982; Zander, 1976). It is also clear that "vague commitment criteria [lead] to greater incidence of hospital admission and recommitment, and also facilitate involuntary, rather than voluntary hospi-talization" (Peters, Miller, Schmidt, & Meeter, 1987, p. 82). More stringent criteria reduce admission rates, largely by decreasing the number of involun-tary commitments.

Although current commitment standards are based on dangerousness, it is uncertain whether other standards could be applied instead. Before the recent trend toward stricter criteria, some states provided for hospitalization of those who were mentally ill but not seeking treatment or in need of hospitalization but refusing. It seems legitimate to ask if the state does not have a compelling interest in treating mental disorder among its people. There have been a variety of persuasive proposals based on the "need for treatment" justification, basically focusing on the inability of the disordered person to obtain needed care. These concepts would place commitment much closer to the functions of civil incompetency and could help to resolve difficult problems concerning patient's rights. Such positions, advanced by Stone (1976a) and Roth (1979) and adopted by the American Psychiatric Association, generally appeal to therapists, but it is unclear whether they would withstand legal challenge. The Supreme Court has held that it is unconstitutional to hold nondangerous mentally ill persons without treat-ment and has hinted that it may be inappropriate to confine these persons even for the sake of providing them active treatment (*O'Connor v. Donaldson*, 1975).

Some of the consequences of the mix of motivations and rationale for commitment will be discussed at the end of the chapter. Before turning to the pragmatics of civil commitment, however, it is important to note several relevant conceptual issues related to areas of the law presented in earlier chapters. First, commitment is like criminal sanctions in that both are intended to change unacceptable behavior and protect society. Both the criminal defendant and the committed patient do not want this treatment. Unlike criminal law, commitment is focused on what the patient might do in the future, rather than on enacting punishment for prohibited acts. Civil commitment also bears similarities to legal incompetency, because in each case some decision-making power is taken away. In the case of commitment, only the decision to enter the hospital is made for the patient, who is generally viewed as competent to make all other decisions. This distinction between committability (see Chapter 3) and competency is the basis for debates about patient's rights to make decisions regarding treatment, to be reviewed later.

PROCEDURES FOR CIVIL COMMITMENT

The procedures and rules regarding commitment are established on a state-by-state basis, but there are important commonalities. The information presented here is a composite of a generalized civil commitment procedure, but a practicing therapist should be familiar with the specifics of the statute in his or her jurisdiction. Some states have experimented with significant modifications.

Routine commitment procedures begin when someone petitions a magistrate or judge to request commitment of someone else. Petitioners may include family, friends, coworkers, therapists, or other persons who have some knowledge of and relationship to this person. The subject of the petition has an opportunity to respond (hence the term *respondent*) to the assertion that he is in need of confinement for mental health treatment. If it is not an emergency situation, then a hearing is scheduled within the next several days and the respondent is ordered to undergo examination by one or more psychotherapists. The respondent has the right to an attorney and may actively fight commitment. He is also guaranteed the right to be present at any proceedings and to retain his own experts.

Because commitment is, by definition, involuntary, many patients will not agree to be transported to a triage center for evaluation. Consequently, all 50 states provide for some type of time-limited emergency commitment for those believed to be mentally disordered (Schwitzgebel & Schwitzgebel, 1980), and many communities have established centers for emergency confinement. Family members, friends, or other interested parties may contact a special judge or magistrate who handles commitment procedures and ask that an emergency commitment order be issued. The petitioner must explain the basis for his belief that the person requires commitment; if the explanation is satisfactory to the court, a mental health warrant is issued. Much like an arrest warrant, this document authorizes police, marshals or other peace officers to seek out the named individual and transport him or her to the hospital for further evaluation. These procedures serve to insure that persons who may be an immediate risk to themselves or others can be quickly entered into the system, more quickly than would be feasible if full legal proceedings were required. In practice, the majority of commitments are initiated under emergency procedures, possibly because many petitioners resist acting until a crisis arises (Mestrovic, 1982; NCSC, 1982).

Psychotherapists can serve as petitioners; in fact, in many states they may bypass some of the paperwork involved and arrange for the person to be taken to the hospital simply by calling the authorities. For example, if a client discloses an intent to commit suicide, a licensed therapist can generally ask the police to take him or her to an inpatient facility immediately, leaving the paperwork for later. Practicing therapists should acquaint themselves with the pragmatics of commitment procedures in their communities *before* a crisis arises. Magistrates and clerks of court are usually very cooperative in explaining the relevant laws and procedures and may "walk through" a petition to illustrate the entire process. Therapists should understand whom to call to arrange a mental health warrant, the criteria that apply in their jurisdiction, how and where to complete the necessary paperwork, and the location of the community evaluation center. Further, they should be able to explain all of the above to members of the community.

Once at the hospital or evaluation center, whether on an emergency or routine basis, the respondent is examined by one or more mental health specialists. Most states permit psychiatrists, psychologists, and registered psychiatric nurses in various combinations to conduct the examination. If the person is brought in at the request of a psychotherapist, this person generally serves as both the petitioner and one of the examiners. Most states require that at least two professionals agree on the need for confinement. If the person satisfies the criteria for commitment, then he or she can be held for periods of 24 to 72 hours on the recommendation of the experts. If he does not meet the criteria, he is immediately released.

Prior to the signing of a formal commitment order, many jurisdictions allow for expunging records of the commitment process. Many persons react to the initial commitment process by agreeing to enter the hospital voluntarily; if they do so, there is generally no public record of the emergency proceedings taken to hospitalize them. These provisions, intended to reduce the likelihood of stigmatization, have been characterized as a plea bargain in the commitment process. If the detainee continues to refuse admission against the recommendations of the examining therapists, then a public preliminary hearing is held where a judge reviews the need for continued commitment. This is generally followed by a more extensive hearing to finalize the court's decision.

In practice, most hearings are informal and are held without a jury. Attorneys for the state present the case for committing the patient and question the mental health experts regarding their findings. Family members or other witnesses may testify as well, and the patient or his attorney may question any witnesses. Often the respondent himself is questioned directly by the judge. Finally, the detainee is either committed or released, or perhaps the proceedings are dismissed if the patient agrees to voluntary admission.

RELEASE OR CONTINUATION OF COMMITMENT

Until the last two decades, indefinite commitment was the rule, as consistent with the court opinion in *Oakes*, which said that the asylum director should decide when treatment was complete. Presently, most statutes limit the length of commitment to a period of three to six months. The patient may be released at any time that the therapists in the institution decide that he is sufficiently improved to no longer meet the criteria, usually without judicial action. If the patient remains committable, then he stays in the hospital until the mandated limit of commitment. At that time the staff must either release the patient or go through commitment proceedings again.

States which have adopted very limited period of commitment have experienced an increase in readmissions, as many patients are not prepared for release in the allotted time (Peters et al., 1987). In response, some states have provided for extended commitments, on the order of six months to a year, for patients who must be recommitted. In practice, hearings for recommitments are often held at the hospital for the convenience of the therapists and to minimize disruption of the patient's routine.

LAWYERS AND THERAPISTS

The roles taken by psychotherapists and lawyers involved in civil commitment are somewhat different from those in other areas of practice. This can be disconcerting and often leads to problems in implementing the process.

When therapists enter the legal arena, they are typically consultants. Even as expert witnesses in criminal proceedings, they participate as independent parties who provide special information, but have little or no investment in the outcome of the case. Therapists' role in commitment proceedings is quite different. Research suggests that judges are extremely dependent on the opinions of experts in these matters, in effect giving over the decision to therapists. Courts concur with therapists' recommendations in as many as 90 percent of cases (Zander, 1976), perhaps "letting someone else make the tough decisions" (Smith & Meyer, 1987). Also, therapists do have some interest in the outcome of the proceedings. As caretakers for their clients, they may see commitment as a necessary step toward treatment; also, the therapist's involvement does not stop once a decision is made. There is some suspicion that this arrangement invites "therapeutic paternalism," the idea that patients should have little autonomy and should be dealt with simply as therapists see fit.

Lawyers are accustomed to serving as advocates. In adversarial matters such as a criminal trial or a civil lawsuit, the interests of the client are clearly defined and the attorney is obligated to pursue these interests by any legal and ethical means available. In commitment cases the client's best interests are less clear. By definition, commitments are undertaken for people who do not want to be confined for treatment. To do what the client asks, the attorney must keep him out of the hospital—but is this what is best? Often, attorneys are faced with a difficult decision. Most do not actively seek the release of clients (Hiday, 1982). This amounts to "legal paternalism," since the attorney now guesses what the client needs without necessarily giving much weight to what he wants. Attorneys are, of course, less able to judge the clinical needs of their clients than are therapists. Some scholars have argued that "Modern commitment proceedings, therefore, suffer from the worst of both worlds: uninformed legal decision-making concerning [psychotherapeutic] issues and uniformed decision-making [by therapists] concerning legal issues" (Bloom & Faulkner, 1987).

THE REALITIES OF MODERN COMMITMENT

A group of night students contacted the clinic when they noticed a young woman in the lobby of another building. She was dressed strangely, spoke aloud to herself, and appeared to hear things. When approached, she was shy and fearful, but gave her name, Christine. With encouragement she agreed to come to the clinic and talk.

It was December and below freezing outside, but she wore only bedroom slippers, jeans and a flannel shirt, no coat. She shivered visibly as she looked fearfully about the room. Her clothes were dirty and she later explained that to wash them she would lay them in the bottom of a bathtub, then climb in and bathe. She put the clothes back on to air dry. While Christine had an apartment she had not been there in several days; when asked why, she said that there was something evil in her closet. Even though she had cleaned it repeatedly, the evil presence remained and so she was afraid to go home. For the last several days she had sought shelter in public buildings to avoid the cold.

Christine was extremely thin and said she had not eaten for two days. Baskets of fruit were placed in the clinic waiting room for the holidays, and she eagerly stuffed food into her pockets. Her speech was striking. She spoke only in fragments of ideas, struggling to communicate at all. She had difficulty sticking to any line of thought and was easily distracted by outside noises, her own voice, and occasionally by auditory hallucinations. She was obviously frightened by what she heard and repeatedly became alarmed by insignificant stimuli.

At length Christine revealed that the night before a stranger had offered her a ride. She had accepted because it was warm in the car. The man took her to a theater where they showed "pictures of people being dirty." After leaving the theater they drove to a vacant parking lot where the stranger raped her; then he asked her to get out and drove away. Because Christine seemed to be in danger on the streets, at least in her current condition, it appeared that she should be hospitalized. Unfortunately, she feared that the evil presence would follow her to the hospital and that she would be unable to escape it there. She refused to go to the hospital voluntarily and staff members felt that the only ethical action was to seek involuntary commitment. The police were called to detain Christine and a petition was filed with the appropriate magistrate.

The petition asserted that Christine was suffering from a major mental disorder and that she posed a danger to herself, as evidenced by her inability to provide for basic needs including food, shelter and clothing. Further, she was at risk for victimization as indicated by her experience the night before. The magistrate refused the petition on the following grounds: (1) Christine had an established residence and therefore could provide shelter for herself; (2) the petitioner (a psychologist) was not an expert on metabolism and physiology and his speculations about malnutrition were not persuasive; (3) matters of dress and sexual conduct involve considerable leeway for personal expression and were not useful indicators of neglect or dangerousness to self; and (4) there was no indication that she was dangerous to others. Although Christine was mentally ill, she was not, in the magistrate's view, "dangerous" and therefore did not meet the criteria for commitment in that state.

It was later learned that Christine was arrested by local police the following day and charged with indecent exposure. She had been found leaning against an automobile urinating in a rain gutter. The public defender assigned to her case asked the court to order an evaluation of her competency to stand trial. Due to her bizarre behavior this was granted. She was found not competent and returned to a public hospital for treatment to restore competency. Ironically, she was confined in the same state facility to which she would have gone if committed, although in another unit. The net effect of the magistrate's refusal to allow civil commitment was that Christine was confined anyway, but as a criminal defendant and potentially for a longer period of time (see Chapter 3). It is unclear how her best interests were served by this outcome.

This case illustrates the impact of dangerousness criteria on commitment procedures. A number of studies has documented the decline in public hospital admission rates as a result of the more stringent criteria adopted (McGarry et al., 1981; Miller & Fiddleman, 1982; Peters et al., 1987). While some of this decline probably results from a decrease in the number of inappropriate commitments, that is, confinement of persons who really do not require involuntary hospitalization, some of the decline is due to failures in the current system.

Although changes in civil commitment statutes were ostensibly adopted for the benefit of mentally disordered persons who might have been subject to involuntary confinement, the current status of commitment procedures has produced a number of unfortunate consequences and calls into question the real purposes for which changes are undertaken. In many respects practice falls far short of theory.

One unintended consequence of stricter civil commitment laws is that persons who were formerly sent directly to hospitals now take a more circuitous route. The inclusion of "dangerousness" in statutory criteria was intended to reduce the number of committed individuals and has had the desired effect. Between 1955 and 1981, the number of persons involuntarily confined to hospitals under civil order on a given day declined from 560,000 to just 138,000 (Stromberg & Stone, 1983). Admittedly, this in part reflects the general deinstitutionalization movement and the effects of neuroleptic medications, but these factors are unlikely to account entirely for such a dramatic drop. Changes in state commitment criteria produce predictable changes in public hospital population. It is reasonable to ask what has become of those formerly confined to a hospital.

One answer is that some are still hospitalized, but by way of criminal court. Research shows that as states enact stricter commitment laws, the rate of arrest for mentally ill persons rises to compensate (Geller & Lister, 1978). Many individuals who previously would have been subject to commitment are now charged with disturbing the peace or some other minor offense. It is common for these people to be found incompetent to stand trial (see Chapter 3) and required to enter a hospital until competency can be restored. Often, state laws allow longer commitments through this route than under civil commitment procedures. Clearly, these patients are no better off by being "protected" from "unnecessary" mental health commitment when they end up as criminal defendants, potentially confined for a longer time and arguably in less treatment-oriented programs.

A second response is that many persons, like Christine, who would formerly have received treatment, albeit involuntarily, now receive none. "Many individuals who clearly would benefit from short-term hospitalization and treatment are not treated because they do not meet, for example, the 'perceived threat' [dangerousness] criterion extant in many states" (Maloney, 1985). A variation on this theme is the "revolving door" patient, an individual who meets criteria until brought into the hospital and treated, often with medication that blunts the worst of his symptoms. If hospital staff follow statutory procedures closely, they may release the patient in very short order, without substantive progress toward lasting rehabilitation. Once released, many of these patients discontinue their medication and aftercare, only to degenerate rapidly and return to the hospital just long enough to receive medication. The marginal functioning of these individuals and the inability of the current system to meet their needs have led to the development of "psychiatric ghettos" and an entirely new class of disadvantaged Americans (see Bonovitz & Guy, 1979; Brown, 1985).

A final consideration is the effect on hospital environments and conditions. The winnowing of public hospital populations by stringent commitment guidelines may leave only "a 'hard core' of more disturbed and dangerous clients" (Peters et al., 1987; see also DeRisi & Vega, 1983). This shift in clientele may require increased security at state hospitals, special training of staff to deal with an increasingly difficult population, changes in treatment and discharge planning, and greater per patient expenditures on nonclinical services.

CONDUCTING EVALUATIONS OF CIVIL COMMITTABILITY

When conducting an evaluation as an impartial expert retained by the court or as a petitioner seeking the commitment of a current client, the therapist will benefit from approaching the task in a systematic manner. While written reports are rarely requested, the therapist will be more effective if data are systematically collected, organized, and presented, as for a formal evaluation. Obviously, familiarity with local statutes is essential. At least six major factors should be addressed, as discussed below. One of these factors, the assessment of dangerousness, is addressed in detail in Chapter 5. The main topics for a commitment evaluation can be phrased as a series of putative questions by the court.

What is the Nature of the Respondent's Mental Illness, if Any?

Clearly, the most basic element in a civil court's determinations of the need for commitment is the presence or absence of mental illness. In many jurisdictions where commitment evaluations are inadequate, therapists merely give a summary diagnostic statement and indicate that hospitalization is warranted. A more thorough evaluation would go well beyond a diagnostic label. Testimony should describe the patient's current behavior and mental status and focus on the ways that the observations are consistent with a defined diagnostic category. The examiner should emphasize the ways that the subject's behavior differs from the norm, is maladaptive, or represents a decline from prior levels of functioning. Only when the degree of impairment is significant is the court likely to find commitment justified.

It is often useful to provide the court with a broad conceptual explanation of the respondent's disorder in layman's terms. Laypeople, even judges who deal with commitments, use mental health terms in their own ways, which may not be consistent with professional usage. "Schizophrenia," for example, is often confused with multiple personality, and "depression" is commonly used to describe almost any sort of negative feelings. A brief review of the fundamental characteristics of the relevant diagnostic label will help to clarify in the court's mind the basis for the finding that the respondent does manifest a specific, well-defined mental disorder.

Special emphasis should also be placed on characterizing the patient's degree of impairment related to nonclinical populations and to others with mental disorders. Courts often find statements about the respondent relative to other patients more informative than a blanket assurance of "severe" or "moderate" or "mild" impairment. While these issues will become important in another part of the evaluation process, they should be addressed at the outset.

Psychological testing, if available, will often aid in establishing normative statements. As an example, consider a patient who completes the MMPI and produces elevations between 70 and 80 T on scales 6 and 8. The therapist would be able to state clearly that the test results indicate symptoms associated with schizophrenia, paranoid type, and that the patients reports of these symptoms exceeds that of about 90 percent of psychiatric inpatients.

What are the Patient's Special Needs, Based on the Findings Noted Above?

A clear, concise statement of the patient's needs should proceed directly from the types of impairment noted above. A common mistake on the part of therapists is to offer only a vague description of mental health treatment, while courts often prefer a more functional view. A blanket recommendation of "inpatient treatment" is far less persuasive than a carefully reasoned account of the many types of care the detainee may require.

An acutely schizophrenic client might be described as needing: (1) supportive caretakers who will not react inappropriately to psychotic episodes; (2) a simplified and structured environment which will minimize demands on the patient's compromised adaptational abilities and allow for a period of reintegration; (3) intermittent assistance to meet basic needs such as food, shelter, clothing, hygiene, and health care; (4) financial support due to current inability to maintain employment; (5) social services intervention to coordinate acquisition of stable housing and employment when condition permits; (6) temporary drug therapy to suppress some problematic psychotic symptoms; and (7) intensive psychotherapy aimed at developing more adaptive responses to environmental and emotional stresses.

Obviously, different psychological conditions will lead to different needs, and these needs will vary from one client to the next. If the respondent is acutely suicidal, then round-the-clock supervision, the potential for restraint, and availability of emergency medical care would be required. The presence of complicating medical problems might mandate inpatient care. Patients who are addicted to alcohol or drugs require special care associated with detoxification and withdrawal management, whether or not the addiction is the primary focus of treatment. Other specific needs might include physical therapy, vocational rehabilitation, and marital and family therapy.

While many therapists may not view all of these needs as germane to their involvement with the patient, ideally such factors will be considered in deciding whether to commit the individual. Far from an exercise in humoring the courts, this should serve as an opportunity for the psychotherapist to evaluate the patient as a whole person. After all, if the patient is committed to a psychiatric hospital, the responsibility for coordinating all of the services he may require will fall to the staff there. The therapist's evaluation can provide useful guidelines. While many therapists seem to resist addressing "nonprofessional" or ancillary treatment issues, it is often the need for these services that really mandates commitment.

What Are the Patient's Abilities to Provide for His or Her Own Needs?

Once it has been established that the patient has a mental disorder and that special needs arise from it, the court must decide if the patient has the abilities to provide for these needs or for self-care generally. In some areas it may be clear that the patient is largely incapable of satisfying his own needs, as with the patient who experiences command hallucinations that drive him toward suicide. The court should understand that the patient cannot be expected to manage these impulses without considerable support and supervision. Other patients may be reasonably self-sufficient and able to maintain a safe home environment and provide for daily needs with minimal assistance.

The question of the patient's ability for self-care will often boil down to issues of competence. Many acutely disordered patients could be managed through an outpatient or partial hospitalization program that is less intrusive than commitment — *if* they would agree to these kinds of services. If individuals accurately perceive that they do not specifically need treatment, then their decision should be honored. If they cannot accurately ascertain their need for professional care and services, if they are incompetent to make such a judgment, then they should be viewed as unable to provide for any demonstrated needs in this area. Though the patient may have the capacity to arrange for needed psychotherapy or medical care, if their disorder causes them to incorrectly determine that they do not have such needs, then the need will not be met. Issues related to competency to make treatment decisions are discussed later in this chapter, in the section on "Right to Refuse Treatment."

What Sorts of Care and Other Resources Are Available to the Patient Without Intervention by the Court?

Courts have increasingly recognized the possibility that family support and community or personal resources may enable otherwise committable persons to remain at liberty. Potential patients may find that relatives or concerned friends can help satisfy needs other than for professional treatment. In the example of the schizophrenic patient mentioned above, the first four broad categories of need, including emotional support, simplified environment, basic survival needs, and financial support, might be satisfied through placement with a relative, or in a halfway house, or through the agency of a mutual aid group. If social service and treatment needs could be managed on a walk-in basis, then the patient would not require confinement.

From the psychotherapist's point of view, the need for professional treatment seems the most pressing concern, but in reality it is often the need for shelter, food, and simple supervision that demands commitment. It is unlikely that patients will receive greater professional attention in a hospital than they would through day treatment or as outpatients in a community mental health center. In overburdened state hospitals they may actually receive less active care than they would in the community. They will, however, receive significant custodial care in addition to professional services. Both therapists and courts should recognize the value of these basic services provided by nurses, technicians, and aides in the hospital.

Many persons who are the subject of commitment proceedings lack alternative resources. Their families are often unable or unwilling to provide the type of care required, and in some cases actually may be demonstrably harmful to the patient. The therapist should be prepared to address, in a broad way, alternative sources of care and support available to the patient. If these are generally adequate, then commitment may not be required. If they are inadequate or suspect, the expert should be prepared to point out the ways that the patient's needs cannot be satisfied without recourse to active intervention by the court.

What Is the Least Restrictive Treatment Alternative That Will Meet This Patient's Needs?

The need for commitment to involuntary hospitalization (or to other treatment alternatives in jurisdictions where available) should be based on the gap between patients' special needs and their own ability to meet those needs with the help of family, friends and community resources. Clearly, the patient who is in need of full-time supportive care and supervision, who is delusional and does not recognize this need, and who has no family willing to take him in experiences a significant lack of fit between needs and resources. The only effective way to satisfy these unmet needs is through hospitalization. Any court should be able to follow the logic of such a statement. Patients whose condition requires less aggressive management might be suitable for a halfway house. Still others who have a very interested and supportive family may be able to meet all their needs without court intervention. Therapists should be prepared to make reasonable recommendations regarding the appropriateness of several alternative treatment programs (see Keilitz, Conn, & Giampetro, 1985; Zlotnick, 1981), including these and other more libertarian options.

In many respects the courts fail to understand the concept of "least restrictive alternative," though this is a legal phrase. Most courts incorrectly view recommendations for hospitalization as an assertion that less extreme measures could not benefit the patient. Therapists may assist the court by describing a continuum of care along which less aggressive interventions are valid options for some patients and perhaps will be for this patient in the future. If hospitalization is recommended, it should be because that is currently the best treatment option, the one which most clearly satisfies all of the patient's needs for care. The court should understand that hospitalization is intended to enable the patient to take advantage of voluntary, less restrictive modes of intervention in the future.

Does This Patient, as a Result of His or Her Psychological Condition, Present a Significant Danger to Specific Others or to Society?

The issue of dangerousness to self, either through self-destructive impulses or through neglect or incapacity, can be subsumed under the broad issue of the patient's need for care. The question of dangerousness to others is more difficult to conceptualize. While in some philosophical or moral sense persons may have a "need" to be prevented from harming others, these considerations are hard to balance against basic freedoms.

When responding to the court's need to evaluate dangerousness, the therapist must be familiar with the peculiarities of local law. Some jurisdictions make no effort to define the term, while others focus on "threats or attempts to cause harm," again with little elaboration. Other states have swung so far toward police power reasoning that dangerousness must be demonstrated on the basis of a recent violent act, though it is unclear why persons in these jurisdictions are not charged with criminal offenses. Some laws speak of "imminency" of harm and may actually specify that this must be reasonably expected within a short period of time, often three weeks.

Under no circumstances should a therapist/examiner offer an unqualified statement that a given respondent is or is not dangerous. In fact, some experts have argued that it is unethical to offer any opinion at all, in view of research which indicates little predictive validity (see Ewing, 1983). Statements of potential for violence should be couched in probabilistic terms. The expert should clearly indicate that dangerousness is not a trait, but the product of an interaction of the individual with the environment. The examiner should describe factors that would promote dangerous behavior, situations where these factors are common, and, if known, the ways that the respondent's living conditions match these problem situations. The role of substance abuse is a good example. If alcohol or drugs are likely to have a significant disinhibiting effect on the respondent, this should be noted for the court. If the respondent's situation promotes substance use, this may influence the court's decision.

It should also be noted that violence is not synonymous with any diagnostic category, and that the large majority of mentally disordered persons are not violent. A key issue is the relationship of any observed disorder to violence potential. Some respondents are dangerous because of their disorder, as with paranoid individuals who feel that they must defend themselves against attack. Serious ethical dilemmas arise when clearly dangerous, nonpsychotic individuals, such as psychopaths, are evaluated. Their disorder may not warrant commitment, unless the court is willing to consider a severe personality disorder a "mental illness." More frequently, these persons are seen as "bad, not mad." It is crucial that the examiner describe the nature of less acute disorders thoroughly and let the court assume responsibility for disposing of threatening but not disturbed individuals. A related point is that it is inappropriate to exaggerate dangerousness to gain commitment of patients who might benefit from treatment.

These six general questions will guide the therapist who is called upon to testify in commitment proceedings. Thorough consideration of these factors will enhance credibility with the court and promote better decision-making.

RECENT TRENDS IN CIVIL COMMITMENT

An unusual character in many respects, Kenneth Donaldson, 48 years old, divorced, and unemployed, went to visit his parents in Florida. His family became alarmed when Kenneth began to claim that someone was poisoning him. They contacted the authorities, and he was subsequently committed to the Chattahoochee State Hospital. The year was 1957.

Staff at the hospital suggested that Donaldson take medication (neuroleptic drugs had been widely available for about two years). He steadfastly refused on two grounds. The first was that he did not see himself as mentally ill; the second that he was a Christian Scientist and viewed medical treatment as a violation of his religious beliefs. The only other treatment offered during his confinement was "milieu therapy," which in this case consisted of sitting in dayrooms filled with other persons who were deemed mentally ill.

If Kenneth Donaldson had no purpose in life prior to his hospitalization in Florida, he certainly had one after it; that purpose was life as a mental patient (Szasz, 1977). He became driven by two objectives: getting out of the hospital (but only on his own terms), and establishing his right to reject medical treatment. He filed a lawsuit to gain his release and eventually accomplished both of his goals, but at considerable cost to himself. He was released in 1971 at the age of 62. The Supreme Court reviewed the case in 1975 and upheld a monetary judgment against the physicians who had kept him confined for 14 years (*O'Connor v Donaldson*, 1975).

Right to Treatment

Though the process of confining the mentally ill to hospitals was established over 140 years ago, only in the last two decades have courts considered what should happen there. In *Rouse v. Cameron* (1966), the court considered whether those committed could be confined only for custodial care and concluded that there was a constitutional right to treatment. Confinement alone did not serve the purpose of civil commitment; there must be a *"bona fide* effort at treatment." The court in *Donaldson* viewed this as a *quid pro quo* that must be offered to compensate the nondangerous patient for deprivation of liberty. The right to hospitalize rests on the responsibility to provide treatment. The right to "minimally adequate" treatment has also been extended to dangerous individuals confined primarily under the doctrine of police power (*Eckerhart v Hensley*, 1979).

Courts have generally not confronted the challenge of defining *bona fide* treatment. Rather, some cases have focused on basic civil liberties that must be preserved, even within an institutional setting. These include factors such as the right to send and receive mail, opportunities for religious worship, sufficient space for living quarters and day areas, compensation for work performed within the institution, safety from fire and other hazards, and other assurances (see *Eckerhart v. Hensley*, 1979 and *Wyatt v. Stickney*, 1971). Some courts have attempted to describe minimal standards of care in terms of patient to staff ratios, hours of active treatment per week, existence of continuing therapeutic programs, and the utilization of individualized treatment planning. It is interesting to note that most of the above considerations pertain to custodial aspects of care, rather than to real issues regarding adequacy of treatment.

The reluctance of courts to become enmeshed in efforts to define standards of care more precisely may stem from several factors. First, there is relatively little consensus among psychotherapists as to what treatments are effective for given conditions. It is likely that attempts to label one treatment approach superior to another would fail. It is also not clear how standards of care for committed patients should compare to the practice of psycho-therapy at large. Must committed persons receive types of care typically provided to private, voluntary patients? Does commitment justify substandard care? Other problematic issues include defining the client. Certainly, the therapist has a duty of care to the individual client, but commitment is undertaken largely for the benefit of society. Should the treatment aim at serving only the client's needs, or should it try to render the individual palatable to society? Could treatment aimed only at, say, reducing danger-ousness be considered minimally adequate since it might lead to release, or should therapists assume that what is best for the client is ultimately best for society?

A final issue revolves around the lack of cooperation that often arises with involuntary patients. Many types of treatment require active participation. Must hospitals offer such care if the patient continues to undermine these efforts? If not, who should decide what less desirable alternatives should be used instead?

Obviously, these issues are very problematic and the courts have been understandably reluctant to try to resolve them. Rather, they have generally focused on assuring basic civil rights, comfort, and safety, factors that really pertain to custodial care, while simultaneously arguing that custodial care is not enough. At present the courts rely upon the professional community to establish standards of care, which would be difficult to define through legal proceedings. If hospital administrators and employees, state legislators, pol-icymakers, and practicing therapists do not take the lead in assuring the quality of care provided to involuntary patients, it is likely that courts will become increasingly involved.

Right to Refuse Treatment

Though Kenneth Donaldson's case is usually associated with the "right to treatment" movement, from his perspective it really concerned the right to *refuse* certain treatments. As mentioned earlier, commitment is generally viewed as different from incompetence, and involuntary patients often wish to exercise their right to choose the types of treatment they will receive. Committed persons have argued that forcing them to undergo treatment with drugs, electro-convulsive treatment, aversive therapy, and even conven-tional psychotherapy violates their first amendment rights to freedom of religion and speech and their eighth amendment rights to protection from cruel and unusual punishment. Legal scholars sympathetic to this position have characterized *parens patriae* "treatment" as punishment in disguise (Coleman & Soloman, 1976; see also Herr, Aarons, & Wallace, 1983).

From the perspective of hospital staff who must deal with committed individuals on a daily basis, the distinction between commitment and competence is difficult to appreciate. There is little logic in identifying someone as so psychologically impaired that they must be confined, effectively depriving them of decision-making about simple day-to-day activities, and then asking them to make a well-reasoned, informed decision regarding the most important problem confronting them—what to do about their disorder. Since professional and judicial judgments have already overridden the patient's preference not to be placed in a treatment facility, why should they not also override objections to treatment? Legal authorities sympathetic to this view have described the right to treatment as "one right too many" (Rachlin, 1975) and have claimed that treatment-refusing patients are left in the hospital "rotting with their rights on" (Applebaum & Gutheil, 1979).

A right to refuse treatment was established in *Rennie v. Klein*, (1978). Mr. Rennie, who had been hospitalized on 12 previous occasions, refused to take medication ordered by his psychiatrist. A Federal District Court held that involuntary mental patients may have the right to refuse medication or other treatments in the absence of an emergency, founded on the constitutional right to privacy; further, in the absence of an emergency, some type of due process protection is required prior to forced medication. To overrule the patient's refusal, four factors should be considered by an independent party: (1) the patient's capacity to decide on his particular treatment; (2) the patient's physical threat to other patients and staff; (3) whether any less restrictive treatment exists; and (4) the risk of permanent side effects from the proposed treatment. Although the Supreme Court later considered *Rennie*, it did not establish an absolute constitutional right to refuse, as the District Court had, but remanded the case for further attention at the state level. Incidentally, though the court established the basis for a right to refuse treatment, in subsequent action it determined that, based on these four considerations, Mr. Rennie's refusal was properly overridden by the hospital.

The court's reasoning in *Rennie* has been very influential in other jurisdictions. Most recently, a New York court has held that the right to refuse treatment can be invaded only if the patient is dangerous or incompetent (*Rivers v. Katz*, 1986). Under emergency conditions involving dangerousness to self or others, hospitals may administer even invasive treatments over the patient's objection. Without this justification, refusal can be superseded only by a formal determination of incompetency, similar to the process discussed in Chapter 3.

Rather than pursuing formal incompetency proceedings, many institutions have established advocacy boards made up of laypeople, lawyers, and therapists to review conflicts over treatment. It was hoped that these measures would allow more individualized consideration of problem cases, but recent case law indicates that even several levels of administrative review by independent psychotherapists may not satisfy the requirement for due process protection (see *State of Wisconsin ex rel Jones*, 1986). It is increasingly clear that only a formal judicial determination of incompetence to make treatment decisions will justify a therapist's decision to treat an involuntary patient over his or her objections.

Research indicates that these procedural protections may be superfluous. Requests to override treatment refusal are common, the patients involved are almost always severely disturbed, there is generally a high degree of consensus among therapists as to the need to override refusal, excessive or inappropriate treatments are not used, and even with formal procedures the patient's refusals are ultimately overridden in more than 95 percent of the cases considered (Bloom, Faulkner, Holm, & Rawlinson, 1984). There are also considerable costs in terms of time and resources associated with treatment refusal.

Therapists remain largely ambivalent about the right to refuse treatment. On the rationale that they are "only trying to help," they may resent the implication that they would act against an individual client's best interests. At a more fundamental level, confining disordered persons without treatment, even if that is their preference, may be at odds with professional ethics. Is it proper for therapists to assume the role of jailer, detaining the mentally disordered only for the benefit of society? Given the overreliance on dangerousness and police power justification, doesn't commitment with treatment refusal amount to a form of preventive detention? These questions, arising from both the right to refuse treatment and police power reasoning, have spurred numerous calls for reform of the commitment process.

Commitment, Competency and Reform

During the last decade there has been a variety of calls for reform of civil commitment procedures. Stone (1976) and Roth (1979) have eloquently argued that civil commitment procedures should be changed to give greater weight to traditional *parens patriae* issues. Under these proposals, persons who are "gravely disabled" and "in need of treatment" could be confined for treatment simply for their own good. These reforms would go further, however, as they also focus on the patient's capacity to make informed decisions regarding treatment. Persons who are competent to accept or reject treatment should be allowed to reject hospitalization, assuming they are not a danger to society. Those who are found not competent would be confined with the explicit determination that their objection to treatment could be overridden. These measures should help avoid many of the thorny problems surrounding the right to refuse treatment.

Some have argued that a "need for treatment" criterion would make commitment standards too broad and would lead to unnecessary commitments. However, the additional requirement of incompetence should offset this trend. The Stone-Roth model has been adapted into a Model Commitment Statute by the American Psychiatric Association (Stromberg & Stone, 1983:

(1) The person is suffering from a severe mental disorder; and
(2) there is a reasonable prospect that his disorder is treatable at or through the facility to which he is to be committed and such commitment would be consistent with the least restrictive alternative principle; and
(3) the person either refuses or is unable to consent to voluntary admission for treatment; and
(4) the person lacks capacity to make an informed decision concerning treatment; and
(5) as the result of the severe mental disorder, the person is (a) likely to cause harm to himself or to suffer substantial mental or physical deterioration, or (b) likely to cause harm to others.

In defining capacity or competency to make treatment decisions, the statute speaks of an inability to understand the nature and effects of hospitalization and treatment, to weigh the possible risks and benefits, or to engage in a rational decision-making process. This type of law has been adopted in Alaska, North Carolina, Texas, and Washington.

Other authors have emphasized the crucial role that competency should play in deciding who is to be confined and treated against his will (Bloom & Faulkner, 1987; Brown, 1985), and have suggested that commitment should essentially become a special case of incompetency. These proposals would establish at the outset explicit procedures to identify guardians or advocates to aid in treatment planning and approval for patients who cannot competently give informed consent. Incidentally, these types of protections have also been advocated for "voluntary" patients who may not really understand the complex issues involved in their care (Applebaum, Mirkin & Bateman, 1981).

Where would dangerousness to others fit within revised schemes that lean toward *parens patriae* issues? Certainly, the requirement of incompetence to justify commitment makes little sense for someone both mentally disordered and violent, and it is difficult to understand what might be meant by "dangerous, disordered but competent." Does this mean that some persons have the prerogative to remain dangerous? Most authors envision the expansion of settings like current forensic hospitals, where these persons would be held to satisfy society. Treatment would be voluntary, but those who did not comply and recover would obviously have little chance of gaining release. This scenario is generally given little attention, and begs a plethora of very difficult clinical, legal, and moral questions. Radical preventive detention of this sort is objectionable on legal grounds; further, this type of "patient" may present little hope for treatment, even with cooperation. In fact, defining treatment might be impossible. There would certainly be considerable public pressure to use extremely coercive and intrusive measures if these had any chance of success.

The Supreme Court's recent decision in *United States v. Salerno* (1987) indicates that at least some forms of preventive detention will be found constitutional. The case involved denial of bail to a suspected organized crime boss subjected to federal prosecution. Language in this decision indicates that detention may be justified if it serves a compelling interest, such as promoting "the safety of any other person and the community." The court found that denial of bail could be construed as "permissible regulation" and was not punitive because that had not been Congress's intent in the Bail Reform Act of 1984. Commentators have noted that this type of pretrial detention "may become a kind of civil commitment for those who are charged with a crime [read dangerous?] but are not mentally ill" (Smith, 1987). State jurisdictions are likely to adopt similar measures.

If the legal system is willing to endorse more aggressive intervention with dangerous, nondisturbed individuals premised on public safety, then this may signal a willingness to reconsider the basis for commitment of the mentally ill. While the appropriateness of preventive detention is ultimately a legal and political question, perhaps the debate will help refocus the rationale and purpose of civil commitment on care and treatment for those who need it, rather than on thinly disguised efforts to equate criminality and dangerousness with disorder. A return to a paternalistic model might help therapists and institutions to escape their current role as agents of social control in favor of a more therapeutic stance.

CHAPTER 5

Prediction of Dangerousness

> There is no foreseeable time when there will not be some people from
> whom the rest of us will want to feel protected . . .
>
> — Brody & Tarling, 1980, p.2

PSYCHOTHERAPISTS PARTICIPATE in many difficult legal processes, but at
present none is more problematic and controversial than the prediction of
dangerousness. The public often believes that mental health officials release
far too many potentially dangerous persons from our public hospitals. In
fact, there is a widespread belief that mentally disordered persons as a group
are dangerous, despite repeated findings to the contrary (see Cocozza, Melick, & Steadman, 1978; Monahan & Steadman, 1983; Quinsey & Ambtman, 1978).

This perception leads to a belief that preemptive incarceration of the
mentally disordered is in order. Some communities have also witnessed the
repetition of tragic crimes by persons released from prison on parole or
probation and mistakenly attribute these to the mentally ill. Coupled with
the high rates of violent crime, these episodes lend urgency to the public
perception that something must be done to protect society from dangerous
individuals.

There are several reasons for the legal system's difficulty in responding to
these demands; two stand out clearly. First, the concept of preventive detention — the practice of confining someone simply because he may behave
badly in the future — seems to run counter to Anglo-American jurisprudence
(but see the discussion of *US. v. Salerno* at the end of Chapter 4). Lawmakers, judges, and lawyers find it objectionable to deprive an individual of

liberty simply because he frightens others. Punishment may follow violent acts already committed, but should not precede them. Second, our system of justice is incredibly overburdened. There are insufficient resources to deal with past offenses, much less to intervene proactively.

Because of these difficulties, mental health professionals in this country have been increasingly forced to confront the issue of dangerousness and to act as agents of social control in ways that the legal system cannot or will not. The two most significant examples of this process include the change in civil commitment laws to emphasize dangerousness and police power as justifications for involuntary confinement (see Chapter 4), and therapist liability for harm done by clients. These trends have converged recently in civil actions establishing an outright duty of therapists to confine potentially dangerous patients against their will. This shows just how far clinicians have been driven into serving a police function (see the discussion of *Currie v. U.S.* in Chapter 1). Shah (1978) has identified at least 13 other areas of legal process where expert testimony about potential harmful behavior may play a role. In short, society at large, and the legal system in particular, want something done about dangerous individuals, and they expect psychotherapists to do it.

Against this background pressing for aggressive identification and confinement of dangerous individuals is the reality that prediction and treatment of dangerousness are extremely difficult. Empirical studies of dangerousness determinations indicate that therapists are inclined to overpredict violence and classify an excessive number of persons as hazardous. These findings have prompted some experts to conclude that therapists do not contribute significantly to what are primarily legal decisions, and to question their continued involvement in the process (see Dix, 1980; Ewing, 1983).

Alan Stone (1976, 1985) has identified two generations of criticism aimed at psychotherapists by legal scholars. As legislatures and courts expanded legal reliance on the concept of dangerousness, the first generation of criticism focused on the "paternalistic" model of mental health care and delivery as an unworkable system that created a number of social problems. Rather than recognize that many of these problems arose from social indifference and a lack of sufficient resources, the response of lawmakers, judges and lawyers was to revamp many areas of mental health law along more adversarial lines, with many of these efforts relying heavily on the concept of dangerousness. The second generation of criticism ensued when clinicians were unable to conceptualize and predict dangerous behavior in ways that the legal system wanted.

Stone views the prediction of dangerousness as a "battlefield" where lawyers and therapists are locked in conflict. He notes that clinicians are therapists first and foremost, and should repudiate prediction as a trap that leads inevitably to conflict with therapeutic responsibilities. When the courts ask for predictions of dangerousness, therapists inevitably "serve as police officers whose responsibility it is to protect society, the family, and other institutions against the patient" (1985 p. 14). The increasing pressure brought to bear on therapists probably reflects the frustration and impotence of our system of justice in confronting such social problems as crime and poverty. Stone advocates outright refusal to participate in efforts to subsume therapeutic expertise under the rubric of social control.

Aside from the obvious impracticality of refusing to participate in legal decisions where dangerousness is an issue, many therapists consider the prediction of dangerousness an unpleasant but compelling social and legal responsibility (Blau, 1984; Berger & Dietrich, 1979). Referring to professional abstention as a "Pilate-like position," Megargee (1976) encourages therapists to participate in these determinations:

> It is facile, but correct, to point out that someone has to make these predictions. If there are data that show that better predictions are made without [psychotherapist's] input, then by all means a clinician should decline to participate. Otherwise, as long as predictions regarding dangerous behavior are going to be made . . . [therapists] should contribute to the best of their ability. (p. 15)

Other authorities, including Monahan (1981, 1982) and Greenland (1985), advocate that therapists offer predictions to the courts, but within certain limits. Like Stone, Monahan (1981) has identified two generations in the prediction of dangerousness, but his division focuses primarily on research and clinical practice. He describes a first generation marked by naturalistic demonstrations that forecasting the future, particularly regarding aggressive and harmful behavior, is extremely difficult and prone to error. The second generation moves from these findings toward an exploration of the limits and capabilities of expert opinions, identification of better clinical methods, and formulation of rational public policy based on these findings.

This chapter is written in the spirit of this second generation of theory and practice. While there are ample empirical and philosophical justifications to resist the "criminalization" of mental health law, the pragmatic considerations of our current system require that therapists do what they can to assist the legal system in the many important areas where prediction is an issue, while working to improve clinical methods and scientific understanding.

In the following pages we review some basic issues in defining and predicting dangerousness. We briefly set the historical backdrop for the current belief that therapists cannot accurately predict dangerousness, then discuss factors that call into question the accuracy of this first generation of data. Second-generation ideas and their relevance for the practicing therapist are addressed, along with basic factors to be considered in judging dangerousness. Finally, we discuss the pragmatics of translating clinical information and judgment into feedback to the legal system or other agencies.

THE CONCEPT OF DANGEROUSNESS

Like insanity, dangerousness is an explicitly legal concept with no specific meaning to therapists. Attempts to operationalize the concept have usually focused on the proneness of individuals to respond to social and physical environmental cues with overt applications of force that result in harm to others or property. In short, predicting dangerousness usually is assumed to involve judging the probability of violent or assaultive behavior. Here we focus on violence potential, though many other types of harmful behavior may be just as objectionable from society's perspective. For example, nonviolent sexual exploitation of children and trafficking in illegal drugs are demonstrably harmful to both individuals and society. While clinicians are sometimes called upon to provide information about an individual's potential for these kinds of harm, such involvement is rare.

PREDICTION AND ERRORS

Most legal decisions are dichotomous. Persons are committed to the hospital or they are not. They are granted parole or parole is denied. But potential for violent behavior is not all or none. One of the primary difficulties in this area centers on translating clinical evaluations of relative violence potential into discrete legal decisions of dangerous versus nondangerous. Increased recognition that this translation involves value judgments that are beyond the expertise of the therapist will help to resolve some of the disagreements over the role of mental health professionals in dangerousness determinations.

Influential research efforts have generally perpetuated the confusion of violence potential with all-or-none pronouncements. Rather than allowing individuals to be ranked according to their perceived potential for violence, most projects have required that subjects be divided into two mutually exclusive groups. Under these conditions two types of errors in prediction are possible. First, those who are predicted dangerous may turn out to be safe (false positives). Second, predicted safe individuals may engage in violence (false negatives).

FIRST-GENERATION STUDIES

Prior to 1980 several important studies of the accuracy of clinical predictions of dangerousness were reported. These generally revolved around special programs for presumably dangerous offenders, juvenile delinquents, sexual psychopaths, or others. In some cases special treatment programs were established by statute and former patients were followed in an attempt to discern their post-release rates of violence. Some studies involved a comparison of persons released with therapists' recommendations versus those released at the insistence of the courts but against professional advice, the "predicted safe" versus "predicted dangerous" groups. Other projects simply looked at post-release violence among a whole class of individuals summarily released from confinement.

To get a feel for this type of naturalistic research, consider the "Baxtrom patients." In the 1960s, New York state maintained a significant population of "criminally insane" patients in the Mattaeawan and Dannemora hospitals. These were completely separate from the public mental hospitals and served primarily to warehouse convicted offenders believed too dangerous and mentally disordered to be released. In *Baxtrom v. Herold* (1969) the Supreme Court found this system unconstitutional. Johnnie Baxtrom had been convicted of a crime, found mentally ill, and then detained in a security hospital throughout the maximum length of his sentence and beyond. The court ordered that Mr. Baxtrom should be released or processed through state civil commitment procedures, as any other citizen would be, and he and nearly one thousand other criminally insane were either transferred to public hospitals or released.

Subsequent research on the Baxtrom patients (Steadman & Cocozza, 1974) revealed that the frightening predictions of their potential for violence in the less restrictive hospital and community settings were exaggerated. They were anticlimactically docile, with only about 20 percent engaging in assaultive acts during the next four years. Steadman and Cocozza (1974) contend that all of these patients were predicted to be dangerous by clinicians, as that should have been the basis for their confinement. According to their reckoning, this makes clinical judgments of dangerousness wrong in 80 percent of these cases. They conclude that their data provide "clear and convincing evidence of the inability of psychiatrists or of anyone else to accurately predict dangerousnes" (p. 1101).

Table 5.1 lists the results of the Baxtrom "study," along with four other naturalistic evaluations of the ability of clinicians to predict dangerousness in several populations.

Some conclusions can be drawn from these studies. First, the rates of

TABLE 5.1
Major Naturalistic Studies of Accuracy In the Prediction of Dangerousness

Study Site or Patient Group	Follow-up	Criterion for Dangerousness	Percentage Meeting Criterion	
			Predicted Dangerous	Predicted Safe
Massachusetts Center for Diagnosis and Treatment of Dangerous Persons[1]	5 years	"Serious assaultive acts"	35	9
Patuxent Institute for "Defective Delinquents"[2]	3 years	Any recorded arrest	41	7
New York Hospitals for the "criminally insane"[3]	4 years	"Assaultive"	20	N.A.*
"Mentally Disordered Offenders"-Pennsylvania[4]	4 years	"Injurious to others"	14	N.A.*
New York State Defendants found not competent to stand trial[5]	3 years	Assault in hospital,	42	36
	3 years	Arrest after release	49	54

*Not applicable: These studies involved follow-up of groups of disordered detainees released en mass as a result of legal actions. They have been interpreted as including no subjects predicted to be at low risk for dangerous behavior
[1]reported in Kozol, Boucher, & Garofalo, 1972
[2]reviewed in Steadman, 1977
[3]described in Steadman and Cocozza, 1974
[4]reported in Thornberry & Jacoby, 1979
[5]reported in Cocozza & Steadman, 1976

false positives or incorrect diagnoses of dangerousness are high. For each correct prediction that violence would occur there were two that were in error. Even with such a bias toward overprediction, not all of the dangerous subjects were correctly identified. Monahan (1982) concluded that "the 'best' clinical research indicates that psychiatrists and psychologists are accurate in no more than one of three predictions of violent behavior over a several-year period among institutionalized populations who both had committed violence (and thus had high baserates for it) and were diagnosed as mentally ill." The bottom line of this first generation of studies was that it did not seem possible to predict dangerousness with any degree of accuracy.

These results have had a significant impact on the professional community. Both the American Psychological Association and the American Psychiatric Association have published official reports and submitted *amicus curiae* briefs to the Supreme Court which assert that experts cannot reliably predict dangerousness. Legal scholars have likened expert testimony on dangerousness to "flipping coins in the courtroom" (Ennis & Litwack, 1974), and there have been widespread calls for the exclusion of such testimony or the elimination of legal procedures, such as civil commitment, which typically employ it. Despite some revisions of these very pessimistic conclusions, the prevailing opinion is that the prediction of dangerousness is imprecise at best.

Difficulties with Early Studies

Various factors have been cited to suggest that clinical predictions of dangerous behavior may sometimes be more accurate than the results of the above studies would suggest. The most obvious complaint is that the criterion measures employed severely underestimate that rates of post-release violence. In general these studies relied on arrest records as the primary measure of dangerousness, though some also took other factors into account. Of course, it is possible that many of these individuals were involved in violent crimes that were not discovered. In fact, between one-third and one-half of all violent crimes are not reported to authorities, and of those that are reported less than one-half are resolved through arrest (Monahan, 1982). Thus, a reasonable estimate is that only one in three violent offenses leads to arrest, probably setting something of an upper bound on the accuracy of arrests as a criterion for clinical predictions.

These general factors may not even reveal the extent of the inaccuracy. Domestic violence, which is arguably the type most likely to involve mentally disordered persons, is far less likely to be reported and is also less likely to result in arrest. For example, only about 8 percent of wife-batterings are reported (Schulman, 1980). Many types of sexual assaults, especially rape and incest, are reported in very small proportion to the actual rates of crime (Osborne, 1982). These factors contribute to the inaccuracy of arrest records in assessing the dangerous behavior of persons involved in civil commitment, parole decisions, sexual psychopath programs, and other contexts that require evaluation of potential for harm to others. Stated simply, some of the persons predicted to be violent appear as false positives not because they were harmless but because they were not reported or caught. While several researchers have indicated that this underreporting does not explain nearly all of the overprediction of violence, it is clear that the "one in three" level probably represents an underestimate of the true positive rate.

A second major problem with the first-generation findings arises from the selection of subjects. A rigorous experimental design would require that all subjects, or at least randomly selected samples from the predicted dangerous and predicted safe groups, would be released and followed until completion of the study. Of course, a true experiment cannot be conducted ethically. Those individuals thought to be dangerous by both clinicians and the courts are not released. Those at the other extreme, seen as safe by judges and therapists alike, are all released. What can be said of the group for whom there is no consensus? It is likely that on a continuum from most to least violent these individuals fall in the middle. The result is that the subjects that therapists feel have some potential for violence are split into two groups. Those who impress judges and magistrates as most dangerous are kept confined, while the impressionistically less dangerous are released and followed *as if* they constituted the entire predicted dangerous group. It is hardly surprising that these middle-of-the-road subjects have modest rates of post-release violence. No one knows how harmful their more extreme cohorts would be, so it is not clear how much more accurate therapists' guesses would appear if they were also given the opportunity to test their definite predictions of dangerousness.

A third and less frequently acknowledged flaw in the early studies and their interpretation derives from the quality of the predictions. This point is best illustrated by returning to the Baxtrom patients. "Few if any of the [therapists] employed in the Matteawan or Dannemora hospitals were professionally qualified or board-certified [psychotherapists]," and most were medical doctors in a variety of non-mental-health specialties (Greenland, 1985, p. 31). The work of these practitioners of uncertain training could hardly be viewed as typical of therapists in general. Also, a variety of political and social factors influenced the system, and the whole project may "provide better evidence of bad practice than of the state of the art of assessing dangerousness . . . " (Floud & Young, 1981).

The above points are not intended to indicate that the studies reviewed above are without merit or that predictions of dangerousness are highly accurate but poorly tested. More recent second-generation studies continue to find high rates of overprediction and modest overall accuracy (see Clannon & Jew, 1985). An accuracy rate of 40 percent has been described as a "forensic sound-barrier" which remains difficult to break (Menzies, Webster, & Sepejak, 1985). The pessimistic view growing out of the first-generation research projects should give therapists pause and instill an appropriate degree of humility, but the task of evaluating the limits and processes of clinical prediction of dangerousness should continue. "The jury is still out on the empirical question of prediction-outcome associations" (Menzies, et al., 1985).

THE PROBLEM OF OVERPREDICTION

Two factors seem to lead to the high degree of overprediction. First, prediction of rare events is an inherently difficult task, and violence is something of a rare phenomenon. The prevalence of aggressive behavior in the general population has been estimated at 200 persons per 100,000, or .2 percent (Cocozza et al., 1978), a rare event indeed. Scrutiny of Table 7.1 reveals that during the three-to-five-year follow-up on these subjects (selected for high risk) the baserates for violence when the predicted dangerous and safe groups are combined are on the order of 15 to 30 percent. Even mild inaccuracy in prediction is likely to lead to misclassification of many subjects under these conditions.

The second bias toward overprediction probably stems from the relative costs of mistaken predictions. Mistakenly labeling an individual dangerous may result in continued confinement to a hospital or treatment program, with little potential for adverse consequences for the therapist. By comparison, incorrectly labeling someone safe who later commits a violent act may expose the predictor to public outcry and civil liability. Since the costs of false negatives are high, therapists are biased to overpredict out of self-defense.

THE INTERACTIONIST PERSPECTIVE

In explaining the low predictive validity of dangerousness assessment in the early studies, numerous authors have noted that "dangerousness" is not a simple trait or predisposition (Megargee, 1981; Monahan, 1981; Steadman, 1981). People who vary along many dimensions may be dangerous or violent at some point, and no one is invariably and constantly dangerous. Under the right conditions, nearly any individual may become assaultive, while even very impulsive, hostile individuals are not violent most of the time. Unlike other characteristics which are viewed as highly stable, dangerousness fluctuates over time in accordance with a variety of environmental factors, maturation, changes in level of adjustment, and so forth. Proneness to violent or harmful behavior is more analogous to mood than to intelligence. While intellectual abilities remain fairly stable over time and help explain behavior in many situations, a person's mood is both changeable and situationally influenced.

Departing from the work of Mischel (1968), many recent investigators have emphasized the situational factors in violence and dangerous behavior. Noting that conditions such as the availability of a weapon or a particular victim will have a powerful effect on the expression of aggression, some have advocated a "situationist" view of dangerousness while minimizing individual predispositions. This position is too extreme, as it is clear that some individual characteristics do contribute to prediction of violence. After all, the best known "predictor" of violence is past violence. Also, aggression has been shown to have a high degree of behavioral consistency under many conditions, even when the predictions were made many years prior to the criterion (Blackburn, 1983). Recent research on biological substrates for aggression would also suggest substantial consistency (see, for example, Brown & Goodwin, 1986; Woodman, 1983). Violence is a "relative, context-bound behavior . . . [and] is attributable to a complex interaction of individual predispositional and situational factors" (Mulvey & Lidz, 1984).

Greater attention must be paid to the interaction of individual factors that contribute to the potential for aggression and environmental precipitants. Clinical evaluation should focus on defining what factors make a given subject act out, with what frequency, severity and probability, and then examine the likelihood that these factors will be present in the social, occupational, and familial environment.

Another second-generation innovation is the realization that there is no single etiological model for evaluating the potential for dangerousness. Often, these assessments proceed as if a single set of factors were associated with harmful acts and so a simple summation of these would be a reasonable basis for prediction. Even glancing study of the literature on violence, aggression, and criminality reveals that persons who engage in dangerous acts are not a homogeneous group. There are, for instance, clear differences between persons who are primarily involved in "instrumental" acts of aggression, such as armed robbery, and those who commit violence acting on delusional motives. Several researchers have described schemes for classifying dangerous individuals (Blackburn, 1983; Hinton, 1983; Megargee, 1976). Greenland (1985) has described a fourfold typology of violent offenders:

(1) *Chronic antisocial*—Habitually undercontrolled and socially maladjusted individuals who commit aggressive acts with little concern for others or for long-term consequences.
(2) *Psychotic episode*—Persons who become overwhelmed by chronic, unbearable problems and suffer an acute loss of reality contact, often with delusional motives for aggression.
(3) *Episodic and situational violence*—Explosive "rage" incidents associated with alcoholism, organic impairment, or mania.
(4) *Extended suicide*—Severely depressed individuals who for "altruistic" reasons kill others in the process of their own suicide. (Other

suicidal individuals may also commit violence as a final attempt to punish others.)

No single set of variables will serve to identify a unitary concept of dangerousness. Rather, different factors will be relevant for different individuals. It is important both to recognize that several etiological models are involved in the production of violent and harmful behavior, and to individualize the assessment of violence potential. As shown below, a number of factors have shown a correlational or predictive relationship to aggression and violence; here we provide examples of the types of data relevant to assessment of dangerousness.

CLINICAL FACTORS IN PREDICTING DANGEROUSNESS

Traditional clinical lore held that a triad of childhood difficulties was pathognomic for juvenile delinquency and later aggressive behavior as an adult. This cluster of symptoms included firesetting, enuresis, and cruelty to animals. While many clinicians continue to assert the utility of these indicators, little empirical work supports this contention, and at best there may be a tenuous connection with dangerousness. The persistence of this speculation appears to result from the richness of dynamic interpretations of these behaviors. Better understood and documented predisposing factors are reviewed below.

Family Atmosphere

Among persons convicted of crimes generally and violent offenses in particular, a disproportionate number come from divorced or single-parent families. Those raised in homes where one parent, typically the father, is estranged or has deserted the family are more prone to engage in aggressive behavior, but this relationship may be more correlational than etiological. Early studies (see Glueck & Glueck, 1968) hypothesized that single-parent homes contributed to criminality because of the relative dearth of parental supervision. Recent reviews of the literature point to parental characteristics (such as alcoholism, impulsivity, unreliability, or hostility) which lead to the breakup of the traditional family unit as directly contributing to poor socialization and subsequent violence on the part of affected children (Wilson & Herrnstein, 1985). In fact, intact homes marked by considerable discord are actually associated with higher rates of delinquency and adult violent behavior than homes where conflict is reduced by dissolution. Although it is not entirely clear how the overall family atmosphere predisposes a young person toward later violence, data on family distress and conflict should be considered. Lack of stability and consistency in family relationships has been identified as particularly important in predisposing toward violence (Maloney, 1985; Marmor, 1978).

One specific family variable bears a clear relationship to subsequent dangerous behavior — violence begets violence. Research indicates that many dangerous offenders were victims of child abuse or witnessed significant violence between parents, other family members, or in the social milieu (see, for example, Patterson, 1982). Such a history predisposes toward dangerousness for several reasons, including desensitizing the individual to potentially aversive consequences of aggression (Maloney, 1985), demonstrating the instrumental use of violence, and establishing a normative expectation that the use of force is a legitimate means to resolve conflicts (Gardner & Gray, 1982). From a theoretical point of view, it has been argued that family dynamics marked by domestic violence are associated with a lack of consistent structure and appropriate adult role models, and may promote dangerous acting-out indirectly by impeding the development of coping skills and of adult moral and cognitive reasoning (Kegan, 1986).

In assessing an individual's history of early exposure to violence, it is important to consider a range of factors. Initial exploration might focus on the methods of parental discipline, including alternatives to corporal punishment, consistency of discipline, balance of participation by both parents, and relationship of discipline to the severity of misbehavior. Often, a discussion of discipline will allow a transition into related topics, such as unprovoked violence towards children, spouse abuse, and physical altercations with neighbors and authorities.

Not surprisingly, individuals most affected by family contexts which promote violence and aggression tend to act out these impulses at relatively early ages. In fact, an early onset of aggressive behavior is one of the strongest predictors of violent actions as an adult (Dietz, 1985; Patterson, 1982; Petersilia, 1980).

The focus here is not on minor fighting common in younger children but upon serious assaultive behavior employing weapons, participation in group assaults or gang violence, aggressive sexual activity, or other acts with a high likelihood of injury to others. As might be expected, early serious aggressive acts are associated with involvement in peer group activities that encourage and maintain further acting-out. Clinical evaluations should assess involvement with gangs and other sorts of juvenile and adolescent contexts where aggression is common and encouraged. These findings often tie in with factors in the individual's current social situation.

Neurological and Physiological Factors

At present the role of physiological factors in the etiology of violence and aggression is poorly understood; however, several general factors may be noted. First, as will be discussed below, impulsivity and low intelligence are often associated with dangerousness. In turn, these characteristics are influenced by problems in health and development.

Covert organic impairment is present in a significant fraction of violent offenders and inpatients (Fowles & Coleman, 1987; Poss & Johnson, 1987). Clinicians should gather information regarding prenatal care, gestational age, birth complications, and neonatal problems, with an eye toward identifying potential sources of subtle neurologic impairment. Particularly when high-risk signs are borne out be developmental delays, learning disability or subnormal intelligence, or "soft signs" of neurological disorder, the possibility of a neurologic substrate for impulsive, violent behavior should be considered.

Other biological factors may also contribute to violence potential. Poor health may be a source of nonspecific stress that taxes a potentially violent individual's already limited resources and makes dangerous behavior more likely. Some conditions, such as those that lead to unpredictable changes in mood or arousal, may have a more specific role in potentiating aggressive impulses. Metabolic disorders such as premenstrual syndrome and hypothyroidism have been implicated in producing severe mood swings that may lead to impulsive rage and acting-out. Consistent with the "frustration-aggression hypothesis," chronic pain may also be associated with increased risk for violence. Finally, rare forms of epilepsy have been associated with "episodic dyscontrol syndrome," marked by intermittent periods of extremely regressed behavior, often including assaultive acts. These episodes may be triggered by alcohol or substance abuse.

Psychological and Personality Factors

Numerous predisposing psychological factors have been hypothesized, generally with only rudimentary empirical testing. Still, at least four factors consistently associated with dangerousness have been identified.

Psychopathy is the most widely researched variable related to violent acting-out. High levels of psychopathy are associated with a chronic pattern of aggression and exploitation toward others. A correlation with substance abuse and criminal vocations heightens the potential for dangerousness. Assessment of psychopathy may be pursued in a variety of ways, including assessment based on criteria in diagnostic manuals, structured interview approaches, and standardized psychological tests such as the MMPI. Various measures are described in detail in Hare's (1985) excellent review article.

Megargee (1976) has reported the development of a scale which seems to assess control over hostility. Interestingly, individuals falling at either extreme have been found to exhibit assaultive behavior, but in different ways. Individuals low on this dimension impulsively act on angry or aggressive impulses, and frequently have a history of multiple episodes of violence. They view aggression as a legitimate social behavior. Individuals at the other extreme, so called "overcontrolled," find it difficult to express anger or hostility in any productive way. They appear to let frustration build up until they explode in a fit of rage. Generally lacking a history of aggression, these persons tend to be involved in isolated episodes of extreme violence or assaultiveness. Persons with midrange scores seem to deal with hostility and anger in effective ways that do not result in violent behavior.

Low intelligence is also associated with increased risk for violence. Explanations of this relationship focus on the inability of individuals to solve problems and manage stresses in more prosocial ways. Some persons with limited intellectual abilities may also be more impulsive or easily frustrated. The observed correlation may represent something of an artifact if persons of borderline intellectual abilities are apprehended at a disproportionately high rate.

Finally, Blackburn (1983) has reported that social withdrawal or introversion also bears a complex relationship to violence potential. Individuals who are exceedingly gregarious or extremely avoidant appear to have higher rates of violence, although this factor probably interacts with other variables. For example, individuals who are extremely introverted and also highly psychopathic may be prone to bizarre crimes involving kidnapping, rape, or murder which serve ego-syntonic functions. More extroverted persons are likely to become involved in violence for instrumental purposes, such as financial gain.

Drug and Alcohol Abuse

Statistics indicate that over half of the crimes committed in the U.S. involve the use of alcohol or drugs, and the figures may be higher for violent offenses. Theoretical reviews (Taylor & Leonard, 1982) cite three main factors that link intoxication to aggression. The most obvious is "pharmacological disinhibition." Simply, the moderating effects of higher intellectual functions on aggressive impulses is reduced. The second, "learned disinhibition," refers to the conditioned expectation that socially disapproved behavior may be more tolerated with intoxication as an excuse. Finally, intoxication may simply represent a peculiar form of stressor that can be seen as psychologically arousing.

Maloney (1985) has pointed out that different intoxicants have varying potentials for precipitating dangerous behavior. Citing phencyclidine, or PCP, as an example, he notes that some substances are well-known to produce aggression in a significant fraction of users. In addition to PCP, other hallucinogens, such as LSD, cocaine, and amphetamines, may be especially likely to promote violence, largely through induction of psychotic and paranoid thinking.

Past Behavior

The best predictor of future violence is past violence. "If there is one finding that overshadows all others in the area of prediction, it is that the probability of future crime increases with each prior criminal act" (Monahan, 1981, p. 104). This statement is no less true of violent acts than of crime in general (Shah, 1978). In a series of highly influential longitudinal studies, Wolfgang and his associates (Wolfgang & Ferracuti, 1967; Wolfgang, Figlio, & Sellin, 1972; Wolfgang & Tracy, 1982; Wolfgang & Weiner, 1982) have documented that as a given individual's number of violent episodes increases, so does the likelihood of future violence. For example, persons arrested four times have an 80 percent chance of being arrested again. Those arrested more than five times "approach certainty" of rearrest (Shah, 1978), and many of the subsequent arrests will involve violence. Research on "high rate offenders" reveals that they report a significant number of violent crimes, the majority of which are not solved by authorities.

It is obviously important to assess both history of violence per se and more general criminal history. To some extent this process can be aided by police and probation records, but the examiner should also question subjects about undetected offenses. Assaultive behaviors toward spouse or children, though rarely reported as crimes, are also relevant to potential for further violence. As noted above, juvenile offenses and other background characteristics, such as fighting in school, should also be considered. One category of past violent behavior need not be related to only that type of aggression in the future, and a broad background of aggressive and antisocial behavior should be interpreted as indicating a generalized predisposition toward violence.

Mental Disorder

Aside from broad personality characteristics, the presence of significant mental disorder may be relevant to an individual's dangerousness. In general, mentally disordered persons are not dangerous insofar as the rate for violent offenses among former patients approximates that for the general population. However, there is an identifiable subset of offenders whose violent acts appear related to their disorder (Howells, 1982, 1983; Taylor, 1985). Individuals who have both a psychotic disorder and a history of violence are often actively symptomatic at the time of their offenses (75 to 85 percent), and motives for the offenses are frequently derived from delusional processes or hallucinations (Taylor, 1985; Taylor & Gunn, 1984). While it remains true that as a group psychotic individuals do not experience hostile fantasies or delusions, those who do may act them out, even in the absence of other primary indicators of violence potential.

The role of nonpsychotic disorders is less well established. A small group of nonpsychotically depressed offenders has been identified, with their offenses often related to murder/suicides. These may be motivated by a desire to end the suffering of children or spouses along with the patient's own. Clinical experience also suggests that another group of depressed, guilt-ridden persons may commit violent offenses in an effort to provoke authorities into killing them in an armed confrontation.

SITUATIONAL FACTORS

Theoretical reviews of environmental factors have identified four etiologic relationships between situational stressors and aggression (Mueller, 1983). These include:

(1) *Arousal*—Stressors increase arousal and the propensity for active behavioral responses, including aggression.
(2) *Stimulus overload*—Stressful environments often lead to misperception or misinterpretation of social cues, increasing the probability of maladaptive behavior.
(3) *Interference with behavior*—Stressors often impede ongoing behavior or render usual behavior ineffective. The possibility of unusual behavioral responses, such as aggression, is increased.
(4) *Negative stimulation*—Many stressors are irritating, annoying, frustrating or uncomfortable. This is true of physical stressors, such as noise, or psychosocial incidents, such as marital discord.

At one level, an assessment of situational factors that could promote violence may be very general and view stress as an aggregate of situational demands. Inventories of "Stressful Life Events" (see Holmes & Rahe, 1967) may be used to assess an overall level of stress (Blau, 1984). Specific situational factors that promote violence have also been identified.

Family Situation

Given that family members are the most common targets of violence by mental patients (Skodol & Karasu, 1978; Steadman, 1981), and that nondisordered offenders are often involved in domestic violence as well, family situation would appear to be a significant factor in eliciting aggression. Such obvious factors as overcrowding, number of children in the home, and presence of extra-nuclear family members are related to the level of stress in the family milieu. Also relevant are changes in family structure, such as frequent moves, a family member's illness or death, and marriage or divorce. Research has shown that spouse abuse is inordinately common toward pregnant women, indicating that stresses related to family size, finances, and perhaps sexual access may play a key role in precipitating aggression (Minchin, 1982).

Peer Group Influences

The peer group may have a significant impact on violent behavior. Since gangs are increasingly involved in street violence, gang membership would imply a greater likelihood of dangerousness. Similarly, criminal vocations, such as drug trafficking, may involve the use of weapons and frequent confrontations with rivals or law enforecement officers. Less obvious peer influences may also encourage violence, such as participation in an extremist political organization or mercenary or paramilitary pastimes (Dietz, 1985). An individual who has been involved in these sorts of activities is at higher risk for violence than an otherwise comparable subject.

Availability of Weapons

Though violence can be done with only "bare hands," the presence of weapons plays a key role in aggression. First, the presence of weapons serves as a cue to elicit dangerous behavior. Second, instrumentality often determines the severity of the assault. "The difference between assault and murder frequently revolves around whether the offender had a knife or only a fist at his or her disposal" (Monahan, 1981). The more lethal the weapons available, the greater the chance that violence will occur and, if it does occur, that it will be serious. Persons whose hobbies involve guns, knives, or martial arts obviously have weapons at hand. Casual access to weapons should also be considered, such as the individual who works with tools such as crowbars that could be pressed into service.

Availability of Victims

For the individual who has an extensive history of violence and antisocial behavior directed at many different targets, it may appear that almost anyone in society could be a future target. Other classes of offenders are more selective. Individuals who are assaultive toward children or spouses tend to continue this pattern, if they are allowed access, but may be no threat to others. Delusional individuals often focus their hostilities on a specific figure. Still other subjects are a threat to "types" of victims. Without a potential victim, violence is unlikely, but assessing this requires insight into other factors that lead the individual to violence.

THE DEMOGRAPHICS OF VIOLENCE

Four demographic variables have been widely studied as predictors of violent criminality. Unlike many of the factors cited above, the baserate of aggression as a function of these variables is reasonably well established. At the same time, many of these factors, such as gender or race, seem to be inappropriate bases for judging dangerousness, particularly in situations where there may be negative consequences for the subject. Perhaps their best use is in defining a baserate expectation of dangerousness for those in a given demographic category as a starting point for prediction. The types of clinical data reviewed above would serve to adjust these expectations.

Age

Rates of arrest for violent crime are very low for children and pre-teens, rise abruptly to extremely high levels at about age 15, then decline steadily throughout the rest of the age range (Wilson & Herrnstein, 1985). Individuals aged 15 to 19 are arrested approximately four times more often than their prevalence in the population. By comparison, rates of arrest for violence exactly match the proportion of 35–39-year-olds. The overall age effect persists even when such related factors as employment and family circumstances are factored out.

Gender

Between 85 and 90 percent of those arrested for violent crimes are males (Wilson & Herrnstein, 1985; Monahan, 1981). As of 1980, Uniform Crime Reports indicated that on an annual basis four of every 100,000 men were arrested for serious violent crimes, with correction for underreporting suggesting a baserate of 12–15 per 100,000. During the same period less than one woman per 250,000 was arrested, only a slight increase over 1960. In fact, accounting for the increase in the population, the proportion of female arrests for *violent* crimes actually declined during that 20-year period.

Socioeconomic Status (SES)

Unemployment and low income are consistently related to increased rates of violent behavior. Lack of job opportunities, employable skills, and stable work history is prevalent among "predatory, violent career criminals" (Mulvey & Lidz, 1984). Some studies have actually found SES to be the strongest demographic predictor of violent offenses (Shannon, 1978).

Race

Ethnic minority groups in many countries have rates of criminal and violent behavior which differ from the population at large. In the United States considerable attention has been focused on crime rates among Blacks. As of 1980, Blacks comprised one-eighth of the population but accounted for 40 to 50 percent of all serious crimes. While some authors have attributed this discrepancy to related factors such as age (the median age of blacks is seven years lower than that of whites), SES, and biases in arrest practices (Maloney, 1985), others contend that these factors do not completely account for the race effect (Blumstein, 1983; Wilson & Herrnstein, 1985). While crime statistics indicate that Blacks are disproportionately involved in violence, it is unclear at present whether this trend involves more than correlation with other demographic factors.

FORMULATING AN OPINION

Integrating the range of data we have described involves two major processes. The first involves evaluating the baserate for violent activity for a given pattern of demographics, as this should serve as a starting point or anchor for judgments of probability. Without this anchoring effect, there is little to connect clinical factors with probabilities in the "real world." Based on the pattern of individual characteristics, an estimate of violence potential derived from baserates may appear to be an under- or overestimate.

At a more global level, the examining therapist must integrate individual and situational information into a coherent picture. Monahan (1981), borrowing from the work of Bem and Funder (1978) summarizes this process as answering three questions:

(1) What characteristics describe situations in which the person reacts violently?
(2) What characteristics describe the situations the person will confront in the future?
(3) How similar are the situations the person will confront in the future to those that have elicited violence in the past? (p. 140)

Obviously, this approach can also be generalized to address situations likely to minimize the potential for acting-out, and this type of feedback is often useful to courts in their efforts to deal with potentially violent persons. Although there are no formulas or set rules to guide the integration of data, careful consideration of individual predisposing factors and their interaction with salient situations will help the examining clinican conduct a thorough and relevant assessment. In this way the therapist can assist the court while maintaining a degree of clinical integrity.

THE FORM OF EXPERT OPINIONS OF DANGEROUSNESS

The above model, while theoretically sound, has a major drawback. It requires some knowledge of the situations the individual "will confront," and it is this factor that confounds the process, for who can say with certainty what environmental stresses will or will not occur? While therapists can evaluate past social, family, work and other situational factors, and make some reasonable guesses about the future, these are at best probabilistic statements. Often it will be difficult to make these inferences with accuracy. For example, members of gangs often assert that they intend to discontinue such involvement, and drug and alcohol addicts say they have "kicked the habit." While recidivism is the rule, some succeed in making a change. How can an examiner know with certainty who will succeed or what pressures will be brought to bear by outside forces?

The vagaries of prediction assure that the best one can do is to describe the general predisposition of an individual toward violence and the factors that will increase and decrease risks. Dogmatic yes or no statements about dangerousness, a legal concept, are not warranted and are unsupportable both theoretically and empirically. Crystal ball predictions are the domain of soothsayers; careful clinical evaluation and description are the domains of scientists and professionals. Ethical therapists must often educate legal practitioners about capabilities and limitations in this area, and reframe naive questions in terms that allow useful, accurate, and professional responses.

Many authorities have argued that determination of dangerousness should be the province of therapists with special training and expertise in the areas of forensic psychology or psychiatry or of clinical criminology. Familiarity with the literature on violence and aggression, particularly research on dangerousness, is in order. Finally, special training in statistical issues in prediction and Bayesian inference are beneficial in preparing to serve courts in assessing the potential for violence.

Perhaps the most important issue facing therapists, given the bias toward overprediction, is the separation of probabilistic issues from value judgments. Inspection of a number of prediction studies suggests that in samples with violence baserates on the order of 20 percent, therapists routinely identify upwards of 60 percent for continued confinement or treatment. This overprediction indicates that therapists consider the "costs" of a false negative to be between 15 and 20 times higher than for a false positive. Since false negatives subject the public to potentially extreme violence, this weighting may not be irrational. As Walker (1983) has pointed out, if therapists know that one of three people will do violence, but not which one, would society want all to be released or all to be detained? Realistically, the bias toward overprediction probably reflects a misguided attempt to protect society from harm (and therapists from liability).

Protecting society is the job of the courts and the police, not therapists. Professionals have special training and expertise in understanding human behavior, and may legitimately describe individuals, their propensity for violence, and factors which will affect their dangerousness to society. It should be up to courts to go beyond this data to decide what risks society is willing to take, for what kinds of violence, and with what alternatives. Therapists should provide a rich database for dangerousness decisions, but should leave to the courts the final decisions. Such a policy will place responsibility for judgments which turn out badly where it belongs, with those whom society has empowered to act on its behalf — judges, not therapists.

CURRENT LEGAL PERSPECTIVES

Legal scholars generally misunderstand the research on prediction, the limits and capabilities of expertise, and therapists' motives for participating. The pessimistic conclusions of first-generation research projects have led lawyers to assert that therapists have nothing to offer. They fail to recognize the inherent difficulties of such naturalistic studies. At the same time, many judges and magistrates continue to request that therapists go beyond their clinical role to state that an individual is or is not too dangerous to be at liberty. Legal thinkers seem to be saying that therapists must either make the whole decision or not participate at all.

This confusion seems to result from a belief that therapists want to decide who will be confined. Scholars perpetuate the myth that therapists wanted to establish dangerousness as the basis for important decisions such as civil commitment, and then insist that they must also be responsible for predicting dangerousness in other contexts, such as potential harm to third parties (see Chapter 1 for more on *Tarasoff* actions and malpractice). Of course, dangerousness has always been a legal contrivance. Although therapists have offered predictions, often with excessive self-assurance, they have done so because the courts have expected it. Recent legal thinking has swung even farther into irrational territory, holding that therapists should have nothing to say about dangerousness in civil commitment, but should still be held liable for failure to predict harm to third parties (*In re William Wilson*, 1983). Such thinking would effectively remove therapists from an area of decision-making where their expertise is clear, while imposing a standard of care that cannot be effectively met.

CHAPTER 6

Family Law, Child Custody, and Child Abuse

So long as little children are allowed to suffer, there is no true love in this world.

— Isadora Duncan

THE FAMILY HAS traditionally been the basic unit of social interaction and order, and despite massive changes in social attitudes toward marriage and divorce, reproduction and sexual variations, child-rearing, and related domestic issues, family life remains a near-universal concern. Psychotherapists are inevitably confronted with clientele experiencing problems in one or more of these areas — families on the brink of divorce, divorced individuals adjusting to their new status, children with abusive or negligent parents, or couples distressed by sexual or reproductive problems — to name but a few. It would be impossible in one chapter, or even one book, to address all of the legal issues related to family and domestic matters, even as they relate to the practice of psychotherapy. (Also see Chapter 12.)

The focus here will be on three key areas of legal process most likely to involve practicing therapists: marriage and divorce, child custody, and child abuse. Although marital problems and divorce may be the single most common problem for clients of psychotherapists, clinicians are rarely directly involved in the legal proceedings to either create or dissolve marriages. Therapists usually function "alongside" the legal process, trying to help troubled couples avoid divorce if possible or cope with the results if not. We will briefly address recent legal trends in the regulation of marriage so that therapists can understand their clients' experiences within the legal system.

Understanding the legal status of marriage and divorce is also important because it is directly related to child custody. Common themes and evolutionary trends underlie theories of divorce, property settlement, and child custody; recognizing these themes gives the therapist insight into legal thinking in all of these areas. Finally, while the law surrounding child abuse has expanded greatly in recent years, it too borrows heavily from traditional thinking about the needs and rights of children following divorce. Abuse as a clinical phenomenon may also overlay other concerns, such as divorce or custodial decisions, and it is not unusual for therapists to be enmeshed in complex proceedings on all three fronts simultaneously.

MARRIAGE

Marriage has been an institution of cultures throughout history. Originally tied to both sociopolitical and religious motives, marriage served to regulate social order, maintain society through reproduction, provide for orderly succession of property and title, and structure division of labor. As society itself has changed, so have legal conceptions of marriage. Although the Supreme Court has recognized marriage as a fundamental right under the Constitution (see *Loving v. Virginia*), it is regulated by state laws established by statute. While each state has had to confront changing needs and social mores on its own, a number of legal concepts are generally accepted and some clear trends are evident.

States are allowed to regulate marriage to serve compelling public interests, hence strictures against marriages of close blood relatives and against polygamy. As the legal concept of marriage has become increasingly divorced (pun intended) from religious and procreative functions, the whole process has been reconceptualized to be consistent with the law of contracts. Potential partners must be competent to enter into a marriage contract to the extent that they understand and accept their duties and prerogatives if the contract is consummated. Marriages can be annulled on the grounds that one partner was not competent to enter the contract due to mental disability, such as mental retardation or severe disorder (see Chapter 3 for more on issues of competency). Similarly, when one individual induces another to marry through coercive or unnatural means (similar to undue influence in testamentary capacity cases), the marriage may be voided. These retroactive negations of marriage are rare, particularly given the tremendous liberalization of divorce laws, but when they do arise therapists are generally asked to aid the courts by evaluating one or both of the parties.

DIVORCE

From a legal perspective, divorce involves three distinct phases. First is the termination of the marital relationship. Next the marital estate, that is, all the assets and liabilities acquired during the marriage, must be settled and distributed to the parties as required by law. The final task is the award of custody of any children, along with arrangements for their future mainte- nance and well-being. The circumstances surrounding the breakup of the marriage affect each of these tasks. Here we will address divorce and marital property to aid therapists in understanding the procedures that may con- front their clients and to point out areas where therapists may become involved.

While marriage may be legally viewed as a contract between two parties (despite sentimental notions about love and affection), it is a contract in which society has a strong interest. Married persons assume many obliga- tions toward one another, some of which are defined by the law. For exam- ple, one spouse can generally be held responsible for debts incurred by their partner, which helps to ensure financial accountability. Because of the broad social and legal implications of marriage, once the contract is made " . . . the law favors marriage, it disfavors divorce. . . . " (*Solomon v. Solo- mon*, cited in Goldzband, 1982).

Because of the state's interest in maintaining the marriage contract, tradi- tional law required extreme justification for divorce, and invariably focused on the concept of fault. Faults that sufficed to end a marriage included adultery, desertion, physical and mental cruelty, venereal disease, confine- ment in prison, and even mental illness. The concept of fault was central to the outcome of the proceedings, because the "guilty" party generally left the marriage without claim to any marital resources, including the children. These laws made the prospect and process of divorce discouraging.

While traditionalists assert that liberalized divorce laws have lead to the "decline of marriage as an institution" and the "breakdown of the family unit," the real relationship is reversed. As in other areas, changes in divorce law have followed social trends at some distance. As divorce became increas- ingly common, the notion that only culpable individuals dissolved their marriages became untenable. Current estimates by the United States Census Bureau indicate that fully 60 percent of "ever-married" women now between ages 30 and 39 will divorce *at least* once (*Newsweek*, 1987). Thus, from a purely statistical point of view, divorce is something of a norm.

Since 1969, 48 states have adopted "no-fault" divorce statutes, that make, or at least add, "irreparability" as a grounds for dissolution (Blau, 1984, p. 107). These reforms were necessary because the traditional fault scheme failed to provide any mechanism for divorce by mutual consent. Under the old system, spouses might have to contrive one of the recognized grounds for divorce or each spouse might have to take the chance of being found at fault. Under the no-fault system, couples who agree to divorce can do so while reducing the emotional and monetary costs of an adversarial trial.

The no-fault divorce system is not without opposition. Critics argue that it is too easy and has accelerated the increase in divorce rates. Others suggest that without proof of fault, it is difficult for the court to determine proper division of the marital estate. This arguably prejudices the outcome against women, who may not have worked outside the family home, producing no separate monetary income or assets during marriage.

Traditional jurisdictions followed the common law doctrine of separate property. According to this principle, each spouse owned all the property that he or she had before marriage, as well as that which came to him or her through personal earnings, investments, inheritance, or gifts. These were deemed the separate property of the individuals and not part of the joint marital estate. A spouse could acquire interest in the other's property only by way of gifts or, where permitted, through a business relationship.

Following divorce each spouse was left with his or her separate property. From its inception, this policy severely prejudiced women who divorced, because they rarely owned any separate property or earned substantial income. Divorced women were generally left with nothing, except perhaps some china and linen from their trousseau. Many common law jurisdictions adopted the use of alimony as a partial redress for this failure. Alimony is, of course, monetary support for a financially dependent ex-spouse. It is completely distinct from child support, in that it is solely for the needs of the dependent spouse. Alimony could be provided *pendente lite*, i.e., only while the matter is being litigated, for rehabilitative purposes on a temporary basis after the final decree, or indefinitely until death or remarriage.

In the mid-nineteenth century, Emancipation Acts or Married Women's Acts reflected increased recognition of women's rights and legal identity separate from their husbands. These laws began to establish the legitimate interests of both genders in the marital estate, regardless of social and occupational roles. This trend, along with the recent advent of no-fault divorce, led many jurisdictions to adopt the doctrine of community property, which recognizes that marriage is a structure of joint and concurrent ownership. In community property jurisdictions, usually there is an equal division of the marital estate upon divorce. Each spouse theoretically owns one-half interest in the estate developed during the marriage, though separate property acquired before or through gift, devise, or descent during the marriage remains with the individual. Each partner has the burden of demonstrating that a given part of the estate is his or hers alone, with all other property being equitably divided. Factors such as marital misconduct, duration of marriage, health of spouses, or age of spouses may also be taken into account by the court. Alimony is rarely used in community property jurisdictions.

Therapists' Involvement in Divorce

Therapists working with couples on the verge of divorce find themselves at the crossroads of the legal system, the mental health system, and often a religious system. The legal system will focus on giving priorities to and protecting the rights of the individual participants. The therapist will attempt to address their well-being in a more holistic way.

The underlying assumptions and operating procedures of the two systems differ dramatically. The legal system is adversarial. Lawyers make every effort to win their client's case and to discredit the other's arguments concerning property, custody, and visitation. The system aims to highlight and focus on areas of conflict and the differing perspectives of each party. Therapists, in contrast, will usually attempt to support each person as a member of a family system. Their approach is to emphasize commonalities and motivations for cooperation.

The issue of confidentiality is also handled very differently. The adversarial nature of the legal system promotes competition, guardedness, and mistrust. Family therapy fosters cooperation, open communication, and trust. Because these agendas conflict so strongly, therapists must initially ascertain whether their clients are already involved in the legal system. What is their purpose in coming to counseling? Is it because their lawyer suggested it or because they are motivated to work things out? Does the patient intend to call the therapist to testify against the spouse? If the case involves child custody, are both parties willing to accept the therapist's opinion of what might be in the child's best interests or are they trying to buy the therapist's expertise and authority to support their claims in court? These diverse goals, all of which have some validity, must be recognized and understood.

Such complex problems can be handled by the therapist; we mention them here to alert practitioners that they must be prepared to help their patients clarify expectations before becoming involved in individual or family therapy when divorce looms on the horizon. When the legal system is actually involved, the therapist and patient may have highly divergent goals at the outset. Further, it is common for those enmeshed in a potential divorce to have motives which they do not recognize — desires to punish the spouse, to perpetuate the marriage by contesting the divorce, to act as if they are unaffected by the divorce, or to prove that they are "better" by winning custody of the children. Making these hidden agendas explicit may help clients adopt more adaptive coping skills.

Particularly problematic are cases in which allegations of marital misconduct are made by one or both parties. Unsuspecting therapists may be lured into trying to validate allegations as a prelude to working actively with the family or couple. In these cases it is especially likely that a hidden agenda underlies the consultation, and the possibility that one or the other spouse intends to utilize the counseling as a battlefield or as a tool in the legal process is heightened. Therapists are well-advised to focus narrowly on clarifying what is to be accomplished. Do the spouses really want to work through this crisis and remain married? Is only one partner invested in preserving the marriage? Do the spouses want or expect the therapist to mediate a negotiated divorce settlement? If the motives at hand are contradictory to effective intervention, then the therapist must consider referrals to attorneys or separate therapists or other actions more likely to aid the clients without compromising the professional's integrity.

As an alternative to conventional adversarial divorce procedures, some jurisdictions have adopted mediation as a primary method of settling divorce disputes. Growing out of the older "conciliation courts," which aimed to avert divorce, mediation has been broadened to serve families in completing divorce in a less destructive and costly way. The couple is generally aided by a team consisting of a lawyer, a psychotherapist, and sometimes a social worker. This team helps the couple decide on the division of the estate, spousal support, child custody and visitation, and child support. The process of mediation appears to work best in cases where the spouses maintain some degree of respect for one another and can focus on the needs of their children rather than on personal agendas (Ruman & Lamm, 1985). Unfortunately, attorneys generally have considerable reservations about negotiating without a clear mandate to "win" for one side or the other. Their experience dictates that they must vigorously advocate for one side in any dispute, and this training is hard to abandon. In fact, lawyers who do not advocate as vigorously as possible are usually seen as unethical by others in their profession; nevertheless, it is impossible to advocate aggressively for both sides in the same action. In jurisdictions using mediation, a select group of attorneys and therapists with experience in this area participate, and it is rare for practicing therapists without intimate knowledge of domestic law to be involved in the process.

CHILD CUSTODY

Child custody is most often an issue following divorce. By comparison, a very small proportion of custody decisions arise due to legal severance of parental rights, adoption, or orphanage. The following discussion focuses on post-divorce custody, but many of the same principles in determining proper custodial arrangements guide courts and clinicians when dealing with children on other grounds. Brief reference to specific issues in adoption and termination of parental rights will be made at the end of the chapter.

When parents ask a court to terminate their marriage, the law requires that a separate decision be made regarding the future care and custody of their children. Even when the arrangements are settled in advance subject to the court's approval, this aspect of the divorce is extremely stressful. Goldzband (1982) has termed the outright custody battle the "ugliest litigation," and most therapists are loath to become involved. Cases that proceed to litigation may involve numerous unspoken motives that really have little to do with the children themselves, such as desires to punish the ex-spouse, to satisfy narcissistic strivings by "winning" custody, or to prove to the children that each parent was willing to "fight" for them. To the extent that such motivations operate, the custody proceedings are likely to be expensive, destructive to all concerned, and unhelpful to the family as it attempts to adjust after divorce. On the other hand, some cases involve legitimate differences of opinion regarding the best interests of the children and genuine concern for their welfare. Experience suggests that these are the minority of litigated custody suits.

Court-ordered custody decisions are significant for a variety of reasons, but the importance of custody law and its effects on most children of divorce may be exaggerated. While 60 percent of couples who have difficulty resolving divorce disputes go to court (Blau, 1984, p. 107), only one-sixth of these involve disagreement over custody. In 85 to 90 percent of all divorces, custody and visitation arrangements are agreed upon by the parties, with subsequent approval by a court (Wallerstein & Kelly, 1980). Still, the number of children affected by divorce continues to grow, now estimated at 1.2 million annually (U.S. Department of Commerce, 1984), and those whose custody is decided by a court number over 100,000 annually. By 1990 about one-third of all children in the U.S. will have experienced the divorce of at least one set of parents (Clingempeel & Reppucci, 1982). Since courts must ultimately agree even to stipulated custody arrangements, trends in statutory and case law probably influence negotiation of these agreements, indirectly affecting even more children.

Divorce custody proceedings can be broken into three phases. As soon as spouses undertake a legal separation, well before the actual divorce proceedings, the court may intercede to establish a temporary custody arrangement. If there are indications of potential harm to the children or if one party asks the court for formal custody while the divorce is pending, then some action is usually taken. These provisions are important because most judges favor continuity of care and are likely to make the temporary arrangements permanent following the final divorce decree. Therapists are rarely involved in temporary custody decisions.

The bulk of this section will address issues connected with outright legal contests for permanent custody. The small number of cases that reach this stage of litigation typically involve spouses who each feel they have a great deal at stake in winning the case. Actually, families usually lose as a result of custody trials, although in their anger and rage at one another parents may not be able to see this. Expert testimony is almost always sought at this stage, consistent with the common, "win at all costs" mentality.

Courts may also exercise jurisdiction over custody even after a final decree has been issued. While many parents who are dissatisfied with the outcome of the initial round of proceedings threaten further legal action, in reality courts are reluctant to consider changes in custody. Many states actually forbid alterations for a set period of time, usually two years, to foster stability as the family adjusts to the divorce and new living arrangements. Only if the complaining party clearly establishes some suspicion that the existing arrangements may cause the children harm will the court initiate a new trial. In these few cases experts are virtually always asked to evaluate whether the children are actually being emotionally or physically harmed. If not, the court will not make significant changes.

Evolution and Limits of the "Best Interests" Standard

In the preceding discussion of divorce and property settlement, two major trends were noted: the destigmatization of divorce, including the abandonment of fault-finding, and increased attention to gender-fair property division. The same themes have reshaped the law of child custody, particularly in the last decade (Levy, 1985). A brief review of historical trends in child custody will provide some context for recent developments and indicate reasons for persistent problems.

Historically, ancient Roman law dictated that the father had absolute power over his offspring and was always awarded custody. Children were viewed as "chattel," and under the doctrine of *parens potestas* only men could hold legal title to their offspring. Since the developmental and emotional needs of children were not considered significant, custody was treated strictly as a matter of title over property. This orientation carried over into English common law and persisted into the nineteenth century, by which time it was also firmly established in America.

The doctrine of *parens patriae* gained influence in the latter half of the nineteenth century and eventually led to greater recognition of the state as guardian of helpless and needy individuals (see earlier discussion in Chapter 4). These themes were adapted to child custody matters in the form of judicial efforts to structure custody decisions according to the needs of children rather than the "property rights" of parents. Following reasoning similar to the 1881 case of *Chapsky v. Wood*, many courts aimed to "promote the welfare and interest [of children of divorce as] the paramount consideration" in custody decrees. In theory, gender-bound and parent-oriented notions regarding child custody were replaced by concern for children themselves.

Perhaps due to social and political realities, the legal view of "welfare and interests" remained strictly paternalistic. Courts took a monetaristic approach to "welfare and interests," such that a child's welfare was equated with material benefits; more humanistic concerns such as emotional nurturance were not considered. Custody decisions still overwhelmingly favored fathers because they had the financial resources to provide for a child's material needs. Thus, the status quo was preserved, albeit with a new set of rationalizations.

By the early twentieth century, the view that custody decisions should reflect only the "best interests of the child," a phrase usually associated with the 1925 case of *Finlay v. Finlay*, was firmly established. Gradually, courts in the United States began to pay greater attention to the emotional and developmental needs of children, rather than focusing on financial support alone. This change in emphasis led courts to completely reverse the gender bias, claiming that "there is but a twilight zone between a mother's love and the atmosphere of heaven" (*Tuter v. Tuter*, 1938). Courts acted on the assumption that a child of "tender years" should be placed in the custody of the mother, absent a clear demonstration of unsuitability on her part. The development of the "tender years doctrine" led to a complete reversal of favoritism toward fathers in custody decisions. During the twentieth century fully 90 percent of all divorce decrees involving minor children have given the mother primary legal custody (Marafiote, 1985, p. 4), most without contest by the father (Weitzman & Dixon, 1979).

During the last two decades there has been an increasing effort to truly consider the best interests of the child as the basis for child custody decisions. The Uniform Marriage and Divorce Act (National Conference of

Commissioners for Uniform State Laws, 1971), which has influenced legislation in many states, specifies five general factors to be considered in custody decisions:

(1) The wishes of the child's parent or parents.
(2) The wishes of the child.
(3) The interaction and interrelationship of the child with his or her parents, his siblings, and any other person who may significantly affect the child's best interest.
(4) The child's adjustment to his home, school, and community.
(5) The mental and physical health of all individuals involved.

While these criteria represent something of an improvement over simplistic notions that all children are best served by placement with the more financially secure parent or that all children benefit most from placement with their mother, the factors to be considered remain vague and the guidelines unhelpful. It is noteworthy, for example, that the first item listed is the wishes of the parents. Of course this makes sense in stipulated decisions where the parents agree on custody arrangements. In contested cases, by definition the mother's and the father's wishes are mutually contradictory. Statutes based on the Uniform Act have been instrumental in reducing gender bias and excluding from consideration factors that do not directly bear on the suitability of proposed caretakers. For example, parental homosexuality, promiscuity, or unusual religious practices cannot become *de facto* disqualifications, and could only be considered as they directly affect parenting. The best interests doctrine "has been interpreted to mean that children have the right to a loving, stable home with adequate provision for their maintenance, education, and continued contact with the noncustodial parent" (Howell & Toepke, 1984, p. 57).

Despite gradual progress, the law remains reluctant to rely totally, or even primarily, upon the "best interests" standard in custody decisions. For example, Georgia, which has largely retained fault-finding in divorce law, simply assigns custody to the party not found at fault in the divorce. In practice courts continue to place a strong emphasis on the competing "rights" of biological parents to custody of their offspring over the offspring's rights to a suitable home. Even when both divorcing parents are relatively poor custodians, one or both will almost invariably retain custody.

This bias is seen most clearly in the "reversion doctrine," which states that under a variety of conditions a child's custody will revert to a biological parent over others. In one case a young girl resided with her mother and maternal grandparents; the father had abandoned his family before her birth. When the child was 15 months old her mother died, and she was raised by her grandparents until age 11. At that time the biological father reappeared, sued for custody, and won. The Supreme Court of Nebraska eventually held that "Courts may not properly deprive parent of custody . . . unless it is affirmatively shown that such a parent is unfit . . . or has forfeited *that right* [emphasis added] (*Raymond v. Cotner*, 1963). Nearly all child development experts would agree that in this case the courts acted not in the best interests of the child, but with the property rights of her father in mind.

The situation above highlights the differences between legal and psychotherapeutic views of children's psychological and developmental needs. The most influential therapeutic contribution to this debate derives from *Beyond the Best Interests of the Child* (Goldstein, Solnit, & Freud, 1973). These authors argue that divorce is invariably troublesome for children, and that courts had best seek the least detrimental alternative in custody actions.

> The least detrimental alternative . . . maximizes, in accord with the child's sense of time and on the basis of short-term predictions given the limitations of knowledge, his or her opportunity for being wanted and for maintaining on a continuous basis a relationship with at least one adult who is or will become his (or her) psychological parent. (pp. 53–54)

The concept of psychological parenthood has gained considerable attention among therapists, lawyers, and judges. Goldstein et al. argue that the most crucial element in a child's psychological development is a continuing relationship with a parental figure who is unconditionally responsible for the child, accepts and wants that responsibility, and exercises that responsibility without debilitating interference from others.

The most controversial outgrowth of this thinking is the argument that legal custody should always be given to only one parent. Even when either adult could be a good parent, these authorities would advise courts to choose only one permanent custodian, who would then be responsible for all childcare decisions, including visitation. This view, which contrasts sharply with the legal tradition's presumption that both parents have rights to custody or visitation, has not been widely accepted. Still, *Beyond the Best Interests* has been widely read in judicial circles (Ellis, 1984), and at least the broad concept that parenthood is a function of a continuing relationship rather than genetic heritability has taken hold. Courts are increasingly willing to take account of children's emotional and developmental needs as against conflicting parental motives.

Types of Custody Arrangements

In summarizing extensive research on the outcome of divorce for children, Wallerstein and Kelly (1980) noted that it is the quality of postdivorce relationships, not the fact of the divorce itself, that determines the long-term effects. The most significant predictor of successful adaptation appear to be (1) a reduction in parental conflict, anger, and expressed hostility, and (2) a continuing constructive relationship between each parent and the child(ren). It is interesting to consider the potential of various custody arrangements to meet these goals.

It is important to recognize that custody may refer to two distinct realms. Legal custody refers to the role of exercising decision-making control over children. A child's legal guardian is responsible for choices in medical care, schooling, financial interests, and so forth. Physical custody refers to actual residential care and day-to-day supervision of children. In some cases these roles may be split; for example, a child's father may retain legal custody while the mother has permanent physical custody. More often, one parent is the primary caretaker and full legal custodian.

Sole Custody. The traditional custody arrangement is for one parent to have both legal and physical custody, while the noncustodial parent has modest financial responsibility and exercises minimal visitation rights. Many aspects of sole custody perpetuate the assumption that one parent is unsuitable, or at least that one is clearly preferred over the other. While this assumption may apply in some cases, there are clearly situations where the two parents are almost equally good (or poor) candidates. Sole custody may not address the needs of these families. Advantages of sole custody derive from the stability of the child's life-style. Disadvantages stem from minimal contact with the noncustodial parent. Further, child support payments and visitation can often become weapons by which the parents seek vengeance on one another through the child.

Various legal developments have addressed some of the problems associated with sole custody. As mentioned above, sole custody typically requires that the noncustodial parent pay child support, but noncompliance is extremely high. Many states have enacted stiff legislation that allows courts to seize assets or wages or to incarcerate those who are delinquent in paying child support. Parental "childnapping" has also received considerable attention in recent years. Since custody is controlled by states, parents dissatisfied with existing conditions could become residents of another state, take their children to that location, and seek a new custody decree there. States often simply ignored or were unaware of decisions made elsewhere, so these ploys were often successful. The Federal Parental Kidnapping Prevention Act of 1980 was adopted to prevent states from issuing custody decrees to supersede those of another state, and to increase the federal role in enforcing childsnatching laws. The Uniform Child Custody Jurisdiction Act, adopted by all states but Massachusetts and Texas, serves to clarify jurisdictional issues and promote cooperation among state courts handling custody issues.

Split Custody. Split custody is rarely employed. In this arrangement each parent has primary legal and residential custody for one or more of several children. Split custody is probably best employed when the relationships among the children are particularly destructive (Hodges, 1986) or when the quality of relationships between parents and the individual children varies markedly. For example, one adult might be a generally superior parent but have specific problems with one child. In this case the one disaffected child could be placed with the other parent or some other guardian, while the rest of the children remained with the preferred parent. Separating the children has obvious disadvantages, and these should be clearly outweighed by the fit among the proposed subsets of the family before split custody is considered. These arrangements are usually associated with very problematic cases, where courts prefer to give custody to biological parents and must attempt to minimize the weaknesses of each.

Joint Custody. Joint custody, in which both parents share child-rearing responsibilities, is a relatively new phenomenon. This trend seems to follow both the destigmatization of divorce and the focus on gender-fair distribution of marital assets. As divorce law abandoned the idea that one of the parties was severely flawed or at fault for the breakup, it became untenable to retain the notion that one of the parents had to be inadequate. Logically, some divorce cases must involve two potentially good, separate parents. At the same time, the focus on equal division of assets in community property jurisdictions seemed at odds with the bias toward maternal custody. Consequently, many jurisdictions have followed the lead of California's 1980 statute and adopted joint custody as a standard for family courts. These states mandate equal legal and custodial responsibility unless the court finds clear reasons to minimize the role of one parent. At least 22 states have specific provisions for joint custody, while others follow this procedure on an informal basis (Howell & Toepke, 1984).

The term "joint custody" has been applied to situations in which legal custody is shared although physical custody is given to only one parent. This arrangement is obviously similar to sole custody with visitation. However, it may provide greater opportunity for the noncustodial parent to remain involved with the children. It may also increase the potential for fighting among the parents.

Most often, joint custody refers to near-equal division of both legal and physical care for the children, also called coparenting. This arrangement presents considerable logistical challenges, as children are passed back and forth between the parents. Common arrangements rotate care on a short-term basis, each week or half-week. At the other extreme, joint custody may be implemented with one parent as custodian for the school year, the other during summer and winter vacations. This latter arrangement is most often used when parents live far apart, and may also involve visitation by the currently noncustodial parent.

The response to joint custody of psychologists, psychiatrists, and child development specialists has been quite mixed. From the philosophical background of *Beyond the Best Interests of the Child*, some therapists have noted that children who are shuttled between the parents on an equal basis may be effectively denied access to either adult as "psychological parent." To the extent that joint custody leads to feelings of being constantly uprooted or divided between the parents, the child may not develop a secure sense of either parent as an unconditional caretaker.

In contrast, Roman and Haddad (1978) have argued against cutting children off from either parent through traditional single custody arrangements. They suggest that parents divorce each other, not their children, and so both divorced parents and children have the right to continuing substantial relationships. Proponents suggest that joint custody maintains the emotional attachment of both parents to the child, prevents an adverse impact on the parent who would not have obtained custody in a conventional arrangement (usually the father), and reduces the burden on each adult as a single parent. Advocates in the legal community have indicated that it may simplify divorce negotiations and reduce the rates of relitigation (see Ifeld, Ifeld, & Alexander, 1982).

A critical view of joint custody holds that it perpetuates the treatment of children as property, with each parent staking an equal claim à la community property. Unlike King Solomon, who had no intention of really dividing the child claimed by two different women, modern judges are often required by statutorily mandated joint custody to do just that. Ironically, it has been argued that family court judges may perceive joint custody as a means of escape from the burden of extremely difficult and wrenching custody decisions.

Outcome studies of voluntary joint custody arrangements, those established as part of a negotiated divorce settlement, have been generally positive. It is important to note that these findings are based on self-selected and often small samples, and findings may not be applicable to other types of families. For the most part, families studied to date have been cooperative and interested in shared parenting, so that outcomes may have been more positive than can be expected under other circumstances.

Taken together, a number of studies of joint custody (Abarbanel, 1979; Ahrons, 1980; Irving, Benjamin, & Trocme, 1984; Luepnitz, 1982; Steinman, 1981) suggest consistent themes. Children are generally more satisfied with the amount of contact with each parent than they would have been with single custody. Some are able to maintain a " . . . sense of being loved and wanted by both parents" (Steinman, 1985, p. 92). Problems arise from home-switching, disruption of school functioning and peer relationships, and confusion over family relationships, values, and identity. Parents in general are satisfied with joint custody. Both adults can preserve significant parental roles while enjoying greater freedom than they would as single parents. The additional free time afforded the adults may help smooth acceptance of the divorce, changes in employment, and entry into new relationships. Interestingly, a significant fraction of joint custody arrangements, perhaps as many as one-third, eventually evolve into a more traditional primary custodial arrangement. These changes are more common as children reach adolescence and insist on greater autonomy and consistency in their affairs. Parental changes in residence which makes joint custody difficult may also terminate shared parenting. Finally, when one or both parents remarries and acquires new children, existing custody arrangements must often be simplified, obviating the complexity of joint custody.

Despite the generally positive findings, there are significant problems with joint custody. The bottom line appears to be that it is demanding for children but may allow them greater access to both parents. Steinman (1985) noted that " . . . With joint custody legislation now being applied to parents who are unmotivated and even bitterly hostile to one another, it is especially urgent that we understand how joint custody works for parents and children in less-than-ideal circumstances" (p. 89). In her study among highly motivated families committed to coparenting, about one in three children experienced significant problems and felt "burdened" by the routine, even after several years. While it is not known how many of these children would have had ongoing problems in other custody arrangements, it is clear that joint custody may work for some families but is not a perfect solution. "The myth that joint custody will prevent divorce from changing children's lives should not be encouraged" (Blau, 1984, p. 112).

Based on available information (Hodges, 1986; Irving et al., 1984; Steinman, 1985), several factors suggest that joint custody is a viable alternative for a given family:

(1) General parental agreement on child-rearing and discrimination between issues for shared parenting (usually longer-term, "policy" matters) and non-sharable matters; acceptance of some divergence in parenting styles and goals.
(2) Acceptance and respect between parents; sense of equality.
(3) Recognition and appreciation of benefits of coparenting.
(4) Parental ability to make joint decisions without escalating hostilities, or at least without allowing conflict to affect or be communicated through children.
(5) Compatibility of children's needs and developmental tasks with shared parenting.
(6) Parents' commitment to living in close proximity.
(7) Family recognition of child's legitimate needs for continuing relationship with both parents; parental ability to show empathy with each other's sense of loss after divorce.
(8) Availability of psychological, financial or other resources that promote flexibility in accommodating the logistical demands of joint custody.

Contraindications to joint custody include the following:

(1) Different values in child-rearing which cannot be resolved or accepted (e.g., religious orientation), especially if these contributed to the divorce.
(2) Intense, unremitting hostility that spills over to using children as weapons, conduits, or targets.
(3) Lack of respect or tolerance between parents, or marked differences in power.
(4) Joint custody as court ordered rather than the product of voluntary negotiation.
(5) Preschool or adolescent children or children of widely divergent ages.
(6) History of family violence.
(7) Major disturbance in one or more family members, including drug or alcohol abuse.
(8) Inability of one parent to accept the reality of the divorce or incorporate failure of marriage into self-image.

While it should be apparent that no single custody arrangement is right for all divorcing families, advocates of specific custody schemes often miss this point. Proponents try to align their preferred arrangement with children's rights, arguing that children have the right to a consistent relationship with a parental figure, or that children have the right to continuing relationships with both parents. Who could argue with such reasoning? On the other hand, the conclusion that children have a right to pure single custody, as suggested by Goldstein et al. (1973, 1986), or that children have a right to joint custody à la Roman and Haddad (1978) is based upon a variety of assumptions or biases.

These biases can work to the disadvantage of children when enacted as legislation. Statutory preference for any specific custody arrangement cannot be in the best interests of all children; the circumstances of divorcing families are simply too diverse. For those who do not fit well into the preferred model, the law's preference becomes an unfair burden. All of the good intentions of child development experts might best be subsumed under the rubric of a *child's right to a thorough, open, and unbiased evaluation of his or her specific needs and the ways that these can be met*. Therapists should advocate not for legislative enactment of increasingly rigid structures for divorce, but for a commitment that family courts will fully embrace the best interests of each and every child as the sine qua non for judging custody arrangements.

Gender, Custody, and Child-Rearing

Traditional, sole custody is a phenomenon usually associated with the "weekend father," given the overwhelming predominance of mother custody. Stereotypic views that males are generally less adequate parents than their female ex-spouses continue to influence both negotiated and court-ordered custody arrangements, though many states have recently forbidden court-ordered custody based on gender alone. To date relatively little research has addressed the role of fathers in parenting within intact families, much less as single parents.

Research on father custody suggests that the small number of fathers who do press suits for primary custody are successful about half the time (Atkinson, 1984). In general these men are financially secure, have good jobs, are socially stable, and are described as highly nurturing, assertive, confident, and well-organized (Berry, 1981). Although these may be a select group of fathers, there are indications that "most fathers can be successful single parents" (Levy, 1985). Smith and Smith (1981) identified five factors which predicted successful adjustment by single fathers in the first postdivorce year:

(1) Direct child-rearing experience.
(2) Participation in domestic activities and decisions prior to the divorce.
(3) Active involvement in setting limits, providing structure, and administering discipline before the divorce.
(4) Nurturing and supportive style in interactions with children.
(5) Training or education in child development or related fields.

Of course, these same criteria apply equally well to successful single mothers.

Research on longer-term adjustment indicates that divorced fathers resemble divorced mothers in terms of life-style and strategies for coping with the demands of single parenthood (Defrain & Eirick, 1981). Luepnitz (1982) studied general family environment and functioning, parental adjustment to divorce and custody arrangements, and children's self-concept in father custody, mother custody, and joint custody. She found no significant differences in these three domains for the two groups of single-parent families.

Warshack and Santrock (1979, 1983) examined the effects on children of living in single-parent homes with parents of the same gender versus those of the opposite gender. Their findings were complex, but were interpreted to suggest that children may do better with parents of the same sex, particularly in terms of social competence (e.g., honesty, self-esteem, cooperation, less complaining, "pleasantness"). Girls living in father-only homes seemed more affected than male children in mother-only custody. Subsequent research indicates that individual differences in parenting style are more important than the parent's gender, and that an "authoritative parenting style with warmth, clear rules, and open verbal interchange" will optimize children's long-term adjustment.

These results indicate that any remaining bias against fathers as custodians, even in sole custody arrangements, is unwarranted.

CONDUCTING THE CUSTODY EVALUATION

Perhaps more than any other area of interface with the legal system, custody evaluations require a broad and complex intervention by the psychotherapist. Focused evaluation of a given individual, the rule in forensic work, is not adequate to respond to the court's needs in custody trials. Rather, the entire network of the divorcing family, along with their collaterals and community resources, must be understood. Often, the therapist must draw inferences about the systematic interactions that would result under several potential custodial arrangements, with an eye toward selecting the "best," or perhaps least detrimental, outcome. While the criterion for choosing the most desirable plan is clearly established as the "best interests of the child," the range of relevant information is quite broad and makes the task of identifying a single recommended custody plan challenging.

Accepting and Negotiating the Referral

The conduct of a thoroughgoing evaluation is fraught with problems; most stem from the very nature of the divorce proceedings. When therapists are contacted to conduct a custody evaluation, it usually means that the divorcing parents have been unable to reach an agreement. By this stage in the divorce, tensions run high and the process tends to become increasingly adversarial. This polarization does not promote consideration of the needs of children, instead accentuating many hostile motives between the parents. The first task for the responsible evaluator is to clarify his or her role in the process and to make an explicit commitment to advocate for the best interests of the child or children.

While therapists may view the acceptance of a referral as preliminary to the evaluation per se, this is properly a stage for careful and diligent work. Referrals for custody evaluations generally come from attorneys representing one parent. Attorneys hope to find a sympathetic expert whose opinion will be advantageous to their client, but it is unlikely that a professional therapist could ethically conduct any type of evaluation "for" only one parent. The ideal situation is to be retained by the court as an impartial "friend of the court" or by a guardian *ad litem* representing the children. A guardian *ad litem* is appointed by the court to represent only the child's legal interests as separate from those of either parent. Either of these arrangements firmly establishes the impartiality of the consulting therapist.

Every effort must be made to involve both parents equally in the evaluation. Balanced participation assures more accurate information if the evaluator is not seen as an enemy by either party. It also allows clearer comparison of the strengths and weaknesses of each party and a matching of each parent's characteristics with the needs of the children. Both the therapist's commitment to advocate only for the children and the need to evaluate both parents should be immediately brought to the attention of the referring agent. If the referring party is an attorney, he or she should be encouraged to contact the opposing counsel to discuss a unified evaluation of both parents. In the absence of such cooperation it may be necessary to refuse involvement in the case.

The best way to demonstrate neutrality, professionalism, and concern for the interests of children is to carefully explain the rationale and procedures required for a thorough evaluation up front. If the parents are informed about and understand the nature of the evaluation, they are more likely to agree to participate, cooperate and provide accurate information, and to accept the legitimacy of the findings. There are a variety of complex issues which must be addressed. For example, both parents must understand that there can be no confidentiality; all pertinent information will be shared with the court. Also, a thorough study of the child will often require contact with extended family, physicians, schools, or others; the parents should agree to this in advance. It is important to note that both parents usually retain full legal custody until a final decree is issued by the courts, so that pursuing any evaluation of the child without the consent of *both* parents may expose the therapist to legal liability. Also, it is prudent to discuss fees and make arrangements for advance payment, as these matters may become hopelessly confounded in a complex and acrimonious case.

The negotiation of such sensitive issues requires a joint meeting with both parents and their attorneys. In addition to working out the details of the evaluation, such a meeting can serve to establish the necessary sense of cooperation with an eye toward the long-term welfare of the children. If such cooperation is lacking, the therapist should strongly consider declining to participate. Obviously, the strength of any recommendations to the court would be greatly reduced if the examiner were able to address the suitability of only one parent, or were hindered in seeking highly relevant information from collateral sources.

Weiner, Simons, and Cavanaugh (1985) suggest several important issues to be addressed in planning the evaluation. The presence of even one of these issues should alert the therapist to the need for thorough study and clarification, often with recourse to collateral sources of data:

(1) Are there charges of physical or sexual abuse?
(2) Is there a history of alcoholism, drug abuse, or previous psychiatric hospitalizations?
(3) Is anyone presently in therapy? Has anyone been in therapy in the past? Why?
(4) Are the children showing adjustment problems?
(5) If the custody dispute centers on only one or two children in the family, why is there no dispute about the other children?

The Conduct of the Evaluation

The following paragraphs describe a general model for custody evaluations. While many key areas of content are described, it is impossible to specify in advance what characteristics must be considered or how they should be weighted. For example, differences in parents' intelligence are rarely an important consideration, provided that both fall somewhere in the broad range of "normal" functioning. Often other factors outweigh any nonspecific advantages of higher intelligence. In some cases, however, the relative intelligence of parents may be quite significant, such as when the child is extremely bright or has medical problems which require sophisticated management. Thus, the exact content to be addressed must be determined on a case by case basis.

As the welfare of the child will ultimately serve as the sole criterion for the adequacy of any custody arrangements, it is logical to begin by evaluating the child or children affected by the divorce. It is crucial to remember that they deserve the same consideration as their parents. The therapist should describe, in age-appropriate language, how the children will be involved in the study and answer any questions they may have. It is often useful to give parents guidance on how to introduce the children to the initial contact with the evaluator. Also, the therapist must remember that the children are already stressed by the conflict within their families, so that establishing rapport may require extra effort.

Emphasis should be placed on clarifying the child's developmental progress on many fronts, including cognitive, emotional, physical, and social levels. Often developmental theories, such as those of Piaget, Erikson, and Kohlberg, may provide a model for understanding the child's progress within a meaningful framework. Other factors, such as temperament, receptivity to structure or discipline, or need for emotional support, may also be relevant. If there are many children, at least some individual assessment is warranted. The focus of data collection should be identifying specific strengths and weaknesses that must be addressed by any custody recommendations. Data regarding the above issues should be derived from a variety of sources.

It is recommended that the child or children be observed in at least one "naturalistic" setting, such as during school or daycare or in a community or recreational activity. During these observations the impact of the examiner on the child's behavior should be minimized. Direct observation of this type may be especially useful in revealing the peer relationships and social behavior of children; it may also provide some insight into how the child might be affected by changes in normal activities attendant on the divorce. The examiner should strongly consider direct observation in any setting where clear behavioral problems are reported, such as at school or when visiting specific family members.

Clinical evaluation in an office setting, which is commonly used, may include both formal testing and unstructured activities. Psychological testing may help clarify intellectual level, educational progress, and the potential for psychopathology. A variety of projective techniques is useful, particularly with younger children. These may include traditional projective tests, such as the Thematic Apperception Test, as well as family drawings, which often provide a vivid picture of the child's view of family dynamics, particularly important alliances. Similarly, play activities using puppets can help children act out important family themes; simple doll houses and small human figures may provide even greater verisimilitude. Other activities, such as the *The Talking, Feeling, and Doing Game* (Gardner, 1973), may also be useful.

Older children will respond to more direct interview techniques, although they may have difficulty knowing how to express the complex feelings aroused by the divorce process. Also, many children feel trapped in impossible loyalty conflicts and strive to be very noncommittal so as not to alienate either parent. The examiner may respond to these concerns if they become apparent, but becoming overly involved at a therapeutic level probably will not serve the child well in the long-run (Goldstein, Freud, Solnit, & Goldstein, 1986). It is often easier for the child to respond to nonthreatening, specific questions about family relationships and their own feelings. For example:

- What is the very earliest thing you can remember? Tell me about that.
- If you could have three wishes, what would you ask for? Or, if you had magical powers or could travel in time, what would you do?
- Desert Island Game (see Lazarus, 1971): Through magic you may travel to a remote island, a beautiful paradise. You can take one person along. Who would that be? (Skafte, 1985, suggests allowing the child to then add other persons, and eventually resolving the fantasy by having everyone return home and live happily.)
- Act out how you think a mother/father should be when her/his child is sad, happy, or disobedient. Tell how your mother/father is like this. How is she/he different?
- Tell about the most recent time you were angry with your father/ mother.
- What have been the best and worst times in your family?

Such probes or questions may be modified and expressed in appropriate language for the child, and fantasy-oriented procedures intermixed with direct inquiry.

There has been considerable debate over whether children should be asked for their preferences regarding custody and visitation. While many state laws explicitly make this one of the criteria for custody decisions, especially with children older than 10 or 12, most child development experts argue against this practice (see Franklin & Hibbs, 1980; Hodges, 1986). It is generally recognized that most children are quite conflicted over the divorce and related issues, and that it is unfair to coerce them into participating in the dissolution of their families. Many children will infer that if they express any preference they are then responsible for the outcome of the proceedings.

Even when children spontaneously express a preference for one parent or one type of custody and visitation, it is crucial to explore their motives. For example, as parents become focused on their conflict with one another, they may allow or even prompt their children to become increasingly undercontrolled. Under these circumstances the child might prefer the custody of the more *laissez faire* parent, though a firmer parental style might be more advantageous for them. Other motives for choosing one parent over another might include attempts to rescue the adult who seems more vulnerable. Such parent-child role reversal can be very destructive. Likewise, it is unfortunately not uncommon for one parent to try to persuade the children that the other does not care for them. Children in the midst of divorce, with their heightened susceptibility to fears of abandonment and rejection, may cling desperately to a parent who paints himself or herself as the only source of love and protection. Of course, the suitability of a parent who actively manipulates a child in this fashion is questionable. In many cases, the manipulation is subtle and unintended, but the effect on the child is similar.

Although many legal scholars assert that for children's preferences to be taken into account they should be expressed clearly in the court or at least in the judge's chambers, it is often possible to comply with the spirit of state custody laws without going to these extremes. Most statutes speak of the "wishes" of the child, which are often very apparent through interview techniques such as those described above and can be persuasively conveyed to the court without placing the child under undue pressure.

Important data regarding the children can also be collected from pediatricians, teachers, babysitters, and others who have significant contact with them. Pediatricians may be the single most valuable source of information if the child has been seen regularly. As they have worked with hundreds if not thousands of children over time, these physicians often have very pertinent observations regarding physical and psychological development, though the busy pace of their practices may limit observations of emotional and social processes. Of course, any medical problems and childhood illnesses should be noted, and any history of repeated, unexplained injuries that might suggest abuse should be thoroughtly evaluated. Teachers will have their own perspective on the child, often emphasizing cognitive development, peer relationships, and behavioral control. They are key contacts in gathering and interpreting school records. Finally, long-term babysitters or daycare workers may observe important trends in development and behavior, particularly in response to the acute stress of the divorce. While these individuals are often quite objective, it is wise to be sensitive to the possibility of an alliance with one parent that might derive from motivations other than concern for the child. As mentioned earlier, contacts with collateral sources such as these should be cleared with *both* parents in advance to avoid liability for breach of confidence.

The possibility of psychopathology must be considered, though it is important to differentiate between situational problems associated with the stress of divorce and parental conflict and more ingrained difficulties that are less likely to remit. Consequently, it may be best to take a long-term, developmental view in understanding behavioral problems or apparent emotional conflicts. If there are any indications of ongoing harm to the child, either unintentional or through abuse or neglect, these should be immediately communicated to the court so that some protective measures can be instituted. Only with a clear rationale and concrete recommendations will the court take action. If need for treatment or other intervention following the divorce is evident, this should be specifically recommended and also taken into account in discussing custody and visitation suggestions.

Once a thorough understanding of the child(ren) is developed, the therapist may focus on the parents. It is crucial that the evaluator be fair and equitable to each party, and that impartiality is clearly conveyed. Parents may generally be evaluated in the therapist's office in separate interviews. While most parents come primed to discuss the details of the divorce, it may help to break the ice by asking them to first recount the family's history, beginning with how the couple met, courted, and became married. Information on the early marital relationship may elucidate current dynamics between the parents. Also, families evolve through a series of developmental stages, and each parent may have his/her perspective on this process. The parents' perceptions of the family's life-cycle will reveal what aspects of family life they consider important, how they have participated in the family, and how they are likely to cope with the process of becoming a binuclear family.

Parents should also be asked to describe in detail the addition of children to the family. Key issues include whether pregnancies were planned and/or wanted, whether the parents agreed on this, and how important decisions about child-rearing have been made. A thorough account of each child's history, including developmental milestones, special events, accidents and illnesses, major achievements or crises, and important relationships, should

be elicited from each parent. In addition to clarifying the child's background, this information reveals how each parent understands the child,
what he/she views as significant, and how actively he/she has participated
in the children's upbringing. Even in families where one parent has been
primarily a homemaker while the other has served as breadwinner, the employed spouse may have remained actively involved in parental decision-
making and may be highly invested in the children.

It is often helpful to inquire about the structure of the family prior to
divorce. The following sorts of inquiries may serve as examples:

- What was the marital relationship like?
- How were the domestic responsibilities divided between the parents?
- How was discipline handled?
- Which family members were "close" to one another and why?
- What was the family climate like?
- How were problems resolved?
- How were emotions expressed and by whom?
- Did the family do things together or were the members relatively
  disengaged?

Answers to these questions may shed light on important dynamics and
alliances. While these may change somewhat after the divorce, they are
likely to continue in postdivorce relationships.

Each parent should be encouraged to explain perceptions of the most
recent phase in the family's developmental course, the causes of the divorce.
It is often crucial to know whether the motives for divorce were largely
focused on the parents (e.g., infidelity), on the children (e.g., how many to
have), or on other issues. While some have argued that "parents divorce each
other, not their kids," this may not always be accurate. It is important to
know how the separation was handled. Was it negotiated or unilateral? Did
one parent abandon the family, even briefly? Were adequate provisions
made for the children, or did one or both parents lose track of their needs?
Often, the character of the separation and divorce will provide clear indications of the quality of future interactions between the parents.

Parents in heated custody battles may make various allegations about one
another, which are difficult or impossible to verify or disprove. It is recommended that all complaints of domestic violence, improper sexual conduct,
child neglect, substance abuse, or other significant problem behavior be
taken seriously. Every effort should be made to gather data from independent sources to clarify these issues. Potential sources include police, witnesses, child protection and welfare services, family physicians, probation de-
partments, hospitals, insurance carriers, schools, neighbors, daycare

workers, and relatives. Biased sources may, of course, provide a prejudiced account. When solid collateral information is not available, the therapist has little choice but to note the allegations as unsubstantiated. Under no circumstances should a therapist report any simple allegation as fact; even with supporting documentation caution should be exercised.

Especially challenging is the evaluation of past problem behavior, particularly prior episodes of mental disorder and treatment, substance abuse, and criminal activity. When one or both parents have such a history, this must be taken into account but should not be viewed as an automatic disqualification for custody. Although traditionally courts used these as grounds to terminate parental relationships, increased attention to the constitutional rights of parents deriving from the 14th Amendment has reversed this trend, at least under certain conditions.

When a parent has a history of treatment for mental illness, the key issues are the nature of the disturbance, its effects on the children, and the likelihood of future episodes. Successful past treatment and readjustment should largely negate the importance of previous bouts of mental illness, and even when future episodes are likely these may not be given great weight. For example, courts have held that disordered parents who capitalize on periods of lucidity to make appropriate arrangements for a child's welfare during subsequent periods of incapacity may retain legal custody (see *Williams v. Mashburn*). The Supreme Court has ruled that clear and convincing evidence that a parent's disability (psychological disorder, mental retardation) has a detrimental effect on children must be produced before a state can alter the legal relationship (*Santosky v. Kramer*).

It is likely that similar logic would be applied to those with a history of substance abuse or criminal convictions. To the extent that these problems are clearly past, they may have no effect on the custody decision. On the other hand, if these are current complaints or there is a high likelihood of future recurrences, the effects of such activities on the children should be considered and conveyed to the court.

From a pragmatic point of view, a major focus in evaluating the parents is on parenting skills and attitudes toward child-rearing. These will inevitably be shaped by direct experiences in the parents' own families of origin. Their recollections of discipline, family values, problem-solving, and other characteristics are useful in understanding their own current values, especially if significant enmeshment in the family of origin is evident. Childhood experiences of divorce or domestic violence are relevant. If either parent played a significant role in caring for younger siblings, this may have shaped his/her skills and attitudes in raising children. Grisso (1987) reviews several formal methods of evaluating and interpreting child-rearing skills and attitudes.

While obviously important, the parents' expressed ideas about custody are often inadequately evaluated. Each parent deserves an opportunity to explain ideas or plans and the motives for these. Parents should be encouraged to identify potential difficulties. The ability to realistically anticipate problems and engage in thoughtful problem-solving is a sign of good potential to manage as a single parent.

Areas of potential compromise should be discussed, but it is especially useful to ask about areas where compromise is out of the question, and the reasons for this. Each parent should clarify how he would involve the other through visitation, shared custody, or other procedures, as courts often place emphasis on selecting the custodian most likely to promote a continuing relationship with the other parent. Parents may also be encouraged to express their fears or their anticipated reaction if things do not go their way. Therapists may take this opportunity to remind the principals that they still have a chance to negotiate a settlement. If the parents do show renewed interest in a self-determined custody arrangement, they should be encouraged to contact their attorneys. It is not advisable for the evaluator to try to switch roles and become a mediator, especially since that effort might fail and necessitate completion of the assessment.

A variety of logistical issues must also be considered. Often, both parents will need to work after the divorce. Plans for daycare should be addressed, possibly including a visit to the daycare center, daycare home, or relative's residence where the children would be placed. The geographic proximity of parents' homes may have some bearing on the feasibility of joint custody. Locations of schools and recreational facilities may even become important in planning details of visitation. Finally, each parent's work should be considered, including stability of employment. Those on "swing" shifts may be confronted with severe scheduling problems. If one or both parents work for companies that frequently transfer employees, joint custody and frequent visitation are likely to be short-lived. If the parents are willing and able to obtain other employment, these factors may be negated.

After individual sessions with children and parents, the therapist is prepared to observe parent-child interactions, again looking at both naturalistic and structured interactions. A visit to the home of each parent is recommended. These observations should focus on routine family activities and the quality of parent-child interactions. The therapist should expect considerable tension due to recognition by all family members that they are being evaluated.

Office visits may consist of both unstructured play time and more structured tasks such as planning a family outing or negotiating family rules or policies. During this phase the examiner should begin to formulate a structural model describing the interactions of all the individuals previously assessed. Important dynamics or structural problems should be identified, with particular reference to how these factors will evolve through the divorce.

Often children have significant relationships with adults other than their parents. Relatives, such as aunts and uncles or grandparents, may play significant roles as caretakers, and it is common for these roles to expand after a divorce. The availability of extended family support may be a significant factor in the adjustment of both adults and children following divorce. Divorcing parents may also rely upon close friends or lovers. Whenever a parent is involved in a significant romantic relationship, particularly if the children are aware of it, then the potential contributions or liabilities of this third party should also be addressed. This is especially true if there are any indications that the paramour is a "spouse in waiting." Negotiating to evaluate a parent's boyfriend or girlfriend can be very sensitive, especially if infidelity is the cause of the divorce.

It is often helpful to simply ask each parent to make a list of family members and close associates who will have continuing contact with or responsibilities for the children, and to arrange a single meeting of all of these individuals. If necessary, separate interviews with a significant collateral figure and one or more children may be arranged. For example, if a mother would rely upon her own parent for daycare during working hours, then the compatibility of the child and grandparent should be assessed. The quality of this relationship would have a strong bearing on the suitability of giving primary custody to that parent.

To review briefly, the following procedures are generally useful in conducting custody evaluations:

(1) Observation, interview, and assessment of children, individually and collectively.
(2) Collection of information from pediatricians, teachers, daycare facilities, neighbors, and others.
(3) Interview and assessment of parents individually.
(4) Observation and assessment of each parent with children.
(5) Interview of each parent with various significant others.
(6) Collection of any other information which appears important given the needs of the children.

Obviously, such a thorough evaluation can require dozens of hours of professional time and may cost several thousand dollars. If done by an individual clinician the series of interviews and visits alone may take several weeks. For this reason complex evaluations are often done by a team of several experts working together. Because these evaluations may be prohibitively costly, many potential clients may attempt to negotiate a less comprehensive undertaking. Therapists should be receptive to these requests; however, it is important to remember that the welfare of one or more children may be influenced by any inadequacies in the evaluation. The therapist must be prepared to decline the case if the quality of the evaluation would be jeopardized.

Formulating Recommendations

There are really two consumers of the resulting recommendations: the family or juvenile court, and the divorcing parents. To this point the parents may have been unable to resolve their differences regarding custody, but with feedback from the evaluator they may be able to agree on an appropriate compromise without the tremendous financial and emotional costs of a custody trial. Many authorities advocate a post-evaluation meeting with the parents for this reason, though the potential for acrimony is great.

If the custody dispute continues and a report to the court must be prepared, the evaluator must translate the findings into workable information for the court. The report should be concise, free of jargon, and clearly focused on the question at hand. Often, the report can be structured according to the logical progression of steps in the evaluation, first explaining the children and their developmental progress and needs, followed by the parents' individual characteristics, and finally focusing on the quality of relationships within the family. The factors identified as central to the welfare of these specific children should be made explicit, along with supporting documentation. Any subsequent recommendations should be expressly tied to these factors.

Some courts prefer to receive the opinions of experts in child custody without specific recommendations. Others prefer to receive suggestions on custody, visitation, and related matters. The examiner should expect that courts will make every effort to allow shared custody or regular visitation, and that biological parents will be strongly favored over stepparents or other caretakers. Still, if a nontraditional decree is believed to be in the best interests of the children, then it should be recommended (Goldstein, Freud, Solnit, & Goldstein, 1986). If postdivorce family or individual treatment would seem to be beneficial, this should be clearly recommended.

Special care should be taken in addressing sensitive issues. While it is inappropriate to withhold information from the court, delicate matters that may add little other than embarrassment of one of the parties should generally be excluded from a formal report. Likewise, diagnostic labels, test scores, and other information not directly useful to the court should be translated into sensible everyday language. Particular care is in order in protecting the privacy and sensitivities of the children involved. It is inappropriate to report information or testify in a way that will victimize the children.

For more information on the general style of expert witness contributions through deposition or testimony, see Chapter 8.

What Factors are Considered in Divorce Custody?

Goldzband (1982, p. 30) has noted that "Judges have inherited the impossible task of dispensing the Wisdom of Solomon in custody cases, and few have it. This is no slap at judges; no one seems to have such divinely inspired guidance these days." It is wise for the mental health expert involved in a custody evaluation to remember that professional opinions in this area are difficult to buttress with any empirical research. Training, experience, and logic must often suffice in guiding a choice among many less than satisfactory alternatives. Perhaps most distressing, no matter how well-developed the proposed custody resolution, it is likely that the divorce will have a significant negative impact on the children, at least in the short run.

Many child development experts note the discrepant philosophical assumptions of the legal and therapeutic professions and view judges and lawyers as adversaries in the custody process. Much as parents are encouraged to set aside their differences when dealing with their children, therapists should be encouraged to develop a working alliance with family courts to seek the best interests of children. While it is important to maintain the integrity of professional role boundaries (Goldstein, Freud, Solnit, & Goldstein, 1986), beneficial cooperation is possible.

It is interesting to examine the factors that judges, family court administrators, and lawyers, on the one hand, and therapists such as psychologists and social workers, on the other, consider important in making custody determinations. Lowery (1981, 1985) has conducted a series of surveys to address this issue. Table 6.1, adapted from these reports, presents the rank order importance of 20 different considerations for each professional group. The similarities and differences in relative values of these factors are revealing. Both legal and therapeutic professionals appear to value responsibility, emotional stability, and simple bonds of affection highly. Therapists also focus on factors such as the "quality" of parent-child relationships and parenting skills. Judges place less emphasis on these considerations and instead look to issues such as biological relationships, "moral character," and the physical health of the parties. Still, the high degree of overlap indicates considerable agreement about the priorities in custody determinations.

TABLE 6.1
Legal and Therapeutic Factors in Custody Determinations

Legal	Rank	Therapeutic
Mental stability of each parent	1	Quality of the parent-child relationship
Each parent's sense of responsibility to the child	2	Each parent's sense of responsibility to the child
Biological relationship to child (vs. stepparent)	3	Mental stability of each parent
Each parent's moral character	4	Parenting skills
Each parent's ability to provide stable community involvement	5	Amount of contact with the child by custodial parent
Each parent's affection for child	6	Each parent's affection for child
Keeping the child with siblings	7	Parents' wishes (if they agree)
Each parent's ability to provide access to schools	8	Maintaining sibling relationships
Keeping a young child with mother	9	Parent's moral character
Physical health of each parent	10	Stable community involvement
Parents' wishes (if they agree)	11	The child's wishes
Professional advice	12	Access to schools
Biological parent over adoptive	13	Professional recommendations
Each parent's financial sufficiency	14	Relationship with ex-spouse
The child's wishes	15	Amount of contact with the child by the noncustodial parent
Length of time each parent has had custody	16	Parent's physical health
Parent's ability to provide contact with other relatives	17	Parent's financial sufficiency
Access to child's peers/agemates	18	Access to peers/agemates
Each parent's ability or intention to provide a two-parent home	19	Length of temporary custody
Placing child with same-sex parent	20	Potential for child's contact with other relatives

CHILD ABUSE AND NEGLECT

Child abuse and neglect are frighteningly pervasive in our society. There are between one and two million complaints or reports of abuse per year in the United States (U.S. Study on Child Abuse and Neglect, 1981), and knowledgeable estimates place the actual incidence at more than three million. Approximately 4 percent of the children in this country suffer significant injuries at the hands of adults each year (Heins, 1984); perhaps two-thirds of these children are under two years of age. The problem of sexual abuse and exploitation is more difficult to measure (Goldstein, Keller, & Erne, 1986). Over half of the reports that are made and subsequently investigated cannot be substantiated (Besharov, 1986; Schuman, 1986) indicating the difficulty of verifying these sensitive allegations, as well as a considerable number of groundless reports. (Also see Chapter 12.)

For decades, child abuse was essentially ignored by the legal community. Initial efforts to gain legal redress were undertaken by the Society for the Prevention of Cruelty to Animals, under statutes designed to prevent abuse of animals. Maloney (1985) describes the increase of interest in abuse as pediatricians in the 1940s and '50s began to document the shocking frequency of serious injury by parents. In 1963, the United States Children's Bureau proposed a model statute detailing child abuse as a legal problem distinct from general criminal and civil wrongs. At that time no state required the reporting of abuse by professionals or citizens; now all states have some type of abuse-reporting requirement.

Child abuse is defined and controlled on a state-by-state basis. Many laws are extremely vague; generally, however, abuse is defined as the voluntary or intentional application of force in a manner resulting in injury to a child. Many states also forbid child neglect, generally defined as failure to provide adequate food, shelter, clothing, medical care, education, support, or supervision. Generally, before the state can allege neglect an adult must occupy some recognized relationship (almost always parental) to a child where an appropriate level of care is expected. Several states have also developed statutes which address the concept of psychological abuse or emotional neglect (Shapiro, 1984). These laws usually speak of causing emotional distress or psychological harm or of failing to provide for the emotional, moral, or psychological development of the child. The majority of these laws are extremely vague and some have been successfully challenged as too broad an intrusion on constitutionally protected parental rights (see *Wisconsin v. Yoder* and also *Bothman v. Warren B.*).

In reality, social service agencies, child welfare services, and courts exercise considerable leeway in enforcing child abuse laws. Since corporal punishment is overwhelmingly approved and employed by parents in America, most agencies are reluctant to pursue any allegations unless they involve significant harm. Some child development researchers have reported that as many as two-thirds of American children are the targets of "parental violence" each year, a finding which calls into question the definition of violence (Strauss, Gelles, & Steinmetz, 1980). Though the majority of therapists may oppose corporal punishment, it is unlikely that society at large or the legal system will accept the idea that most parents are abusive. Ultimately, the line between corporal punishment and abuse becomes difficult to draw. Similarly, neglect may be hard to specify, especially when parents justify their actions on the basis of religious or political beliefs. Given that all sexual contact with children is widely disapproved, it is at least easier to agree on what behaviors should elicit formal intervention.

Allegations of abuse and neglect are typically reported to a designated public welfare agency for investigation. Most jurisdictions have established a specific child protective service to respond to these complaints. If the allegation concerns sexual exploitation or serious injuries, then criminal charges may be filed. The police are often involved in the investigation. Some communities have developed special joint task forces with trained representatives of police, welfare, and prosecutor's offices working together to smooth the investigative process. On the rationale that it is in the child's long-range interests and the interests of society to punish the offender, investigations typically focus on validating the allegation and taking action against the perpetrator. Ideally, there is also an emphasis on identifying the needs of the child victim and planning for future therapeutic efforts.

When allegations arise, child protective services must normally make an initial assessment to determine if the child is safe from further harm. If not, as when allegations are against parents, the child or children may be placed in foster care until the legal proceedings are completed. In reality, few cases lead to such extreme measures, and most are dropped after preliminary investigation. If evidence of significant abuse is adduced, then the juvenile court (which usually hears such cases) may have considerable discretion in resolving the situation. Often court-ordered treatment is pursued, with close supervision by protective services. Unfortunately, research indicates that recidivism is high and that treatment for abusive adults is extremely costly and time-consuming (Goldstein, Keller, & Erne, 1986).

In extreme cases involving severe abuse or neglect by parents, the state may seek termination of parental rights. In these cases a state attorney or a prosecutor seeks to prove that the likelihood of future harm to the children justifies making them wards of the state. If there is proof beyond a reasonable doubt that the children are neglected or subject to harm within the state's definition, then the legal bond between the children and their parents is severed. Such children are placed in foster care until adoption can be facilitated. Some authors have been critical of the informal handling of many parental abuse cases, particularly in view of the poor prognosis for change, and have argued for much more aggressive use of legal termination (see, for example, Williams, 1983).

Investigation of Abuse Allegations

Most investigations of abuse are traumatic for children, and if the case ultimately goes to trial, that may actually be more traumatic than the abuse itself. Unfortunately, many jurisdictions do little to protect children from an overly intrusive investigation process conducted by numerous representatives from various agencies. These individuals, strangers to the child, may approach him/her at home or at school, take him/her to their offices or even to a police station, and proceed to question him/her in detail. It matters little whether the allegations are true or not — insistent questioning and demands that the child "tell the truth" are punishing. Often the allegations concern a parent or other relative for whom the child cares. While the child may be frightened or confused or hurt by this adult's actions, it is common for the child to want to continue the relationship. Subtle or overt threats about what should be done to the perpetrator place the child in an impossible bind. It is common for children to seem confused, reticent, or contradictory in their reports under these conditions. Parents who resist excessive intervention are often threatened with legal action or made to feel like accessories to the abuse. In short, it is often clear that child protective services are more interested in a prosecutorial than therapeutic role. An unintended consequence of aggressive investigation may be that it reduces the utility of any information the child does provide.

Therapists, often brought into the picture after the investigation of abuse or sexual exploitation is underway, may be asked to fill one of two roles. The first is as a consultant in the investigation who evaluates the child to assess the likelihood that the allegations are true. At present there are strident disagreements about the appropriateness of this role.

Therapists may also be contacted to provide therapeutic services to children who may have been abused. If so, it is important to clearly define this role as outside the investigation itself. Becoming enmeshed in the investigation inevitably compromises the confidentiality and integrity of the therapy relationship.

The therapeutic community widely accepts the notion that children do not lie about abuse, particularly sexual abuse, and that evaluation by a therapist is a reliable way to "validate" abuse allegations (Sgroi, 1982). Others have argued that while children do not lie, they may be coached or pressured into statements consistent with the alleged abuse so that high-pressure investigations may actually lead to inaccurate assessment of children (Underwager et al., 1986). Finally, others have objected to therapist participation on ethical grounds, as it conflicts with therapeutic considerations and may serve the courts or welfare agencies rather than the child.

If therapists do participate in an investigation, particularly if they may testify at trial, then they should recognize that this may prevent them from helping the child in a significant way. It is probably wisest to make completely separate arrangements for therapy if this is indicated, and to protect the child's therapist from any direct involvement in civil or criminal proceedings.

In assessing the child it is important to remain free of any preconceptions or biases. For this reason it may be best to gather as little background information as possible prior to the evaluation. The examiner must recognize that the child is inevitably under terrific pressure, and should endeavor not to compound the excessive demands already placed on the potential victim. It is important to establish rapport and reduce the child's anxiety; spreading the evaluation out over several short periods may help in this regard, although care should be taken not to establish inappropriate expectations for future contact. The interviewer should refrain from directive questioning and should never badger the child. What the child reports needs to be placed within the context of his or her cognitive development. If legal proceedings are anticipated, then it is wise to record the interviews. Finally, the examiner should gather and interpret supporting information, including medical examinations where appropriate.

To date there are no clear data to guide the examiner in inferring that abuse has taken place in the absence of clear statements by the child victim. It is often suggested that indications of acute emotional distress and anxiety are indicators, but often the investigation itself is sufficiently stressful to produce this effect. Clinical wisdom suggests that when children do verbally confirm allegations, they are genuine. False allegations generally involve clear manipulation by adults, such as by a vindictive divorced parent attempting to "get even" with the ex-spouse. Other false reports may be made by adolescents who are having significant behavioral problems.

Child Abuse Reporting Laws

All states have laws designed to encourage reporting of abuse and neglect. Most simply require that any "reasonable suspicion" should be reported, and that proof need not be immediately available. Most states also protect those who report in good faith from liability when the allegations turn out to be unfounded. States vary as to who is covered by these laws. Some, such as Kentucky, require that any adult citizen with a reasonable suspicion must report. Others only impose this duty on doctors, therapists, and other professionals. Psychotherapists are obligated by law to report in every state, and usual therapist-patient confidentiality does not apply. That is, even when a parent enters therapy and reveals that he or she is seeking help because of abusive behavior, the therapist must make a report, even though it may be counterproductive.

This places therapists in an ethical bind. Arguably, what is best for the child and parent will be sacrificed to comply with the law. Many therapists have argued that a therapist-offender privilege should be created, such that those who are trying to help themselves and actively participate in treatment would not have to be reported (see Coleman, 1986; Newberger, 1983; Smith & Meyer, 1984). To date these suggestions have not been heeded. Therapists who have stood on principle for therapist-patient privilege have been arrested and incarcerated for failure to report. More troubling, therapists who determined that parents were not abusive have been disciplined by courts that did not agree with them (Denton, 1987). At present, therapists must be willing to report their patient's abusive behaviors or go to jail. If therapists choose to report, they should also volunteer to intercede in any way possible for their client, and be prepared to advocate for continued treatment in lieu of other sanctions. Obviously, there is need for professional advocacy and change in state laws.

ADOPTION AND GUARDIANSHIP

Adoption is a legal procedure which terminates one parent-child relationship and creates a new one. Most adults are technically eligible to apply for adoption, yet some are effectively excluded by policies of specific agencies. As most adoptions are either processed or supervised through an agency, there is little uniformity regarding qualifications. Consequently, knowledge of local practices is important when counseling potential adoptive parents.

Adoption is usually sought by childless couples or by the spouse of a biological parent who wishes to formalize the legal relationship with a stepchild. There are three basic alternatives for childless persons who want to adopt — application to a public welfare agency, application to a state-licensed private agency, or seeking a private, "arranged" adoption. Private adoptions are not legal in all jurisdictions. Stepparents wanting to adopt their spouse's children need only proceed with the necessary legal steps to complete the adoption. Regardless of the circumstances, adoption culminates in the child's being treated legally as if he had been born to the adoptive parents in marriage. Note, however, that in some jurisdictions the child may retain rights to inheritance from the natural family.

Adoption typically requires the following: (1) consent of the birth parents or guardians, (2) consent of the child if over 12 to 14 years of age, (3) an investigation by the placing agency to assure the suitability of the prospective home, (4) a trial period with the adoptee in the adoptive home under appropriate supervision, (5) issuance of a final decree, withheld pending evidence of satisfactory adjustment of the adoptive parents and child to one another, and (6) secrecy of the legal proceeding and provisions for alteration of the child's birth certificate. It is important to note that children who are wards of the state may be adopted without consent of the biological parents. This means that orphans, whose parents obviously cannot consent, may be adopted. When children of abusive or neglectful parents are made wards of the state through termination of parental rights, they may also be adopted without the birth parents' consent; the agreement of the state suffices as parental consent.

A private or independent adoption takes place without the intervention of an agency, although often with the assistance of a professional intermediary such as a physician, an attorney, or both. Independent placements often come under scrutiny because of concern regarding kidnapping and trafficking in "stolen" children. In legitimate private adoptions the biological mother selects the parents and offers her child to them. The intermediary's function is to arrange meetings between the respective parties. Usually, there is no financial consideration given to the mother beyond the reasonable expenses allowed by the court. Adopting parents ordinarily pay for medical expenses, legal fees, and court costs. Some jurisdictions allow reimbursement for the birth mother's living expenses during the prenatal and recovery periods, but it is flatly illegal to buy children. Recent surrogate parenting arrangements strain the distinction between legitimate reimbursement and child peddling.

An issue which may involve therapists grows out of the traditional secrecy of adoption records. During the 1970s adoptees organized and began to assert a "right to know" the truth about their birthparents, their genetic background, and the circumstances of their adoption. Many states now permit adult adoptees to have limited access to their records, though only upon a showing of good cause. Both biological and adoptive parents have a legitimate interest in preserving the confidentiality of relevant information, but increasingly courts have recognized a "right to know" about one's own history. States which permit release of information usually attempt to minimize any adverse effects on the parties involved.

Traditionally, it has been very difficult to place children who have special needs, despite an overall shortage of eligible children. Most couples seek to adopt a baby free of any potential problems, yet many children eligible for adoption are no longer babies and not all are without special needs or physical or emotional problems. Often, these children have become wards of the state through abandonment or termination of parental rights, as described earlier. For this reason, many couples seeking to adopt apply to private rather than state agencies. Because there are so many children with special needs waiting to be adopted, most states now subsidize adoptions to help defray the costs of raising a child with special needs. In addition to state financial assistance, federal and state income tax laws permit deductions by parents who have adopted such children.

Guardianship

In many respects, guardianship is similar to adoption, except that the arrangement is much less binding and may be viewed as temporary. Whereas adoption simulates a parent-child relationship by birth, a child's guardian is explicitly a stand-in for natural caretakers. Also, guardians need not assume all functions of parenthood, but can take on only those responsibilities for which the child is in need of adult guidance or supervision. Children who are wards of the state often have formal legal guardians who are representatives of a state welfare agency. This arrangement allows the designated adult to make important decisions for the child's medical care, education, residence, and other issues when there is no legally recognized parent to be responsible. If the child is eventually adopted, this arrangement is superfluous and is dissolved.

CHAPTER 7

Personal Injury

"That's crazy," The Bad Czech said. "Dogs ain't got brains like that."
"He [Ludwig-K-9 Core Dog] wouldn't have a single beer tonight," Hans
said.
"I tell you he *knows*. He saw Gertie all busted up and covered with
blood, and he knows his pal's gone for good."
"I don't doubt nothin no more," Cecil Higgins said. "You tell me Ludwig
knows, I believe it. You tell me Ludwig wants a stress pension, I believe
it. I don't know what's real and what ain't real no more."

— Joseph Wambaugh, *The Delta Star*, p. 135

THERE IS ENORMOUS variation among personal injury suits. However, the
following case demonstrates many of the issues that commonly arise.

Charles left a party at a friend's house at about 11 p.m. He had had a few
drinks but certainly did not appear to be drunk. Driving home, he passed a
cluster of movie theatres, just as most of the patrons were leaving and
walking toward their cars. Some teenagers bolted across the thoroughfare in
front of his car. Somehow Charles lost control of his car and veered into a
car parked at the curb. A man and his 13-year-old son and 11-year-old
daughter were in the car. The father was severely injured, and died later that
night at the hospital. The son sustained a number of injuries, including a
badly broken arm and a concussion. The daughter was unharmed except for
a cut across her cheek and mild whiplash.

Charles' case brings up many of the types of questions that courts must
deal with in personal injury cases, as, for example:

(1) Is Charles' liability reduced by the illegal actions of the teenagers in
bolting in front of his car?

(2) Is his liability shared by his friends who served him the alcohol and let him drive home?

(3) Could Charles in any way be reasonably construed as an alcoholic, and how would that status affect his liability?

(4) How much long-term damage will the son's head injury produce?

(5) How much redress should the daughter have for any long-term emotional upset over the scar on her face?

(6) How much redress should either the son or daughter have for witnessing the terrible injuries to the father that led to his death? Would the son have less claim because he had been unconscious, and then very disoriented, until after the father had been taken away in an ambulance?

(7) Does the mother have any claim for emotional upset from the loss of her husband and injuries to her children, even though she was not even a remote witness to the accident itself?

Much of the testimony about possible damage from a personal injury incident (PII) will be provided by medical experts, engineering experts, and the like. However, psychotherapists can become involved in personal injury litigation in several ways. In an automobile accident such as Charles', the psychotherapist's testimony about the plaintiff's mental status before and after the accident or personal injury incident (PII), as well as the victim's degree of psychological recovery (and potential recovery), is important evidence for the court. A second avenue for involvement occurs when a person who is affected in some fashion by a personal injury incident (PII) is referred to a psychotherapist to help heal the emotional damage. Eventually, that psychotherapist likely will have to produce a report or even testimony about the patient's progress for the court. In a third and less common situation, a psychotherapist may be referred a person who has caused a PII, to help heal the trauma and guilt about causing the injury.

Personal injury litigation generally involves attempts to provide proof that a person has suffered harm or loss as a result of another person or entity's action or negligence. An issue encountered frequently by psychotherapists is that of chronic pain (Aronoff, 1986; Grote, Kaler, & Meyer, 1986). Courts often ask psychotherapists to determine whether the client's pain is a result of the PII, how dysfunctional psychologically the client is and will be from the pain, and whether the person is truly suffering the pain or is only imagining or deliberately faking it. (Also see Chapter 11.)

As Weissman (1985) notes, psychotherapists who are called upon to testify in personal injury cases usually will be asked to speak to the following elements:

(a) the extent to which the accident or exposure constituted a substantial factor in causing a new disorder or in aggravating or accelerating a pre-existing disorder.

(b) whether a disorder would have occurred at all but for the instant event(s), traumatic or cumulative.

(c) the relative contributions to the presented disorder of proximate, pre-existing, and co-existing factors.

(d) the extent to which a pre-existing disorder in its natural progression or evolutionary course would have resulted in the observed impairments, in the absence of the instant event.

(e) whether motivational factors associated with malingering, convenient focus, and secondary gain are present.

(f) whether a factitious disorder is present, where psychological symptoms are being voluntarily produced and presented (as in malingering), but where the goal is to assume the "patient role." (pp. 138–139)

LEGAL ISSUES IN PERSONAL INJURY CASES

Personal injury claims typically occur within the parameters of tort law, which falls within civil, rather than criminal, law. *Tort*, derived from the Norman word for "wrong," refers to intentional or negligent wrongs to another person for which the person may be liable. Rather than implying some sort of moral judgment, tort law is intended to distribute the results of frequently occurring risks in accordance with social policy. As Stromberg (1987, p. 3) describes it:

> The basic rule of Tort law is that you may recover money damages from someone if they violate ("breach") a "duty of reasonable care" which they owe to you, and that breach is the immediate ("proximate") cause of provable injury to you (including discomfort), and you are not also partly ("contributorily") negligent, and the other party is not immune from suit for some reason. (p. 3)

A wide range of civil wrongs can be conceptualized as torts, including false imprisonment, invasion of privacy, sexual harassment, malpractice, product liability, defamation that results in personal injury of some sort, and intentional or negligent infliction of emotional trauma. The basic elements typically include (a) negligence, (b) duty, (c) proximate cause, and (d) damages.

The Impact Rule

While psychotherapists are aware of the likelihood of psychological damage resulting from a PII, whether or not there is actual physical trauma, it was not until 1773 that English law first explicitly recognized pain and suffering (Kerns & Turk, 1984). Indeed, the prevailing legal view up and into the nineteenth century was that emotional suffering or psychogenic pain from a PII was not appropriate for evaluation or commentary, let alone remedy. This is probably most clearly seen in the 1861 case of *Lynch v. Knight*, in which that court stated, "Mental pain or anxiety the law cannot value, and does not pretend to redress, when the unlawful act complained of causes that alone." So, the basic concept at that time was that, in order to allow redress for emotional trauma, that trauma had to be directly related to evident physical disorder which was in turn a direct result of the "impact" in the PII. Following this rule, the girl injured in Charles' accident would be allowed no redress for any emotional upset over the scar on her face. An English case of that era, *Victorian Railways Commission v. Coultas* (1888), probably best summarizes the reasons why nineteenth century courts were loathe to recognize such damages, citing (1) a lack of legal precedent, (2) the possibility of fictitious lawsuits, (3) the difficulties of tying emotional distress to a physical event, and (4) the danger of a huge flood of litigation if precedents were overturned and emotional damage was recognized. Courts still warn of many of these problems, and reasonably so. Yet, as psychotherapists are so well aware, emotional trauma and pain are very real and hence warrant redress.

Interestingly enough, while English courts rather quickly abandoned the "impact rule," two years later, in the case of *Bell v. Great Northern Railway Company*, American courts embraced the impact rule. Then, two years after Bell, in 1892, the court in *Ewing v. Pittsburgh Railroad Co.* further supported the impact rule as a liability-limiting concept by stating, "If mere fright, unaccompanied with bodily injury is a cause of action, the scope of what are known as accident cases will be greatly enlarged." They were, of course, correct in this prophecy.

Although there were continuing exceptions to the impact rule, it became the dominant legal concept for many years. The absurdity of the impact rule was probably best demonstrated in the case of *Jones v. Brooklyn Heights Railroad*. The defendant in that case alleged that a miscarriage occurred because of being in an automobile wreck with a train. Even though there was no true physical injury from the accident, the plaintiff was eventually allowed to recover simply on the basis that a small light bulb had fallen from the roof of the defendant's automobile when hit by the train and hit the plaintiff on the head.

The Zone of Danger Rule

Until the last decade or so, the concept under which a litigant was permitted to recover damages for psychological harm was the fear that the person felt for his or her own safety because of being in the "zone of danger" that was generated by the defendant's negligence or malice. The zone of danger approach had its roots in *Palsgraf v. Long Island Railroad* (1928), in which the judge articulated his "orbit of danger" idea. Under this concept, a person could recover damages as a witness to a trauma to a close relative, though the victim actually had to be within a range where he or she could have been injured also. For example, in a later case, *Waube v. Warrington* (1972), in which a woman witnessed the death of her child when the child was struck by an automobile, the mother was not allowed to recover because she was observing this from a window in her house.

In a critical case in the development of the "zone of danger" rule, the plaintiff in *Dillon v. Legg* witnessed her daughter being struck and killed by a car as the daughter crossed at an intersection. Interestingly enough, the dead girl's sister was with the mother but a few yards closer to the actual point of impact. Following precedents, a lower court in California permitted the surviving daughter to recover for damages, asserting she was in the "zone of danger," while dismissing the mother's claim.

The clear set of facts in *Dillon* then allowed the California Supreme Court, when reinstating the mother's claim, an opportunity to point to the rather absurd artificiality of the zone of danger rule by stating:

> We can hardly justify relief to the sister for trauma which she suffered upon apprehension of the child's death and yet deny it to the mother merely because of a happenstance that the sister was some few yards closer to the accident.

The *Dillon* court generated three criteria that helped to clarify the zone of liability: (1) The plaintiff must have a close relationship with the victim; (2) the plaintiff must be in close proximity to the scene of the accident; and (3) the emotional shock has to be the "sensory and contemporaneous result" of the incident.

Modern Issues

In the several states, there have been many and varied interpretations springing from *Dillon*. A major question that continues is: What is a "close relationship"? Certainly mother-child or brother-sister would qualify. But what about stepfather-stepdaughter, good friends, tennis partners? In *Leong v. Takasaki*, upon an appeal, a 10-year-old boy who saw his step-grandmother struck and killed by an automobile was allowed to recover for psychological injuries and nervous shock by order of the Hawaiian Supreme Court. Many states, however, would not find this a compelling relationship, and some states do not even accept the zone of danger or liability concept. Yet, the trend is clearly reflected in a 1984 New York case of *Bovsun v.*

Sanperi, in which the court held, by a slim margin, that a plaintiff may collect, when (1) the defendant's negligence has generated an unreasonable risk of bodily harm to the plaintiff, and (2) the plaintiff suffers emotional trauma from directly observing death or serious physical injury to an immediate family member.

A variation that has developed since the 1960s is the adoption of a rule that a person can recover for emotional trauma if it were "foreseeable" that he or she could later suffer some form of damage or would later be a witness to harm to a close loved one by watching an injury to that loved one. For example, one federal appeals court held that workers who had long been exposed to asbestos could recover for psychological fear of getting cancer, even though they showed no current physical evidence of cancer, if they could show a "reasonable medical probability of future harm" (Stromberg, 1987).

Thus, the trend is toward recognizing that there can be emotional harm without necessarily either an actual physical injury or a direct observation of the event. For example, in *Molien v. Kaiser Foundation Hospital,* a husband successfully sued a physician who had negligently misdiagnosed his wife's condition as syphilis, leading to marital upset and eventual divorce. While there was no physical harm to anyone involved and while there was no direct observation of the relevant situation as it occurred, the court recognized a right to gain compensation because of psychological distress.

CONTROLLING EXCESSIVE SETTLEMENTS

Concerns about excessive settlements if awards were to be allowed for psychological injury alone are not restricted to nineteenth century commentators. For example, Blinder (1977, pp. 934–960) notes:

> Psychiatric claims seem only to arise when there is someone other than the claimant at fault or at least able to assume financial responsibility for the effects of the injury. By contrast, the number of claims of psychiatric disability following trauma consequent to an athletic injury or to the plaintiff's drunkenly driving his own car into a tree are infinitesimally small.

Blinder also expresses disquiet about the effects of compensation for such claims:

> . . . "traumatic neurosis," "functional overlay," . . . in some jurisdictions . . . account for fully 15 percent of successful claims — and their number continues to grow. . . . [These claims] are difficult to define, no less defend against, resulting in intolerable financial burdens for compensation funds, employers and carriers alike, substantially higher costs to the consumer, and ultimately, loss of coverage.

In response to such concerns, Burley (1982) argues that courts should consider five factors before compensating the deserving to avoid creating potentially unlimited liability. First, the court should look to the factual relationship of the victim and plaintiff, as opposed to their legal relationship. This would compensate plaintiffs who had a close relationship with the victim that was not legally recognized, such as a couple who had been living together for a period of years.

Next, Burley would require that the plaintiff observe the act which caused the injury or the results of the act before the victim is moved. This approach focuses on the shock of the observation, as opposed to the shock of learning of the injury, which he presumes to be milder and perhaps more difficult to prove. In the same vein, Burley would require that the plaintiff appreciate the severity of the injury at the time of the observation.

Finally, in order to prevent unwarranted claims, Burley suggests that the plaintiff show that the emotional distress was in fact caused by the observance and that the emotional distress was severe.

Another effective method of limiting recovery is to impose a higher burden of proof on the plaintiff (O'Connell & Carpenter, 1983). Normally, in civil cases the burden of proof required is only that of preponderance of evidence. However, certain jurisdictions have moved toward the more stringent "clear and convincing" standard for emotional distress claims. It is thought that the clear and convincing standard requires of expert witnesses more consistency and credibility in their testimony.

One reason why contemporary juries may find the concept of providing redress for emotional trauma more acceptable is because in recent times there has been more allowance for expressing such disorder, whereas in decades past it was considered unseemly or weak to verbalize such concerns. Psychotherapists may help not only by validating and clarifying the existence of these issues, but also by articulating various components of the defendant's situation, e.g., describing a sense of fright, as well as certain physical symptoms such as chest pain, nausea, headaches, and fatigue. The jury is then better able to relate to these symptoms and sense the reality of the emotional trauma.

EVIDENCE ON LONG-TERM EFFECTS

There is now more research evidence available to jurors and the courts that emotional accompaniments to a PII can have long-ranging and altering effects on the personality of the individual (Krupnick & Horowitz, 1981; Meyer & Salmon, 1988; Steketee & Foa, 1987). A follow-up study of children victimized by vicious dog attacks found that they later had personality styles characterized by overcaution, constriction of thought, inhibition of action, and impairment in the ability to experience gratification (Gislason & Call, 1982). Reflecting the early theory and observations put forth by Kardiner (1941), a later analysis of victims suffering from emotional shock showed that they feared noises and the dark and had marked difficulty in concentration and falling asleep. These problems commonly lingered years after the provoking incident (Ben-Eli & Sela, 1980). As with chronic pain, the emotional reaction to the trauma can become a vital part of the personality (Aronoff, 1986). The individual's reactions become self-reinforcing, despite their inappropriateness.

In addition, many jurors can empathize with the detrimental effects on the family. Children of parents who suffered psychological trauma will in turn be less likely to develop healthy personalities (Davidson, 1980; Steketee & Foa, 1987). These stressed children are also at risk to develop ulcers (Wessel & McCullough, 1982) or even to be afflicted with psychosomatic symptoms that resemble the malady that killed the parent (Kolevzon & Green, 1985; Lehmkul, 1982). When it is stressed by the serious injury of one of its members, the family, in general, is subject to breakdown, and its members have an increased risk of heart disease (Jenkins & Zyzanski, 1980), and a wide variety of infectious diseases (Frederick, 1982–83). Thus, the PII is not a static event. Psychotherapists can help jurors become aware of and sensitive to the PII's catalytic effect, as well as the ramifications that the injury has on the victim's social network (Aldrich, 1987).

PRIOR STATUS OF THE VICTIM

Psychotherapists who testify in personal injury cases always have to contend with the issue of prior status (Singer & Kolligan, 1987). If an individual claims emotional damage, the opposing attorney is likely to attempt to indicate that there was already some preexisting emotional disorder. For some jurors, simply hearing that the plaintiff had once seen a mental health professional for therapy strongly supports this contention. Psychotherapists have to be prepared to explain that therapy does not necessarily indicate any significant emotional disorder, but rather may be a response to situational distress or may even be an attempt to "grow beyond the average" in certain areas. Courts, as well as jurors, vary markedly as to how they accept data about preexisting status. On the one hand, there is the concept of "take the body as you find it." This means that even if a person is predisposed toward emotional trauma, the defendant who generates the incident that pushes the person over the edge is responsible for all of the accumulated trauma. On the other hand is the "thin skull" doctrine, which suggests that, if there is clear evidence of a preexisting condition, that should limit compensation in a substantial way. The relevant law varies from state to state, yet it often is the jurors' perception of the issue rather than the law itself that determines the settlement. While jurors are inclined more toward the "take the body as you find it" doctrine when there is physical injury, they appear more inclined toward the "thin skull" doctrine with emotional injury. Overall, experience has shown that if there is some evidence of preexisting emotional disorder, juries are much more reluctant to allow recovery of any significant amount (Grote et al., 1986; Weissman, 1985).

Two other important factors are, first of all, the degree to which the person's body was injured, disfigured, or subjected to pain. The more extreme each of these conditions is, the more likely the person is to suffer eventual psychological trauma. The second variable is the personality and coping patterns the person had prior to the trauma (Singer & Kolligan, 1987). Individuals who have shown patterns of high physiological reactivity or a number of phobias in the past are particularly likely to be traumatized in this manner again.

There are a number of other prior status conditions that can influence the severity of the trauma as it is experienced psychologically. A person's previous experience relevant to the trauma could be important. Someone who has had a close relative or friend traumatized by rape is indeed more likely to be sensitized to that issue (Steketee & Foa, 1987). Yet a clever attorney might argue that prior experience would have allowed the development of good coping defenses. This, obviously, is a very individual factor.

In a similar vein, individuals who are naive about the world and expect the world to be a generally positive place may be more traumatized than those who are worldly wise. There are individuals who seemingly go through much of life without encountering great difficulties or who have been sheltered from such experiences. When they encounter a trauma, they may be more devastated than individuals who have been forced by prior experiences or the style of parenting to learn to respond to traumas with adequate coping mechanisms.

Prior skills or vocation are also relevant (Grisso, 1986). Mutilation of several fingers may be devastating to a professional athlete or someone who uses fine motor movements to work, such as a watchmaker, yet may not be as much of a problem for someone who works in the more cerebral professions, such as teaching history.

The site where an individual is traumatized or violated is also relevant. A woman who is raped in her home is likely to be more traumatized than a woman who is raped out on the streets. The former woman has been doubly violated, in that there may be no sense of a safe haven after the incident.

RULING OUT HYPOCHONDRIASIS, FACTITIOUS DISORDER, OR MALINGERING

There are three possible specific prior statuses that a psychotherapist must invariably take into account in a PII case, and these are especially relevant to the task of limiting excessive claims (Landis & Meyer, 1988; Meyer, 1983; O'Connell & Carpenter, 1983; Prasad & Oswald, 1985). In order to provide useful and effective service to the courts in PII cases, the psychotherapist has to rule out (or at least compartmentalize as to their specific contribution in an individual case) *hypochondriasis, factitious disorder* (sometimes referred to as Munchausen's syndrome or compensation neurosis), and *malingering*. While these patterns are also discussed in Section II (see Chapter 11), we will go into some detail here as to how psychotherapists can make a decision about the presence or absence of these patterns, since this is often a critical decision in a PII case.

Hypochondriasis is one of the somatoform disorders (along with the somatization disorder, conversion disorder, and psychogenic pain disorder), all of which are denoted by complaints of physical symptoms that have no identifiable physiological base and are *not* under voluntary control.

The factitious disorders are designated by a pattern of complaints of psychological or physical symptoms that have no identifiable basis in fact but which *are* under voluntary control. The term Munchausen syndrome is usually reserved for those factitious disorders that focus primarily on physical rather than psychological symptoms. The motivation for the factitious disorder is idiosyncratic to the individual, is usually largely unconscious, and typically involves a need to gratify dependency, manipulative, and other neurotic needs through being responded to in a medical and/or hospital setting.

Malingering also encompasses the voluntary production of physical and/or psychological symptoms, but the motivation is largely conscious and easily comprehended by others, e.g., to receive a large insurance settlement or escape the draft (Landis & Meyer, 1988).

As noted, psychotherapists who are engaged in a PII are often called upon to determine if any of the above three conditions exist. Figure 7.1 shows a decision tree to apply to such a situation.

In order to facilitate this decision process, the checklists for each of the three categories shown in Tables 7.1, 7.2, and 7.3 were developed by the senior author and Elizabeth Salazar. Each of the three checklists should be applied to the case in question. In the great majority of cases, a high percentage (approximately 75 percent or more) of positive or "yes" answers will predominantly occur on one checklist, indicating support for that pat-

FIGURE 7.1
**Decision Tree Used to Determine Presence of Hypochondriasis,
Factitious Disorder, or Malingering**

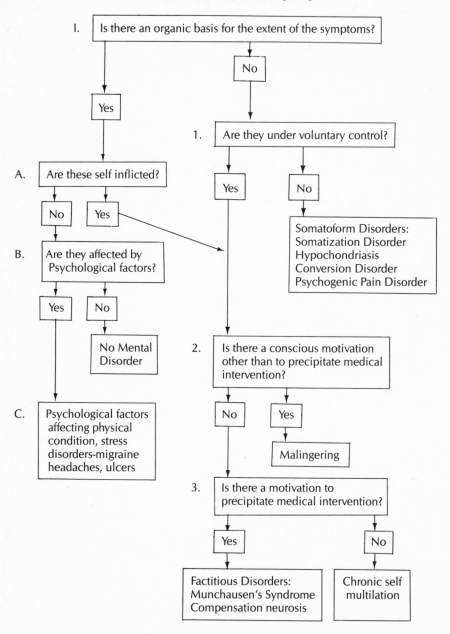

TABLE 7.1
Hypochondriasis Checklist

1. Is there a morbid preoccupation with the body or a part of the body which is felt to be diseased or functioning improperly?

2. Is there a long-term pattern of social or occupational impairment?

3. Are normal bodily functions/fluctuations exaggerated as indications of disease?

4. Are beliefs about the issue sustained in spite of consistent medical information to the contrary?

5. Is there a general indifference to the opinions of people in the client's environment?

6. Is the client anxious, worried, and concerned about this "illness"?

7. Does the client dwell excessively on the symptoms, turning interviews into monologues, i.e., an "organ recital"?

8. Does the speech content consist almost solely of symptoms, their effect on his or her life, and the difficult search for a cure?

9. During conversation, does the client frequently point out afflicted areas of the body?

10. Is there an expression of obsessive-compulsive traits such as defensiveness, obstinacy, miserliness, or conscientiousness?

11. Is there an indication of narcissistic traits, such as egocentrism or oversensitivity to criticism?

12. Is there a lack of a sense of inner worth, self-esteem, or adequacy?

13. Does the client appear to have a preference for being ill, showing positive emotions if any real sickness is found?

14. Are there indications of an affective disorder, such as significant depressive tendencies?

15. Is there a history of frequent doctor visits with one physician or "doctor shopping"?

16. Is there an unusual and wide-ranging familiarity with psychological or medical terms and jargon?

17. Is there an apparent addiction to reading medical journals, health magazines, and other related written materials?

18. Does the client follow unusual health fads, diets, or exercise plans?

19. Has the client often made appeals for extensive tests, examinations, and prescriptions?

20. Do the symptoms commonly deal with the head, neck, abdomen, chest, or gastrointestinal system, or generally the left side of the body?

21. Are there indications of a dependent relationship in which affection is not effectively displayed outside of sickness situations?

(continued)

Table 7.1
(Continued)

---

22. Do the symptoms seem to fulfill an ego-defensive purpose?
23. Do the symptoms enable the client to ease an intolerable personal situation, avoid anxiety or personal responsibility, or gain needed attention?
24. Do the symptoms appear to be an attempt to control a situation that seems to be getting out of his or her control?
25. Did the pattern appear to have an early onset?
26. Did the client grow up in an "atmosphere of illness," e.g., with a bedridden or terminally or chronically ill family member, or a family member in the medical field who brought his or her work home in some fashion?
27. Were the client's parents, especially the mother, overprotective, strict, or overly sanitary in health tendencies?
28. If the client grew up without parents for a substantial period, was there a pattern of self-mothering?

---

tern. If no condition shows a substantial percentage or clearly predominates, these three patterns can usually be ruled out. There are some cases in which two (or even in very rare cases, all three) of these patterns will occur.

STAGES OF TRAUMA RECOVERY

While hypochondriasis, factitious disorders, and malingering are central to false claims in the PII arena, true victims commonly go through the following stages after a trauma (Gislason & Call, 1982; Krupnick & Horowitz, 1981; Meyer & Salmon, 1988):

(1) *Shock period*. Victims are disoriented and feel helpless. Initially victims may be emotionally flat, but they soon become highly suggestible to cues and influences from others. Immediate intervention to provide a supportive structure is very important.

(2) *Denial period*. After the shock has worn off, many victims shift into a denial phase, even to the development of a spirit of quasi-celebration. For example, victims of a devastating tornado in 1974 in Louisville, Kentucky, banded together in a spirit of friendly solidarity that occasionally spilled over into partylike celebrations. In this way they effectively denied the devastation for a period of time.

(3) *Reality phase*. When individuals eventually face the actual impact

TABLE 7.2
Factitious Disorder Checklist

1. Is there an absence of evident or obvious gain that the client would achieve as a result of the presented disorder pattern?

2. Is there gut-level sense that the client has been inducing the symptoms?

3. Could the problem fulfill a masochistic need, such as relieving guilt, or a need to identify with the "sadistic" doctor?

4. Does the client show any counterphobic responses to other disorder patterns or syndromes?

5. Are there indications that deceiving others acts as a defense mechanism, e.g., against low self-esteem or a sense of powerlessness?

6. Are there indications that the presented disorder provides distance from frustrating objects, internal conflicts, or anxieties, or that it provides a temporary identity while egofunctions are reorganized?

7. Is there any evidence that dependency needs are being gratified in the pattern?

8. Was childhood marked by institutional placement or sadistic, abusive, or rejecting parents?

9. Did the patterns apparently start in adolescence or early adulthood?

10. Is there a history of multiple hospitalizations?

11. Is there any evidence of multiple surgeries?

12. Do the symptoms appear to have symbolic meaning or to have been derived from a previously suffered disorder?

13. Does the client have a background in the health professions or some other access to medical knowledge?

14. Did the client grow up in an "atmosphere of illness"?

15. Is there any indication of wandering to many different hospitals or clinics?

16. Has the client accumulated diagnostic labels, medical biographies, radiographs, or thick hospital folders?

17. Is the medical history inconsistent with known pathophysiological courses?

18. Have there been any inconsistent lab or test results?

19. Have there been any unusual recurrent infections?

20. Has the client failed to respond to therapy as expected?

21. Has the client falsified his or her history in any manner?

22. Does the client dramatically present one or more symptoms with elaborate stories, while interacting on a narcissistic level?

23. Is the client's attitude toward staff threatening, aggressive, hostile and/or impatient?

24. Are there frequent requests for surgery, direct patient observation, or invasive procedures?

(*continued*)

Table 7.2
(Continued)

25. Does the client impassively or even eagerly submit to agonizing examinations and treatments, expressing high pain tolerance and/or exhibitionist traits?
26. Does the client show "pseudologia fantastica," attention seeking, or restlessness?
27. Has the client ever discharged himself or herself or retreated indignantly when confronted?
28. Are there indications of any underlying histrionic, antisocial, narcissistic, or combinations of such personality disorder patterns?

---

of the trauma, reality intrudes and delayed depression, anxiety, and phobic responses occur. Many of the issues described subsequently in this chapter deal with this phase.

(4) *Recovery period.* Recovery occurs, even though in some cases post-traumatic responses surface and must be dealt with. Even people not seriously affected may have a continuing need to talk over the events.

In addition to testifying about the immediate effects of a trauma, the psychotherapist will often have the task of dealing therapeutically with the traumatized individual and then reporting on the progress, or lack thereof, of the treatment.

TREATMENT OF PII CASES

The standard of care for therapeutic response during the shock period has evolved from the treatment of combat stress during warfare and incorporates the following principles (Meyer & Salmon, 1988; D'Zurilla, 1986):

(1) *Immediacy* includes three major subprinciples: (a) early detection, (b) prompt treatment, and (c) a speedy return to the conflict area. Treatment personnel who are in a position to observe victims are taught to recognize signs, such as mild confusion, sleep disturbance, crying spells, or anxiety, as probable indicators of combat exhaustion.

(2) *Proximity* was derived from the observation that it was more difficult to return soldiers to combat if they had been removed to a location distant from the combat zone. Consequently, intervention

TABLE 7.3
Malingering Checklist

---

1. Would the client obtain any obvious gain by being considered ill or disordered?
2. Does the client seem to perceive interviews as a challenge or threat?
3. Does the client appear to be annoyed at what he or she considers to be unusual tests?
4. Does the client appear suspicious, overly evasive, vague, or unusually lacking in comprehension of issues?
5. Are there seemingly exaggerated concerns for the symptoms?
6. Is there an easily expressed pessimism about recovery?
7. Is there a relative lack of concern about treatment for the presented disorder?
8. Is the client quick or especially explicit in denying concern for financial (or other goal-oriented) matters?
9. Is there a focused rather than wide-ranging familiarity with medical or psychological terminology?
10. Does the client show an overly self-confident or assertive manner?
11. Are there any indications of antisocial or psychopathic personality traits?
12. Are there any indications that either of the parents showed manipulative or psychopathic patterns?
13. Do some symptoms seem to contradict symtomatology the client should have?
14. In cases that should supposedly show a long-term deficit or problem, is there an unusual lack of previous exams?
15. Are there other discrepancies, contradictions, omissions, or odd exaggerations?
16. Is there poor test-retest reliability in testing or interview patterns?
17. Whether or not there are discrepancies, exaggerations, etc., do some portions of the client's presentation just seem too "neat," as if coming out of a textbook?

---

is first attempted in a place near to where the person lives and works.

(3) *Expectancy* that the person will not avoid the situation is implied in the two previous principles. But expectancy embodies the explicit communication of four ideas: (a) Fear and anxiety are not indicative of abnormality; (b) many persons have such experiences; (c) these experiences are part of life; and (d) reinforcement by escaping future situations will not be tolerated to the degree this is feasible to enforce.

The shock period, during which the person often does not report many negative emotions, will vary among individuals. However, most often this is only a period of days to a few weeks. Denial of physical and psychological damage is already being generated at this time. The person is engaged in trying to cope with the details generated by the damage, and in many ways those details provide a therapeutic distraction. This is often combined with supportive responses from individuals, family, and friends. However, with time these support individuals interpret the shock responses of the victim as indicating healing. So, either because they are now reassured or because they are in some way tired of giving the support responses, they begin to withdraw. At the same time, the immediate details have been taken care of and the person now has to look at the true effects of the trauma. As such permanent effects as disfigurement or loss of functioning in certain areas become all too evident, the reality phase sets in. Now, as well as later in the recovery phase, there may be flashbacks to the traumatic event. These in turn can engender anxiety and phobic responses not evident immediately after the trauma (Thyer & Himle, 1987).

During the first stages after the trauma, the victim's functioning is often analogous to that of the paranoid. He or she has a distorted view of reality. The difference is that the paranoid maintains the distorted view indefinitely, while it is only temporarily held by the trauma victim. In any case, as with the paranoid, the therapist needs to be able initially to accept such individuals' presently distorted view of reality to give them a sense of understanding. At the same time, the therapist should not reinforce or buy into that same belief system. Hence, while empathizing, psychotherapists need to begin to provide alternate views of the world, to offer alternate perspectives on the specific situations, and to gently question and probe the person's distorted reality.

This distorted reality is often accompanied by one or more of three separate, though related, components (Davidson, 1980; Meyer, 1983): shock, depression and anger. In dealing with these components, the therapist must first help the person let go of the denial that evolves from shock. Then, while helping the person face the reality of the situation, the therapist has to be aware that, as that denial breaks down, depression is likely to follow. The therapist must be ready to help the person mobilize to cope with the experiences. Many of the techniques that are standard for depression are useful here. Also, ethics, potential liability, and good sense all demand that an assessment be made as to whether this depression is accompanied by suicidal feelings.

The reality phase is marked by internal rumination, often centering around the classic issues of "If only . . . ," and "Why me?" Even though friends and family may be quick to offer reassurance, unfortunately this does not resolve anything and the questions continue. Thus, they are a central focus for the psychotherapist at this point. Guilt about prior perceived misdeeds or "sins" now has a specific focus. The psychotherapist has the task of helping the person break the linkage of these prior guilts with the present trauma. At the same time, the therapist may have to help the person deal with some true existential guilt or clarify the neurotic sources of the guilt.

Friends and family also will be happy to advise the victim to "just don't think about all that" or "put it out of your mind whenever it comes up." Such advice is usually well-intentioned but may also be self-serving, since by this time family and friends may have found the victim's ruminations tedious or irritating. However, victims simply cannot just put all this out of mind. They need help to (a) work through the emotions generated by the trauma, (b) accept the fact that random events can happen to us in a positive or negative manner, and (c) realize that the key issue at this point is what to do about it rather than what happened.

Just as some family members and friends can retard progress by supporting a denial process, others can retard it by reacting in an exaggerated or hysterical manner. Unfortunately, this puts the victim in the position of being a caretaker. Such victims must reassure the friend or family member, using words that they themselves don't believe but feel they must say.

The person may come out of the depression into anger. Sometimes experienced as a diffuse emotional state, anger can lead to inappropriate reactions, which can be directed toward a specific person or individual or channeled into inappropriate litigation (Weissman, 1985). The therapist's role is to provide a more effective view of reality and, at the same time, help the client learn to manage his anger.

Throughout treatment, the therapist has to be aware of how vulnerable such individuals feel and of how much they are in need of support. This is easiest to see during the depressive phase; however, it's just as important to provide that support (and make them aware that they need to elicit it in others) during the denial and anger phases. Also, the therapist needs to encourage awareness that the person is not alone in experiencing trauma and to clarify that there is a recognized sequence of emotions that he or she will pass through. In that sense, the therapist becomes a guide through this rite of passage. Also, as the person progresses, it is important to help him or her reinvigorate skills and regain a sense of control over his or her world. Explanations of how people cope with trauma (such as through defense mechanisms) or of the expected stages of recovery are often useful to a client, enabling her to realize that the process is normal and feelings should not be viewed quite as ominously.

Factors in Generating Needed Changes

Throughout the process of helping the victim to the recovery phase, and eventually to a "letting go" of all that is related to the trauma, the psychotherapist uses techniques that induce change in the following ways (Daly & Wulff, 1987; D'Zurrila, 1986; Meyer & Salmon, 1988; Waller, 1987) and often in this sequence:

(1) *Consciousness raising*, or the development of awareness of one's needs and conflicts. It is a prime component in group therapy and existential therapy.
(2) *Behavioral stimulus control*, manipulating various environmental settings and stimulus conditions in order to generate behavioral change and then later to maintain recovery.
(3) *Catharsis*, the expression of emotions and feelings that have been suppressed or repressed. This element is particularly important in psychodynamic and Gestalt approaches.
(4) *Choosing*, which consistently forces clients to take responsibility for the consequences of their behavior. This is particularly characteristic of confrontation, reality and existential therapies; yet making a choice is a critical point in any therapy, including the behavior therapies.

Either separately, or in combination, these mediation strategies produce the two most important conditions for change: (1) the ability to *confront* and cope with feared stimuli, and (2) the ability to *generalize* the changes out of the psychotherapy situation and into the ongoing world.

In order to provide an optimal context for healing, the psychotherapist may need to bring family members and friends into the treatment process (Kolevzon & Green, 1985). Courts are resistant to providing financial support for such endeavors, so it is incumbent on the psychotherapist to have a good case for extending the therapeutic effort. Without such efforts, secondary undesirable reactions, such as divorce or deviant response by children, can further the negative pattern already in place.

THE VICTIM AND THE CRIMINAL ARENA

When their client has been victimized, psychotherapists often need to participate in the criminal court system. In many cases the victim may have to go to a hospital because of injuries, and the response to those injuries may not always be of a supportive nature. Victims may be subjected to extensive questioning, and this questioning may take on an aura of skepticism, at least in the mind of the victim. Police interrogators may make tape recordings and/or take an adversarial approach, in effect cross-examining the victim. Victims may even be asked to take a lie detector exam. All of this is likely to be experienced as further violation on top of the initial trauma. Since at this point in the trauma recovery cycle victims are often inclined to distort their view of reality and even to become somewhat paranoid, such violations can result in further psychological disruption.

If given the opportunity to participate early in the process, therapists can help by preparing such victims for these events, e.g., trying to make them understand the positive benefits of the process and explaining how it is not directed in a negative way toward them as individuals. The therapist can even accompany victims through some parts of this process. Many therapists have found this to be an especially useful way of preventing a worsening psychological state. Therapists can also encourage the presence of family and friends and coach them to act as a supportive presence.

Feelings of victimization and exploitation may be reexperienced if the victim eventually has to become a witness in a criminal trial. This is stressful for virtually anyone who is unfamiliar with the criminal process, but it can be doubly destructive to the person who has already been a victim of the crime. There is always the sense of "Why are you attacking me? I'm the victim," especially when the victim encounters the adversarial and even hostile questioning of the accused's attorney. The psychotherapist can help the person prepare for this experience through discussion, by attempting to make him aware that trauma may be reexperienced, and possibly even by using such techniques as relaxation training or systematic desensitization.

Some psychotherapists even work with the prosecuting attorney to put the victim through a mock interrogation (Smith & Meyer, 1987). This benefits the prosecutor, who finds out how the victim will perform in court, so he or she can gauge questions accordingly. It also is a great help to victims, who become familiar with the process. The therapist can explain why certain cross-examination techniques are used. It's analogous to the finding that one of the best ways to help an individual pass a lie detection exam is to have him take several of them before taking the actual exam. It's as if the anxiety of the initial exam makes it more likely that the person will fail the exam, regardless of whether or not he is telling the truth. The mock interrogation similarly allows the person to function more efficiently, and with less stress, in the actual trial.

THE VICTIM IN THE CIVIL COURT ARENA

Victims who go into a civil court arena have to deal with many of the issues that are faced in the criminal arena. In addition, the choice of whether they ever go to court in the first place is often up to them, so they have to bear a sense of responsibility about putting themselves in a situation which then causes them upset. Although the psychotherapist can help them decide whether or not to proceed with litigation, this should never be done without substantial reflection. Victims should understand that it is likely to be a long-term process, and, because of periodic events such as depositions, motions, etc., the trauma can be reactivated.

It's also important that victims realize that they may be more personally vulnerable in some respects in the civil arena. Some protections of their personal privacy that they retained as a victim in the criminal system are absent when they become the plaintiff in the civil system. For example, since they probably raised the issue of psychological damage, the defendant's attorney may go into their personal life, issue subpoenas for indications of prior psychological disorder, and, in addition, request examinations by the defense's own mental health experts. Much personal material will come into the public domain. In such situations, the victim's psychotherapist can be pushed into a dual role. The therapist will likely need to be available as a support throughout the process. At the same time, the therapist may be called on to provide expert data. Victims may be uncomfortable upon hearing some of the comments, conclusions, and assumptions that their therapist is required to make in open court. This, in turn, can easily become a negative factor in the therapy.

In making reports in personal injury cases, psychotherapists need to be aware that lawyers often express frustration with them in terms of getting reasonable estimates of their clients' long-term impairment (Shapiro, 1984). Psychotherapists are inclined to believe that they will be able to change their client for the good; however, this optimism can sometimes cloud an estimate of long-term impairment, which in turn may hamper the lawyer's effort to win the maximum monetary settlement for his client.

QUALIFYING AS AN EXPERT WITNESS IN PII CASES

As in all areas of expert witness work, those testifying can expect to go through a rigorous examination of their credentials, as well as attempts to impeach the credibility of their credentials and their testimony (Shapiro, 1984). Since testimony in this area, as well as in many areas of mental health law, may involve theories or techniques that are somewhat novel, or at least not totally accepted by that scientific community, admissibility of that technique or theory is often challenged. The Federal Rules of Evidence tend to be more liberal than state rules, in that these federal rules generally admit any scientific technique if it has some indication of reliability and relevance, despite its novelty. However, in most states, there is a more conservative approach, based on the 1923 case of *Frye v. United States*. The *Frye* test was based on that court's decision to reject the early form of the lie detector test. The Frye test holds that, in order to be admissible, the technique or theory must be generally accepted by the relevant scientific community. When the Frye test is the dominant concept in a court system, the mental health professional is pushed to use much more traditional techniques, some of which may not have as much validity as a newer technique.

CONCLUSION

A century ago, courts had little interest in recognizing damages for either the negligent or intentional infliction of emotional distress. The occasional exception was when there was clear accompaniment of observable physical damage that was caused by a direct impact. Even here, very small settlements were the rule. However, this attitude has been extensively altered as a result of (1) changing views about the need to protect such an interest in a modern, highly interdependent society, (2) society's allowance for increased personal litigation, (3) developments in psychology and medicine recognizing the reality of emotional distress and pain, and (4) recognition by courts that the costs to society and to the courts themselves were not outweighed by the need to afford a legal remedy for such tort situations (Smith & Meyer, 1987; Waller, 1987).

Concomitant with these developments, psychotherapists have played an increasingly important role in the adjudication of tort actions arising from personal injury incidents (PII). Psychotherapists can help the victim recover from, or at least learn to cope with, the effects of a PII, or may help the victim in the decision as to whether or not to proceed into a civil action for redress and adjust to the stresses of either a civil or criminal action. Psychotherapists also are called upon to provide reports to courts in PII cases and often to provide oral testimony.

While psychotherapists need to become more skilled in fulfilling these roles, courts need to develop more flexibility to accommodate the complexities of each individual case and the rapidly developing findings of modern science, while maintaining the traditional concern for predictability in decisions and ultimately a respect for the needs of society as a whole.

CHAPTER 8

The Psychotherapist as a Witness in Court

Melrose said: "But, of course, perjury seldom plays a role in the testimony of so-called expert witnesses. It is only too easy for both defense and prosecution to find honest authorities who oppose each other diametrically in regard to the same phenomenon, even in such a supposedly exact science as ballistics, and when the human element enters, consistency goes right out the window. Dr. Brixton, for example, believes that a man who has tried to get himself mutilated can be held responsible for no subsequent act however criminal. I wager that the prosecution psychiatrist will find the same fact utterly negligible.

—Thomas Berger, *Killing Time*

DR. JAMES WAS being cross-examined in a personal injury case involving one of his long-term psychotherapy cases. The attorney focused for quite a while on Dr. James' familiarity with the 16 PF Test, a commonly used test of personality (Meyer, 1983) and one of the tests Dr. James had administered when he first saw this client. Through careful questioning, the attorney put Dr. James in the position of being on the record regarding the value of the 16 PF, both in general and in this case. He then asked Dr. James to repeat one of the scoring steps. Dr. James did so and came up with a different score than he had listed on the test protocol that had been presented to court. Then, by direct statement, by innuendo, and through some of Dr. James' direct admissions, the attorney made it appear that his opinions about the case in general could be in error. The attorney then shifted to asking Dr. James if he was familiar with certain specific studies on the 16 PF, and Dr. James had to admit that he was not.

220

By the time he left the witness stand, it was evident to everyone concerned that Dr. James was a shaken man. The jury eventually found for the position opposite to the one supported by Dr. James' testimony.

The irony here is that the 16 PF had no real effect on the essence of Dr. James' position in this case. Also, none of the specific literature about which he was questioned was particularly relevant to the case. Any clinician could have made a similar error; even those clinicians who regularly use the 16 PF probably would not have been aware of the specific studies the attorney mentioned.

Unfortunately, Dr. James had little previous experience testifying in court. Also, the attorney he was working with was not very sophisticated in the mental health area, and had not even helped Dr. James prepare for testifying. It's unclear how much influence Dr. James' problematic testimony had on the eventual jury verdict, but it is clear that the negative image he conveyed could have been muted. This chapter points to many similar problems and pitfalls a psychotherapist who provides testimony to the court is likely to encounter.

For obvious reasons forensic psychologists and psychiatrists frequently appear in court. Issues such as competency to stand trial and criminal responsibility involve consultation with attorneys or judges and typically require direct testimony (Kennedy, 1986). But *any* practicing psychotherapist may be asked to testify regarding these issues or others that affect his or her own clients. Because many persons who seek the services of a psychotherapist are having difficulty in life, they are likely to come into contact with the justice system, occasionally as criminal defendants and more often as litigants in civil courts (Shapiro, 1984). Considering, for example, the high divorce rate in this country, it becomes clear that there is a high likelihood that practicing clinicians will be called to testify in divorce and related child custody hearings at some time during their career. Most clinicians also will become involved in civil commitment proceedings on occasion. It is possible that a client may become involved in personal injury litigation where his/her psychological condition before the injury is at issue. Therapists may be drawn into court to describe acceptable levels of care in professional liability cases or even as defendants in malpractice suits.

The law has procedures, concepts, and language that are unfamiliar to most therapists. While earlier chapters have dealt with some of the legal issues specific to the types of proceedings mentioned above, this chapter serves to orient the therapist to the courtroom and to some practical concerns in serving as an expert witness, regardless of the context. Even though many clinicians may try to avoid courtroom involvements, it is prudent to have some knowledge of how to survive as an expert witness.

ESTABLISHING EXPERTISE

Formal legal procedures have evolved to aid courts in arriving at the truth. One of the most basic principles of legal process is that only factual data should enter into decisions. Consequently, most persons who appear in court are allowed to testify only to what they themselves saw, heard, or did. Hearsay and opinion are not tolerated, only objectifiable statements of fact. Nevertheless, for a variety of reasons the courts find it useful to allow some witnesses to offer their opinions in testimony. These special witnesses are "experts" in a given field of study, profession, or trade. While their opinions are recognized as fallible, they are also seen as having special value in deciding the case. The Federal Rules of Evidence (702) indicate that a witness qualifies as an expert:

> If scientific, technical, or other specialized knowledge will assist the trier of fact [usually a jury] to understand the evidence or determine a fact in issue, a witness qualified as an expert by knowledge, skill, experience, training or education, may testify thereto in the form of an opinion or otherwise.

Any or all of the five criteria—knowledge, skill, experience, training, or education—may qualify the witness as an expert and enable him/her to go beyond the concrete facts of the case to offer conclusions and inferences, even upon hypothetical data given by attorneys in the case. The fundamental test of an expert's value to the court is whether he or she can provide information that the jury could not possibly determine on its own. Because laypeople cannot perform ballistics tests on guns and ammunition, the opinions of people with special training and skill in this area are admitted. Though this testimony is fallible, it allows the jury to reasonably consider material that would otherwise be "beyond their ken" (Kargon, 1986). Mental health experts, including psychologists, psychiatrists, and in some cases psychiatric social workers and nurses, are qualified for the same sorts of reasons. Jurors cannot collect, integrate, and interpret data on human behavior and mental disorders, at least not in the sophisticated ways available to these professionals (Wells, 1986).

Practicing psychotherapists generally will be admitted as experts in most courts (see *Jenkins v. United States*, 1962). Minimum requirements for expert status should include the highest degree offered in the specific discipline, or at least a degree sufficiently advanced for independent practice of the specialty. Further, the expert should be licensed, certified, or registered as provided by law in that jurisdiction. We believe there are six primary standards for establishing expertise:

(1) education;

(2) credentials and honors;

(3) relevant experience, including previous diagnostic and intervention work and positions held;

(4) research and publications, including books and articles;

(5) knowledge and application of scientific principles; and

(6) use of specific tests, procedures, and measurements.

EARLY COURT INVOLVEMENT

In a real sense, testifying in court is the final stage in an elaborate series of legal proceedings. In fact, many times, when a therapist is consulted by an attorney, the matter will be resolved without actually reaching the courtroom. It is important to understand the progression of proceedings and how they may involve the therapist.

The most fundamental issue in court-related consultation centers on developing a working arrangement with an attorney or judge. While attorneys sometimes accept cases on a contingent fee basis, the ethical therapist cannot. It is best to develop a written contract at the outset specifying that the clinician will perform specific procedures for a set hourly fee. The first stage of consultation generally involves evaluating a client and rendering an opinion to the attorney. If the opinion turns out to be compatible with the theory of the case as envisioned by the lawyer, then further work may be requested, with an eye toward eventual testimony. If the opinion does not fit with the attorney's plans, then the consultation may end at that point. Avoid the temptation to become an advocate for a position requested by the attorney. Don't "squeeze the data." Remain as an advocate only for the truth of the position as you see it (Barrett, Johnson & Meyer, 1985).

In any event, written reports should not be prepared unless requested, since they may be "discoverable" by counsel for the other side of the case (Weiner & Hess, 1987). It is wise for the expert to keep track of the dates when first retained, dates of evaluative services, the date an opinion was formed and communicated to the consulting attorney, and the date the attorney subsequently conveyed more specific information about the facts of the case, legal theories and strategies, and other information that should not be considered until a preliminary opinion has been formed.

At this stage, it's important to observe the following principles of general case preparation:

(1) Avoid taking any case in which you don't have a reasonable degree of expertise. There are numerous instances of mental health profes-

sionals taking on cases in which they only have a passing awareness of the issues or the requirements of practice. If you are trying to branch into a new area, make sure that you receive appropriate background education and supervision. It is also appropriate to inform the client, in a nonthreatening fashion, that this is a new area for you, and to talk about the limits of what he or she can expect from your participation.

(2) Take thorough notes on your encounter with the client and of other related events. This is especially true in diagnostic cases, since these often will have implications in the forensic area or in other decision-making agreements. Make sure that when you return to the case after a lengthy period of time, you will be able to clearly reconstruct what went on between you and the client, and be sure you can report clearly what the client told you. Additionally, it is worthwhile to record your overall impressions at the time in which you first summarized the data in your own mind.

DEPOSITIONS

If your involvement in the case continues, the next phase of preparation centers on preparing depositions for each side. Depositions are basically a way for attorneys to discover what all the potential witnesses in a case will say before the trial. They are often called "discovery devices" because they are used to discover the details of the other side's case. Prior to the advent of depositions, courtroom showdowns often took on the character of "trial by ambush," since each side endeavored to spring testimony on the opposition, testimony that it would be unprepared to effectively rebut. Depositions also have become important because they save professional time, often leading to out-of-court resolutions.

The testimony that is recorded in the form of a deposition can be used in the same way as trial testimony. The person being deposed is under oath and is required to answer questions fully and honestly. In fact, you should assume that any responses given in a deposition should be of sufficient quality that they would be presentable in court. Often the testimony given, at least in part, will be read in the courtroom.

There are at least five major purposes to taking a deposition from expert witnesses:

(1) the discovery of facts;
(2) discovery of theories underlying expert testimony;
(3) preservation of the witness's testimony;

(4) development of content material; and
(5) obtaining of information relevant to the settlement of the cause of action.

Discovery of Facts. If the expert has evaluated someone or some aspect of a case, part of the deposition will be aimed at finding those facts upon which the expert has based his or her conclusion. If all of the data were supplied by the attorney who retained the expert, the deposition will be aimed at finding what general factors are important for the expert and which might lead to alternative conclusions. More frequently, the opinion is based on direct examination, and the deposition aims to discover the methods and procedures used and the results obtained. Often this information will be presented to other experts for critique, in an effort to determine the strength of the opinion and possible avenues to discredit it. Of particular importance are factors such as the completeness of the evaluation, time invested, reliability of methods used, and the thoroughness of recordkeeping.

Discovery of Theories Underlying Conclusions. The expert's training, philosophical or scientific orientation, and other characteristics may lead to bias in his or her opinion (Buckhout, 1986). The nature of any theory used to interpret the facts of the case will be discovered through the deposition. Again, there is an emphasis on evaluating alternative conclusions. The possibility that different theories or interpretive strategies could be used will be explored with independent expert consultants.

Preservation of Testimony. Depositions are not intended to replace live testimony, and their impact is less substantial than actual testimony in court. Because they are legally admissible as trial testimony, depositions can sometimes be used when the expert becomes unable to attend the trial proper, and the deposition is clearly better than no expert opinion at all. Still, the utility of a deposition may be quite limited, particularly when juxtaposed with a live presentation by a competing expert. As a rule therapists should not count on giving depositions in lieu of live courtroom appearances.

Development of Material for Impeachment Purposes. Perhaps the central function of the deposition is to allow the parties to formulate strategies for discrediting one another's case. When experts are deposed, the attorney for the "other side" will be looking for any avenues to impeach the witness or the conclusions. The facts relied upon, tests given, and the general thoroughness and objectivity of the evaluation will all be examined. It is also common for counsel to inquire into the qualifications and possible personal or professional biases of the expert. Finally, it is common for the opposing lawyer to experiment with tactics to upset or compromise the expert (Shapiro, 1984). While personal attacks on the expert are risky in court (they may alienate or antagonize the jurors), they may be very wide-ranging in a deposition.

Development of Material Relevant to Settlement. Though these issues are of little interest to the therapist, they may play a key role in the resolution of the case. In civil matters any cause of action has some value, whether nuisance or real. The discovery process underlying the deposition allows each party to make some estimate of this value and of the respective strength of its own case. The better one side, and by inference one expert, does in preparing for trial, the more likely that a case will be settled. In fact, more cases are settled than not. Frequently, the tests and reports described in the deposition are used to justify a settlement value. This is a legitimate use of psychological data. For example, in personal injury cases, presentation of the expert's findings regarding the injured party may lead to a fair monetary settlement without going to court.

Preparing for a Deposition

Preparation for the deposition should be similar to that for trial testimony. All material pertinent to the case, including notes, test data, and other materials should be gathered and reviewed in detail. If you have been retained by an attorney to this point, it is because your expert opinion is consistent with a legal strategy. It is crucially important that the expert and attorney hold a predeposition conference to review the opinion and its relationship to the case. This session should involve mutual education, with the attorney elaborating on relevant legal standards and theories. The expert must explain clinical data in commonsense terms and outline the limits of the opinion. Even the most informed and professional opinion will appear sparse if it is not fully elaborated in the deposition. The expert must depend on the attorney to ask proper questions to elicit not only the opinion but also the data and inferences that support it. This will require close cooperation between the lawyer and expert. Witnesses should generally insist on predeposition conferences to insure that the process goes smoothly.

Conduct During the Deposition

Most importantly, answer all questions truthfully. Answer only the questions asked and do not volunteer information. If the attorney retaining the expert objects to a question, do not answer until or unless the conflict has been resolved. If necessary, the expert may check specific information in notes or other records, but it is important to remember that any records used may be subject to subpoena. This can create an unusual bind. The expert wants to be thorough and accurate and may really need records, but most jurisdictions hold that files are fully discoverable, at least in civil actions. Even though they may not be admissible as evidence, these records may be used to develop the case. Just because a given set of records could be subpoenaed does not mean it should be released, and the disclosure of confidential information under the wrong circumstances could lead to a malpractice suit. When in doubt the therapist may (1) insist that the attorney requesting the information provide a valid authorization from the affected person, (2) request a court order before releasing the information (in some jurisdictions even a court order is not sufficient), or (3) obtain independent legal advice before acting. Retaining independent counsel can be costly, but civil suits for wrongful disclosure can be even more costly. Under no circumstances should the therapist take the word of the requesting attorney that disclosure is permissible.

It is common practice to have copies of business cards and curriculum vitae available at the deposition for all attorneys. A listing of your relevant education and experience may help to establish the weight of your opinion. At the same time, if the expert does an impressive job during the deposition, the other attorney may want consultations in future matters.

The following practical suggestions are adapted from Danner's Pattern Deposition Checklist:

(1) Be courteous and polite to all concerned.
(2) Speak in a voice that can be heard by everyone, but especially by the stenographic reporter.
(3) Think about and understand each question *before* you answer. Your testimony even at this stage can markedly affect the case.
(4) Base your answers only on information you have obtained yourself as part of your study. Be willing to say, "I don't know."
(5) If the attorney who hired you objects, stop talking. It is best to let the lawyer deal with the point in question.
(6) Be aware that the opposing attorney will be evaluating you as a witness and may try many things in deposition that won't be used in trial.
(7) Read the deposition when a copy is sent to you for your signature; do not waive your right to sign it. Correct any errors in it as your attorney instructs. Keep a copy of the deposition with your other records pertaining to that case.
(8) Review your copy of the deposition prior to going to court, and take it with you to the witness stand.

SUBPOENAS

A subpoena is a command by a court for a witness to appear at a certain time and place to give testimony in a specific matter. Though subpoenas sometimes refer to depositions, they generally pertain to court appearances. It is important to distinguish between two types of subpoenas: the *subpoena ad testicandum*, and the *subpoena duces tecum*. The first is what most people assume, a summons to the court at a specified date and time. The second has an additional function in that it requires experts to bring specific materials with them to court. These are generally written so that therapists will be directed to bring *all* records, notes, files, test protocols and other relevant documentation. These directives must be honored; failure to provide the required documentation can result in a contempt of court citation.

As an expert, you are entitled to a degree of courtesy from attorneys and court personnel. While it is rarely possible to specify the exact time and duration of an expert's testimony, those concerned should endeavor to give as accurate an estimate as possible. Given that witnesses are generally not allowed to sit in the courtroom and hear the testimony of other witnesses, it is best to inquire if you may remain at your office until requested to appear by telephone. If you must be present at the courthouse, plan to bring work to fill the time productively.

REPORTING TO THE COURT

At some time in the process, and usually at this point, you may be requested or ordered by the court to provide a report on the client. The outline in Table 8.1 has been found to be useful in report writing. The psychotherapist collects all relevant data and then goes through the sequence point by point as the report is dictated or written. Sequence, exclusion of subsections, or inclusion of other information sections, is easily adjusted to the requirements of an individual case and/or the court's request.

In order to be most effective here, the psychotherapist should use a combination of information sources (Grisso, 1986; Meyer, 1983). These generally consist of (1) psychometric approaches, (2) observational approaches, (3) clinical interviews, (4) collateral interviews and documentation, and (5) other peripheral methods, such as hypnosis.

TESTIMONY IN COURT

An expert's testimony is divided into direct and cross examination. Each serves to present useful information to the court. Understanding the purposes of each segment of the testimony will help the expert prepare for and cope with the demands of courtroom testimony.

TABLE 8.1
Outline of Data to be Covered in Report to the Court

Name of Client:

Name of Examiner:

A. Introductory variables:
    1. Age
    2. Sex
    3. Educational background
    4. Socioeconomic status
    5. Occupational status, responsibilities

B. Referral Source and Related Information

C. Circumstances of examination:
    1. Place of examination
    2. Length of exam
    3. Present medications and last time used
    4. Tests administered

D. General appearance:
    1. Physical characteristics
    2. Dress and grooming
    3. Unusual behavior or mannerisms

E. Level of response:
    1. Answers questions fully
    2. Volunteers information
    3. Protocols adequate
    4. Attitude toward testing and examiner

F. Presenting problem and dimensions of that problem:
    1. Duration
    2. Pervasiveness
    3. Severity
    4. Frequency

G. Consequences and implications of presenting problem:
    1. Functional aspects of impairment regarding:
    job
    family
    school
    social milieu
    2. Legal status (e.g., pending litigation); this incident or others
    3. Necessary changes in habits, roles (especially if acute)
    4. Adoption of coping skills, defense mechanisms, both healthy and unhealthy

H. Historical setting:
    1. Onset of any symptoms (acute? gradual?)—whether perceived as related to referral problem or not
    2. Circumstances surrounding onset of symptoms
    3. Evidence of, data regarding premorbid functioning in these areas

(continued)

Table 8.1
(Continued)

I. Other historical factors:
　1. Level of adjustment—as child
　2. Level of adjustment—as adolescent
　3. Prior hospitalizations and diagnoses
　4. Parental relationships—then and now.
　5. Sibling relationships—then and now.

J. Other present situational factors:
　1. Marital relationship
　2. Children
　3. Job or school
　4. Other maintaining factors

K. Current physical-physiological condition:
　1. Medication; types and dosages
　2. Medical complications (e.g., removal of limb)
　3. Other factors not directly related to presenting problem

L. Type of affect and level of anxiety:
　1. Amount
　2. Appropriateness
　3. In-session versus ongoing functioning
　4. General mood
　5. Effects on testing and interview behavior

M. I.Q. level:
　1. Subtest variability
　2. Pre-incident versus present level
　3. Educational preparation versus inherent ability
　4. Potential functioning
　5. Personality inferences

N. Organic involvement:
　1. Any significant indicators
　2. Degree, if any
　3. Specific or global
　4. Cause—alcoholism, birth or prenatal factors, trauma
　5. Cause of or coincidental to other disorder

O. Thought processes:
　1. Hallucinations or delusions
　2. Paranoid traits
　3. Degree of insight
　4. Adequate social judgments
　5. Adequate abstracting ability
　6. Orientation to environment

P. Overall integration and statement of personality functioning—diagnosis

Q. Evaluation of patient's current overall attitudes toward his/her situation:
　1. Expectancies regarding recovery

(continued)

Table 8.1
(Continued)

---

2. Attitude toward disorder
3. Motivation for treatment
4. Understanding of status/condition
5. Coping skills, responses to stress and crisis

R. Identification of any need for further referral or consultation

S. Identification of targets for modification, intervention

T. Treatment recommendations:
  1. Individual and/or family and/or group therapy
  2. Chemotherapy
  3. Hospitalization
  4. Predictions of dangerousness to self or to others
  5. Interest in change
  6. Probability of maintenance in treatment

U. Priority of treatment recommendations (including reevaluation and follow-up), based on available resources

V. Judgment regarding prognosis, based on:
  1. Age at time of onset
  2. Phase of disease or disorder
  3. Known morbidity rates
  4. Severity of affliction
  5. Accessibility of family, other social support systems
  6. Test results
  7. Patient's attitude

W. Other summary formulations and conclusions

Qualifications

As mentioned above, most practicing psychotherapists can be qualified to testify in a broad range of matters involving mental health issues. The judge decides who will be admitted to testify, based on the credentials presented. But eliciting the expert's credentials on direct examination serves another purpose; it provides the jurors with background information necessary to appropriately weigh the testimony provided by the witness (Blau, 1984). The expert's qualifications are demonstrated through a process known as *voir dire*, which means to "speak the truth." The attorney who wishes to call the expert asks a series of questions designed to persuade the jury that the expert is a respected authority in the matter at hand.

This phase of testimony is important, not just in terms of qualifying the witness, but also in presenting credentials that are impressive to the jury and in casting the later evidentiary testimony of the witness in a good light.

While this may seem to be an inappropriate use of one's academic credentials and experiences, it is essential for the jury to determine the credibility of the witness. The therapist's testimony is not binding on the court or jury, and its effect depends on the persuasiveness of the expert. During *voir dire* questioning, the expert is asked to give place of residence, an account of academic training, and a history of experiences relevant to the case in point. In some instances, it also may be important to note that the expert has qualified in court in the past. Each of these elements is important in demonstrating that the witness is, in fact, an expert (Kargon, 1986).

The issue of residence may be important for several reasons. Often the judge and jury lend more credence to someone from the local community. Outsiders may be characterized as "hired guns," brought in because local experts do not hold the same opinions. In some jurisdictions there may even be a local practitioner rule. For example, in a malpractice case, the standard against which the defendant is judged may be prevailing standards of care in the local community. Someone from one area is not qualified to testify regarding the standards of care in another jurisdiction. For the most part, courts are moving toward comparisons with a standard of practice in the broader professional community as a whole, rather than within a geographic locality. Some legal matters do not entail local practice rules, such as criminal responsibility, competency to stand trial, or testamentary capacity.

Education and training should be recounted chronologically, beginning with the first college degree earned, the university granting the degree, the date, major, and any honors attached. This process is repeated for all subsequent degrees. Most therapists will have a variety of practicum, residency, or internship training, and these should be recounted in sufficient detail to allow the jurors to understand the nature of the work performed and any supervisory and didactic components that enriched these experiences. Finally, the questioning should turn to past work experience, up to and including the present. Other relevant details, such as academic appointments or consultantships, should also be noted.

It is particularly important that the jury be told about publications and scholarly presentations. This establishes in the mind of the jury and the court not only that you are an expert by reason of experience, but also that you are contributing to the scientific literature. It also may help to demonstrate that you chose your profession for reasons other than financial gain. Publications and teaching experience at the professional level are generally quite impressive, although courts have little sense of the relative merits of specific projects, such as the difference between writing several articles or an entire book.

You should also be asked to cite any honors you have received. Note memberships in professional organizations, committee appointments and elected offices, editorial positions, diplomates or other distinguished professional credentials. The focus here should be on demonstrating professional integrity and commitment.

Well qualified experts will often find themselves in a paradoxical position. The opposing attorney may graciously offer to stipulate that the witness is an expert, particularly if the extent of the therapist's credentials is already known. This tactic serves to demonstrate the attorney's good will before the jury, but is also an attempt to prevent the court from hearing all of the witness's qualifications. The lawyer presenting the witness should never accept stipulation and should pursue *voir dire* to the extent necessary to optimize the expert's standing with the court (Loftus, 1986).

Often, establishing credentials may proceed from the very broad issues described above to demonstrating competence in the specific areas of interest in a given case. For example, if the case involves criminal responsibility, then prior experience in other insanity cases should be described. Often, this is a matter of giving more detail about experience in a narrow area of interest to the court.

The more specific the issues at hand, the more specialized should be the credentials of the expert. Consider a case involving a battered wife who is accused of murdering her husband. The defense intends to argue that repeated victimization compromised the woman's ability to refrain from killing. Special knowledge and background in understanding domestic violence might be called for. This example should demonstrate that, while many issues can be addressed by psychologists and psychiatrists with basic clinical training, some cases call for very specific skills or knowledge beyond those of the average professional. If you possess these qualifications, make sure that they are presented to the court. Otherwise, as a would-be expert, take care to ensure that you participate only in cases where you actually have the necessary expertise.

The opposing attorney may immediately try to impeach you as a witness by arguing that your credentials do not qualify you as an expert. If your background and training are adequate and you are licensed in your profession as provided by law, then your qualifications as an expert in the basic issues of psychotherapy and human behavior can hardly be questioned. A common tactic is to argue that the witness has no knowledge of the specific issue involved in the case. As mentioned above, this strategy should be anticipated, and some effort should be made to establish a level of expertise in the *voir dire*.

Laying the Predicate

There is always a brief transitional phase between credentials and present-ing the opinion. The groundwork for the opinion is developed by describing how the expert became involved. Given that you have qualified as an expert, this part of your testimony demonstrates how your expertise was brought to bear in this specific case. Questions such as "Did you see certain evidence?" or "Have you conducted an examination?" or "Did I provide you with certain facts?" will often serve as the basis or *predicate* for all later testimo-ny. It is important to be as specific as possible about all of the sources of information utilized in forming an opinion. If one or more subjects have been evaluated, the dates of interviews and testing sessions, as well as their duration, should be noted. If records were obtained or reviewed, the time spent on these activities should be documented. *All* sources of information that will be used to support the upcoming opinion should be catalogued at this time. Sloppy or imprecise recordkeeping regarding this basic informa-tion will tend to discredit the rest of the expert's testimony, so good notes should be kept throughout preparation for the trial. Any written report to the court or an attorney should be equally specific and list all sources of collateral information, as well as the dates of original work. A report pre-pared in this way will facilitate testimony when the time comes.

Presentation of Findings and Opinions

The third part of the direct examination will usually begin with a question from the attorney such as: "And did you form an opinion as to . . . ?" If the examiner responds affirmatively, the most difficult part of the attorney's job begins. Contrary to popular belief, the direct examination of witnesses is the trial lawyer's most challenging task. This is the period when the attorney must get into the trial record and the minds of the jurors a clear and persuasive picture of the case, with no surprises and an eye toward preempt-ing the opposition's efforts to present contradictory evidence.

The opinion given by the therapist should be very familiar to the lawyer. Since pretrial conferences should have established exactly what information needs to be presented to the jury, the attorney will generally proceed with a predetermined list of questions. The expert must take care to offer testimony in clear, concise, nontechnical language. In addition to the "bottom line" opinion, the supporting facts and theories must also be presented. If the methods by which the expert gathered the data, integrated the facts, and formulated an opinion are explained in step-by-step fashion, then it is likely that the court will understand and respond to the testimony offered (Wells, 1986).

It is crucial to remember that once the direct examination is concluded, the opposing attorney will undertake to discredit this opinion, your qualifications, or you personally. The expert and attorney should anticipate these attacks during direct questioning (Shapiro, 1984). No case is likely to lend itself to a "perfect" opinion, one that covers every detail of the case and cannot be challenged or interpreted differently. The expert will do well to carefully examine all the data available in a given case and to realistically appraise the least persuasive aspects of the opinion, possible conflicting facts, and alternative explanations. If the therapist has done a thorough, professional job, then he can show why he believes that an isolated fact, though apparently contradictory, does not change the overall opinion. Similarly, he has reasons for interpreting the data in a specific way. During the direct examination it is important to remember that you are the expert, and your reasoning on these points should be explained to the court. It is far better to anticipate and defuse these issues than to appear surprised by them during cross-examination.

The Cross-Examination Phase

The obvious purpose of cross-examination is to neutralize the opinion presented by an opposing expert. The American legal system places great faith in adversarial proceedings. It is assumed that if each party puts forth its best case while trying to discredit the other, then the jury will have the best facts upon which to base a decision (Monohan & Walker, 1985). This perspective is generally foreign to therapists, who tend to seek truth through resolving conflicts, through finding a middle ground where both parties can be satisfied. Consequently, most clinicians are quite intimidated by the idea of cross-examination. While this can admittedly be a taxing experience, if the witness adopts the proper perspective and has done a good job on direct questioning, cross-examination need not be inordinately unpleasant.

It is often stated that a good attorney does not ask a question to which the answer is not known. This is particularly true upon cross-examination. The attorney recognizes that the expert has been called by the other side because of a particular position already presented. If the other attorney has done a proper job, the witness will have fully presented the relevant evidence to the court and jury. In some cases the most efficacious way to deal with a solid opinion is to simply get the witness out of sight of the jury as quickly as possible. For example, if there is any single weakness in the opinion, the attorney may point this out and then dismiss the witness without asking any questions.

Frequently, an attorney will attempt to limit the expert to yes or no answers (Blau, 1984). These efforts should be resisted if a categorical response would be less than accurate. It is best to remember that the cross-examining attorney cannot force you to choose between the lesser of two inaccurate answers. If the question cannot be answered yes or no, then ask that it be rephrased or clarified, or point out that the biological and mental sciences involve complex processes and theories, and that simplistic answers will not help the court to understand these phenomena. Another tactic is to wear down an expert by asking a series of complicated but essentially irrelevant questions, each requiring long and elaborate answers. This practice has at least an equal effect on the jury, who may simply become tired of listening to the witness talk. This practice can be effectively stopped only by objections from counsel.

A favorite approach is to confront the witness with conflicting testimony from other experts, often in the form of books or articles submitted as a written authority (Shapiro, 1984). If the witness gives an unqualified endorsement of a given source as authoritative, the attorney may be able to find some part of it that apparently contradicts the expert's opinion in the case at hand. For this reason, it is best for the witness to indicate that he or she recognizes the contribution of the author, but does not consider this an unfailing authority. Often, noting others who have also made substantial contributions to research literature will serve as an effective disclaimer.

The procedures used by the expert witness may also be major targets for cross-examination. For example, psychiatrists often speak of the mental status exam as if this were a standardized, formal procedure. Sophisticated attorneys may point out, or more correctly lead the witness to point out, that the components of such an evaluation vary according to the preferences and biases of the clinician, and that the results are interpreted subjectively. Psychologists may be taken to task for wholly opposite reasons. Standardized tests such as the MMPI may be criticized based on the content of single items (Ziskin, 1981). For example, the first item on the MMPI may be read to the court, followed by the question, "Doctor, is true or false the 'normal' answer to that question?" or "What does that have to do with mental disorder?" Obviously, the witness needs to be familiar with the basics of his or her own evaluation techniques, and should take this as an opportunity to clarify the logic behind these procedures. Of course, the simplest way to discredit an examiner's methods is to demonstrate he spent negligible time on the case. We have observed a number of cases where the opposing expert spent less than 30 minutes in conducting an insanity evaluation. Obviously, the ethical clinician spends sufficient time and should be prepared to document this.

Often attorneys try to suggest alternative interpretations of the facts and findings in a case (Kennedy, 1986). If these alternatives are possible, they should already have been dealt with in direct examination. If they have not been, they should be acknowledged during cross-examination, along with the expert's reasons for rejecting them. The attorney may ultimately ask, "Isn't that idea possible?" or "Are you saying that this explanation is impossible?" Dogmatic positions such as these will make the expert appear rigid and unreasonable, and usually backfire. Hence, it's best to offer a response such as, "Just about anything is possible, but for the reasons I have already given I find that explanation extremely unlikely." The degree of certitude expressed (extremely, highly, rather, somewhat) should correspond with the expert's own conviction about the opinion given.

A related strategy is to offer hypothetical information and ask if this would change the expert's opinion. Refusing to consider new information would again make the witness appear committed to defending a position rather than weighing the information fairly. On the other hand, indicating that a specific piece of information would definitely change one's opinion may be very problematic. Often the information is not hypothetical at all, but has been provided by an earlier witness. The attorney may then indicate that someone else has already sworn to this new information, and that the expert should revise his conclusions accordingly. Realistically, it is rarely possible to put hypotheticals offered by the cross-examining attorney into context. If a clear response is possible, then it may be offered, but more often than not a reasonable response is to indicate that isolated facts have little significance and that the posited information would have to be considered along with everything else known about the case. If the attorney wishes to provide new, factual information, the expert should be willing to reevaluate the entire case, but not in the form of freewheeling speculation from the stand. The expert should point out that professional practice does not admit off-the-cuff speculation in important matters, and that the court is best served by careful deliberation.

Demonstrating that the witness might be biased is an extremely effective way to impeach testimony (Blau, 1986). The most common method is to portray the expert as a "hired gun" by asking, "How much were you paid to give that opinion?" This innuendo should be calmly confronted. If the expert bills on an hourly basis, as suggested here, then it can be demonstrated that fees received are for professional services, not in exchange for the opinion requested by the attorney. This point can be made more clearly if there is a written contract specifying the arrangements under which the expert will consult. The contract should specify that it is the evaluation that is paid for, regardless of the opinion offered—something along the lines of, "I will perform the evaluation and give my honest opinion. If it turns out to be consistent with your theory of the case we can proceed from there."

The spectre of bias can also be raised by portraying the expert as a professional witness, one whose livelihood consists of taking the stand and offering an opinion in exchange for hefty fees (Ziskin, 1981). Clinicians who accept primarily forensic evaluations will obviously be vulnerable to such a characterization. It is appropriate to indicate that one's training is specifically in this area, and so by nature frequent courtroom testimony is required. A brief account of how the expert receives referrals, becomes involved in the cases, and is eventually asked to participate in court may help educate the jury regarding the realities of forensic practice.

Other efforts to imply unfairness center on the expert's record in prior cases. Those who always testify for the prosecution or only for the defense may obviously appear biased. Most clinicians will have a more mixed record and should be prepared to explain, without defensiveness, the factors that have determined their "personal statistics." For example, an expert who has testified for the prosecution four out of five times might point out that research indicates that the majority of insanity pleas are unsuccessful, so that a predominance of clinical opinions consistent with that trend is hardly surprising.

RECOMMENDATIONS FOR COURTROOM PRESENTATION

The following is a reiteration of some of the points already made in this chapter, along with a number of other suggested practices for effective functioning as an expert witness in court.

Practices that Promote Effective Participation in Courtroom Process

- Develop a written agreement with referring attorneys. Set your fee schedule in the first appointment so that there is no dispute later, and do not accept a contingent fee. Therapists should be extremely cautious with lawyers who suggest such arrangements, as they should know that this is an ethical violation.
- Be prepared to be questioned about the issue of fees. Attorneys like to ask questions like, "How much are you being paid to testify for this client?" You need to correct that and state that you were asked to do an evaluation, and to give your full and honest opinion to the best

of your knowledge, and that it was then up to the attorney to decide whether he or she wanted to go ahead and use you in the courtroom. Also, make sure that you state that you are not being paid for your testimony, but that you are being paid for the time that you put into this trial, no matter what testimony would emerge from that time spent. For that reason, you probably will look better to the jury if you charge by the hour rather than charging a flat fee for a case.

- Many cases will involve assessment of one or more individuals involved in the case at hand. Always advise clients of the nature of your involvement in a case and, when performing evaluations, discuss the purpose of the examination and how the results will be used. Aside from legal concerns, this is simply a matter of ethical practice.
- When you are examining a client on referral from an attorney, use standardized measures or techniques, follow routine procedures, and be thorough. If you deviate from standard procedures or are less than meticulous, then you, your opinion, and your testimony can be more readily attacked (Gutheil, 1986). Make your preparation and approach to the case as solid and professional as possible. Important legal decisions will depend upon your input, and during live cross-examination it is too late to remedy any shortcomings in your development of the case.
- Once the opinion has been formed, insist that the attorney who employs you provide the basic facts of the case, as well as the relevant statutory and case law, and explains the theory under which the case is to be pursued. Understanding of these issues is crucial to your preparation for the case, and reports and testimony should specifically address these legal issues.
- Always remember that you are being paid for your time and not for your opinion. The ethical psychotherapist cannot allow fees to play a role in shaping their clinical opinion.
- Know legal procedure. If you intend to serve as an expert witness on a regular basis it is a good idea to become familiar with courtroom procedures in both criminal and civil matters. Observations of an entire trial in each domain would be a good learning experience, especially regarding the pragmatic problems of coordinating the many witnesses and participants.
- Hold conferences with the attorney who retained you before giving a deposition or going to court. Be prepared to educate the attorney regarding proper procedures for questioning in your area of expertise, including establishing credentials, the details and limits of your opinion, the facts upon which the opinion is based, and the theories

and procedures which logically lead from the facts to the opinion. Be prepared to be educated as to the way that your opinion fits with the lawyer's view of the case, and the connections that must be drawn between the clinical opinion and the fine points of the law.

- If you have given a deposition, reread it before you testify in court. Bring the deposition and your report with you to the stand and refer to them if necessary. Do not bring other materials that you do not wish to share with both attorneys, unless they are specified in a *subpoena duces tecum*. While you may bring reference materials with you to the stand, any of this material may be requested by the cross-examining party, and marked as evidence.

- When presenting testimony, talk to the judge and jury. Though the attorneys are asking the questions, they already know the case and are merely trying to elicit your testimony for the benefit of the court.

- The therapist should present expert testimony in simple, nontechnical language that the judge and jury can reasonably be expected to understand. For example, "emotion" is more easily understood than "affect." "Thought processes" is a straightforward term that will be less confusing than "cognitive operations." The therapist should not "talk down" to the jury, however. Clinically astute therapists should be able to judge the jury members' level of understanding by observing their behavior.

- Avoid weak or insipid-sounding speech patterns, commonly marked by (a) hesitation forms such as "Uh," "You know," "Well," (b) hedges, such as "sort of," "I guess," "I think," (c) overly polite speech, (d) the use of a questioning form of sentence structure rather than straightforward sentences.

- Avoid using any graphs, tables, or exhibits that will not be easily visible, readable, and comprehensible to the average juror.

- Respond only to the question asked. If you are uncertain of the question, ask that it be rephrased. Or, if the questions seem to miss the point of your testimony, you can rephrase the question yourself so as to focus on relevant issues: "If what you are asking is . . . , then. . . ."

- Assert your opinion as positively as is reasonable within the bounds of scientific and clinical inference, but be honest. Do not offer undefendably rigid pronouncements. Also avoid getting too far from the data at hand (Halleck, 1986). If the information available does not allow for an opinion regarding a particular point, then say so. If you do not know a specific piece of information, be willing to admit this.

- Rescore any objective and projective tests to make sure you have not made a mistake. Oftentimes a mistake in addition, as in the opening case of Dr. James in the scoring of a subtest, will not really have any major bearing on the case. But if the opposing counsel discovers it and makes it public, it is likely to taint your entire testimony.

- Prepare your testimony in language that will be meaningful to the court. Remember that jurors are going to be put off by jargon or will misunderstand and thus not give proper weight to your testimony.

- When you're close to actually presenting the case in court, make sure you can be comfortable in your knowledge of the client. This may entail bringing the client in for visits shortly before the court testimony. In many court cases the professional may do the evaluation even years before actually coming into court. In such a case one really ought to see the client again, if at all possible, so as to check on prior data that was collected and to update one's impressions and inferences.

Practices to Avoid

- Do not talk to the attorney for the other side without obtaining permission from the attorney who retains you. Therapists generally value cooperation, but the legal system constrains openness to the courtroom.

- Do not prepare a report in a case until asked to do so by an attorney. If your opinion cannot help the referring lawyer, he or she will probably choose to terminate your services. If a report is already written, this may be discoverable, a legal term meaning that it can be subpoenaed and scrutinized by the other side. When a report is written, you should assume that it will become a public document and prepare it appropriately.

- Do not bring test materials or overly detailed notes to the courtroom unless required to do so. These will merely provide a rich source of material for cross-examination that will miss the main points of the opinion.

- Do not disagree with the judge. Judges have a difficult and exacting role which most try to fill to the best of their abilities. While some may be unkind to expert witnesses, you must respect the trust and honor of their position, independent of any personal eccentricities.

- Do not personalize exchanges with the attorneys. Attacks upon you, your work, or your profession are simply "part of the job" for lawyers. During cross-examination the attorney for the other side believes that to help get out the truth he must point out any weaknesses in your presentation. React appropriately by giving nondefensive answers to the questions that may ensue. Remember that a very hostile cross-examination usually indicates that the opinion present- ed is persuasive and that the attorney must try extreme measures to defuse it. Many therapists are surprised when an attorney who has been very aggressive during cross-examination, later asks for a busi- ness card and suggests employing the expert in the future.

- Do not overqualify your testimony. Try to state conclusions clearly and accurately. Excessive qualification will reduce the jury's under- standing and make your opinion unpersuasive. Still, do not state conclusions so simplistically that they are inaccurate or misleading.
- Do not assume that the court will conclude the same things from your findings as you do. Courts are notorious for applying their own idiosyncratic reasoning to the opinions and research results of be- havioral and social scientists (Hays & Solway, 1972; Monohan & Walker, 1985).
- Be honest in your testimony and do not try to hide anything. The worst possible error is to appear less than honest or forthright.
- Do not anticipate where a line of questioning is going. Confront one question at a time and give the best answer you can.
- Do not be led into overgeneralizations on cross-examination.
- Avoid becoming an advocate for a position. Stay with giving an honest and thorough account, and avoid exaggeration or deception for the purpose of "winning" the case.
- Avoid the three classic errors of the expert witness—becoming (a) too technical, (b) too complex in discussion, or (c) too condescend- ing and simplistic in approach. Any of these approaches is likely to lose the attention of the jurors and may also turn them against you and the content of your testimony.
- In that vein, try to avoid long and repetitive explanations of your points. If at all possible, keep your responses to two or three state- ments. If you feel more is needed, try to point out that you can't fully answer the question without elaboration; then, again, keep your elaboration as clear and concise as possible.

SUMMARY AND CONCLUSIONS

The foregoing discussion has focused on a number of pragmatic issues that arise when psychotherapists are consulted by attorneys or testify in court. Other more esoteric roles, such as advocate, court-ordered therapist, or "pure" consultant, have been discussed elsewhere (Barrett et al., 1985; Wells, 1986); for the majority of psychotherapists they are not critical.

While this chapter has emphasized the importance of cooperating with legal professionals, particularly attorneys who retain expert witnesses, it is important to remember that therapists cannot become advocates for any side of a legal conflict. Valid clinical opinions require a degree of objectivity that is sometimes threatened by the highly charged and confrontive legal arena (Barrett et al., 1985). The therapist in court must endeavor to present only an accurate opinion based on the unique knowledge, skill, experience, training, or education that qualifies him or her for participation in the first place.

> Whenever one testifies in court . . . one should not consider oneself an advocate for the patient, for the defense, or for the government. One is an advocate only for one's own opinion. When the expert witness allows himself or herself to be drawn into a particular position, because of a feeling that the patient needs treatment, that the patient should be incarcerated, or that society needs to be protected, the credibility and validity of one's testimony invariably suffers. (Shapiro, 1984)

Experts in psychotherapy can only legitimately be advocates for the scientific or clinical merit of their conclusions.

Perhaps the best way to cope with the rigors of courtroom testimony is to develop a thorough understanding of the legal procedures involved. This process may be played out with each new case, as the context of a given cause or proceeding will have important implications for the participation of the expert. Ultimately, the expert must rely on his own expertise and hard work.

Although courts are not bound by the opinions of experts, they depend on them heavily. In the absence of solid contributions by psychotherapists, the courts must depend on amateurish speculation and simplistic notions of human nature. Consequently, those with special training in psychiatry and psychology bear a heavy responsibility to support and assist the legal system (Buckhout, 1986). Though this system's methods are foreign to many therapists, just decisions in many areas can be made only within the context of the most sophisticated and evolved understanding of human behavior available.

Specific Disorders and the Psychotherapist

CHAPTER 9

Issues of Reality Contact

LOSS OF REALITY contact is the inability to gain adequate information from the environment, to process it in such a way as to generate an adequately realistic portrayal of that environment, and then to generate behaviors appropriate to reality. Psychoses such as schizophrenia have typically been defined as disorders in which there is inadequate reality contact, and so we considered them first. However, whether there is adequate reality contact is often also the central issue, especially within the legal arena, for disorders such as amnesia, multiple personality, and even the post-traumatic stress disorder.

SCHIZOPHRENIA

"Your secret dreams that grow over the years like apple seeds sown in your belly, grow up through you in leafy wonder and finally sprout through your skin, gentle and soft and wondrous, and they have a life of their own . . . "
"You've done this?"
"A time or two."

—W. P. Kinsella, *Shoeless Joe*

When people use the term psychosis, they often mean schizophrenia because the question of adequate reality contact is such a clearly evident issue with this disorder. Of course, there are other mental disorders that are labeled psychotic, e.g., severe depression and paranoia, and these are discussed later in this section. Nevertheless, most psychotherapists who have worked with schizophrenia would argue that it is the most serious of all mental disorders. About one out of every 100 people in the United States will be diagnosed as schizophrenic at least once in his or her lifetime.

Schizophrenia has often been confused with "insanity", not only in the layman's mind, but of attorneys, and even mental health professionals as well. The authors have witnessed numerous instances wherein mental health professionals testified that they thought there was insanity because the accused was schizophrenic. But, a) the "loss of reality contact" found in schizophrenia does not necessarily fit with the definition of insanity, b) the loss may be evident in areas of thinking or times unrelated to the crime, and c) other disorders can just as easily fit the legal definition of insanity.

From a perspective of potential legal liability, the psychotherapist needs to be aware of those premorbid predictors that may indicate the possibility of schizophrenia (Meyer & Salmon, 1988; Kay & Lindenmayer, 1981):

(1) A schizophrenic parent or parents, with a less reliable indicator being the presence of other schizophrenic blood relatives. There is evidence that for women, the earlier that their mother became schizophrenic, the higher is the likelihood that they, too, will become schizophrenic. For sons, however, this is not as critical, with a more important issue being the time of separation from a disturbed mother. The earlier the separation occurs, the more damaging it is for a son.

(2) A history of prenatal disruption or birth problems.

(3) Low birthweight and/or low I.Q. relative to siblings.

(4) Hyperactivity; cognitive slippage; any signs of central nervous system dysfunction, particularly in the left hemisphere, such as convulsions; evidence of enlarged cerebral ventricles; significant reaction time problems; or an abnormally rapid recovery rate of the autonomic nervous system.

(5) An early role as the scapegoat or odd member of the family.

(6) Parenting marked by emotional and/or discipline inconsistency, including double messages.

(7) Rejection by peers in childhood or adolescence, and perception by either teachers or peers as being significantly more irritable or unstable than other children.

(8) Rejection of peers, especially if accompanied by odd thinking processes, ambivalent emotional responses, and/or a lack of response to standard pleasure sources.

The personality of individuals who later become schizophrenic can often be described as eccentric and isolated, mildly confused and disorganized, suspicious, and/or withdrawn.

Psychotherapists also should be aware of those prognostic indicators that point to a good chance of remission once schizophrenia does occur:

(1) Sexual-marital status — being married or at least having a previous history of stable, consistent sexual-social adjustments.
(2) A family history of affective disorder rather than schizophrenic disorder.
(3) Presence of an affective pattern (either elation or depression) in the acute stage of the schizophrenic disorder.
(4) Abrupt onset of the disorder and onset later than early adulthood.
(5) Adequate premorbid vocational adjustment.
(6) Evidence of premorbid competence in interpersonal relationships, and higher socioeconomic status.
(7) A short length of stay in the hospital, and an absence of electro-convulsive therapy (ECT) treatment.
(8) A relatively high score on the WAIS-R similarities subtest.
(9) Evidence of clear precipitating factors at the onset of the disturbance.

A multifaceted treatment plan is generally required as the standard of treatment of schizophrenia (Meyer & Salmon, 1988; Nasrallah & Weinberger, 1986). Chemotherapy, usually with the phenothiazines, the butyrophenones, or the thioxanthenes, is useful as one component in the treatment of many schizophrenics, particularly for those who are hospital-prone clients of low competence. Since there can be major problems with their ability to take the medication after they are released from the hospital, the long-acting agents, such as the phenothiazine Prolixin, can be useful, although they do have a restricted range of effectiveness and numerous side effects. At least 35 percent of all clients taking antipsychotics show muscular problems and feelings of lethargy alternating with restlessness. Approximately 5 percent (up to 40 percent in the elderly) develop tardive dyskinesia (T.D.), a typically irreversible syndrome that may involve grimacing, lip-smacking, and involuntary neck and head movements. The majority of patients who develop T.D. experience only mild to moderate symptoms, however. Also, some drugs, particularly the phenothiazines (the most commonly used drugs), tend to suppress gag reflexes and have caused a significant number of deaths due to aspiration asphyxiation. In addition to these side effects, there can be a loss of creativity and spontaneity and a reinforcement of the patient role, since the client sees the treatment as totally external to oneself. Although chemotherapy can be useful, antipsychotic drugs are no doubt prescribed too often (Helman, 1981; Taub, 1986), and the severe side-effects offer some grim potential for malpractice liability in the event of

misdiagnosis or a too routine use of chemotherapy or other physically invasive techniques.

Since its discovery, ECT has been intermittently used with schizophrenics. However, ECT has not shown marked success with schizophrenia
(Scovern & Kilmann, 1980). Psychosurgery, dialysis and megavitamin therapies have been tried with increasing frequency in recent years, but there is
little significant evidence as yet that these treatments are successful (Diaz-
Buxo et al., 1980; Nasrallah & Weinberger, 1986).

Paranoid Schizophrenia

Paranoid schizophrenia presents somewhat different characteristics for
the psychotherapist to consider. Most importantly, paranoid schizophrenics
are more likely than other schizophrenics to be dangerous. Also, the paranoid schizophrenic is typically brighter and more socially competent than
other schizophrenics and has judgment that is less impaired. Since accurate
discrimination has both treatment and legal considerations, paranoid schizophrenia is possibly best conceptualized in contrast first to schizophrenic
disorders and then to the other paranoid disorders, as in Table 9.1 (Meissner,
1978; Nasrallah & Weinberger, 1986; Turkat, 1985).

Since paranoid schizophrenia is marked by a greater overall level of disorder and more obvious and bizarre disturbance, it may warrant more intrusive methods of treatment, thereby increasing the psychotherapist's liability.
ECT has been used with some paranoid schizophrenics in an apparent attempt to disrupt the consistency of the belief system. However, ECT contains all the risks of any intrusive procedure; this is so particularly important
here since a fear of being intruded on in any number of dimensions is central
to the paranoid disorders. In addition, there is the probability of short- and
long-term memory loss, which could easily increase the sense of vulnerability central to many paranoid disorders (Squire, Slater, & Miller, 1981).

Because establishing trust in a series of psychotherapy contacts may be
extremely time-consuming in the more bizarre paranoid disorders, the therapist may have to crash through the defenses erected by the paranoid systems.
Direct analysis (Karon, 1976; Rosen, 1953) has been useful in this regard.
Interpretations are forced on the paranoid individual to break through his or
her massive avoidance procedures. These interpretations usually center on
what are thought to be major inner conflicts, notably in the areas of aggression, sexuality, and inadequacy.

Discerning the relevance of an individual's insane delusions has taken on
a new twist in light of the 1986 Supreme Court case of *Colorado v. Connelly*. Connelly confessed to an unsolved murder to a police officer, and then

TABLE 9.1
Features of Paranoid Schizophrenia

Other Schizophrenic Disorders	*Paranoid Schizophrenia*
More often show depression or other mood disorder or anxiety	Depression or anxiety not that common
Show first manifestations in adolescence or late adolescence	Manifestations develop later in life
Approximately equal incidence in males and females	More common in males
Appear more disoriented or withdrawn	Often show some reasonably normal-appearing outward behaviors
Often of lower than average intelligence	Higher intellectual ability than other schizophrenics
More impaired in specific judgment and cognitive tasks	Less impaired in specific judgment and cognitive tasks
Approximately equal occurrence across cultures	Seldom occurs in rural non-Western cultures
Tend toward long periods of hospitalization	Proportionately shorter hospital stays
Average body build	More often tend to be mesomorphic (the body of the powerful athlete)

Other Paranoid Disorders	*Paranoid Schizophrenia*
Irrational beliefs may not be so severe as to constitute a delusion; when existent, they tend to be fewer in number, and they don't often change	Delusional system is poorly organized and may contain a number of delusions that change over time
Belief system disorder is the fundamental abnormality	Schizophrenia and the belief system disorder are both fundamental to the abnormality
Appear normal	Present a generally bizarre appearance and attitude
Relatively good reality contact	Problems in reality contact
Delusions are of persecution or delusional jealousy	Delusions are more wide-ranging, including persecution, jealousy, grandiosity, irrelevant thoughts
More consistent relation to early developmental patterns	More often develops later in life
Psychological factors are generally the primary causes	Biological factors may be significant contributing causes

later repeated and expanded his confession to other officers, stating that "voices" or "the voice of God" had told him to confess. (He was given *Miranda* rights throughout.) He was later determined to be incompetent to stand trial and hospitalized for six months where he was treated with medications before he was restored to competency and stood trial. His attorney sought to have his confession suppressed on the basis that it and the waiver of attorney were not voluntary. A mental health professional who examined Connelly found that he suffered from "command hallucinations" which interfered with his "volitional abilities; that is, his ability to make free and rational choices," but did not, however, interfere with his cognitive abilities, and thus he probably understood his *Miranda* rights.

The Supreme Court rejected this claim. They asserted that claims that the defendant was not exercising "free will" or were the result of psychotic episodes involving hearing the voice of God were not relevant to determining whether the confession was voluntary because they did not demonstrate that the police coerced the confession. The Court concluded that the notion of "free will" has no place in this area and that the defendant's perception of coercion flowing from the voice of God "is a matter to which the United States Constitution does not speak."

THE PARANOID DISORDERS

The *DSM-III-R* paranoid disorders, the most important of which is the delusional (paranoid) disorder, are also psychotic conditions. The symptom picture is dominated by persistent persecutory delusions or delusions of jealousy. There are no significant hallucinations. Unlike paranoid schizophrenia, there is not much fragmentation of thought in the delusions. Also, there is seldom as severe an impairment in daily functioning as there is in paranoid schizophrenia. Paranoid schizophrenics typically have more than one delusional system, but a single focus in the delusions is not uncommon. Individuals with paranoid disorders often experience disruption in marital and interpersonal functioning, though disruption rarely occurs in occupational functioning or in intellectual activities.

Paranoid disorders are relatively rare disorders, and since these individuals are usually coerced into treatment, they are not always cooperative in a diagnostic situation. Since anger is often a factor in the personality makeup, therapists must be concerned about issues of danger to others.

Although the paranoid system is often based on bizarre premises, it is marked by a well-integrated personality; therefore, intrusive techniques are likely to backfire and further alienate the client from the treatment process. The development of some minimal trust in the relationship is crucial, as this gives paranoids a much needed feedback resource, a person with whom they might test out the adequacy of their delusional system. The therapist must accept and empathize with the paranoid and yet not lose integrity as a therapist by participating in the delusional system. For example, the therapist may note correlates between his or her own life and the client's, which give the client a potential new frame of reference as well as a new model for coping with vulnerability and fear. Humor, notably absent in many paranoids, can be modeled, as can other cognitive coping systems.

Also, paranoids are likely to be litigious. Hence, some psychotherapists are not willing to see them in psychotherapy. It is no doubt wise to make extensive use of upfront informed consent documents, made in front of valid witnesses, before engaging in psychotherapy with a paranoid.

Shared Paranoid Disorder

Traditionally termed *folie à deux* (i.e., "the madness of two"), the shared paranoid disorder, which appears in *DSM-III* but not in *DSM-III-R*, involves one person who is originally paranoid in some form, and a receiver who passively incorporates the paranoid beliefs into his or her own system. These receivers are in a close and intimate relationship with the dominant individuals and have a history of being dependent psychologically on this controlling person. When they break away from the relationship, the paranoid belief system dissipates. Certain cult-based crimes involve this type of relationship, and in such cases a critical task is parceling out degrees of criminal responsibility between the original paranoid and the receiver.

AFFECTIVE DISORDERS

Major Depression

Since suicidal feelings often accompany depression, it is important for the therapist to recognize the symptoms of severe depression—not only to provide proper treatment, but also to avoid legal liability. Consistent and significant depression is marked by (1)dysphoria (feeling bad) and/or apathetic mood, (2) a loss or decrease in the potency of stimuli, e.g., through the death of an important other—a condition referred to as a "stimulus void," and (3) "anhedonia"—or a chronic inability to experience pleasure.

These primary symptoms are then often associated with a various mixture of the following secondary symptoms: (1) withdrawal from contact with others, (2) a sense of hopelessness, (3) rumination about suicide and/or death, (4) sleep disturbance, especially early-morning awakening, (5) psychomotor slowing or agitation, (6) decrease in and/or disruption of eating behaviors, (7) self-blame, a sense of worthlessness, irrational feelings of guilt, (8) lack of concentration, (9) lack of decisiveness, (10) increased alcohol or drug abuse, (11) crying for no apparent reason (Murphy et al., 1985; Roy, 1987).

In the United States, about 30 million to 40 million persons have experienced a serious depression of some type, a rate of about 12–14 percent, which has remained reasonably stable for several decades (Murphy et al., 1985). It is also estimated that up to one-fourth of the office practice of physicians who focus on physical disorders is actually concerned with depression-based symptomatology. About 85 percent of the psychotropic medication dispensed for depression is prescribed by nonpsychiatrists, primarily internists, gynecologists, and family practitioners.

Since a severe level of depression, possibly including psychotic components, is often found in major depression, more intrusive techniques are likely to be used. ECT has often been used for severe depression; this is probably one of the few syndromes for which there is good evidence of ECT's effectiveness. However, that effectiveness must be balanced against the high psychological and physical costs of the technique. Similarly, psychosurgery, in which a lesion is placed in areas that control emotional response, such as the limbic system, has been used.

Drugs (notably alcohol and other self-medications) have long been used to alleviate depression. The two major subcategories of antidepressants used in recent times are the tricyclics and the monoamine oxidase inhibitors. Both require substantial trial and error adjustment on dosages (titration). Also, both require from several days to several weeks before any positive effects occur, so suicidal prevention procedures are especially critical during this lag period. Since the monoamine oxidase inhibitors have more significant side effects and require dietary restrictions, the tricyclics have been favored. They are most effective with severe depressions that have a significant endogenous component, but the rate of effectiveness is seldom better than 70 percent (Fabry, 1980). When the tricyclics are administered to someone who is actually in the depressive phase of a bipolar disorder, there is a very real danger of stimulating a manic episode.

The intrusive techniques have many risks, which, of course, can be balanced by gains in controlling the depression, and secondarily, in preventing any suicide behaviors. Yet it is most important that they be implemented in an overall treatment that includes a variety of techniques designed to control the depression psychologically and to upgrade the skills needed to prevent future depression.

Dysthymic Disorder (Depressive Neurosis)

The dysthymic disorder is symptomatologically similar to major depression, except that the symptoms are less severe and yet typically of greater duration. A duration of two years is required for the diagnosis (except for children and adolescents, where the requirement is one year), and periods of dysphoria cannot be separated by periods of normal mood of more than two months.

The dysthymic disorder is often treated with chemotherapy, but this treatment is not as appropriate as it is for more severe depressive episodes. Since learned helplessness is often a factor in this disorder, chemotherapy, ECT, or similar treatments can easily exacerbate this component by indicating that patients cannot play a major role in redirecting their life situation.

Cognitive-behavioral treatment techniques, derived primarily from Beck (1976), are probably the most important psychological treatment methods of depression. Along with chemotherapy, they comprise a standard of care for most cases. Through discussion and consciousness-raising techniques, clients in cognitive-behavioral treatment are taught to view their thoughts more objectively (i.e., to distance themselves from these maladaptive thoughts). For example, such common depressive thoughts as "I am totally worthless" are confronted as hypotheses rather than facts, phenomena rather than reality (Ellis, 1987; Ellis & Dryden, 1987).

Bipolar Disorder

Bipolar disorder is the modern term for what is traditionally known as manic-depressive disorder (or psychosis). The diagnosis of bipolar disorder is made whenever manic features are observed, regardless of the presence of depressive features. The range of behaviors that typify mania is wide and most commonly includes (1) hyperactive motor behavior, (2) variable irritability and/or euphoria, and (3) a speeding-up of thought processes, called "flight of ideas." Manic speech is typically loud, rapid, and difficult to understand. When the mood is expansive, manics take on many tasks (seldom completing them), avoid sleep, and easily ramble into lengthy monologues about their personal plans, worth, and power. A number of manics become dangerous if they become "frustrated" during a manic episode. When the mood becomes more irritable, they are quick to complain and engage in hostile tirades. The manic phase is contrasted to typical depression (either as a phase of a bipolar disorder or simply as depression alone) on the dimensions outlined in Table 9.2.

TABLE 9.2
Comparing Mania and Depression

	Manic Phase	Depressive Phase
Behavioral	Hyperactive	Slowed motor behavior
	Socially gregarious	Socially withdrawn
	Impulsive	Tentative or non-responsive
	Variable appetite	Decreased appetite
	Increased sex drive	Decreased sex drive
	Energetic	Easily fatigued
	Decreased need for sleep	Disrupted sleep patterns
Emotional	Euphoric	Melancholic
	Agitated irritability	Dispirited, glum
	(on occasion)	
	Stimulation-seeking	Stimulation-avoidant
Cognitive	Flight of ideas	Slowed thought processes
	Optimistic	Negativistic, tentative
	Pollyannish	Sense of hopelessness
	Positive self-image	Negative self-image
	Delusions of grandeur	Delusions of guilt and/or
		disorder

Psychotherapists need to be aware that during a manic phase, an individual is likely to make commitments and contracts he cannot fulfill. Steps (e.g., gaining the cooperation of relatives and friends) should be taken to protect him in this regard.

Psychotherapists occasionally have difficulty making an accurate differential diagnosis regarding this disorder. For example, psychotic manic reactions involve grandiose delusions, bizarre and impulsive behavior, transient hallucinations and explosiveness. As such, these reactions may be confused with schizophrenic episodes. However, whereas schizophrenics (and schizoaffectives) are distracted by internal thoughts and ideas, manics are distracted by external stimuli that often go unnoticed by others. Also, whereas schizophrenics (and schizoaffectives) tend to avoid any true relationships with others during an active phase, manics are typically open to contact with other people.

In this same vein, psychotherapists who work with children should be aware that children are at risk for a bipolar disorder with a clear manic component if: (1) they have a family history of bipolar disorder; (2) they have shown affect problems, particularly hyperexcitability; (3) they show significantly higher ability on the verbally based items (rather than those depending on visual-motor performance) on the Wechsler Intelligence Scale for Children (WISC-R); and (4) there is evidence of EEG irregularity in the frontal lobes of the brain (Kestenbaum, 1979; Klein, Depue & Slater, 1985).

Until recent decades, a wide array of treatments received anecdotal support as useful for mania. Hopes were high for each, but empirically valid data confirming their effectiveness were never forthcoming. One good reason is that spontaneous remission is common in mania. Thus, therapists who coincidentally happened to do something unaccustomed (such as bring up a new topic, give a new drug, or even fall asleep) at the same time one or two of their manic clients spontaneously remitted would infer that the new method was responsible for the cure. If they were sufficiently ambitious to publish a clinical report, the new technique would become the focus of attention until someone else discovered another presumed cure.

However, it is now clear that the standard of care for the treatment of mania is a combination of lithium and psychotherapy (Klein et al., 1985; Mester, 1986). Lithium is usually administered as lithium carbonate, a chemically convenient form that also contains a high percentage of lithium per weight. Lithium therapy is a bit more demanding than other chemotherapy. Because the kidneys absorb lithium rapidly, it must be taken in divided dosages to avoid damage to the renal system. Educating clients about its use is most important; they must, for example, take it continuously and on schedule even though they may feel well (and manics feel quite well at times). A lack of informed consent in regard to this education leaves the clinician liable if the manic is damaged by abuse of the medication regimen.

PSYCHOGENIC AMNESIA

Psychogenic amnesia often has legal ramifications, as it essentially involves a temporary and sudden loss of ability to recall personal information (Schachter, 1986). This loss of information can be about a specific topic, or it can be memories of the immediate or distant past. Although media portrayals lead people to believe that the memory for all past events is lost in amnesia, this is rare. This disorder is most often observed in adult and adolescent females who are undergoing significant stress and also in young males experiencing the stress of an identity conflict. Recovery of memory is usually rapid, whereas the recovery is gradual in organic conditions, if it takes place at all (Schachter, 1986). The alcohol amnestic disorder differs from psychogenic amnesia. In the former, the person is able to recall information for only a few minutes after it is obtained, since the ability to transfer information from short-term memory into long-term memory has been lost.

The memory failure in psychogenic amnesia is too significant to be explained by ordinary forgetfulness, and it is not explained by the alcohol amnestic disorder, by other organic conditions, or by such disorders as catatonia and stupor. It also needs to be discriminated from malingering, and such discrimination is often quite difficult. The findings of faking scales on psychological tests are helpful here; the reader is referred to the sections on malingering in Chapters 1 and 11. Interviews with the use of sodium amytal or hypnosis can also be helpful.

It is unclear exactly what mechanisms underlie psychogenic amnesias and fugues. However, three main hypotheses have been proposed (Kopelman, 1987); the treatment response, as well as possibly the legal response, depends upon which theory one subscribes to. The first hypothesis holds that such amnesia experiences result from faulty encoding of information at initial input, i.e., the information is not even stored. The deficit is thought to occur because the extreme mood or emotional arousal that often accompanies the first appearance of such amnesias can hamper the acquisition of the information. Kopelman sees this first hypothesis as being the one best supported by the data. The second hypothesis is that the memories do exist but have been "repressed," i.e., there is "motivated (at a subconscious level) forgetting." A third hypothesis is related to the second in that the information is believed to be actually stored somewhere in memory. This third hypothesis suggests there is a primary retrieval deficit, and that the amnesiacs reflect mood-state- (or ego-state-, in psychodynamic terminology) dependent phenomena, similar to those described in depression. Thus, the experiences could be retrieved if the subject could be restored to a subjective state similar to that in which the experiences first occurred.

With few exceptions, e.g., *Wilson v. U.S.* (1968), courts have not accepted amnesia by itself as a primary defense supporting either incompetency to stand trial or insanity. And the exceptions have usually involved incidents in which there is severe head injury. Certainly amnesia caused by true physical trauma is seldom ever total, nor is it selective for issues pertaining only to the relevant incident (Meyer & Salmon, 1988). The abuse of drugs and alcohol can, of course, distort memory, although, again, there's little evidence that people with any significant degree of functioning during the incident have totally impaired memories because of such abuse. While hypnosis can be useful in refreshing memory in all of the above conditions, psychotherapists should be aware there was an increasing trend in the legal system to reject any testimony which has been "enhanced" by hypnosis (Edmonston, 1986; Orne, 1979).

However, this trend has certainly been slowed, if not stopped by the findings of the 1987 Supreme Court case of *Rock v. Arkansas*. In this case, Vickie Rock was charged with shooting her husband. She had a partial amnesia for the details of the shooting. She was hypnotized to enhance her memory, and after hypnosis she remembered that the gun had misfired because it was defective. The trial court refused to permit this testimony because it had resulted from hypnosis, and was therefore considered unreliable.

The Supreme Court held that it was a violation of her constitutional right to testify in her own defense arbitrarily to prevent the defendant from testifying concerning the memory recalled under hypnosis. It was the absolute rule prohibiting the defendant from presenting hypnotically enhanced testimony that the Court found objectionable, stating "In applying its evidentiary rules a State must evaluate whether the interests served by a rule justify the limitation imposed on the defendant's constitutional right to testify."

Justice Blackmun noted that a number of courts had imposed limitations on the use of hypnotically enhanced testimony and that "the most common response to hypnosis, however, appears to be an increase in both correct and incorrect recollections." This difficulty with hypnosis, the Court felt, could be cured by good cross-examination, or rules regulating hypnotically enhanced testimony without prohibiting it altogether. Presumably a state could enforce such rules as procedural safeguards to help reduce hypnosis-caused bias.

Ironically, the five justices making up the majority in this case are generally among those who are most likely to rely on social science data in their decisions. Yet, they seemed to pay little attention to the very serious problems associated with hypnosis and memory that have been identified by social science research. In the long run, this decision, which technically is aimed at protecting the rights of the accused, is likely to harm rather than help defendants. If states are required to permit defendants to present hypnotically refreshed testimony, most will probably allow the prosecution the same right. This in turn is likely to result in the use of eyewitnesses who under hypnosis "remember" details that point to the defendant's guilt. Given the very limited training of those police officers who most often conduct criminal hypnosis, this is not a happy prospect.

Psychogenic Fugue

This specific form of amnesia is one in which people are unable to recall the essentials of their previous identity. In addition, they are likely to wander away from their home environment and assume an entirely new identity. Although they are seldom able to recall their behaviors while in the fugue state, the recovery is usually complete. This syndrome often occurs as a reaction to a severe psychosocial stressor, such as the unexpected breakup of a marriage or the loss of a job without warning. It is facilitated by heavy alcohol or drug use. Kopelman (1987) points out that a history of amnesias based on actual organic damage is a typical precursor to psychogenic fugue. The psychogenic fugue often "serves a purpose" in the life of the individual. This is commonly an escape from negative circumstances, but it is not unusual for it to facilitate a collection for damages in the legal arena.

The traditional treatment for amnesia, and the most generally effective, involves using hypnotic techniques to gain access to subconscious material. Psychotherapy, with an emphasis on interpretation of possible conflicts before adequate realization of them, is also useful, particularly if a supportive atmosphere both in and out of the therapy hour can be generated. This gives clients the sense of safety and potential for reintegration that they so desperately need.

MULTIPLE PERSONALITY

Because the concept of multiple personality receives much attention from the media, it is often thought to be a relatively common disorder. However, in 1978 Winer noted that there had been only about 200 reasonably well documented cases. There have been reports which would lead one to believe there are a large number of multiple personalities but, as Gruenewald (1978) and Schachter (1986) have shown, these reports are often spurred by (a) inadequate observation, (b) a therapist's great readiness for various reasons to find such clients, and (c) the eagerness of many clients to produce multiple personalities. The multiple personality should be considered rare, and many clinicians never see a true multiple personality in their entire career. It occasionally has been put forth as a defense to crime, although seldom with any marked success.

There have been attempts to have multiple personalities avoid legal responsibility by pleading that the original personality was not aware of the offense. Success here has been mixed. Nevertheless, it is an attractive approach for malingerers (since it is both dramatic and only requires the energy for dissimulation for part of the time). A healthy skepticism is always warranted when there is a claim for this rare disorder some time after an accusation of criminality is made.

Multiple personalities come into treatment because they note some peculiarities in their world—forgetting of certain interactions with people, general confusion, and loss of memories (Kluft, 1987). A different personality is then discovered through psychotherapy, which is often supplemented by hypnosis. In some cases, personalities continue to be produced, first by the indirect suggestion of the therapist's interest and reinforcement, and then by the reinforcement of the therapist's reinvigorated concern for the person's problems (Gruenewald, 1978).

Precipitating factors in the genesis of the multiple personality disorder include psychological stress and previous amnestic episodes. The multiple personality, according to *DSM-III-R*, is a person who is consecutively dominated by separate and distinct personalities that determine separate behavior patterns. The personalities are complex and reasonably well-integrated, and the transition from one to another is sudden. The next and later personalities are usually crystallizations of various, often opposing, facets from the original one.

The traditional treatment for the multiple personality is hypnosis (Gruenewald, 1978; Kluft, 1987), which is used to get in touch with the dissociated subpersonalities. In the few cases that have been available to clinicians for study, hypnosis has generally been reasonably successful, though the cost in time has been high. Also, it is arguable that since hypnosis itself may involve a dissociative experience, it may iatrogenically increase the tendency to produce multiple personalities, particularly in the short run.

POST-TRAUMATIC STRESS DISORDER (PTSD)

Psychotherapists involved in the legal arena commonly encounter or offer diagnoses of post-traumatic stress disorder (PTSD) (Henden & Haas, 1987). The difficulty with this is that the link between the current alleged disorder and a prior situation is hard to establish; the "face valid" nature of the symptomatology, e.g., nightmares about the prior incident, is often the only clear support for the diagnosis. Hence, it is amenable to conscious and unconscious faking (Sparr & Atkinson, 1986).

For example, in *Pard v. U.S.* (1984), Mr. Pard received a verdict of not guilty by reason of mental disease or defect on two counts of attempted manslaughter and one count of attempted murder, stemming from an attempt to kill his ex-wife and a consequent shootout with police officers. The jury accepted his assertion that he was suffering from a PTSD, generated by alleged extensive combat experiences in Vietnam. Subsequent to the criminal trial, Mr. Pard lodged a civil suit for related damages against the U.S. Government and the Veterans Administration. During that trial, the defendants provided extensive evidence that, at most, Mr. Pard had only been marginally exposed to combat.

While post-traumatic stress disorder evolved as a *DSM-III* category out of the Vietnam War (Henden & Haas, 1987), it is frequently seen in individuals involved in various traumatic events. According to the *DSM-III-R*, it is marked by: the existence of a recognizable stressor that would evoke significant symptoms of distress in almost anyone; some method of reexperiencing the trauma, such as flashbacks and nightmares; numbing of responsiveness to or reduced involvement with the external world beginning some time after the trauma; and various symptoms, including hyperalertness or exaggerated startle response, sleep disturbance, guilt about surviving when others have not or about behavior required for survival, memory impairment or trouble concentrating, avoidance of activities that arouse recollection of the traumatic event, and/or intensification of symptoms by exposure to events that symbolize or resemble the traumatic event (see Table 9.3).

"Flashbacks," vivid reexperiencings of the traumatic event, are commonly reported in cases of PTSD that make it into the legal arena (Sparr & Atkinson, 1986). Certainly the dramatic quality of such symptoms is very impressive to most jurors. The difficulty for the psychotherapist who is involved in such a case comes in deciphering the veracity of such reports. In conjunction with the general concepts noted in our discussion of malingering in Chapters 1 and 11, the following criteria (Blank, 1985; Sparr & Atkinson, 1986) are effective in helping to make such discriminations:

(1) The flashback is sudden and unpremeditated.
(2) The flashback is uncharacteristic of the individual.
(3) There is a retrievable history of one or more intensely traumatic events that are reenacted in the flashback.
(4) There may be amnesia for all or part of the episode.

TABLE 9.3
Traumas and Their Effects

Traumatic Stressors	Common Psychological Effects	Common Physical Consequences of Psychological Reactions
combat	emotional numbing	diminished sex drive
natural disasters	depression	insomia
man-made disasters	guilt over survival	hypertension
(car accidents)	flashbacks and nightmares	tension headaches
torture	obsessive thoughts about	stomach and intestinal
kidnapping	the traumas	disorders
hijacking	anxiety	excessive fatigue
assaults	tendency to be startled	heart palpitations
severe abuse	inability to relax	
rape	problems in memory and	
	concentration	
	impulsiveness	

(5) The flashback lacks apparent current and specific motivation.
(6) The current trigger stimuli reasonably resemble the original experiences.
(7) The individual is at least somewhat unaware of the specific ways he or she has reenacted some of the prior traumas.
(8) The individual has, or has had, other believable symptoms of PTSD.

The psychotherapist who is treating someone who is in a crisis that could later lead to a PTSD is advised to keep in mind the standard principles of crisis intervention (Kasl & Cooper, 1987). These are usually articulated as immediacy, proximity, and expectancy. These principles were developed in World War II to decrease the consequent problems of the severe distress of combat. Immediacy emphasizes early awareness and detection by others close to the person, treatment as quickly as possible, and an emphasis on returning clients to their typical life situation as quickly as possible. Proximity emphasizes the need to treat clients in their own world — not distancing them from their upset by hospitalization. Lastly, the psychotherapist must communicate a clear expectancy that although fear and anxiety are normal processes here, they do not excuse clients from functioning adequately. The sick role is not reinforced, and there is an emphasis on experiences that demonstrate that clients are regaining control of their world. An innovative alternative would be to use carbon dioxide inhalation therapy. Single inhalations of high concentrations of carbon dioxide have been effective in markedly reducing free-floating anxiety (Wolpe, 1987), the type of anxiety that is thought to generate later flashback experiences.

CHAPTER 10

Issues of Impulse Control

THE CONCEPTS OF impulsive behavior and "compulsion" occur throughout criminal law and are usually interpreted in legal parlance as "irresistible impulse." This is a difficult concept, however, to sell to most jurors. The difficulty comes in applying to any one individual, since irresistibility cannot be measured objectively. In many cases, judgment is based on history; that is, the number of times the person has not resisted the impulse is offered as de facto evidence of the irresistibility of the impulse. The removal of culpability as a result of such a definition, however, would paradoxically place the legal system in the position of rewarding those individuals who have most often committed a particular criminal act! This difficulty of "irresistible" repetitive behavior is especially relevant in the legal response to the antisocial personality. In most insanity defense statutes, repetitive behavior does not support insanity or an irresistible impulse to commit a crime. Ultimately, the discrimination is between an irresistible impulse and an impulse that was not resisted.

In kleptomania the "addictive" behavior is itself illegal, so the diagnosis itself is more logical as a legal defense. Of course, the difficulty of discriminating an unresisted impulse from an irresistible impulse is highlighted here. As such, good history taking, external corroboration, and a high level of attention to the possibility of malingering are important whenever a claim of impulse disorder is part of a legal dispute.

OBSESSIVE-COMPULSIVE DISORDER

This disorder is marked by obsessive-compulsive patterns that are experienced by the person performing them as irrational and ego-alien. At least initially, the person attempts to resist the obsession or compulsion. The most common obsessions seen by psychotherapists are repetitive thoughts of contamination, violence, doubts about religion and one's duties, and self-doubts. The most common compulsions include checking behaviors, handwashing, and repetitive acts. If there is a violation of the law, the question quickly arises as to how much legal responsibility is mitigated by an inability to resist the compulsive components.

Persons coming from middle- and upper-class backgrounds are more likely to develop obsessive-compulsive syndromes. This should not be surprising, especially in a society that so highly values achievement, since those with compulsive patterns are often quite efficient and productive. Obsessive-compulsives are brighter on the average than individuals with the other anxiety disorders; this also makes sense, since obsessions are intellectual coping strategies for anxiety (Rachman, 1980). Thus "white-collar" criminals often combine obsessive-compulsive patterns with psychopathic traits.

A central feature of standard treatment for the compulsive components of this disorder is a clear consistent program of response prevention (e.g., taking all soap and towels away from a handwasher), combined with constant exposure to the eliciting stimuli to promote extinction. Thought-stopping is especially effective in dealing with the obsessions, while paradoxical intention helps control both the obsessive and compulsive aspects of the disorders. As progress occurs on these fronts, standard group therapy and/ or psychotherapy can be used (Kozak, Foa, & McCarthy, 1987).

A diagnosis of obsessive-compulsive disorder (or obsessive-compulsive personality disorder) does not often qualify for an irresistible impulse defense. The one exception may be the individual who had experienced obsessions of violence and then acted on them. The difficulty here, of course, is establishing after the fact that these thoughts and acts were truly obsessive, in the sense that the person felt compelled to carry them out against his or her own desires (Kozak et al., 1987). Establishing that the person sought treatment for this behavior at some prior time supports this defense, although the therapist has to be aware that a clever individual might have gone to seek treatment to establish an alibi for later, rationally deliberated criminal behavior.

PERSONALITY DISORDERS

Personality disorders are chronic and pervasive patterns of perceiving and responding to the environment that are sufficiently maladaptive to cause disruption in functioning (Rutter, 1987). Anxiety is usually present primarily as a result of environmentally generated subjective distress, e.g., in the face of marital or legal problems. As psychotherapists are usually well aware, persons with a personality disorder typically do not seek therapy out of a perception of intrapsychic deficit or conflict (Millon, 1981). Their presence in therapy has usually been stimulated by some social or legal coercion. For the clinician in private practice, this is most likely in the form of distress generated among the client's intimate others.

A relevant diagnostic issue for the clinician is whether or not the personality pattern is an outgrowth of another disorder, such as major depression. For that reason the clinician needs to assess carefully the issues of chronicity and pervasiveness of behavior.

Obsessive-Compulsive Personality Disorder

Persons with an obsessive-compulsive personality disorder, sometimes described as "workaholics without warmth," are overly controlled emotionally and find it hard to express warmth or caring. They are formal and perfectionistic, and they place inordinate value on work and productivity.

While this disorder is occasionally confused with the obsessive-compulsive disorder, there are significant differences between the two syndromes. First, the obsessive-compulsive personality seldom becomes obsessed about issues. Second, the term "compulsive" here refers to a life-style in which compulsive features are pervasive and chronic, rather than to a specific behavior. Third, the person with an obsessive-compulsive personality disorder is not especially upset, anxious, or distressed about his or her life-style, whereas anxiety is generic and often obvious at times in the functioning of individual with an obsessive-compulsive disorder (Kozak et al., 1987).

A *DSM-III-R* diagnosis of an obsessive-compulsive personality disorder requires consistent evidence of: (1) overemphasis on details to the exclusion of an overall perspective (they see the trees rather than the forest, and not even all of the trees); (2) constricted emotionality; (3) excessive devotion to vocation and productivity; (4) need for dominance in personal relationships; and (5) indecisiveness. These individuals can be obnoxious if their efforts are frustrated, and also can be litigious. One psychotherapist who had worked with a number of obsessive-compulsive personalities exclaimed, in a moment of frustration and sarcasm, "This is the type of person who can get a complete physical from a proctologist."

Paranoid Personality Disorder

The paranoid personality disorder does not involve a thought disorder, and well formed delusional systems are not present. There is no loss of reality contact. It is not a psychotic condition, and it is not listed under the *DSM-III-R* paranoid disorders. Modeling of parental or other significant others is more important in this disorder than in the psychotic paranoid conditions. Since paranoid personalities manifest hyperalertness toward the environment and have a chronic mistrust of most people, their information base is consistently distorted and their affect is constricted. Consequently, they find it difficult to adapt adequately to new situations or relationships, which is paradoxical because of their hyperalertness to their environment. So they may often be right in assuming that other people are against them; yet the paranoia is usually a disabling overreaction to low initial level of scrutiny by the others.

It is rare for paranoid personality disorders to come into therapy without significant coercion from others. Then, unless these individuals have almost absolute trust in another, they cannot develop intimacy; consequently they are continually seeking various ways to be self-sufficient. Thus, they are hard to involve meaningfully in a therapy relationship. They avoid the emotional complexities of working out a meaningful relationship and tend to be litigious. For example, they may write negative letters to public figures or bring lawsuits on minimal grounds, and both patterns can in turn make them the target of legal authorities.

As noted in the prior chapter, aside from avoiding taking such clients, psychotherapists are advised to provide detailed informed consent statements to such clients, and to have receipt and understanding of such forms validated by signatures and witnesses. Maintaining consistent contact with such clients is important.

Antisocial Personality Disorder

This disorder is characterized by the chronic manifestation of antisocial behavior patterns in persons who are amoral and impulsive. They are in general unable to delay gratification or to deal effectively with authority, and they show narcissism in interpersonal relationships. The pattern is apparent by the age of 15 (usually earlier) and continues into adult life with consistency across a wide performance spectrum, including school, vocational, and interpersonal behaviors (Herbert, 1987).

There is good evidence that the antisocial personality disorder can be further subdivided into the categories of primary psychopath and secondary psychopath, although the *DSM-III-R* does not make this distinction (Hare & Jutai, 1986; Lykken, 1957; Zuckerman, Buchsaum, & Murphy, 1980). Primary psychopaths are distinguished by the following characteristics: (1) They have a very low level of anxiety and little avoidance learning; (2) they are significantly refractory to standard social control procedures; (3) they are high in stimulation-seeking behaviors, particularly the "disinhibition" factor that refers to extroverted, hedonistic pleasure-seeking. Secondary psychopaths generally fall in the middle between normals and primary psychopaths on these dimensions; they are closer to the primary psychopaths on the amount of stimulation-seeking and closer to normals in the potential for guilt responses.

Especially relevant with antisocial personalities is the problem of getting clients meaningfully involved in therapy. Since they see no need to seek help, treatment is usually coercive. Confrontive therapies can be effective (Meyer & Salmon, 1988; Yochelson & Samenow, 1976), but some form of coercion, such as institutionalization, is still required to keep the person in therapy. Outside of institutional settings, a therapist is unlikely to see an antisocial personality disorder except in a disturbed family situation.

The stimulation-seeking nature of these clients deserves some attention. This need can be interpreted as being similar to that of an alcoholic, in that the person needs somehow to fulfill this drive or will likely go off into deviant patterns. Therapists can work with psychopaths to develop means of gaining stimulation in less self-destructive ways. Consistent engagement in sports and other strenuous and/or exciting activities and jobs that provide for a high level of activity and stimulation is helpful. Stimulant drugs, as used for hyperactive children, may have a paradoxical effect with a small subgroup of the more manic psychopaths, but much care must be taken in management.

Aside from the question of how to rehabilitate the antisocial personality (which psychology or psychiatry cannot do with any great success), there is the related problem of the legal response to persons with antisocial personalities who break the law (Herbert, 1987). The paradox is that these individuals are not "crazy," and, in fact, may appear to be quite normal, even charming. Yet they manifest an inability to profit from experience and show chronic patterns of maladjustment and aggression. Should they be held responsible for their behaviors or are they "mentally disturbed"? In practice, the legal system has usually assumed that individuals with antisocial personalities are responsible for their behaviors. While an "irresistible impulse" defense has been successfully employed in some cases involving antisocial personalities, this defense is usually more successful for otherwise respectable citizens who argue that some isolated defect in their character was the cause of the criminal behavior.

In summary, individuals with an antisocial personality present the legal system with a paradox inherent in these four consistently substantiated conclusions: (1) They show apparent rationality; (2) they do not seem able to profit from experience; (3) at least a substantial portion of their behavior can be related (at least by correlation) to such behavior-determining variables as genetics and brain dysfunction; and (4) there is no clarity as to how these latter factors are "compelling" in the specific behaviors that lead to a criminal behavior. Things become even more confusing when one tries to include the issues of free will and determinism, as well as the variable level of ongoing public opinion about the "coddling of criminals."

Indeed, recent Supreme Court decisions suggest that society's views that persons with such personality disorders (or who in any way fall into the upcoming category of "criminal personality") will be treated more as criminals than disordered personalities. For example, the Supreme Court, in the case of *Turner v. Safley* (1987), noted that individual needs and rights and even constitutionally based rights may be subordinated to "penological interests." That same court's stamp of approval for "preventive detention" in *United States v. Salerno* (1987) in many ways buttresses the notion that penological interests should be primary.

The Criminal Personality

DSM-III-R considers the overall category of antisocial personality, but does little to distinguish the various types of individuals who are easily subsumed under the label of criminal personality (Meyer & Salmon, 1988). By far the most exhaustive and elegant research on the psychological test discrimination of the criminal personality has been carried out by Edwin Megargee and his colleagues (Megargee & Bohn, 1979). Their typology, based on empirically derived and validated MMPI research, has been exhaustively studied by Megargee and his colleagues and students in a variety of settings and has also received strong and independent verification from other researchers (Edinger, 1979; Gearing, 1979). It is relevant throughout most state and federal penal institutions and is applicable to women with almost the same accuracy and efficiency as it is to men, the sample from which it was derived. Race was considered throughout Megargee's research, so this does not seem to be a disqualifying factor.

With both the antisocial personality and the broader concept of criminal personality, it's evident that prevention is more effective than cure. As with virtually all areas, no predictions of future behavior are highly accurate. However, children and early adolescents who show many of the following characteristics have a good chance of later becoming criminal (Bornstein, Schuldberg, & Bornstein, 1987; Goldstein & Keller, 1987; Reid, Dorr, Walker, & Bonner, 1986; Wilson & Herrnstein, 1985); birth disorder; any handicap that is not effectively remediated or coped with; hyperactivity; learning disorder; absent, alcoholic, abusive, or psychologically disturbed or distant parent; bed wetting; early stealing; gratuitous lying; truancy; persistent irresponsibility; refusal to obey parents; early experimentation with drugs or homosexual behavior; lack of any affectionate or solid friendship; absence of guilt or remorse over misdeeds; persistent violations leading to discipline by school or juvenile court.

The probability of late adolescent and adult criminal behavior is then markedly heightened to the degree the adolescent becomes (1) involved in a deviant or delinquent subgroup, (2) drops out of school, (3) is unemployed, and (4) is involved in drug or alcohol abuse. (Also, see the section on juvenile delinquency in Chapter 12.)

Individuals who fit this profile need to be recognized by psychotherapists for the future risk they present. More extensive and radical treatment than is usually employed should at least be recommended in reports. The difficulty is that if society waits until close to 100 percent probability in such predictions, no intervention will ever be made.

Borderline Personality Disorder (BPD)

Borderline personality disorder (BPD) may superficially be confused with schizophrenia. Yet, those in the former category are neither as withdrawn socially nor nearly as bizarre in symptomatology as are schizophrenics. BPD is thought to be relatively common. Persons in the BPD category show significant emotional instability, are impulsive and unpredictable in behavior, are irritable and anxious, and avoid being alone or experiencing the boredom to which they are prone. There is some evidence that as these individuals improve they show more predictable behavior patterns, yet this is combined with increasingly evident narcissism (Widiger, Frances, Warner, & Bluhm, 1986).

A diagnosis of BPD requires at least five of the following: (1) unpredictable impulsivity in two areas such as sexual behavior, drug, or alcohol use; (2) physically self-damaging behaviors; (3) uncontrolled anger responses; (4) unstable interpersonal relationships; (5) unstable mood; (6) unstable identity; (7) persistent boredom experiences; (8) avoidance of being alone.

The BPD category is actually a relatively new diagnostic entity. Since its introduction to the mental health community, its usage has rapidly increased (Widiger et al., 1986). This is probably because the borderline diagnosis can be used for that large grouping of clients who manifest a wide range of emotional instability symptoms, and as a result don't easily fit other more specific diagnostic categories. In addition, BPD covers those clients who show some psychotic (though not primarily schizophrenic) symptoms, but not enough of them to warrant a psychotic diagnosis.

The popularity of the BPD diagnosis, however, means that it is being used with too many different types of clients, thus losing a degree of its explanatory value. As a result, the psychotherapist who is testifying in court about a BPD is quite vulnerable to sophisticated cross-examination.

The problems with the BPD diagnosis are compounded by increasing evidence that in some clients organic factors may play a role in this disorder. Gardner, Lucas, and Cowdry (1987) have presented interesting research on the incidence of "soft signs" of neurological disorder (brain or nervous system) in BPD clients. "Soft signs" include such behaviors as (a) awkward foot tapping and hopping, (b) difficulty in finger-thumb coordination, (c) right-left confusion, (d) difficulty in coordinating repetitive rapid movements, (e) mild problems in speech fluency, etc. Soft signs *suggest*, but are not conclusive evidence of, neurological disorder.

Gardner et al. (1987) gave thorough physical and psychological exams to matched BPD clients and normals. As hypothesized, significantly more soft signs were found in the BPD clients. However, it's also interesting that the majority of normals showed at least one clear soft sign.

Gardner and his colleagues conclude that degrees of subtle, nonfocused neurological dysfunction may be spread across the general population. This mild (in most cases nondebilitating, and in many cases not even noticeable in normal functioning) dysfunction could come from many sources: prenatal or birth trauma or infections, later high fevers, blows to the head, viral infections, etc. As a group, BPD clients simply have more of this disorder, and it is significant enough to add to their psychological and physical dysfunction. A critical question is whether deficits related to "soft signs" should be accorded the same respect in the legal arena, e.g., allowance for diminished capacity, as is usually accorded harder evidence of neurological disorder, such as CAT scan results.

Because the BPD is so variable in its symptomatology, equally variable treatment responses are required. The impulsivity demonstrated in this disorder suggests that the reader should refer to comments about the antisocial personality disorder, as well as those about substance abuse or sexual deviations. The comments on the antisocial personality regarding stimulation-seeking are particularly relevant, since boredom is common in both personality disorders.

Passive-Aggressive Personality Disorder

The passive-aggressive personality is marked by hostility that is not directly expressed, with consequent "double messages" to others. The underlying hostility affects significant others, yet the passive-aggressive denies, often as if insulted, any aggressive or hostile motivation. The actual behavior expressed may be either passive or aggressive, but physical aggression seldom occurs. Slander and libel are more likely offenses than are direct, violent assaults.

PATHOLOGICAL GAMBLING

The essential feature of this disorder is a progressive and chronic preoccupation with the need to gamble, with consequent disruption in some area of the individual's world. Since more states have moved toward legalized gambling, thus making it increasingly accessible to people, it is expected that the rate of this disorder, which is already high, will rise. Compulsive gamblers, like antisocial personalities, are stimulation-seeking, and both specifically show "disinhibition" or the inability to control impulses. The initial streak of compulsive gambling is usually set off by a first big win (Malkin & Syme, 1985; Zuckerman et al., 1980).

It is increasingly popular to argue that pathological gambling is an addiction, and thus may void at least some responsibility for related criminal events. The difficulty here is that in the standard addictions it is evident that the addiction may operate as a motive and, more importantly, impair many areas of functioning, whereas pathological gambling is often functional only as a motive, e.g., robbing a bank in order to cover gambling debts.

Psychotherapists in a forensic situation may have a problem distinguishing pathological from nonpathological gamblers. Nonpathological gamblers seldom have shown prior antisocial or psychopathic patterns, have more stable work and interpersonal commitment histories, and do not typically show the manic or frenetic (or depressive) patterns that are often seen in pathological gamblers when they gamble. Most pathological gamblers report that they only feel alive when they are gambling and experience the rest of their life experience as boring. They are generally nonconformists and are narcissistic and aggressive (Dell, Ruzickah, & Palisi, 1981).

Most pathological gamblers are extroverted and competitive individuals who are brighter than average; they, surprisingly, often experienced learning difficulties as they grew up. Most had placed their first bet by the age of 15. Other factors that predispose to pathological gambling are: an overemphasis in early family life on material symbols, with little value placed on financial planning and savings; an absent parent before the age of 16; and availability of a gambler in the family as a model.

Treatment typically includes individual psychotherapy, family therapy, and involvement with Gamblers Anonymous. Since stimulation-seeking is often a critical variable in the reinforcement pattern for pathological gambling, the comments about fulfilling the need for stimulation-seeking in the section on the antisocial personality disorder are relevant here.

KLEPTOMANIA

Statistics annually compiled by the United States Department of Commerce indicate that approximately 140 to 150 million instances of shoplifting occur every year, and as much as 25 percent of business losses is accounted for in this fashion. Also, about one in every 12 shoppers is a shoplifter, although no more than one in 35 shoplifters is ever apprehended.

Many people steal simply because it seems so easy to get something free, for a lark, or to be one of the crowd. Only a small proportion of these individuals show kleptomania. Kleptomaniacs are distinguished from typical thieves in that they seldom have any real need or use for an object and may even throw it away. They usually prefer to steal while alone, and there is an "irresistible impulse" quality to their behavior. There is usually evidence of depressive features, reflecting an inability to control the behavior, as well as some problems in interpersonal relationships. For example, many older women who show a kleptomaniac pattern are widowed or emotionally neglected by their husbands; the behavior gives them a thrill, sometimes sexually tinged, although they often pay for it with remorse. In fact, many show a clear sense of relief when apprehended. Kleptomaniacs are usually not significantly disturbed psychologically in areas other than this lack of specific behavioral control. Yet, the condition is often chronic.

Treatment approaches for withdrawal and/or depression may be appropriate here since these patterns often precede kleptomania. For the specific behaviors of kleptomania, the aversive therapies are often used. Kellam (1969) employed a particularly ingenious aversive procedure to control shoplifting in a chronic kleptomaniac. Kellam required this person to simulate his entire shoplifting sequence, which was filmed. As the film was played back, the client was asked to participate with internal imagery in what was going on, and a painful shock was administered at crucial points. Such a technique could be amplified by having a person take a portable shock unit and self-administer shock whenever the impulse arose. If the shock unit is clumsy, the patients can be instructed to hold their breath until discomfort ensues, since this acts as an aversive cue.

Another aversive technique that can be used is to have such clients go into a store. If the impulse to shoplift becomes so severe that they feel they will not be able to resist, they are to take an expensive and fragile object and drop it on the floor. Embarrassment, the need for a coping response with store employees, and the need for restitution all act to create a very aversive moment.

PYROMANIA

Deliberate fire-setting behavior is certainly not uncommon in modern society, yet most cases of arson are not indicative of pyromania. It is now estimated that as many as 80 percent of business property fires are caused by arson. In these cases, the perpetrator is far more likely to be an antisocial personality who is being paid — a "torch." Cases of arson in which there is no clear reward for the individual who started the fire could indicate pyromania, but mental retardation should also be considered (Foust, 1979).

Borderline intellectual ability and neurological dysfunction have been seen as common in pyromaniacs (Kuhnley, Hendren, & Quinlan, 1982; Mavromatis & Lion, 1977). To the degree this is substantiated, there may be grounds for legal incompetency or mitigation of criminal responsibility. Any psychotherapist doing an evaluation on such individuals has to be aware of this possibility.

A buildup of tension prior to the fire-setting behavior occurs in pyromaniacs, along with a release on performing the behavior. The behavior is often first seen in childhood and adolescence and is seldom the only antisocial behavior displayed (Kuhnley et al., 1982). Hyperactivity, problems in school, poor peer relationships, and stealing are commonly associated behaviors. It has been asserted that fire-setting in childhood, when combined with either enuresis and/or cruelty to animals, is predictive of assaultive crimes in adulthood, but these crimes may or may not include fire-setting. Pyromania is much more common in males than in females and is often found in individuals who have had trouble making transitions through developmental stages. They are either indifferent to destruction or stimulated by it. The significant disturbance that usually accompanies pyromania suggests inclusion of a wide variety of treatment options. Since these individuals are often adolescents or young adults, family therapy is especially warranted.

With regard to behavioral therapeutic techniques, two specific approaches are typically employed. Overcorrection requires the individual to make a new and positive response in the area of specific disorder. For example, public confession and a restitution of damages through working for the individual who is offended would be one type of application for pyromania. Negative practice has also been used. The pyromaniac is required to perform a behavior "ad nauseam" until it takes on aversive qualities. For example, the client is required to strike thousands of matches in sequence, over several sessions. These techniques would be embedded in the overall treatment program.

EXPLOSIVE DISORDER

A sudden eruption of aggressive impulses and the loss of control of these impulses in an individual who normally inhibits or does not experience them are the main features of the explosive disorder. Not surprisingly, such individuals are frequently encountered in the legal arena. There is usually evidence of regret and guilt, and the behavior is disproportionate to any environmental stressors. Because physiological or mood symptoms are occasionally reported and because there is occasional consequent partial amnesia for the behavior, the pattern has traditionally been referred to as "epileptoid." However, a concomitant clear diagnosis of organic epilepsy is not common, although in a number of cases there are some nonspecific EEG abnormalities or minor neurological signs. When present, these are almost always introduced as evidence of lessened legal responsibility. These signs are not so rare, even in a sample of apparently normal individuals, but clear evidence of a physiological contribution should be thoroughly considered (Monroe, 1981).

Getting clients in touch with their often suppressed ongoing anger responses is standard in the treatment of this disorder, as is teaching them more effective ways either to abort the anger or to deal with it productively. Awareness techniques, such as those found in gestalt therapy, can put clients in touch with the anger that is typically not evident in their usual functioning (Zeig, 1987). Group therapy can provide the feedback essential to breaking down their defenses against seeing themselves as having chronic anger. Keeping a diary or writing letters (not necessarily delivered) to significant others who may be a factor in generating the anger (Kirman, 1980) also enables clients to get in touch with their anger. Once this is accomplished, the therapist can help the client develop a controlled relaxation response, possibly through biofeedback training (Schwartz, 1987).

Individuals with an explosive disorder report the aggressive act as being something they were compelled to do (thus, they expect less legal culpability), and they show a variable degree of remorse for the results. In that sense, the pattern is similar to aggression manifested during an incident of psychomotor epilepsy, a rare epileptic condition in which orderly sequences of behavior are performed, though the person has complete amnesia for it. The difference is that psychomotor epilepsy reflects an established physiological brain disorder, e.g., disturbed EEG patterns. The explosive personality disorder, on the other hand, shows little or no evidence of a physiological brain disorder, but appears instead to reflect an inability to deal effectively with interpersonal aggression, resulting in part from childhood experiences and conflicts.

The use of such terminology has occasionally been a "last resort" when the person has been caught red-handed, e.g., "with a smoking gun" in a crime of aggression. A classic instance of this was the case of Jack Ruby, who killed Lee Harvey Oswald in front of many Dallas police officers, as well as many television viewers. The assertion that Jack Ruby had suffered from psychomotor epilepsy was viewed with little sympathy, except by himself and his attorney. However, given the evidence against him, this may have been the only defense left, especially since he was found to be rational and had no apparent significant history of severe emotional disturbance. Paradoxically, within a year of this murder, Jack Ruby died of a brain tumor, which tends to confirm the defense used.

SUICIDE

Psychotherapists are occasionally called on by the court to make predictions about suicide potential, which they know to be a difficult task (Monohan, 1981). Though suicide is still an issue of concern in legal arenas, it is no longer considered a crime. Only in this last century has our legal predecessor, England, stopped hanging those who attempted suicide. An even more flamboyant approach, driving a stake through the heart of the offender, was used before hanging.

Most authorities believe that the suicide rate has been rising, but it is not clear whether this is a true increase in suicide or a greater willingness on the part of the coroners and police officers to use the term.

Women are three times as likely as men to *attempt* suicide, although suicides are three times as common among men (Schneidman, 1985). About 90 percent of suicides are committed by whites, and most of the data about suicide concerns whites. Table 10.1 (adapted from Schneidman, 1985) indicates the relevant differences in genuine versus manipulative suicide attempts, always a difficult discrimination for psychotherapists.

In this same vein, the following typology of suicidal individuals is also relevant to clinical and legal decisions:

(1) *Realistic*: These are suicides precipitated by such conditions as the prospect of great pain preceding a sure death.
(2) *Altruistic*: The person's behavior is subservient to a group ethic that mandates or at least approves suicidal behavior, such as kamikaze pilots in World War II.

TABLE 10.1
Genuine vs. Manipulative Suicide Attempts

Common Characteristic	Genuinely Suicidal	Manipulative
1. Stimulus	Unendurable psychological pain	Intense, potentially endurable, psychological pain
2. Stressor	Frustrated psychological needs	Frustrated psychological needs
3. Purpose	To seek a solution to an overbearing problem	To reduce tension and to evoke a response
4. Goal	Cessation of consciousness	Reordering of interpersonal patterns
5. Emotion	Hopelessness-helplessness	Loss and rejection; disconnectedness and disenfranchisement
6. Internal attitude	Ambivalence	Trivalent among living (life), suffering, and dying (death)
7. Cognitive state	Constriction	Obsessional, though with some planning
8. Interpersonal act	Communication of intention	Communication of unhappiness; a call to rescue
9. Action	A leaving behind	Communication; a request for contact
10. Consistency of behavior	With lifelong adjustment patterns	With lifelong adjustment patterns

(3) *Inadvertent*: The person makes a suicide gesture in order to influence or manipulate someone else, but a misjudgment leads to an unexpected fatality.

(4) *Spite*: Like the inadvertent suicide, the focus is no someone else, but the intention to kill oneself is genuine, with the idea that the other person will suffer greatly from consequent guilt.

(5) *Bizarre*: The person commits suicide as a result of a hallucination (such as voices ordering the suicide) or delusions (such as a belief the suicide will change the world).

(6) *Atomic*: An abrupt instability in economic or social conditions (such as sudden financial loss in the Great Depression) markedly changes a person's life situation. Unable to cope, the person commits suicide.

(7) *Negative self*: Chronic depression and sense of chronic failure or inadequacy combine to produce repetitive suicide attempts eventually leading to a fatality.

Accurately predicting suicide attempts is an area of significant potential legal liability for psychotherapists. A number of potential primary behavioral clues appear to predispose an individual to successful suicide attempts (Hawton & Catalan, 1987; Mehrabian & Weinstein, 1985; Shneidman, 1985). These are:

(1) Previous suicide attempts; in this context, the first axiom of psychology could well be "Behavior predicts behavior." The second axiom would be "Behavior without intervention predicts behavior."
(2) Statements of a wish to die, especially statements of a wish to commit suicide.
(3) A prior suicide note that is terse, concrete, and matter-of-fact rather than flamboyant and manipulative.
(4) Certain *consistent* life patterns of leaving crises rather than facing them: e.g., in relationships, "You can't walk out on me, I'm leaving you," or in jobs, "You can't fire me because I quit."
(5) Suicide attempts by an important identity figure, be it a parent or a hero.
(6) Feelings of failure, together with a loved spouse who is competitive or self-absorbed.
(7) Early family instability and parental rejection of one's identity.
(8) A recent severe life stress, or the presence of a chronic debilitating illness.

Various factors can then increase this potential:

(1) A cognitive state of "constriction"—i.e., an inability to perceive any options or a way out of a situation that is generating intense psychological suffering.
(2) Easy access to a lethal means; for example, drug overdose is the prevailing form of suicide among physicians.
(3) Absence of an accessible support system (family and good friends).
(4) Life stresses that connote irrevocable loss (whether of status or of persons), such as the relatively recent death of a favored parent. This factor is particularly important if the person at risk is unable to mourn the loss overtly.

(5) High physiological responsiveness—high need for stimulation-seeking in spite of suicide thoughts.

(6) Serious sleep disruption and abuse of alcohol or drugs.

(7) Depression, particularly when combined with a sense of hopelessness or the loss of a sense of continuity with the past or present.

Psychotherapists can work at both societal and individual levels to lower the incidence of suicide (Harlow, Newcomb, & Bentler, 1986; Shneidman, 1985). Promoting public education on the myths and facts of suicide is an important first step. Even some very well-educated individuals hold odd and misinformed beliefs about suicidal individuals, as evidenced by this quote from an interview with the eminent bacteriologist, Dr. Carleton Gajdusek:

> It's like the craze of the American public about the Golden Gate Bridge. Some say ten people a year jump off it, some say hundreds. No one knows how many really do, and some people think it's important to count or to look. I wouldn't waste one cent, even if it were my son, my mother, my father, or me. Who the hell cares? For anyone who's irrational, depressed, or demented enough to go way out there to commit suicide, I'd have a ramp for their wheelchairs, small steps for kids, assistance booths, and little signs along the way saying, LEAVE YOUR WALLETS HERE FOR CHARITY. IF YOU HAVE ANY FURTHER NOTES OR LETTERS, DROP THEM HERE AND THEY WILL BE DELIVERED. I would have a little elevator to help them over.
>
> As a doctor I am awed by human life, but, Jesus Christ, when people are rational enough to know they want to end it, I'd help them! Why spend a penny trying to stop them at such a reasonable suicide place as a bridge? It's better to have them jump from there instead of from an apartment house onto your head. (*Omni*, 1986 *8(6)*, p. 68)

Second, there is evidence that suicide-prevention hotlines and centers can at least slightly decrease the suicide rate. Lastly, suicide prevention at the societal level requires a balanced and restrained attitude in the media toward reporting suicides.

Psychotherapists can help to educate the public, as well as individual clients, that precautions can also be taken for prevention of suicide at the individual level. These are:

(1) Attend seriously to people who voice a desire to kill themselves or "just go to sleep and forget it all." About two-thirds of those people who actually kill themselves have talked about it beforehand in some detail with family, friends, or others.

(2) Attend especially to depressed individuals who speak of losing hope.

(3) To the degree possible, keep lethal means (guns, large prescriptions of sedatives) away from suicidal individuals.

(4) Generate a personal concern toward a suicidal person; a suicide attempt is most often a cry for help. Suicidal individuals need a temporary "champion" who can point them toward new resources, suggest new options, at least in a small way diminish the sense of hopelessness.

(5) Try to get the person to perform some of the following behaviors: (a) engage in regular physical exercise; (b) start a diary; (c) follow a normal routine; (d) do something in which he or she has already demonstrated competence; (e) confide inner feelings to someone; (f) cry it out. Try to get the person to avoid self-medication and other people inclined toward depression.

(6) Make every effort to guarantee that a suicidal person reaches professional help. Making an appointment is a good first step; getting the person to the appointment is the crucial next one.

Police officers and physicians have the highest suicide rates. While it could be argued that the high level of frustration in the work of both of these groups may be an important variable, most suicide experts believe the critical variable is their high access to lethal means — guns and poisonous drugs respectively. In light of this data, the psychotherapist should be especially alert to any apparently suicidal person who has access to lethal instruments and take positive steps to eliminate this access.

As a general rule, those people who are severely depressed and suicidal are more dangerous to themselves when they begin an upswing out of the depths of depression. If successive testings by an MMPI or a specific depression scale reveal an initial upswing in a depressive who has discussed the possibility of suicide, precautions should be emphasized at that time.

HOMICIDE

The potential for a client's acting-out toward others is often a major issue for the psychotherapist. Homicide, an ultimate form of such acting-out, is the killing of a human being. Murder is defined legally as nonjustifiable homicide. In the United States it is commonly subclassified as first- or second-degree murder or first-degree manslaughter or negligent homicide, depending on motivation and premeditation. Yet there is no common "killer personality" (Goldstein & Keller, 1987). Although persons with a paranoid disorder are more likely to be dangerous to others than most others with an emotional disorder, there is a slight negative correlation between diagnosed mental disorder and murder. In fact, the per capita percentage of murders is higher in the general population than it is among former mental patients (Lunde, 1976).

The MMPI can be useful in predicting potential for aggression against others (Meyer, 1983). In addition, as in all areas of psychopathology, certain specific scales have been developed to assess aggression potential. Ironically, in the general testing situation, the examiner would have to already know the "answer," i.e., that the client may well be aggressive, at least to a degree, to employ such scales. They are of help when there are prior cues, and it is worthwhile for the clinician to keep a range of specific tests available for such situations. An example in this area is the overcontrolled hostility scale (O-H), devised and refined by Megargee and his colleagues (Megargee & Cook, 1975). This scale is a subset of MMPI items and effectively identifies a subgroup of assaultive criminals who are generally overcontrolled in their response to hostility but who sporadically are extremely assaultive.

As noted in earlier sections, extreme violence can easily emerge from either the paranoid or the antisocial personality patterns, and the standard of care for response to such violence is dictated by the dynamics of those disorders. However, there may be other components of the violent response, as noted below, along with consensus or standard treatment responses.

A. *Violence as an inherent part of human nature*:
  (1) Traditional psychotherapy to modify basic personality patterns
  (2) Medications to diminish anxiety and minimize inappropriate reactions
  (3) Psychosurgery to change or interrupt patterns of brain functioning
B. *Violence as a consequence of social learning*:
  (1) Family therapy to change home environment or facilitate coping in family setting
  (2) Group therapy to enhance appropriate coping in social situation
  (3) Assertiveness training and social skills training to give concrete training in self-assertion without violence

(4) Systematic desensitization (SDT) to desensitize client to the precipitating stimuli, so as to diminish inappropriate or excessive reactions

(5) Token economy, time-out, social isolation to extinguish violent behavior through removal of environmental reinforcers, as well as to strengthen appropriate responses

(6) Classical conditioning to extinguish violent behavior, as in aversive conditioning

(7) Parent effectiveness training, Parents Anonymous to enhance adequate coping skills and provide a supportive peer group

C. *Violence as a consequence of frustration and other situational factors*:

(1) Traditional psychotherapy to release frustrations and to change coping patterns

(2) Family therapy — see B1 above

(3) Group therapy — see B2 above

(4) Assertiveness training, social skills training — see B3 above

(5) Token economy — provide opportunities for positively reinforcing experiences while extinguishing the violent behavior

(6) Parent effectiveness training , etc. — see B7 above

D. *Violence as a means of communication*:

(1) Expressive therapies to substitute alternate means of expression of feelings underlying violent acting-out

(2) Assertiveness training, etc. — see B3 above

(3) SDT— see B4 above

(4) Parent effectiveness training — see B7 above

E. *Violence and aggression as protection of territorial integrity and body space*:

(1) SDT— see B4 above

(2) Assertiveness training — see B3 above

Because murder, as well as certain other violent patterns, is a discrete and usually nonrepetitive behavior, as opposed to a pattern of cognitive or affective symptoms, the goal is prevention rather than cure. Four strategies that would help are: (1) finding better methods of treating the antisocial and paranoid disorders; (2) providing more therapy for violence-prone families; (3) controlling the modeling of violence in the media; and (4) curtailing the availability of cheap handguns, whose only apparent function is killing other humans.

THE SEXUAL DEVIATIONS (PARAPHILIAS)

The sexual deviations (referred to in *DSM* as "paraphilias") consist of sexually arousing fantasy behavior associated with nonhuman sexual targets or nonconsenting humans, and/or sexual activity with humans that involves either simulated or actual pain or humiliation. The central defect is in the lack of capacity for mature and participating affectionate sexual behavior with adult partners. Traditionally, these disorders have been far more common in males, but this discrepancy has decreased in recent years. Occasionally engaging in such fantasy or behavior does not usually qualify one as a paraphiliac. Exclusivity, persistency, and pervasiveness are hallmarks of the disorder (Levin & Stava, 1987). The main paraphilia categories included in *DSM-III-R* are: (1) fetishism, (2) transvestism, (3) zoophilia, (4) pedophilia, (5) exhibitionism, (6) voyeurism, (7) frotteurism, (8) sexual masochism, and (9) sexual sadism.

The number of criminal sexual offenses committed by persons because of psychosis, central nervous system impairment, or alcoholic delerium is probably no more than five percent (Malamuth, 1986; Miller & Welte, 1986; Prentky & Knight, 1986). This five percent can clearly argue for incompetency or insanity or at least diminished capacity, whereas the remaining individuals, who supposedly are operating from "free choice," can at best primarily argue a defense of irresistible impulse.

The bulk of the traditional clinical and research literature would lead one to believe that people who show a sexual deviation (or paraphiliac) pattern consistently stay within that pattern. However, more in-depth and recent research by Abel and his colleagues (1986) found at least 50 percent of the paraphiliac clients evaluated in their studies showed multiple diagnoses that overlapped a wide variety of paraphilias. Table 10.2 shows the paraphiliac arousal pattern that developed initially for all of their clients who were as adults diagnosed as either rapists or child molesters. These findings together suggest that those persons who are shown to have one pattern of paraphilia should be questioned extensively about other categories of deviant sexual arousal.

An interesting method of corroborating reports of sexual preference among persons accused of and/or referred for psychotherapy for criminal sexual offenses is the psychophysiological assessment of sexual arousal (Abel, Rouleau, & Cunningham-Rathner, 1986). The client wears a circumferential penile transducer that accurately measures not only the existence of an erection, but its rigidity and persistence as well. While wearing the transducer, the client is presented (by audiotape and/or 35 mm slides or video-

TABLE 10.2
Initial Deviant Behavior Patterns of Rapists and/or Child Molesters

First Paraphilia	Rapists	Pedophiles
Pedophilia	25.8%	75.0%
Rape	43.8	3.4
Exhibitionism	7.9	12.9
Transvestism	1.1	1.3
Fetishism	2.2	1.3
Voyeurism	9.0	3.0
Sadism and Masochism	2.2	1.3
Obscene telephone calls	0	0.4
Frottage	5.6	1.3
Bestiality	1.1	0
Arousal to odors	1.1	0

Adapted from Abel, Rouleau, & Cunningham-Rathner (1986)

tape) a variety of sexual scenes representing various normal and sexually deviant patterns. Abel et al. (1986) used this technique with 90 consecutive cases where there was some sexually deviant interest. In 45 percent, the client's self-reported deviant interests were consistent with indications from physiological measurement. The remaining 55 percent were confronted with the discrepancy between self-reported and physiologically-indicated preferences. In 62.2 percent of these cases, the clients subsequently admitted that they had been deceptive, and it is very probable that some of the others were also being deceptive or were not consciously aware of an unconscious or emerging deviant preference.

By stating when the client is "cured" or making predictions about future behavior, the psychotherapist takes on an important role when a legal issue is involved in these cases. As in most disorders where a legal issue and a significant course of treatment are involved, deception regarding progress is a possibility. The senior author is familiar with the case of a voyeur whose treatment was apparently successful at the two-year mark. While the client at that time stated that he was doing well, his wife reported to the therapist that he had long ago resumed peeping. This points to the need for corroborative statements from significant others, as well as other methods for detecting deception, when a report of the treatment progress will be used in legal procedures (Wormith, 1986).

Exhibitionism

The act of exhibitionism was described as early as 4 B.C. (Cox, 1980), although the term was not introduced into psychopathology until 1877. Exhibitionism is the act of exposing the genitals to a stranger in order to obtain gratification. Exhibitionists constitute about one-third of all sex offenders and show the highest rate of recidivism — most estimates say 25 percent or greater — after being apprehended (Cox, 1980). Exhibitionists are almost always male (although there are exceptions — Grob, 1985), perhaps because there are a number of legal and socially acceptable outlets for exhibitionism available to women, such as exotic dancing. Even when female exhibitionism occurs in an unusual place or situation, males seldom react negatively and are unlikely to report it to authorities. This social attitude, together with society's continuing reinforcement of an aggressive role for males in sexual behavior, is the major reason many paraphiliacs are male.

A number of personality types may engage in exhibitionistic behavior, warranting differing sociolegal responses (Grob, 1985; Levin & Stava, 1987):

(1) *Impulsive*. Obsessional, tense, and sexually confused individuals whose exhibitionism is an impulsive response to intrapsychic distress.

(2) *Inadequate*. For people who are not only obsessional but also shy, introverted, and lacking in adequate social relationships, exhibitionism is an ambivalent combination of an anger response and an attempt at both ego affirmation and socialization.

(3) *Unaware*. For some, exhibitionism is a secondary result of mental retardation, organic brain disorder, or extreme alcohol intoxication.

(4) *Assaultive-characterological*. For people influenced by a strong element of anger and hostility, exhibitionism achieves sexual arousal, but the shock response of the victim is the primary reinforcement, and there is little guilt over the behavior.

In the great majority of cases, exhibitionists are not dangerous, particularly those in the first three categories. However, the characterological exhibitionist occasionally moves into aggressive pedophiliac behavior or even rape and assault on adults.

Standard techniques of psychological treatment are generally ineffective with exhibitionists. A technique that has been helpful with recidivist exhibitionists who are at least willing to try to change is aversive behavioral rehearsal (Wickramsekera, 1976). In this treatment, the exhibitionist performs the usual exhibitionistic pattern in front of both an audience and a mirror. It is best if the audience can both respond authentically (laughs, comments such as "It isn't all that big, is it?") and at the same time keep questioning and talking to the exhibitionist so that he does not indulge in the reinforcing fantasies that usually accompany his behavior (Simon, 1987). Most, but not all, exhibitionists experience marked anxiety during such sessions, which facilitates the therapeutic effect. In persons who do not experience that much anxiety, it could theoretically be increased by bringing people into the sessions who are close to the exhibitionist, e.g., wife, brother, or by chemically increasing anxiety by injections of sodium lactate prior to the sessions (Liebowitz et al., 1985). Also, videotapes of the person's actual victims saying how he was silly or unimpressive can be effective. In any case, with virtually any technique, booster sessions at some point are necessary to maintain the withdrawal from exhibitionistic urges and behavior (Wickramsekera, 1976; Simon, 1987).

Legal elements required for a conviction of indecent exposure typically include: (1) the person's exposure of the genitals or other private anatomical parts; (2) exposure in a public place; (3) intentional exposure; and (4) exposure in the presence of, or being seen by, others (Smith & Meyer, 1987). While exhibitionists are usually indicted under indecent exposure statutes, they may also be arrested in some jurisdictions under statutes that relate to "public lewdness" or "public indecency," etc. While the elements are rather clear, the interpretation of what they actually mean may vary from jurisdiction to jurisdiction. They can vary depending on: (1) the definition of private parts or public place; (2) whether or not a witness or witnesses to the exposure are necessary; (3) whether issues of intent are considered in the actual court process; and (4) whether or not consent modifies or eliminates the criminality (Cox, 1980).

Voyeurism

The primary characteristic of voyeurs is the consistent search for situations in which they may view individuals or groups of individuals in the nude or in some form of sexual activity in order to obtain sexual arousal (Levin & Stava, 1987). Like pedophiles and exhibitionists, voyeurs show an apparent positive and quick response to any therapeutic intervention, yet again, they also have a high recidivism rate. Virtually all cases of voyeurism reported to the authorities are males. However, there is no evidence that this behavior never occurs in females; our society is organized to respond differently to exhibitionistic or voyeuristic behavior in females. Most voyeurs are not markedly disturbed. Approximately one-third of voyeurs are married. Even though the age of the first voyeuristic act is usually the middle to late twenties, often there has been a significant history of sexual and other offenses throughout adolescence.

Only a small proportion ever act aggressively, though it is important to recognize this potential when it exists. Those that do usually show definite psychopathic qualities, as well as the following specific behavior patterns: (1) they are much more likely to enter a building in order to carry out the voyeuristic act, and (2) they are much more likely to in some way draw attention to themselves while in the voyeuristic act.

As with many other disorders, though, a critical disposition issue in both exhibitionism and voyeurism is whether the person actually wants to change (Wormith, 1986). There are incidents in the literature where individuals have participated in treatment, usually in order to obtain some legal protection of as a condition of probation. In such instances the patient's motivation to change is low.

Frotteurism

A separate pattern of sexual deviation that has recently emerged is frotteurism. Frotteurism is generally defined as touching and rubbing against the body of a stranger in order to attain sexual arousal and even orgasm. The great majority of frotteurs are males, and the most common sexual target is the buttocks, though attempts to touch other body parts also occur (Levin & Stava, 1987). The act is usually done in a crowded public place like a bus or subway or crowded dance floor.

Also inherent to the frotteur's pattern is a system of coverup plans, ways to avoid either the embarrassment of being caught and publicly humiliated or apprehended. Such plans, e.g., similar to the exhibitionist who sets it up to appear as if he was only urinating in an appropriate spot when he exhibits, are often so effective that they act to shift the "burden of proof" from the frotteur to the victim. Reporting an unclear and ambivalent situation to the authorities is aversive, hence the great majority of frotteuristic incidents go unreported. Those who are willing to report these and similar crimes need to be given protection from embarrassment or legal retribution, or there will be even less inclination in the public to respond appropriately.

Sexual Sadism and Sexual Masochism

Sexual sadism and masochism are obviously interdependent patterns. People engaging in these deviations often pair up to satisfy each other, and in some persons both patterns coexist (Luria, Friedman, & Rose, 1986). Psychotherapists occasionally see a client who manifests the rare pattern (a form of sexual masochism) known as "terminal sex." A man (usually) hangs himself by the neck with a noose to increase his sexual pleasure while masturbating. Releasing the noose just before unconsciousness allegedly increases the pleasure, probably by developing an oxygen debt that facilitates the orgasm. This practice of eroticized hanging is more likely to occur among adolescents and young adults. It is estimated that this practice may cause as many as 150 deaths in the United States each year. In an analogous process, some women can only reach orgasm if they are mildly strangled when they get sexually aroused (LoPiccolo & Stock, 1986). The risk, of course, is linking up with a man who easily moves into a true assault and rape, and discriminating the degree of invitation from the degree of coercion is especially difficult if there is a legal issue.

Homosexuality

Homosexuality continues to be a controversial topic within legal and professional groups as well, as in the society at large. *DSM-I* listed homosexuality as a sociopathic personality disturbance, and in the *DSM-II* it was shifted into the personality disorder category. However, in 1974 the American Psychiatric Association decided by a vote of 5,854 to 3,810 to exclude homosexuality per se as a mental disorder. Yet, the group immediately developed the term "sexual-orientation disorder" to apply to individuals who experience distress as a result of their homosexual behavior. This was followed by the term "ego-dystonic homosexuality," and a subsequent move to eliminate the term homosexuality in any diagnostic category.

When a homosexual comes to a psychotherapist requesting help in changing the sexual orientation, the psychotherapist must first help the client to authentically decide whether or not he or she wishes to reject the homosexual orientation; hence, psychotherapy should precede any direct attempt to change the sexual orientation. If a decision to change is made, the aversive conditioning techniques can be used to suppress the homosexual arousal pattern, and then sex therapy and social skills training are used to help develop a heterosexual pattern. Some have argued (Davison, 1976, 1978) that the therapist should always refuse to participate in changing the sexual orientation. This runs counter to the tradition of the field, if not the culture, that persons who have made an aware choice ought to be aided in actualizing their "self" as they see fit, particularly since it does no harm to others (Eichelman, 1987).

There have been a number of related legal issues that reflect the extensive controversy that has surrounded homosexuality. A basic issue for society at large is whether or not homosexuality can be viewed as a criminal behavior. Though it traditionally has been viewed this way and has been encompassed under sodomy statutes, there has been a tendency during the last couple of decades toward "decriminalization" of homosexuality in most jurisdictions, at least in practice if not statute.

The trend toward decriminalizing homosexuality by statute, however, was first dealt a severe blow in the Supreme Court case of *Doe v. Commonwealth's Attorney for City of Richmond* (1975). This decision did not find any inherent criminality in homosexuality, nor did it support the reasoning of the relevant state statute that argued that it is a criminal behavior. However, it did clearly allow that a right to privacy concept would not prohibit criminal sanctions and it affirmed the rights of states to legislate against such behaviors. So while this didn't actually criminalize homosexuality, it did take away the excuse that many state legislators had used to argue for decriminalization prior to this decision, which was that the courts were decriminalizing homosexuality anyway.

While the criminalization of homosexual acts under certain conditions is legally permissible, there have been many ironic changes in the rights for homosexuals in other areas, particularly in child custody decisions and vocational status. Though courts have varied markedly in their acceptance of a homosexual mother as a fit parent in custody decisions, the general trend has been to accept that homosexuality is not a sufficient cause alone to sustain the removal of the child. The same trend holds true for the teaching of children.

However, since there is now a potential for labeling homosexuality as criminal, the homosexual can lose status in these areas because of "criminal behavior" rather than homosexuality, though the effect is obviously the same. Still, the recent trend had been toward increasing acceptance of admitted homosexuality in government jobs, as well as in many areas of the private sector. A major step was the decision by the National Security Agency to allow an avowed homosexual employee to keep his job and security clearances.

One of the thorny legal and psychological issues here is how a person is to be defined as a homosexual (Money, 1987). Courts have labeled as homosexual married persons who had admitted engaging in same-sex activities in their late teens; persons who had mostly bisexual friends; persons with one conviction for a same-sex "crime"; women in "mannish" attire; and even a man who admitted to be a homosexual in preference, yet who had not admitted or even been proven to have committed any overt homosexual act (*Gaylord v. Tacoma School District of Washington,* 1975). A major reason for the varied treatment of this issue by the courts appears to be the fact that they are usually dealing with stated *preferences* as opposed to overt *acts*. Regarding preferences, there are considerable constitutional protections, such as freedom of speech, privacy, etc.

Rape

About five percent of all violent crimes are rapes. About one in every 2,000 women is a reported rape victim every year. However, it is estimated that only about 10 percent of actual rape victims ever report the crime to police. Also, only about one in 10 rapists are ever arrested, one in 30 prosecuted, and one in 50 convicted. More than 50 percent of reported rapes take place in the victim's home, and in about 40 percent of the cases the rapist is known to the victim.

Most jurisdictions have made changes in their rape statutes in recent years. Giacopassi and Wilkinson (1985) conclude that the five major modifications that have appeared in rape statutes are: (1) abolition of capital punishment as a sanction for rape; (2) a graduated continuum of offenses and penalties for rape; (3) a lowered sentence structure; (4) the reformulation of rape statutes to a sex-neutral definition of participants; (5) a change of terminology away from "rape" to such nomenclature as "criminal sexual conduct." They argue that while the intent of these legal reforms is to ensure fairness, the unintended effect of many of the changes may be to trivialize the rape and devalue the victim.

Rape can be broadly defined as taking anything by force or very narrowly defined as the undesired penetration of a female's vagina by a male's penis, enforced either by physical control, fear, or some other form of coercion (Frazier & Borgida, 1985). Present laws usually fall somewhere in the middle. They do not restrict rape to an act of intercourse and allow for the possibility of the rape of males by females. An example would be where references to rape in statutes have been replaced by phrases such as "criminal sexual assault" and "involuntary sexual battery." This makes sense since, though rape has traditionally been thought to be a sexual crime, recent theorists consider it more a crime of violence. "Sexual battery," for instance, could be defined to include the following acts: anal, oral or vaginal penetration by or union with the sexual organs of another; or the anal or vaginal penetration of another by any other object, provided, however, sexual battery shall not include acts done for bona fide medical purposes.

While the emission of semen is not required under the above definition of sexual battery, and so it may not be legally necessary for the male to ejaculate, the presence of semen is often a critical piece of evidence in rape trials.

Yet, it is estimated that in as many as a fourth of all rapes the rapist is unable to deposit semen because of a potency problem.

Aside from rapes that occur as an incidental result of such disorders as severe organic brain dysfunction or schizophrenia, and rapes that are an impulsive and ritualistic gesture (the plunder of war), there is reasonable agreement that there are three major rape patterns (Malamuth, 1986; Smith & Meyer, 1987). In the first aggression is the major component and sexual satisfaction is somewhat irrelevant. These rapists are hostile toward females and in general carry a high level of aggression potential. The second type of rapist needs to administer pain to another person to obtain sexual satisfaction. For the third aggression is an avenue toward sexual contact and satisfaction, yet rape is also thought by the rapist to be a way of making longer-term interpersonal contact.

Some researchers have found elevated levels of plasma testosterone in some samples of the most violent rapists (Rada, Laws, & Kellner, 1976). However, in general there is not much correlation between rape and physiological measures. An impossible problem is obtaining such measures at the critical predictive point, the time just before the rape, as many of these physiological variables differ markedly for any one individual depending on when they are assessed. However, measurements of penile response to sexual imagery (Abel et al., 1986; Earls & Prouix, 1986) may be useful here, as well as in making at least some tentative predictions about future behavior when that is important in disposition.

The most frequently used treatments for rapists have been the aversive therapies, and they have shown moderate success. Castration has been a time-honored approach for dealing with the rapist, yet now runs afoul of picky legal considerations and the whims of some "pinko liberals." Nonetheless, chemocastration, via drugs that lower the serum testosterone level, is still used (Walker, 1978; Walker & Meyer, 1981). These drugs lower the likelihood of sexual arousal, but side effects are substantial and, in addition, the drugs are not always effective. Suggestions for the legal disposition of the rapist even include some ironic analogy: Fersch (1980, p. 14) states that in rape "the criminal act ought to be brought under assault and battery with a dangerous weapon. Then the attention could be focused on whether or not the accused possessed a dangerous weapon."

Psychotherapists can provide much needed care in the aftermath of a rape, as the rape victim manifests a wide variety of negative effects (Foa & Kozak, 1986; Frazier & Borgida, 1985). Most show abrasions or bruises, and approximately 5 percent suffer severe injury. Virtually all victims also show some emotional trauma, including anxiety, depression, and loss of self-esteem. While the depression often abates in about three to six months, the anxiety and loss of self-esteem are more persistent (Steketee & Foe, 1987). In addition, psychotherapists can aid in rehabilitating the subsequent long-term sexual satisfaction that is commonly disrupted in rape victims.

The defense attorney's traditional ploy of implying that the rape victim had always been "a loose woman" and had invited the rape was fortunately heavily restricted by Public Law 95-540, passed by Congress in October 1978. This law severely limits conditions under which any evidence of a rape victim's past sexual behavior is admissible in federal court. The majority of states has now passed similar laws.

A psychotherapist can help a rape victim who anticipates a related court appearance by role-playing the expected scenario with the client, exploring sources of surfacing anxiety, and then remedying the situation through techniques such as relaxation training, systematic desensitization, and assertive training.

Transsexualism

Transsexuals are people who strongly and consistently identify with the opposite sex, which is often manifested in cross-dressing, as well as in a desire for appropriate physical change through surgery and hormone therapy. The law continues to wrestle with the legal definition of gender in such cases. Transsexualism is to be differentiated from transvestism, which simply involves taking on the behaviors of the opposite sex, including cross-dressing, but does not involve the sense that the inner self is actually of the other sex, which demarcates the transsexual.

One of the first sex-change operations took place in Europe in 1930, but the surgery did not get much attention until 1953 with the case of Christine Jorgensen. Most changes are from male to female, in large part because such surgery is much simpler than surgery in the opposite direction, which is complex, has many potential negative side effects, is far less likely to succeed, and offers much greater potential legal liability.

Some have argued that surgery is an unnecessary intervention. Psychotherapy and the passage of time may indeed be effective with some transsexuals, and this less dangerous approach should at least be considered with all candidates (Money, 1987). However, in many cases the surgery does appear to be the most effective long-term solution, and it is more accurately designated as rehabilitation rather than cure.

Melvin Belli (1979) has argued that therapists can come under tort liability for being an accessory to a client's transsexual surgery. Noting that it could possibly be considered under the "criminal mayhem" statutes if there is any lack of clarity about the client's consent or ability to consent, Belli asserts that adequate consent is unlikely in most cases because of the "compulsive" quality of the need to change the sex. This, he says, is contradictory to the laws that consent be "an affirmative action of an unconstrained and unconceived will" (p. 498). While his formulation initially sounds worthwhile, it appears as if he confuses "compulsive" with "a strong desire." In addition, under such a formulation, almost anyone with any kind of disorder would fit within that context, hence virtually no therapy of any sort could take place.

CHAPTER 11

Issues of Biological Disruption

CERTAINLY MANY OF the disorders we have discussed in the preceding two chapters may have important biological components. For example, schizophrenia is thought by most experts to have a primarily biological etiology; however, in the legal arena that probable biologic component does not typically receive nearly as much scrutiny as the issue of degree of reality contact as manifested in hallucinations or delusions.

In the disorders discussed here, e.g., mental retardation and alcoholism, the degree of biologic disruption is often the determining factor in any related legal decision. We start with the disorder where the issue is obviously most crucial—"brain damage" or, more accurately, central nervous system impairment.

CENTRAL NERVOUS SYSTEM IMPAIRMENT (CNSI)

Many psychotherapy clients present problems requiring differential diagnosis of a central nervous system impairment. (Throughout this section we will refer to central nervous system dysfunction as CNSI, though it is often called organic dysfunction or organic brain damage.) Missing the presence of CNSI in a client can lead to substantial legal liability.

Psychotherapists should be aware of the common signs of CNSI in the standard tests and in behavior even if the possibility of organic dysfunction has not been mentioned by the referring party (Meier, Benton, & Diller, 1987). For example, cerebral impairment and affective disorders must be distinguished. When a syndrome shows a gradual onset of a wide range of affective symptomatology and is accompanied by neurological and cognitive deficits, along with aphasia or agnosia and/or a loss of sphincter control,

294

irreversible CNSI is probable. If the affective symptomatology is unaccompanied by the latter symptomatology, and the depression and/or mania are severe and possibly accompanied by persistent delusions, a bipolar affective disorder is more probable. On the other hand, when there is a rapid onset of symptoms focusing on confusion, agitation, attentional problems, and disrupted sleep patterns, along with problems in self-care (including impaired sphincter control), and primarily visual hallucinations, there is a high probability of acute CNSI.

Psychotherapists should be especially alert to speech quality and problems, dress, grooming, gait and coordination while walking, and affect; all of these behaviors can provide important clinical signs (Hersen & Bellack, 1987). It's especially worthwhile to observe such clients whenever they are unaware they are being observed, e.g., as they walk to their car. Any signs of asymmetry should certainly be noted. For example, one person with visual field deficits neatly shaved one side of his face, but only roughly and sloppily shaved the other side. Obtaining some subject-as-own-control data is also useful, such as finger-tapping tasks or touching body parts with either hand with eyes open and closed. There are also normative or test data specifically collected for neuropsychological assessment, and where there is any reasonable possibility of CNSI, the psychotherapist is obligated to perform such an exam or to refer the client to someone who can.

If the situation requires a substantial neuropsychological assessment, more extensive methods of obtaining normative data, such as the Halstead-Reitan or Smith-Michigan batteries are appropriate (Meier et al., 198; Meyer, 1983). Such batteries are prognostic as well as diagnostic. A good intermediate level screening battery for CNSI might include a WAIS-R; MMPI; specific tests for lateralization, such as the Purdue Pegboard and/or grip strength and tapping tests; tests for sensory response, and other tests that help cover the required variety of modalities and functions (Benton Visual Retention Test, Rey Auditory Verbal Learning Test, Symbol Digit Modalities Test, Sklar Aphasia Scale).

When it comes to routine screening, psychotherapists should consider including a test like the Reitan Aphasia Screening Test (a shortened version of Halstead and Wepman's Aphasia Screening Test) in the test battery. This test takes only about 10 minutes to administer and is a rough assessment of spatial and verbal factors, as well as aphasia. It is a good gross screening measure for significant cerebral impairment, as normals seldom make errors and perform effortlessly. If a client makes even two or three errors, taking a deeper look for more signs of cerebral impairment is worthwhile.

Drawings that are commonly collected by clinicians can also provide helpful initial cues. For example, an analysis of the differences in the style of drawings between those with right hemisphere CNSI and left hemisphere CNSI is shown in Table 11.1.

Several inaccurate "uniformity myths" have unfortunately been pervasive in the traditions of CNSI assessment and rehabilitation (Meier et al., 1987; Meyer, 1983). Psychotherapists who appear to subscribe to any of these *myths* when they provide court testimony become very vulnerable to competent cross-examination:

- The term *brain damage* is an accurate description of the effects of central nervous system impairment.
- Individual differences do not significantly affect the manifestation, course, or outcome of CNSI impairments.
- Lesions of CNSI tissues constitute a homogeneous class of phenomena.
- Brain injuries are relatively static events, and are comparatively insensitive to the effects of time.
- The clinician's role in neuropsychological investigation is confined primarily to diagnostic activities.

Admissibility of Neuropsychological Data

The ability of health professionals other than physicians to assess brain injury has been challenged in the legal arena. While a Florida court disallowed testimony by a neuropsychologist in one case (*GIW Southern Valve Co. v. Smith*, 1986), the opposite occurred in a recent critical case, *Horne v. Goodson Logging Co.* (1987). The "plaintiff," Mr. Horne, was injured when a 1,000-pound log fell 14 feet and struck him on the head. As a result he

TABLE 11.1
Drawing Characteristics

Right Hemisphere CNSI	Left Hemisphere CNSI
scattered and fragmented	simple and coherent
loss of adequate spatial relationships	spatial relationships are adequately retained
corrective lines are added	gross lack of detail
drawings are made energetically, almost driven	drawings are made slowly and laboriously, haltingly at times
orientation to the general task is faulty or lost	orientation to the general task structure is reasonably accurate

suffered compression fractures and disc injuries in his back, the loss of his teeth and multiple lacerations in his face. These injuries were compensated by the Industrial Commission. However, Mr. Horne also suffered a complete personality change, transforming from a gregarious, family-centered and secure person into a paranoid, depressive recluse who had auditory and visual hallucinations and could not control his temper.

Horne's estimated 60 percent permanent brain disability was documented in a psychologist's 17-page report based on an exhaustive neuropsychological examination and extensive interviews with him and members of his family. However, the deputy commissioner who served as the hearing officer in this case refused to consider this evidence, and his refusal was affirmed on appeal by the full commission. The commissioners chose instead to believe the conclusion of a neurosurgeon who had examined Mr. Horne for 15 minutes almost one year after the accident, and who had concluded, without any medical history of the case but based on a negative X-ray and CAT scan, that Horne had suffered no permanent brain injury.

> The North Carolina Appeals Court agreed that it had been an error for the Industrial Commission to conclude that the testimony of the neuropsychologist was "incompetent." However, a two-judge majority on the appeals panel ruled that because the Industrial Commission is the sole judge of the believability of all witnesses, the case should be remanded to the Commission for consideration of the neuropsychologist's credibility. The majority also found that, since the neurosurgeon in this case qualified as an expert witness and testified that plaintiff had suffered no permanent brain disability, it would not reverse the lower decision as a matter of law, but would rely on the commission's reconsideration.
>
> The dissenting judge on the appeals panel agreed that the case should be remanded, but he would have gone much further. This judge would have remanded the case with explicit instructions to consider the evidence presented by the neuropsychologist. (*APA Practitioner*, 11(1), 1987, pp. 6–7)

MENTAL RETARDATION

Particularly in cases of incompetency (see Chapter 3), psychotherapists are asked to direct their expertise to mental retardation. About 1 percent of the population falls into the category of mental retardation (Broman, Nichols, Shaughnessy, & Kennedy, 1987; Matson, 1987). *DSM* requires indication of subaverage intellectual functioning in an individually administered test, correlated problems in adaptive coping behaviors, and onset before the age of 18. If onset is later than the age of 18, the term *dementia*, subcoded as an organic mental disorder, is appropriate. The criteria for severity are noted in the following four subcategorizations:

Mild mental retardation (I.Q. scores of 50 to 70) applies to about 75 percent to 80 percent of the overall retarded population; such persons are commonly referred to as educable. While many persons in the mild category may be found incompetent to stand trial, many are competent, especially if they are handled with patience and care. *Moderate mental retardation* (I.Q. score of 35 to 49) comprises about 12 percent of the retarded population. They usually require at least moderate supervision and are seldom competent to stand trial. *Severe mental retardation* (I.Q. score of 21 to 34) comprise about 7 percent of the retarded population. This group is not likely to profit from any vocational training, though they can usually learn elementary self-care skills. *Profound mental retardation*, 1 percent of the retarded population, is designated by I.Q. scores of 20 or below.

When significant intellectual retardation is apparently present, with functioning below an approximate I.Q. of 70, and for some reason the individual is untestable, the term *unspecified mental retardation* is used. The diagnosis of *borderline intellectual functioning* requires evidence of problems in adaptive coping, and an I.Q. score of 71 to 84.

Severely retarded persons who have been accused of crimes are very likely to be declared "incompetent to stand trial." Some years ago this meant they were very likely to then be confined to an institution. However, the 1972 Supreme Court ruling in *Jackson v. Indiana* held that confinement subsequent to a finding of incompetency could occur only if there were some real chance of remediating the condition that led to the finding of incompetency. Psychotherapists are still occasionally requested to remediate incompetency that is primarily based on retardation (Matson, 1987); in such cases they need to take a hard look at whether any remediation is truly possible.

The static view of mental retardation, along with other images that plague retarded individuals, such as being "dangerous," "subhuman," and even "holy innocents," has resulted in society's taking over a caretaking role "for the best interest of the retarded." As in many cases where the clients themselves are not advocates for their own rights, this has resulted in the loss of some very important rights (Killenbeck, 1986). For example, for many years retarded individuals have been sterilized, usually based on the consent of a third party. Court rulings in most states now prohibit this, but as yet the Supreme Court has not dealt definitely with this encroachment on their privacy.

The whole issue of right to treatment is particularly important in the area of mental retardation. *Wyatt v. Stickney* (1972) and subsequent cases have served to affirm this principle specifically within the area of retardation.

There is an increasing attempt through such cases to define the retarded as having a right of "habilitation," which is basically a quest for normalization by the mentally retarded (Killenbeck, 1986). Following from this concept, the institutional staff is required to assist retarded individuals to develop skills that will enable them to best cope with their environment and ultimately to live in the least restrictive environment.

SUBSTANCE USE DISORDERS

There are an increasing number of substances in our modern culture that are available for abuse, such as alcohol, heroin, the barbiturates, the amphetamines, cocaine, caffeine, tobacco, and marijuana. Psychotherapists should be aware that the MacAndrew Alcoholism Scale (MacAndrew, 1965; Streiner & Miller, 1981), an MMPI content scale, is particularly useful in diagnosing substance abuse disorders, especially problems with alcohol, heroin, and heavy marijuana and polydrug use. This scale is also useful with adolescents in predicting later abuse patterns. Setting a cutoff point (using raw scores) at 24 picks up about 80 percent of the abusers and potential abusers; a score of 27 very strongly suggests an addiction problem of some sort; and a score over 30 indicates that addiction is nearly certain. Since blacks and obese persons tend to score a bit higher on this scale, adjusting the cutoff points two points higher is suggested for these clients. Streiner and Miller (1981) provide guidelines for prorating short or incomplete Mac-Andrew scale protocols.

Physical signs of substance abuse, such as needle marks, abscesses over veins, or constriction of pupils should be noted. Additionally, adequate physiological screening, such as urinanalysis, should be conducted (Van Hasselt, Milliones, & Hevsen, 1981) when substance abuse is suspected.

In treating any substance abuse pattern, the psychotherapist's first critical task is helping the client to generate a strong decision to change. Since the experience-seeking subfactor of the stimulation-seeking variable particularly characterizes the substance abuser (Zuckerman et al., 1980), the therapist needs to help the client channel this need into more legitimate and constructive pursuits. Family therapy is also usually necessary.

ALCOHOL ABUSE

Alcohol is still the main drug of abuse. More than 100 million Americans now drink alcohol at least occasionally, and one in eight is on the way to having a significant alcohol problem, that is, *alcoholism*. The costs of alcohol abuse in terms of personal distress and societal disruption are enormous (Blane & Leonard, 1987). For one thing, alcoholics live about 19 years fewer than the norm; for another, their irresponsible behavior while "under the influence" often lands them in court. Some argue that alcoholics should not be held responsible for either their alcoholism or any criminal offenses that ensue from their alcoholic problems. This defense is strengthened to the degree that it can be argued they are genetically compelled into alcoholism. However, as is noted later, courts are reluctant to give so much legal leeway.

In most cases alcohol dependence develops in progressive stages (Donovan, 1986; Parsons, Butters, & Nathan, 1987). The sequence of behaviors and symptoms listed below is not necessarily inevitable, but is common and should be recognized by the psychotherapist.

(1) Prealcoholic phase:
  (a) Social drinking and an occasional weekend drink are the major symptoms.
  (b) Both tolerance and frequency of drinking increase, usually slowly.
  (c) Alcohol use serves primarily as an escape from anxiety, mild depression, or boredom.
(2) Initial alcoholism:
  (a) Tolerance, frequency, solitary use, and abuse increase.
  (b) More is drunk per swallow; often there is a shift to more potent drinks.
  (c) Depression increases along with loss of self-esteem over drinking patterns.
  (d) Occasional blackouts occur.
(3) Chronic stage:
  (a) True loss-of-control patterns (such as drinking throughout the day and using any source of alcohol) predominate.
  (b) Inadequate nutrition affects functioning and physical health.
  (c) Signs of impaired thinking, hallucinations, paranoid thoughts and tremors emerge.

There is certainly good evidence that a predisposition to alcoholism can be inherited (Donovan, 1986; Heath, 1986; Vaillant, 1983). There are clear individual differences in how individuals respond to a drink of alcohol. Indeed there is evidence that certain genetic strains of rats prefer alcohol virtually undiluted, some prefer it diluted, some prefer either to water, and some will totally avoid alcohol. Similarly, some people react very sensitively to a small amount of alcohol with an increase in pulse rate, respiration, and skin temperature, often accompanied by marked facial flushing. Others can ingest a drink or two without noticeable effect but quickly "feel drunk" if they take in more, while others can take in huge amounts and appear relatively normal (Heath, 1986; Parsons et al., 1987). Unfortunately, in this latter group motor and perceptual processes have been markedly disrupted, and since they may perceive themselves as "normal," they can put themselves and others at great risk, e.g., by driving. Nevertheless, any evidence related to such individual differences may be critical to a psychotherapist's testimony in a particular case.

Since there are marked individual differences to alcohol within any cultural group, based on genetic factors, it's not surprising that there are differences across cultural and racial groups. Psychological expectancies can influence such differences, but there still are primary differences in how the alcohol is metabolized. For example, a high proportion of people from Oriental races (including Eskimos and most Native American groups) shows the sensitivity reactions (flushing, etc.) to small amounts of alcohol. This innate aversive response may act as a block to developing alcoholism. Only 3–6 percent of Caucasians shows this response.

This contrast reflects genetic differences that are manifested at the molecular level. For example, Caucasians and Orientals show differences in two different enzymes that are critical to the metabolism of alcohol: alcohol dehydrogenase (ADH) and acetaldehyde hydrogenase (ADLH—also referred to as acetaldehyde). Some individuals (e.g., a higher proportion of Orientals) have lower rates of these enzymes or show a variant form of ADH or ADLH. This results in the accumulation of pure acetaldehyde (not ADLH) in the body, causing the sensitivity reaction, a process parallel to that generated by Antabuse.

There are a variety of other possible "sites" for genetic differences that generate different responses to alcohol—speed of neurotransmitter processing systems, differences in brain nerve-cell membrane permeability as a response to alcohol, etc. (Parsons et al., 1987). Nevertheless, whatever the site, it is clear that genetic differences do affect an individual's response to alcohol. Such racial differences may be the basis for differential legal strategies at trial, as well as for differential treatment plans proposed to the court by the psychotherapist.

Treating the Alcoholic

Since alcohol abuse is a multifaceted disorder, with strong psychological, social, and biological factors, the standard of care for most cases will involve many, if not all, of the following approaches (Brown, 1985; Heath, 1986; Parsons et al., 1987).

(1) *Detoxification*. An initial phase of hospitalization to "dry out" is needed in most cases. This allows symptoms to readjust to a lack of alcohol, and hospital supervision controls the impulse to return to alcohol.

(2) *Antabuse and/or aversion therapy*. Antabuse is of help to alcoholics who want to change but are likely to relapse by giving in to a temporary impulse to drink. Aversion-behavioral therapy can be helpful in controlling the cues that are unique to the client in eliciting a strong desire to drink.

(3) *Alcoholics Anonymous*. Involvement with AA or a similar group provides many helpful factors, especially the opportunity for consistent associations with nondrinkers.

(4) *Family and/or marital therapy*. Since alcoholism is extremely disruptive to family life, family and/or marital therapy to repair the damaged relationships is often necessary.

(5) *Psychotherapy*. Alcoholics commonly experience conflicts, anxiety, and self-esteem problems. For these, a variety of psychotherapy techniques (such as rational-emotive therapy or traditional insight therapy) can be of help.

The implantation of time-release drugs similar in action to Antabuse is a recently developed option, although there are potential legal liabilities, since it is possible for the client to fatally overdose with alcohol and the drug.

Although the treatment of alcoholism *has made* progress, only a few of those alcoholics in treatment will remain abstinent for as much as a year. Most resume drinking and are rehospitalized. Gorski and Miller (1986) and Barrett (1986), agreeing that the one-year period following a client's entering treatment is critical, focus much of their effort on this period. Virtually all experts advise support groups such as AA during the first year of abstinence. Gorski and Miller (1986) systematically teach clients about the "relapse process" and emphasize that resumption of drinking does not occur suddenly. This counters the myth that alcoholics are "suddenly taken by drink."

In addition, Barrett argues that it is necessary to "use a chemical to fight a chemical." Since the therapist's task is to have the client abstinent long enough for biological functions to return to normal, clients are required to come to the hospital for disulfiram (Antabuse) daily for one year. Unfortunately, above all else, alcoholics act to protect their opportunity to drink alcohol again if they choose to do so. Alcoholics assume that alcohol will be *needed* at some future time. Therefore, Barrett has devised a number of strategies to influence alcoholics to comply with his disulfiram-based program, e.g., having employees contract with employers so that the latter are to be notified if the client does not show up daily for medication and therapy. Most who do make it past the year mark are well on the way to recovery.

Treating Other Abuse Patterns

In treating the abuse of harder drugs such as heroin, cocaine, and the amphetamines, the confrontive group experience, which first evolved with the opioid disorders in institutions like Synanon and Phoenix House, is often necessary (Washton & Gold, 1987). Such groups are effective with some clients, although they have been burdened by problems resulting from their resistance to reliance on professionally trained staff. As a result, there is a lack of objectivity in assessing techniques and outcome and a lack of awareness about the wide range of treatment techniques discussed in the professional literature, not to mention the techniques that are being developed.

Just as heroin was once used to treat morphine addiction, methadone, also an addicting drug, is now used to treat heroin addiction. It appears to be effective in certain cases, though the clinician must be aware of possible secondary abuse of the drug used for treatment, particularly in addicts who are psychopathic. Although it would probably appear to be a frivolous suit to most health care professionals, and hopefully most jurors, a suit for malpractice based on secondary addiction is a potential risk in using methadone.

Legal Issues and Substance Abuse

Alcohol and other drugs have been a central issue in innumerable cases in both the civil and criminal law. Three cases — *Robinson v. California* (1962), *Easter v. District of Columbia* (1966), and *Powell v. Texas* (1968) — are critical to the legal thinking concerning alcoholism and drug addiction. The landmark *Robinson v. California* case concerns a heroin addict who had been convicted of violating a federal statute following a jury trial in the Municipal Court of Los Angeles. Two police officers testified to having examined his arms one evening and at that time noting scar tissue and needle marks. They also testified that he had admitted to using heroin. The judge in that trial instructed the jury that the accused could be convicted if they found him to have either committed the act or be of the status in violation of the statute under which the offense was being considered.

However, the Supreme Court's decision, delivered by Justice Stewart, held that Robinson could not be convicted on the basis of his *status* as an addict. They noted that he would still retain the status of "addict" even if he were "cured," in which case the indictment, if upheld, would allow for his repeated arrest. In addition, it was held that to punish an individual because of such a status would be cruel and unusual punishment, in violation of the eighth amendment. The decision in *Robinson* was buttressed by the *Easter v. District of Columbia* decision, in which the U.S. Court of Appeals for the District of Columbia held, in similar fashion to *Robinson*, that punishment for the "disease" of alcoholism constituted a violation of the "cruel and unusual punishment" aspects of the eighth amendment. The statute under which Easter was convicted is more of a condition than a status.

The Supreme Court then clarified other critical components of this issue in *Powell v. Texas*. Powell, who had been arrested for being intoxicated in a public place, was found guilty and fined $20 in Austin, Texas. Throughout subsequent appeals, his attorney argued that he was a chronic alcoholic (a fact which was not really disputed), and that his appearance in public was not of his own free will, thus seeking to bring this under the cruel and unusual punishment aspects of the eighth amendment, following *Easter* and *Robinson*. However, Justice Marshall, who delivered the majority opinion, stated that this would not come under the *Robinson* holding since Powell was not convicted for the status of being a chronic alcoholic, but rather for the *behavior* of being in public while drunk on a specific occasion. As such, it was asserted that there was no attempt to punish a status or even a condition, but simply to regulate behavior. This may seem like splitting hairs, but there has to be some sympathy with the court's belief that to find Powell innocent would open the floodgates for other types of criminal defendants going free on the basis of other "compulsions," such as to steal, set fires, etc.

Much of the reformists' thinking in *Robinson*, and also in the testimony provided in *Powell*, reflects the disease model of substance abuse, particularly the theories from Jellinek (1960), which the court often cited. This disease model assumed that (1) substance abuse disorders, particularly alcoholism, reflect a physiological disorder, possibly genetically determined, (2) abusers have virtually no control over their intake of the substance because of this dysfunction, and (3) with some substances, especially alcohol, they permanently retain their status, even when they are able to abstain.

The assumptions in the disease model of substance abuse have been shown to be not entirely true in their implications (Donovan, 1986). For example, some alcoholics are able to return to a pattern of social drinking even after many years of chronic alcohol abuse (Peele, 1984). There is also clear evidence that many alcoholics, even while in the status of chronic alcoholism, can refrain from the first drink (a bedrock assumption in Alcoholics Anonymous). Together, this suggests that exempting alcoholics from criminal liability is unwarranted. This is not to say, however, that alcoholism is not a mitigating factor, and psychotherapists are often called upon to offer such relevant testimony in the dispositional stage of a criminal proceeding.

There have been some cases in which persons have ingested substances inadvertently. For example, certain individuals who unknowingly ingested substances like LSD (e.g. "spiked punch" cases) have committed acts destructive to themselves or to others. It has been consistently held by the courts in such a case that the person who was responsible for the ingestion of the substance is the one legally responsible for any resulting destructive acts. So, for example, if LSD is given to someone by a prankster at a party, and a subsequent destructive act occurs, the prankster would bear the legal responsibility for the act in civil cases, and even to a degree in criminal cases.

THE SOMATOFORM DISORDERS

Complaints and symptoms of apparent physical illness for which there are no demonstrable organic findings to support a physical diagnosis are characteristic of persons with somatoform disorders and factitious disorders. Persons with the somatoform disorders are naturally quite suggestible. However, unlike the symptoms of the factitious disorders, those of the somatoform disorders are not under voluntary control. Thus, the diagnosis of somatoform disorder is made when there is good reason to believe that the person has little or no conscious control over the production of symptoms (Kellner, 1986). While factitious disorders are more common in men, somatoform disorders occur more frequently in women.

The four major subcategories of the somatoform disorders are: somatization disorder, conversion disorder, psychogenic pain disorder, and hypochondriasis. The somatization disorder is chronic, with multiple symptoms and complaints, usually presented in a vague fashion. The conversion disorder focuses on one or two specific symptoms suggestive of a physical disorder: on closer examination these reflect primarily a psychological issue, either as a reflection of symbolic conflict or from the attainment of secondary gain. Psychogenic pain disorder is functionally a conversion disorder that refers specifically to psychologically induced pain states. Hypochondriasis is the consistent overresponse to and concern about normal and/or insignificant bodily changes, in spite of expert reassurance that there is no reason for concern.

Conversion Disorder

Conversion disorder is still commonly referred to by the traditional term "hysterical neurosis, conversion type," and such individuals are said to manifest "la belle indifference," an attitude in which there is little concern about the apparent serious implications of the disorder. However, it is now clear that the attitude of "la belle indifference" is not found in all conversion disorders. While a common pattern at the time of Freud, conversion disorders not involving pain are now relatively rare (Kellner, 1986). Persons with a conversion disorder appear to be aware at some level that their complaints do not predict the further dire consequences that others might infer from them. Although indifferent to their presenting symptoms, emotional lability in response to other stimuli is commonly noted.

The dispute in many personal injury cases centers on whether the individual has an actual injury or whether the claimed injury is malingering or a conversion disorder.

Somatoform Pain Disorder

The somatoform pain disorder is a conversion disorder that specifically involves pain not due to a physical cause. As such, it is commonly involved in legal cases, especially civil cases. As with the other somatoform disorders, a history of physical disorder involving the actual symptom is common (Kellner, 1986). The pain seldom follows known anatomical or neurological patterns, and extensive diagnostic work reveals no evidence of organic pathology. In the more sophisticated patient, it may mimic well-known diseases such as angina or arthritis (Grote, Kaler, & Meyer, 1986).

There are broad individual differences in pain thresholds, and description of pain by clients can be very subjective (Rutter, 1987). For these reasons the intensity and etiology of pain are very difficult for psychotherapists to assess. Thus, for the psychotherapist, the question of severity of pain is also accompanied by various other questions related to credibility, motivation, etc. Further, as is the case with permanent and total disability, the identification of pain as part of the definition of an individual's self-perception in a legal proceeding may lead to a self-fulfilling prophecy. Focusing upon pain as a justification for pursuing litigation increases the likelihood of chronicity of the condition (Keefe & Gil, 1987). Documented loss of time from work or the projected likelihood of continuing to need to lose time from work for recovery, physical therapy, stress reduction, or other reasons, represents a compelling argument for increased damages. Conversely, one's ability to continue on the job despite pain or some limitation in functioning capacity suggests that a claim for large damages may not be meritorious.

When pain is in dispute, it tends to be because the intensity of the described pain does not fit the objective medical findings. Thus, the psychotherapist is frequently in the unique position of being able to clarify whether there are functional benefits to be gained from the pain. Again, the psychological profile of the individual contributes to this understanding, as do observations taken within the office upon entering, leaving, or sitting in the waiting room. The psychotherapist's assistant or secretary can be a tremendous aid in unobtrusively observing the client's reactions when he or she is not being observed by the professional. In addition, a well-timed trip to a water fountain or restroom down the hall can unobtrusively provide information about how limiting the pain is after the person is out of the office, waiting for the elevator, etc. Similar information can be provided if one's window provides the opportunity to observe the degree of discomfort and postural adjustments required by the client in walking, getting into a car, etc. On the other hand, a great deal of clinical observation in the office can be directed toward the issue of pain. For example, does the person who is alleging pain seem to have no difficulty sitting through several hours of testing without changing position — or does the intensity of his pain necessitate premature termination of the session?

There are indications that people from certain life-styles or family backgrounds are more likely to use pain as a manipulator (Keefe & Gil, 1987; Whittington, 1982):

(1) People who have a history of taking significant dosages of pain medicine.
(2) People who have a history of extensive medical treatment and multiple surgical procedures.
(3) People with a history of hypochondriasis or of factitious disorders.
(4) People who are highly suggestible.
(5) People who had stressful childhoods and/or are from large families.
(6) People who began working full-time at an early age.
(7) People who had children at an early age.
(8) People who complain of too little pain for their injuries as well as those who complain too much.

Membership in this group does not necessarily indicate that the pain is less real or objective. Pain experienced by these people is as sharp and discomforting as it is for a patient who does not share any of these familiar experiential factors. Rather than discounting their pain, we should think of these individuals as being predisposed to pain and as more likely to have a higher emotional input in their pain.

In all cases of somatoform pain disorder, potentially exaggerated or even malingered responses require (a) a very detailed and complete description of the pain; (b) a thorough history; (c) checking of the description and history against other information sources; (d) administration of psychological tests, e.g., the MMPI and 16 PF, that have validity scales; and (e) employment of other techniques, e.g., polygraph. Other methods can be specifically helpful in discriminating psychogenic from organic pain. Cortical evoked potentials have shown promise as a diagnostic instrument in this area, as well as in many other diagnostic situations. Also, certain EEG patterns appear more consistently in organic than in psychogenic pain, and assessment of blood plasma cortisol can be a helpful discriminator.

Hypnosis has traditionally been considered appropriate in most of the conversion disorders (Edmonston, 1986). David Cheek (1965) has pioneered the use of hypnosis for the reduction of chronic psychogenic pain. He uses hypnosis to find the subconscious causes for the pain. In addition, while such clients are under hypnosis, Cheek asks them gradually to release this symptom, often having them point to a date on the calendar designating when they might be willing to give up the symptom. He then makes an appointment for that day and gradually ties the insights under hypnosis into conscious awareness. With chronic pain, the musculature has often conformed over time to a bodily posture that continues the pain. Hence, even psychogenic pain may have an overlay of real pain (Keefe & Gil, 1986).

With the conversion disorders, secondary gain by the client is frequently a factor. Therefore, the clinician should look at the potential momentary payoffs as well as family and marital situations for possible reinforcement patterns and sites for intervention.

Hypochondriasis

Hypochondriacs quickly interpret the natural physiological flux of the body as disorder and then present themselves to health care professionals as disordered. As such, hypochondriasis is potentially confused with both the factitious disorder and malingering (see Tables 1, 2, and 3 in Chapter 7). Hypochondriacs are constantly alert to an upsurge of new symptomatology, and since the body is constantly changing, they are bound to find it. In one sense, hypochondriacs do not fear being sick; they are certain they already are, and a misdiagnosis leaves the clinician open to liability claims for unnecessary treatments. The following common factors have been observed in the development of hypochondriasis (Kellner, 1986; Meister, 1980):

(1) At some point, often early in life, most hypochondriacs directly experienced an atmosphere of illness. This could include identifica-

tion with a significant other who was hypochondriacal or early exposure to a family member who was an invalid.

(2) Hypochondriacs often have had a strong dependency relationship with a family member who could express love and affection in a normal or intense fashion during periods when the hypochondriac was ill, yet remained distant or nonexpressive at other times.

(3) Hypochondriacs often channel their psychological conflicts and their needs for existential reassurance into this pattern. As a result, the hypochondriac pattern of behavior may mask a mid-life crisis or some other challenge that is not being met effectively.

(4) A certain subgroup of hypochondriacs is postulated as having a predispositional sensitivity to pain and body sensation. This could be stimulated by prior physical disorder in systems in which the hypochondriacal pattern is now manifest.

THE FACTITIOUS DISORDERS

Since factitious symptoms are under voluntary control, these disorders are often thought of as malingering. The difference is that in a factitious disorder the goal or reinforcement sought is not obvious or inherent in the apparent facts of the situation. Instead, the motivation is understandable only within the person's individual psychology. These patterns have been traditionally confused with the conversion disorders, but in both the somatoform and conversion disorders of *DSM* the symptoms are not under voluntary control. Factitious disorders are probably the most difficult *DSM* category to diagnose. To start with, they are rare. Secondly, the feigned symptoms are often accompanied by more subtle, though actual, physical disorder (Pankratz, 1981). Further, when diagnosticians become aware of what they perceive as deception, they are inclined to make a diagnosis of an antisocial personality instead of a factitious disorder, and then give the person little attention (Pankratz, 1981).

Factitious disorders are subdivided into: (1) factitious disorder with psychological symptoms, and (2) chronic factitious disorder with physical symptoms, the latter often referred to in the literature as Munchausen's syndrome. In the factitious psychological syndrome, the symptoms are mental rather than physical, and as a result they are often less well defined. Munchausen's syndrome was named after Baron Von Munchausen, an eighteenth century German equivalent of our own Paul Bunyan, both of whom are associated with tales of exaggeration. The all-time champion victim of the Munchausen's syndrome may well be Stewart McIlroy, whose path through 68 different hospitals (with at least 207 separate admissions) in England, Scotland, Ireland, and Wales was retraced by Pallis and Bamji

(1979). Though he used false names and different complaints, he was eventually identified by scar patterns and other permanent medical characteristics.

Biofeedback is useful for most physiological disorders (Schwartz, 1987). However, the factitious disorder is a different story, as the essential aspect is the deception. Not surprisingly, such persons are openly hostile and avoidant of psychological treatment, so unless they are coerced by a significant other they are not likely to become involved in therapy.

The deception involved in this disorder is not as commonly an issue in legal proceedings as is malingering, since a person faking disorder in order to avoid prosecution would present an understandable motive to most people, and thus would not be diagnosed as having factitious disorder. Obtaining narcotics as a result of such a fraudulent admission to a hospital is one aspect that would clearly have legal ramifications.

CHAPTER 12

Child Issues

MANY OF THE ISSUES examined in the previous chapters can involve children as victims or even as perpetrators; however, in the disorders discussed in this chapter, the child is clearly the central figure. The response in an individual case is in large part determined by the overall politico-psychological concept of children held by those people who handle the case, from police officer or caseworker to judge or psychotherapist.

Melton (1987) suggests four major positions in this regard. The first group, the "kiddie libbers," sees children as more like than unlike adults. Thus, they handle cases and promote public policies designed to preserve the independence and privacy of children. They tend to see problems in children as emanating from a lack of opportunity to exercise options and choices. They are the group that is most likely to recommend individual psychotherapy or peer-dominated group therapies.

A second group, the "child savers," also immediately leans toward the child's position, but they emphasize children's incompetency, dependency, and significant vulnerability. They are inclined to quickly bring the state into the parental role. Interestingly enough, the third group, termed the "family libbers," starts with the same presumption of significant vulnerability in children as does the second group. However, the family libbers also believe the presence of parents is critical to healthy psychological development. They will go to great lengths to keep the family structure intact and to institute programs that increase the positive functioning of the family of a distressed child.

Metton's fourth group, "parent libbers," emphasizes parents' rights for their own sake. Parent libbers see children as legal nonpersons. This is most clearly voiced by those parents who assert they should retain substantial control over any late adolescent, or even early adult, who is still economically dependent on the parent, regardless of level of psychological maturity. Parent libbers are especially concerned about the freedom to socialize their children in whatever fashion they choose. Conflict over this view quickly emerges in cases concerning the first topic discussed in the section, child abuse. Indeed, it is clear that, whatever the psycho-political view held by those persons dealing with cases of child distress, it will directly influence the disposition of that case.

In some of these disorders, e.g., juvenile delinquency, the child is the perpetrator (though in one sense also the victim). In others, the child is the victim. We start with a common problem in which the child is clearly the victim.

CHILD ABUSE

Child abuse is a well-recognized problem in modern society. Indeed, in the spectacularly short time of about five years in the late 1970s and early 1980s, child abuse in the United States went from a virtual non-issue to a focus of national legal and political concern. This is in contrast to most issues, which percolate politically for about 25 years or more before gaining such national attention (Nelson, 1984). It now seems ironic that the first formal legal intervention in a child abuse case, that of Mary Ellen in New York in 1875, had to be prosecuted through animal protection laws and primarily as a result of the efforts of the Society for the Prevention of Cruelty to Animals (Cross, 1984). That irony derived from the preeminence at that time of the view that parents held all rights and children were legal nonpersons.

At present, all 50 states, partly spurred by the federal Child Abuse Prevention and Treatment Act, have legislated methods for the identification of abusive families. However, because of the private nature of abuse and the reluctance of both perpetrators and victims to reveal it (Dale et al., 1986), clearly identified cases of child abuse are generally believed to represent only a portion of actual cases.

Psychotherapists commonly become involved in cases of child abuse in a number of ways. First, in treating a child, they may come upon direct reports or indirect indicators of physical or sexual abuse. Second, in treating a parent, they may be told about abuse by that individual or be told about the pattern in the spouse. Third, though therapists may not be told directly about abuse, they may become aware of a client's (or the spouse's) propensity toward violent behavior or toward drug and/or alcohol abuse. This should encourage psychotherapists to seek other relevant information. In all of these instances, psychotherapists may gain equally important information about conditions of neglect, which are usually much harder for social agencies to detect. From another direction, psychotherapists may be asked to evaluate an abuse situation to report to the court, or they may be referred either the parent or child for treatment. In all of these roles, it is important for psychotherapists to be aware of those factors that are likely to generate an individual case of child abuse.

A specific episode of physical and/or sexual child abuse is usually the result of a number of factors (Belsky, 1980; Browne & Finkelhor, 1986; Cross, 1984; Herrenkohl, Herrenkohl, & Egolf, 1983; Walker, 1987) within three contributing systems: (1) sociocultural; (2) familial; and (3) individual. To the degree these factors are present, the probability of an occurrence of child abuse is increased.

At the most basic level the following *sociocultural* factors increase the likelihood of episodes of child abuse:

(a) lack of affirmation and support of the family unit
(b) lack of emphasis on parent training skills as a prerequisite to parenting
(c) acceptance of and high media visibility of violence
(d) acceptance of corporal punishment as a central child-rearing technique
(e) emphasis on competitiveness rather than cooperation
(f) unequal status for women
(g) low economic support for schools and daycare facilities
(h) an attitude of acceptance in the media toward any coercive or demeaning behavior(s) towards women or children

These sociocultural factors heighten the probability of abuse in conjunction with the following *familial* factors:

(a) low socioeconomic and educational level
(b) little availability of friends and extended family for support
(c) a single parent or merged family structure
(d) marital instability
(e) family violence as common and traditionally accepted
(f) low rate of family contact and information exchange
(g) significant periods of mother absence
(h) high acceptance of family nudity
(i) low affirmation of family member privacy
(j) "vulnerable" children, i.e., to the degree they are young, sick, disturbed, retarded, or emotionally isolated

The probability of abuse in a specific instance is then in turn increased by the following *individual* factors:

(a) history of abuse as a child
(b) low emotional stability and/or self-esteem
(c) low ability to tolerate frustration and inhibit anger
(d) high impulsivity
(e) lack of parenting skills
(f) high emotional and interpersonal isolation
(g) problems in handling dependency needs of self or others
(h) low ability to express physical affection
(i) unrealistic expectancies for child's performance
(j) acceptance of corporal punishment as a primary child-rearing technique
(k) presence of drug or alcohol abuse

The great majority of the above factors acts to generate physical child abuse, and most of them are also relevant to cases of sexual child abuse. However, a number of factors are specifically relevant to sexual abuse (Walker, 1987). Psychodynamic features here include the interaction of such parental factors as marital discord, personality disorder, loss of an important relationship or fear of disintegration of the family, and emotional deprivation. Sexual abuse has also been related to extreme masculine socialization practices and views, which include the equating of sexuality and affection, the importance of heterosexual success to self-identity, a focus on sexual acts rather than relationships, and the acceptance of younger and smaller sexual partners.

All states now mandate psychotherapists to report cases of abuse, and many states require anyone aware of abuse to report it. Most states also require the reporting of any cases of "suspected" abuse. In most states, failure to report constitutes a misdemeanor, usually involving a fine and/or short jail term. Failure to report would also open the psychotherapist to civil liabilities (Meriwether, 1986). Of course, such reporting breaks confidentiality, but state laws typically provide protection from civil suits when breaking both the ethics principle of confidentiality and legal statutes regarding privileged communication.

However, there is no way to guarantee protection of the therapy relationship once the reporting occurs (Meriwether, 1986). Most would agree that the value of reporting actual cases of ongoing abuse overrides the cost of disrupting the therapy relationship. The situation becomes less clear when one is required to report an inactive situation (e.g., a parent admits to abuse some time ago but it's clear to the therapist that there is no apparent present or future danger). Also, there is the question of whether the therapy relationship should be interrupted for a mild suspicion of abuse. Most state laws clearly say it should. As a result, many argue that psychotherapists should inform clients that if they divulge information indicating possible abuse, the therapist must report this.

The depth of societal feeling in this matter became clear in the 1987 Supreme Court decision of *Pennsylvania v. Ritchie* that held that people accused of sexually abusing children have no right to see confidential state records that might help in the preparation of their defense unless a judge determines it is material and important to the defense. Ritchie was convicted in 1979 of rape, incest, and corrupting the morals of a minor for sexually abusing his daughter over a four-year period, beginning when she was nine. State appeals courts set aside the conviction because the state's Children and Youth Services had withheld records from Ritchie.

The Supreme Court, citing the "vulnerability and guilt" of young victims of sexual abuse, then ruled 5 to 4 that the Pennsylvania Supreme Court was wrong in ordering child welfare officials to make confidential records available to Ritchie.

Chief Justice William Rehnquist and Associate Justices Byron White, Sandra Day O'Connor, and Harry Blackmun joined Justice Lewis Powell in the majority in this case. Powell wrote for the majority: "A child's feelings of vulnerability and guilt . . . are particularly acute when the abuser is a parent. It therefore is essential that the child have a . . . person to whom he may turn . . . with the assurances of confidentiality."

The 1987 Supreme Court case of *Kentucky v. Stincer* involves the issue of the defendant's presence at preliminary stages of a case preceding a criminal trial, but has implications for probable future decisions. In that case, the judge conducted a hearing to determine if the child-victims were competent to testify and then excluded the defendant from the hearing. This exclusion was intended to permit the girls to testify at the competency hearing without the trauma of having to face the defendant. However, the defendant's attorney was permitted to be present and participate in the hearing. The girls were determined competent to testify, and later testified in open court, in front of the defendant. The defendant was convicted and appealed on the grounds that his constitutional right to confront his accusers had been violated when he was excluded from the competency hearing.

The Court emphasized that the defendant was present during the substantive direct and cross-examination of the girls, that the defense attorney was present and fully participated in the earlier hearing, and that the legal question addressed in the competency hearing did not particularly depend on the defendant's presence. Thus, the actual holding in the case was somewhat narrow, although press reports of the case claimed a much broader holding involving substantive testimony in sexual abuse cases. The Court did not address in this case the issue of whether the defendant could have been excluded from the courtroom (to watch on closed circuit) during witnesses' substantive direct and cross-examination at the actual trial. The Court's emphasis on the opportunity for cross-examination as the right protected by the confrontation clause may suggest that it will permit the exclusion of the defendant from the courtroom during some child-witness testimony.

Because child abuse cases often come down to a conflict of testimony by the only two people who know what happened—the defendant and the witness-victim—it is important to encourage the witness to testify fully and without trauma. At the same time, the right of confrontation is especially important in these cases. Confronting a child-witness face to face may be both a way of ensuring the child does not lie, and a way of so threatening a child if he or she cannot tell the truth. Eliminating a defendant from a preliminary competency hearing, as in the *Stincer* case probably does not seriously threaten confrontation rights. Removing the defendant from more substantive testimony would be another matter.

Several factors influence the seriousness of consequent disorder in the victim of sexual abuse (Browne & Finkelhor, 1986; Fromuth, 1986; Walker, 1987). More serious problems are likely if (1) the offender is in a close relationship to the child, such as the father; (2) the sexual activity included genital contact, and especially if this includes penetration; (3) the child is older, e.g., adolescent, at the time of abuse; (4) the abuse is frequent and/or of long duration; (5) the child has strong negative feelings about the abuse and/or is somehow aware of its wrongness; and (6) much upset and/or distress occurs around the event, e.g., court testimony.

There is a general consensus that there is a very high recidivism rate in child abuse, with or without intervention. Even where there is intervention, the available data suggest the recidivism rate is still very high, though not as high as when there is no intervention (Browne & Finkelhor, 1986; Goldstein & Keller, 1987; Nelson, 1984). In addition to individual psychotherapy, three core approaches comprise the standard of care here:

(1) *Family therapy*, since the family is virtually always disrupted.
(2) *Parent training*. When a parent is the abuser, training is necessary to deal with not only the problems that led to the abuse, but also those generated by the abuse (Goldstein, Keller, & Erne, 1986).

Parent training to deal with this latter factor also is important when the abuser is not a family member.

(3) *Support systems.* Community-based counseling and support groups should be available to abusing parents. Parents Anonymous works in the same manner as Alcoholics Anonymous or Gamblers Anonymous; a similar group is Parents United.

INCEST

Socially prohibited sexual interaction between close family members is referred to as incest. It is extremely rare between mother and child but relatively common between brother and sister. Father (or stepfather)-daughter incest is the usual target of legal and public health authorities (Frazier & Borgida, 1985). Several situational factors increase the probability of incest. These include geographic isolation of the family, long periods of separation between father and daughter, a family pattern of nudity or semi-nudity in the house, the mother's consistent absence from the house, and alcohol abuse. Male children who have been the target of father-son incest or who have had a long period of brother-sister incest are more likely to repeat the pattern in their own families (Blair & Justice, 1979; Trepper & Barrett, 1986).

Three basic subpatterns are found in father-daughter incest, requiring different psycholegal responses:

(1) *Pedophilic incest.* This psychosexually immature and inadequate father is functionally a pedophile, meaning that he has incestuous contacts with other children as well as his sons and daughters. Responses appropriate to pedophilia (see next section of this chapter) combined with family therapy are appropriate.

(2) *Psychopathic incest.* This psychopathic father relates to most people as objects, shows little or no guilt about his behavior, and is usually promiscuous with both adults and children, both in and out of the home. Removal of the father from the home is usually necessary.

(3) *Family-generated incest.* The father is passive and the mother has a personality disorder. The marriage is shaky, and the child who is the target of the incest, often the eldest daughter, takes on more than just a sexual function. She becomes a mistress in all meanings of that word. The mother is likely to be aware of the incest but helps keep it a secret. Family therapy, along with individual-assertive therapy is usually necessary.

PEDOPHILIA

The core disorder in pedophilia, most commonly in middle-aged males, is a persistent pattern of sexual experiences with children. Ironically, pedophilia literally means "love of children." Psychotherapists need to be aware of the significant differences between pedophilic men who are inclined toward sexual experiences with male children and those who seek out females. Heterosexual pedophiles are more likely to be married and prefer a younger target, usually females age eight to ten. Homosexual pedophiles prefer boys, usually in the 12 to 14 age range. Homosexual pedophiles have a poor prognosis for change, are less likely to know the victim, and are more interested in proceeding to orgasm, rather than focusing on the touching and looking behavior often preferred by heterosexual pedophiles. Many heterosexual male pedophiles have problems with potency and are likely to prefer ejaculation achieved through voyeuristic-exhibitionistic masturbation. When they do attempt intercourse with a child, they are likely to generate trauma and pain and in that way increase their chances of being reported and eventually apprehended (Levin & Stava, 1987).

A common catalyst for this behavior is alcohol abuse. Another catalyst (which does not detract in any way from the pedophile's responsibility for the act) is victim behavior. Finkelhor (1979) collected interesting data that showed that an unusually high percentage of sexually victimized children had lived without their mothers for a significant period before the age of 16. It is possible that they may have missed subtle training in behaviors for fending off this type of sexual coercion. When the pedophile is mentally retarded or schizophrenic, evidence shows that in a number of cases the victim initiated the contact (Virkunen, 1975).

The typical treatment approaches for pedophiles are somewhat coercive, probably because of the perceived revolting nature of the act. Also, pedophiles rarely bring themselves into treatment and are typically coerced by sociolegal pressure. Castration is still a favored response in some cultures, and in our society, chemocastration is still considered to be a reasonable option. Antiandrogens, such as cyproterone acetate (in Europe) or medroxyprogesterone acetate (in the United States), suppress the sexual libidos of male pedophiles; these drugs have also been used with rapists and exhibitionists (Walker, 1978; Walker & Meyer, 1981). They function by reducing serum testosterone levels to a level at which sexual arousal is diminished or is absent. The drugs are moderately successful when combined with psychotherapy.

An interesting issue is whether or not such offenders can be forced into such treatments, even if it is apparent that the treatment is the most effective treatment for an offender who is not highly motivated to change. At present, no such coercion is allowed. However, if there is more of a shift away from prisoners rights to the rights of potential victims and society in general, such treatments may become more common.

An intriguing approach was developed by Forgione (1976). He filmed pedophiles while they reenacted their pedophilic behaviors in response to a child-like mannequin; simply watching the playback proved aversive and reduced the pedophilic behavior. The clinician could vary this procedure by taking selected slides from the tape and pairing electric shock with them to further the aversive response.

GENDER IDENTITY DISORDER OF CHILDHOOD

The child who shows a gender identity disorder of childhood prefers the company, activities, clothes, and toys of the other sex and in some ways indicates dissatisfaction with present sexual anatomy (Money, 1987). The child favors fantasy characters of the other sex, expresses a desire to be a person of the other sex, and rejects standard same-sex activities. Most children occasionally manifest aspects of this syndrome. Only when these behaviors persist for months is concern warranted.

Although, logically, one might expect that abnormalities of the sex organs or sexual hormone levels might be involved in cases of gender disorder, there is actually little evidence, except in rare cases, that this is so (Blanchard, Steiner, & Clemmensen, 1985; Money, 1987). Treatment of gender identity or role disorder in children is usually effective, and the children's long-term adjustment is markedly superior to that of similar children who have received no therapy (Rosen, Rekers, & Bentler, 1978). Family therapy is commonly employed. Vicarious modeling and behavior management counseling also have been helpful in controlling the social learning variables that have fostered the pattern, particularly if therapy begins early. Although aversive treatment of specific behavior patterns is theoretically feasible (Sandler, 1985), it is not advised. Using shock techniques with children involves serious ethical issues and potential legal liability; also, other, less extreme techniques have been effective.

An interesting ethical-legal issue occurs in the treatment of gender confusion problems in a child. Rosen, Rekers, and Bentler (1978) summarize some of the basic treatment elements that lead to the legal issues by pointing out that (1) treatment techniques are effective in changing these behaviors in children; (2) when the change is effected, the long-term adjustment is positive and the behaviors remain changed; (3) much of this can be accomplished without the child's active participation or consent. Some theorists would argue that consent of the child is legally required, while others would hold that the parents have the right to such a decision. This problem is analogous to those discussed in the chapter on child custody. As with child custody, one intervention has been to attempt to get the child to consent, which becomes more important both therapeutically and legally as the child gets older.

JUVENILE DELINQUENCY

Juvenile delinquency refers to a legal status, rather than to a specific pattern of abnormal behavior. It designates someone, in most states a person under the age of 18, who comes under the jurisdiction of a court because of some behavior designated as socially deviant at that age. This may or may not include criminal behavior, as there are two different but related groups of juvenile offenders: delinquents and "status offenders." Delinquency proceedings concern those events that would have been criminal had they been committed by an adult. Delinquency proceedings include many of the aspects of an adult criminal trial, although the labeling of events is somewhat different. Adults are "arrested," juveniles are "taken into custody"; there is "sentencing" of adults, and "disposition" of juveniles. Status offenders are simply juveniles who require supervision because of some condition (e.g., truancy).

Most juvenile offenders are young, impoverished males. Thus, it would seem reasonable to point to poverty, biology, and sex-role expectancies as critical factors in delinquency. However, in recent decades there has been a marked increase in delinquency among young women and among those in the higher socioeconomic classes. Table 2 shows the factors (many of which are usually found in any single case) that generally contribute to the eventual emergence of a delinquent pattern (Bornstein, Schuldberg, & Bornstein, 1987; Herbert, 1987; Quay, 1987). While the model in Table 12.1 deals with delinquent behaviors in general, the one in Table 12.2 is more specific. It describes the evolution of aggressive delinquent behavior, the type most likely to bring the psychotherapists into the legal arena.

The juvenile justice system has resulted in a number of important reforms, including preventing most juveniles from being incarcerated with adult offenders, protecting some information about juveniles from public disclosure, and avoiding some of the relatively harsh punishments of the adult prison system. On the other hand, the system may make it difficult to identify and incarcerate at an early age individuals who will commit a number of crimes during adolescence and early adulthood. The system has also resulted in some juveniles having the worst of both worlds—the absence

TABLE 12.1
Factors Contributing to Delinquency

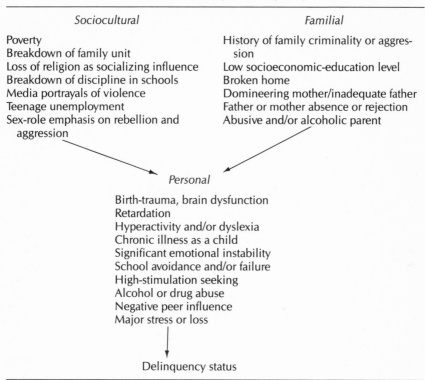

Sociocultural

Poverty
Breakdown of family unit
Loss of religion as socializing influence
Breakdown of discipline in schools
Media portrayals of violence
Teenage unemployment
Sex-role emphasis on rebellion and
  aggression

Familial

History of family criminality or aggres-
  sion
Low socioeconomic-education level
Broken home
Domineering mother/inadequate father
Father or mother absence or rejection
Abusive and/or alcoholic parent

Personal

Birth-trauma, brain dysfunction
Retardation
Hyperactivity and/or dyslexia
Chronic illness as a child
Significant emotional instability
School avoidance and/or failure
High-stimulation seeking
Alcohol or drug abuse
Negative peer influence
Major stress or loss

Delinquency status

of some protections of the criminal justice for minor crimes plus the real possibility that they will be tried as adults for serious crimes.

In the early stages of a juvenile's entrance into the juvenile justice and treatment systems, there is an emphasis on diversion from the quasi-formal juvenile justice system to parents, community treatment, social services, or prevention programs. A diversion is most often generated by the police, who may decide to warn juveniles, reprimand them, or take them home. Perhaps half of the potential delinquency cases are diverted by the police. Many additional juveniles are diverted by the court prior to formal juvenile hearings. A diversion reduces overloaded courts and may speed the process of resolving the juvenile's problems while lowering the cost of the system. However, research has not yet demonstrated a clear drop in recidivism because of diversion (Quay, 1987).

TABLE 12.2
Evolution of Aggressive Delinquency

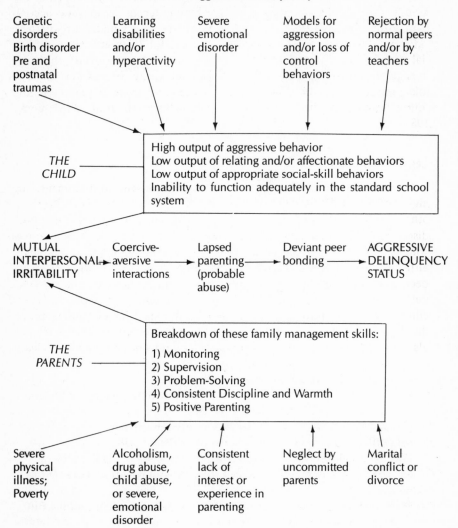

Genetic disorders
Birth disorder
Pre and postnatal traumas

Learning disabilities and/or hyperactivity

Severe emotional disorder

Models for aggression and/or loss of control behaviors

Rejection by normal peers and/or by teachers

THE CHILD

High output of aggressive behavior
Low output of relating and/or affectionate behaviors
Low output of appropriate social-skill behaviors
Inability to function adequately in the standard school system

MUTUAL INTERPERSONAL IRRITABILITY → Coercive-aversive interactions → Lapsed parenting (probable abuse) → Deviant peer bonding → AGGRESSIVE DELINQUENCY STATUS

THE PARENTS

Breakdown of these family management skills:

1) Monitoring
2) Supervision
3) Problem-Solving
4) Consistent Discipline and Warmth
5) Positive Parenting

Severe physical illness; Poverty

Alcoholism, drug abuse, child abuse, or severe, emotional disorder

Consistent lack of interest or experience in parenting

Neglect by uncommitted parents

Marital conflict or divorce

The evolution of the treatment of juvenile delinquency can be viewed as the "three R's." The traditionally favored method of *retribution* gradually gave way to *restraint* (or confinement), which in recent decades was accompanied by *rehabilitation*. However, none of the efforts under any of these categories has been considered markedly successful. Comprehensive residential treatment approaches (a) with dedicated and well trained staff, (b) based in smaller home-like settings, (c) that combine group therapy and merit or token economy programs, and (d) emphasize good aftercare placement and follow-up have had by far the most success (Bornstein et al., 1987; Quay, 1987).

Legal Issues in the Treatment of Delinquency

Several legal issues, especially the child's consent to treatment, are highlighted by the treatment of juvenile delinquents, though they apply to other disorders as well, e.g., the aforementioned issue of treating gender disorders in children. Generally speaking, it is the parent or legal guardian who takes legal responsibility for providing a child's consent to treatment, although, beginning with the landmark case of *In re Gault* in 1967, there has been increasing support for the position that children have separate individual rights, eventually including the right to consent. Nonetheless, many clinicians now seem to favor the inclusion of some type of consent procedures prior to assessment or treatment as standard practice with all individuals, especially minors. The following general guidelines are recommended:

(1) Explain the procedures and their purpose.
(2) Explain the role of the person who is providing therapy and his or her personal qualifications.
(3) Outline discomforts or risks reasonably expected.
(4) Outline benefits reasonably to be expected.
(5) Discuss alternatives to treatment that might be of similar benefit.
(6) State that any questions about the procedures will be answered at any time.
(7) State that the person can withdraw his or her consent and discontinue participation in therapy or testing at any time.

Related to this is the issue of the psychological capacities of minors to provide legal consent, defined as permission given knowingly, intelligently, and voluntarily, even when the general requirement to inform has been met (Grisso, 1986; Grisso & Vierling, 1978). Grisso and Vierling (1978, p. 412) state that clinicians should not "burden some minors with decisions that they cannot make intelligently, or inadvertently deny to some the opportunity to make decisions of which they are fully competent." The results of their work suggest:

(a) There may be no circumstances that would justify sanctioning independent consent by minors under 11 years of age, given the developmental evidence for their diminished psychological capacities.
(b) There appear to be no psychological grounds for maintaining the general legal assumption that minors at age 15 and above cannot provide competent consent.
(c) Ages 11–14 appear to be a transition period in the development of important cognitive abilities and perceptions of social expectations, but there may be circumstances that would justify the sanction of independent consent by these minors for limited purposes, especially when competence can be determined in individual cases. (p. 424)

Research such as this, however, has generally not been used in the development of consent legislation. While some state statutes do specify minimum ages when allowing independent consent by minors for certain types of treatment, the statutory ages employed are often different for various treatments within a given state, and vary widely from state to state. For example, some states allow minors to consent to treatment related to pregnancy without parental consent or knowledge; however, the minimum ages vary from 12 to 14 to 16. For independent consent to treatment for drug-related problems the ages range from early adolescence to no minimum age at all (Grisso & Vierling, 1978).

Interestingly, Melton (1981; 1987) suggests that there are many outpatient clinics that treat minors without parental consent, even though state law may be in opposition to this practice. In one study he looked at the effects of a Virginia state law that permits minors of any age to independently consent to treatment. The results of Melton's study (1981) suggest that: (1) Most clinics do not inform parents of their child's therapy decisions; (2) approximately 50 percent do not allow parental access to records; and (3) there was no significant increase in new cases after the law went into effect. From these results Melton concluded that the primary effect of the law "appears to have been simply to relieve clinicians of liability for treating competent minors without parental consent" (Melton, 1981, p. 51). Clinics who had knowledge of the new law (61 percent) were more likely to seek formal consent from the children themselves and to honor their privacy within the therapeutic relationship; however, 39 percent of the clinics were unaware of the new law more than a year after it was enacted.

The second important issue in the consent literature involves the right of a minor to refuse treatment. Should minors be provided by law or through ethical principle the power to dissent when their parents have already consented to their treatment?

Generally, a minors' ability to refuse treatment has not been recognized by law (Melton, 1987). Problems can quickly arise, however, in determining how much review a guardian's consent to hospitalization and treatment should be given. In *Parham v. J.R.* (1979), minors alleged that they had been deprived of their liberty without procedural due process by laws permitting parents to voluntarily admit minors to mental hospitals. The majority opinion held that parents should be allowed to maintain a substantial, if not the dominant, role in the decision, absent a finding of neglect or abuse, and the traditional presumption that the parents act in the best interest of their child does apply. However, it was further noted that the child's rights and the nature of the commitment decision are such that parent's consent does not always carry absolute and unreviewable discretion to decide whether to have a child institutionalized.

A minor's right to refuse treatment has been raised as an ethical issue in mental health practice, and in general there has been growing support for this, particularly when a proposed treatment is not essential or when the benefits are questionable (Melton, 1987). It is recognized, however, that diminished capacities in some minors to provide meaningful consent may sometimes present such risk to the psychological or physical welfare of the minor so as to offer a compelling reason for denial of the right in certain circumstances (Grisso, 1986; Grisso & Vierling, 1978).

HOMICIDAL CHILDREN

Psychodynamic theorists long ago documented the frequency of aggressive fantasies in children (Gedo, 1986). Many of these fantasies involve murdering others, more specifically, many focus on the murder of a parent. The frequency of such fantasies has commonly been contrasted to the rarity of actual murders by children, either of people in general or of parents.

Within the psychodynamic tradition, facilitating the expression of such fantasies via play and/or talking about them has been seen as effective in reducing any compulsion to act them out in reality. Of course, lack of physical strength, lack of access to lethal means, and immature cognitive abilities relevant to long-term planning also serve to reduce any such acting-out.

However, parricide (the killing of a parent) does occur, and Morris (1987) vividly describes such children and their families. It's somewhat comforting to find that, except for accidents (usually related to easy access to lethal means), most children who kill parents do so in response to chronic physical or sexual abuse. While not making any murder a rational or reasonable response, this makes it more understandable. Another significant group of parricides occurs with severely disturbed children. In this group, especially when the child is schizophrenic, those few who do kill do so quite unpredictably, and even where parents are seemingly loving and concerned.

Children and early adolescents who kill present particular problems for the legal system. Recently, a seven-year-old shot and killed a playmate. After talking to him, the police formally arrested him for murder, citing the fact that he first consistently denied everything, then talked about it in a fashion that indicated rational planning and an awareness of what he had done. The prosecuting attorney's office later dropped the charges.

Since Mozart was writing great works of music at five, it's conceivable that a seven-year-old child could rationally plan a murder and be reasonably aware of the implications of death. Of course, as psychotherapists are aware, most children of that age do not truly understand the implications of death. However, the more important point is that, even if formally fitting the legal requirements for murder, if ever people can agree that the goal of the legal system is rehabilitation, it would be for a seven-year-old offender.

References

Abarbanel, A. (1979). Shared parenting after separation and divorce. *American Journal of Orthopsychiatry, 49*(2), 320–338.

Abel, G., Rouleau, J., & Cunningham-Rathner, J. (1986). Sexually aggressive behavior. In W. Curran, A. L. McGarry, & S. Shah (Eds.), *Forensic psychiatry and psychology*. Philadelphia: F. A. Davis.

Abille v. United States, 482 F. Supp. 703 (N.D. Cal., 1980).

Abraham v. Zaslow, No 245862 (Cal. Super. Ct., 1972).

Abramowitz, S. (1986). Psychosocial outcomes of sex reassignment surgery. *Journal of Consulting and Clinical Psychology, 54*, 183–189.

Addington v. Texas, 441 U.S. 418 (1979).

Ahrons, C. (1980). Joint custody arrangements in the post-divorce family. *Journal of Divorce, 3*(3), 189–203.

Aldrich, R. (1987). The social context of change. In L. Duhl & N. Cummings (Eds.), *The future of mental health services*. New York: Springer.

Alexander, K. (1977). Who benefits from conservatorship? *Trial, 30*, 32.

Allred v. State, 554 p. 2d 418.

American Bar Association (1983), *51 U.S.L.W.*, 2476.

American Bar Association, Commission on the Mentally Disabled (1979). *Exercising judgment for the disabled: Report on an inquiry into limited guardianship.*

American Bar Association Report on Criminal Justice Mental Health Standards (1983).

American Law Institute (1962). *Model Penal Code, Proposed Official Draft 401.*

American Psychiatric Association (1980). *Diagnostic and Statistical Manual III.* American Psychiatric Association. Washington, D.C.

American Psychiatric Association (1985). The principles of medical ethics with annotations especially applicable to psychiatry. *American Journal of Psychiatry, 130*, 1057–1064.

American Psychiatric Association. (1987). *Diagnostic and Statistical Manual III-R.* American Psychiatric Association. Washington, D.C.

American Psychological Association (1979). Ethical standards of psychologists. Washington, D.C.

Applebaum, P. S., & Gutheil, T. (1979). "Rotting with their rights on": Constitutional theory and clinical reality in drug refusal by psychiatric patients. *Bulletin of the American Academy of Psychiatry and Law, 7*, 306.

Applebaum, P. S., Mirkin, G. I., & Bateman, V. (1981). Empirical assessment of competency to consent to psychiatric hospitalization. *American Journal of Psychiatry, 138*, 1170.

Ardrey, R. (1970). *The social contract*. New York: Dell Publishing.

Aronoff, G. (Ed.) (1986). *Evaluation and treatment of chronic pain*. Baltimore: Urban & Schwarzenberg.

Atkinson, J. (1984). Criteria for deciding child custody in the trial and appellate courts. *Family Law Quarterly, 18*, 1–42.

Baker v. United States, 226 F. Supp 129 (S.D. Iowa, 1964).

Baldwin, R. (1962). Confidentiality between physician and patient. *Medical Law Review, 22*, 181–187.

Bales, J. (1987). High court to weigh needs of abuse victims. *American Psychological Association Monitor*, April, 36.

Barrett, C. (1986). Use of disulfiram in the psychological treatment of alcoholism. *Bulletin of the Society of Psychologists in the Addictive Behaviors, 4*(4), 197–205.

Barrett. C., Johnson, P., & Meyer, R. (1985). Expert witness, consultant, advocate: One role is enough. *Bulletin of the American Academy of Forensic Psychology, 6*, 5.

Bartol, C. (1983). *Psychology and american law*. Belmont, CA: Wadsworth Publishing Co.

Baxtrom v. Herold, 383 U.S. 107 (1969).

Beck, A. (1976). *Cognitive therapy and the emotional disorders*. New York: International Universities Press.

Beck, G. (1982). When the patient threatens violence: An empirical study of clinical practice after *Tarasoff. Bulletin of the American Academy of Psychiatry and the Law, 10*, 189–199.

Bell v. Great Northern Railway, L.R. 26 Ir. 427 (1890).

Bellah v. Greenson, 81 Cal. App. 3d 911 (1978).

Belli, M. (1979). Transsexual surgery: A new tort. *Journal of Family Law, 17*, 487–504.

Belsky, J. (1980). Child maltreatment. *American Psychologist, 35*, 320–335.

Bem, S., & Funder, D. (1978). Predicting more of the people more of the time. *Psychological Review, 85*, 485–501.

Ben-Eli, T., & Sela, M. (1980). Terrorists in Nahariya: Description of coping under stress. *Israeli Journal of Psychology and Counseling in Education, 13*, 94–101.

Berger, L., & Dietrich, S. (1979). The clinical prediction of dangerousness: The logic of the process. *International Journal of Offender Therapy and Comparative Criminology, 23*(1), 25–46.

Berry, K. (1981). The male single parent. In J. Stuart & L. Abt (Eds.), *Children of separation and divorce*. New York: Von Nostrand Reinhold.

Besharov, D. J. (1986). Unfounded allegations — A new child abuse problem. *The Public Interest, 83* (Spring), 18–33.

Blackburn, R. (1983). Psychometrics and personality theory in relation to dangerousness. In J. W. Hinton (Ed.), *Dangerousness: Problems of assessment and prediction*. Boston: George Allen & Unwin.

Blackstone's Commentaries, (1898). *4*, 21. (4 Lewis, ed.) at 1427–1428.

Blair, J., & Justice, R. (1979). *The broken taboo*. New York: Human Science Press.

Blanchard, R., Steiner, B., & Clemmensen, L. (1985). Gender dysphoria, reorientation and the clinical management of transsexualism. *Journal of Consulting and Clinical Psychology, 53*, 295–304.

Blane, H. & Leonard, K. (1987). *Psychological theories of drinking and alcoholism*. New York: Guilford.

Blank, A. (1985). The unconscious flashback to the war in Viet Nam veterans: Clinical mystery, legal defense, and community problem. In S. Sonnenberg, A. Blank, & J. Talbott (Eds.), *The Trauma of War*. Washington, D.C. American Psychiatric Press.

Blau, T. H. (1984). *The psychologist as expert witness*. New York: John Wiley.

Blinder, M. (1977). The defense of claims of trauma and disability. *Forum, 12*, 934–9600.

Blocker v. United States, 288 F.2d 853 (D.C. Circuit, 1961).

Bloom, J., & Faulkner, L. (1987). Competency determinations in civil commitment. *American Journal of Psychiatry, 144*, no. 2, 193.

Bloom, J., Faulkner, L., Holm, A., & Rawlinson, H. (1984). An empirical view of patients exercising their right to refuse treatment. *International Journal of Law and Psychiatry, 7*, 315.

Blumstein, A. (1983). On the racial disproportionality of United States' prison population. *Journal of Criminal Law and Criminology, 73*, 1259–1286.

Bonovitz, J., & Guy, E. (1979). Impact of restrictive civil commitment procedures on a prison psychiatric service. *American Journal of Psychiatry, 136*, 1045–1048.

Bornstein, P., Schuldberg, D., & Bornstein, M. (1987). Conduct Disorders. In V. Van Hasselt & M. Hersen *Handbook of adolescent psychology*. Elmsford, NY: Pergamon.

Bothman v. Warren B., 445 US 949 (1980).

Bouhoutsos, J. (1984). Sexual intimacy between psychotherapists and clients: Policy implications for the future. In L. Walker (Ed.), *Women and mental health policy*. Beverly Hills, CA: Sage.

Bouhoutsos, J. (1985). Therapist-client sexual involvement: A challenge for mental health professionals and educators. *American Journal of Orthopsychiatry, 55*(2), 177–182.

Bouhoutsos, J., Holyroyd, J., Lerman, H., et al. (1983). Sexual intimacy between psychotherapists and patients. *Professional Psychology, 14*(2), 185–196.

Bovsun v. Sanperi 61, N.Y. 2d 219, 473 N.Y.S. 2d 357, 1984.

Brady v. Hopper, 570 F. Supp. 1333 (D. Colo. 1983).

Brakel, S. J., Parry, J., & Weiner, B. (1985). *The mentally disabled and the law*. Chicago: American Bar Foundation.

Brenner, D. (1982). *The effective psychotherapist*. New York: Pergamon.

Brody, S., & Tarling, R. (1980). *Taking offenders out of circulation*. London: HMSO.

Broman, S., Nichols, P., Shaughnessy, P., & Kennedy, W. (1987). *Retardation in young children*. Hillsdale, NJ: Lawrence Erlbaum.

Brooks, A. (1974). *Law, psychiatry and the mental health system*. Boston: Little Brown.

Brown, G. L., & Goodwin, F. K. (1986). Human Aggression: A biological perspective. In W. H. Reid, D. Dorr, J. I. Walker, & J. W. Bonner (Eds.), *Unmasking the psychopath*. New York: W. W. Norton.

Brown, P. (1985). *The transfer of care: Psychiatric institutionalization and its aftermath*. Boston: Routledge & Kegan Paul.

Brown, P. (1986). Psychiatric refusal, patient competence, and informed consent. *International Journal of Law and Psychiatry, 8*, 83.

Brown, S. (1985). *Treating the alcoholic*. New York: John Wiley.

Browne, A., & Finkelhor, D. (1986). Impact of child sexual abuse. *Psychological Bulletin, 99*, 66–77.

Buckhout, R. (1986). Personal values and expert testimony. *Law and Human Behavior, 10*, 127.

Burgdorf, R. L. (1980). *The legal rights of handicapped persons*. Balitmore: P.H. Brookes.

Burley, D. (1982). John Dillon revisited: Toward a better paradigm for bystander cases. *Ohio State Law Journal, 43*, 931, 948.

Burling, T., & Saylor, C. (1984). Empirically based assessment of competency to stand trial: Instrument development and preliminary findings. *Behavioral Science and the Law, 2*, 219–226.

Caesar v. Mountanos, 542 F.2d. 1064 (9th Cir. 1976).

Chapsky v. Wood, 26 Kansas 650 (1881).

Cheek, D. (1965). Emotional factors in persistent pain states. *The American Journal of Clinical Hypnosis, 9*, 100–101.

Chodoff, P. (1984). Involuntary hospitalization of the mentally ill as a moral issue. *American Journal of Psychiatry, 141*, 384.

Clannon, T. L., & Jew, C. (1985). Predictions from assessments of violent offenders under stress: A fifteen-year experience. *Criminal Justice and Behavior, 12*(4), 485–499.

Clingempeel, W. G., & Reppucci, N. D. (1982). Joint custody after divorce: Major issues and goals for research. *Psychological Bulletin, 91*(1), 102–127.

Clites v. Iowa, No. 46247 (Pottawattamine County, Iowa, 1980).

Cocozza, J., Melick, M., & Steadman, H. (1978). Trends in violent crime among ex-mental patients. *Criminology: An Interdisciplinary Journal, 16*(3), 317–334.

Cocozza, J. & Steadman, H. (1976). The failure of psychiatric predictions of dangerousness: Clear and convincing evidence. *Rutgers Law Review, 29*, 1084–1101.

Cohen, B. (1978). Protective services and public guardianship: A dissenting view. Paper presented to Annual Meeting of the Gerontological Society, Nov. 20, 1978, quoted in W. L. Schmidt, K. Miller, W. Bell, & B. New, *Public guardianship and the elderly*. Cambridge, MA: Ballinger Publishing Co.

Cohen, R. J. (1987). The professional liability of behavioral scientists: An overview. In L. Everstine & D. S. Everstine (Eds.), *Psycholotherapy and the law*. Orlando, Fla: Grune & Stratton.

Coleman, C. (1986). Creating therapist-offender exception to mandatory child abuse reporting statutes—when psychiatrist knows best. *Cincinnati Law Review, 54*, 1113–1118.

Coleman, D., & Soloman, Z. (1976). Parens patriae 'treatment': Legal punishment in disguise. *Hastings Constitutional Law Quarterly, 3*, 344.

Colorado v. Connelly, 107 S.Ct. 115, 55 L.W. 4043 (1986).

Cox, D. (1980). Exhibitionism: An overview. In D. Cox & R. Daitzman (Eds.), *Exhibitionism*. New York: Garland STPM.

Cross, C. (1984). *Child abuse and neglect*. Washington, DC: National Education Association.

Currie v. United States, 644 F.Supp. 1074 (1986).

Dale, P., Waters, J., Davies, M., Roberts, W., & Morrison, T. (1986). The towers of silence. *Journal of Family Therapy, 8*, 1–26.

Daly, E., & Wulff, J. (1987). Treatment of a post-traumatic headache. *British Journal of Medical Psychology, 60*, 85–88.

Daniel M'Naughten's Case, 88 Eng. Rep. 718 (1843).

Danner, R. A. (1980). *Pattern deposition checklist*. Madison, WI.: University of Wisconsin Extension Law Department.

Davidson, S. (1980). The clinical effects of massive psychic trauma in families of holocaust survivors. *Journal of Marital and Family Therapy, 6*, 11–21.

Davison, G. (1976). Homosexuality: The ethical challenge. *Journal of Consulting and Clinical Psychology, 44*, 157–162.

Davison, G. (1978). Not can but ought: The treatment of homosexuality. *Journal of Consulting and Clinical Psychology, 45*, 170–172.

Defrain, J., & Eirick, R. (1981). Coping as divorced single parents: A comparative study of fathers and mothers. *Family Relations, 30*, 265–274.

Dell, L., Ruzickah, M., & Palisi, A. (1981). Personality and other factors associated with gambling addiction. *The International Journal of the Addictions, 16*, 149–156.

Denton, L. (June, 1987). *APA Monitor, 18*(6), 1.

DeRisi, W., & Vega, W. (1983). The impact of deinstitutionalization on California's hospital population. *Hospital and Community Psychiatry, 34*, 140–145.

Detre, T., & Kupfer, D. (1975). Psychiatric history and mental status examination. In A. M. Freedman, H. T. Kaplan, & B. V. Saddock (Eds.), *Comprehensive textbook of psychiatry II*.

Deutsch, A. (1949). *The mentally ill in America*, 2nd ed. New York: Columbia University Press.

Diaz-Buxo, J., Caudle, J., Chandler, J., Farmer, C., & Holbrook, W. (1980). Dialysis of schizophrenic patients: A double-blind study. *American Journal of Psychiatry, 137*, 1220–1222.

Dickens, B. M. (1985). Prediction, professionalism, and public policy. In C. D. Webster, M. H. Ben-Aron, & S. J. Hucker (Eds.), *Dangerousness*. New York: Cambridge University Press.

Dietz, P. E. (1985). Hypothetical criteria for the prediction of individual criminality. In C. D. Webster, M. H. Ben-Aron, & S. J. Hucker (Eds.), *Dangerousness*. New York: Cambridge University Press.

Dillon v. Legg, 68 Cal. 2d 728, 441 P.2d 912.

Dix, G. (1980). Clinical evaluation of the "dangerousness" of "normal" criminal defendants. *Virginia Law Review, 66*, 523–581.

Doe v. Commonwealth's Attorney for City of Richmond, 403 U.S. Dist. Ct. EVA 1975.

Donovan, J. (1986). An etiologic model of alcoholism. *Archives of General Psychiatry, 143*, 1–11.

Duncan, I. (Autumn, 1929). *This Quarter Magazine* (published in Paris).

Durham v. United States, 214 F.2d 862 (1954).

Dusky v. United States 362 U.S. 402 (1960).

D'Zurilla, T. (1986). *Problem-solving therapy*. New York: Springer.

Earls, C., & Prouix, J. (1986). The differentiation of francophone rapists and non-rapists using penile circumferential measures. *Criminal Justice and Behavior, 13*, 419–429.

Easter v. District of Columbia, 361 F.2d 50 (D.C. Cir. 1966).

Eckerhart v. Hensley, 475 F. Supp. 908 (Mo., 1979).

Edelwich, J. with Brodsky, A. (1982). *Sexual dilemmas for the helping professional*. New York: Brunner-Mazel.

Edinger, J. (1979). Cross-validation of the Megargee MMPI typology for prisoners. *Journal of Consulting and Clinical Psychology, 47*, 234–242.

Edmonston, W. (1986). *The induction of hypnosis*. New York: John Wiley.

Eichelman, B. (1987). The ethics of mental health practice. In L. Duhl & N. Cummings (Eds.), *The future of mental health services*. New York: Springer.

Ellis, A. (1987). The impossibility of achieving consistently good mental health. *American Psychologist, 42*, 364–375.

Ellis, A., & Dryden, W. (1987). *The practice of rational-emotive therapy*. New York: Springer.

Ellis, J. W. (1984). Evaluating the expert: Judicial expectations of expert opinion evidence in child placement adjudications. *Cardozo Law Review, 5*, 587–607.

Ennis, B. (1972). Prisoners of psychiatry: Mental patients, psychiatry and the law. New York: Harcourt, Brace, Jovanovich.

Ennis, B., & Litwack, E. (1974). Psychiatry and the presumption of expertise: Flipping coins in the courtroom. *California Law Review, 62*, 693.

Epstein, J. (1962). Testamentary capacity, reasonableness and family maintenance: A proposal for meaningful reform. *Temple Law Quarterly, 35*, 231.

Everstine, L., Everstine, D. S., Heymann, G. M., True, R. H., Frey, D. H., Johnson, H. G., & Seiden, R. H. (1980). Privacy and confidentiality in psychotherapy. *American Psychologist, 35*, 828–840.

Ewing v. Pittsburgh Railroad Co., 147 Pa. 40, 23A, 340, 14 L.R.A. 666 (1982).

Ewing, J. (1983). Ethical ban on psychiatric and psychological predictions on dangerousness in capital sentencing proceedings. *American Journal of Law and Medicine, 8*, 407.

Exner, J. (1983). *The Rorschach: A Comprehensive System Volume I*. New York: Wiley-Interscience.

Fabry, J. (1980). Depression. In R. Woody (Ed.), *Encyclopedia of clinical assessment*. San Francisco: Jossey-Bass.

Faigenbaum v. Cohen, No. 79-904-736 NM (Wayne County, Michigan, 1979).

Federal Parental Kidnapping Prevention Act of 1980, 28 U.S.C. 1738(A).

Feldman-Summers, S., & Jones, G. (1984). Psychological impacts of sexual contact between therapists or other mental health practitioners and their clients. *Journal of Consulting and Clinical Psychology, 52*(6), 1054–1061.

Fersch, E. (1980). *Psychology and psychiatry and courts and corrections*. New York: John Wiley.

Finkelhor, D. (1979). *Sexually victimized children*. New York: Free Press.

Finlay v. Finlay, 148 N.E. 624 (1925, 1926).

Floud, J., & Young, W. (1981). *Dangerousness and criminal justice*. London: Heineman.

Foa, E., & Kozak, M. (1986). Emotional processing of fear. *Psychological Bulletin, 99*, 20–35.

Ford v. Wainright. 106 S. Ct. 2595 (1986).

Forgione, A. (1976). Instrumentation and techniques. The use of mannequins in the behavioral assessment of child molesters: Two case reports. *Behavior Therapy, 7*, 678–685.

Foust, L. (1979). The legal significance of formulations of fire-setting behavior. *International Journal of Law and Psychiatry, 2*, 371–388.

Fowles, G., & Coleman, C. (1987). Personal communication.

Franklin, R. L., & Hibbs, R. (1980). Child custody in transition. *Journal of Marital and Family Therapy, 6*(3), 285–291.

Frazier, P., & Borgida, E. (1985). Rape trauma evidence in court. *American Psychologist, 40,* 984–993.

Frederick, J. (1982–1983). The biochemistry of bereavement: Possible basis for chemotherapy? *Omega: Journal of Death and Dying, 13,* 295–303.

Fromuth, M. (1986). The relationship of child sexual abuse with later psychological and sexual adjustment in a sample of college women. *Child Abuse and Neglect, 10,* 5–16.

Frye v. United States, 293 F. 1013 (D.C.Cir. 1923).

Fulero, S. (1987). Insurance trust releases malpractice statistics. *State Psychological Association Affairs, 19*(1), 4–5.

Gartrell, N., Herman, J., Olarte, S., Feldstein, M., & Localio, R. (1986). Psychiatrist-patient sexual contact: Results of a national survey, I: Prevalence. *American Journal of Psychiatry, 143*(9), 1126–1131.

Gardner, D., Lucas, P., & Cowdry, R. (1987). Soft sign neurological abnormalities in borderline and personality and normal control subjects. *The Journal of Nervous and Mental Disease, 175*(3), 177–180.

Gardner, J., & Gray, M. (1982). Violence toward children. In *Developments in the study of criminal behavior, vol. 2.* New York: John Wiley.

Gardner, R. A. (1973). *The talking, feeling, and doing game.* Greenskill, NJ: Creative Therapeutics.

Gaylord v. Tacoma School District of Washington, 559 P.2d 1340 (1975).

Gearing, M. (1979). The MMPI as a primary differentiator and predictor of behavior in prison: A methodological critique and review of the recent literature. *Psychological Bulletin, 86,* 929–963.

Gedo, J. (1986). *Conceptual issues in psychoanalysis.* Hillsdale, NJ: The Analytic Press.

Geller, J., & Lister, E. (1978). The process of criminal commitment for pretrial psychiatric examination: An evaluation. *American Journal of Psychiatry, 135,* 53.

George, B. (1976). Emerging constitutional rights of the mentally ill. *National Journal of Criminal Defense, 2,* 35.

Giacopassi, D., & Wilkinson, K. (1985). Rape and the devalued victim. *Law and Human Behavior, 9,* 367–383.

Gislason, I., & Call, J. (1982). Dog bite in infancy: Trauma and personality development. *Journal of American Academy of Child Psychiatry, 21,* 203–207.

GIW Southern Value Co. v. Smith, 471 So. 2d 81 (1986).

Glueck, S., & Glueck, E. T. (1968). *Delinquents and nondelinquents in perspective.* Cambridge, MA: Harvard University Press.

Gobert, J. (1973). Competency to stand trial: A pre- and post-Jackson analysis. *Tennessee Law Review, 40,* 659.

Golding, S., Roesch, R., & Schrieber, J. (1984). Assessment and conceptualization of competency to stand trial. *Law and Human Behavior, 8,* 321.

Goldstein, A., & Keller, H. (1987). *Aggressive behavior.* New York: Pergamon.

Goldstein, A., Keller, H., & Erne, D. (1986). *Changing the abusive parent.* New York: Free Press.

Goldstein, J., Freud, A., & Solnit, A. J. (1973). *Beyond the best interests of the child.* New York: Free Press.

Goldstein, J., Freud, A., Solnit, A. J., & Goldstein, S. (1986). *In the best interests of the child.* New York: Free Press.

Goldzband, M. G. (1982). *Consulting in child custody: An introduction to the ugliest litigation for mental health professionals.* Lexington, MA: Lexington Books.

Goodman, T. A. (1985). From *Tarasoff* to *Hopper*: The evolution of the therapists duty to protect third parties. *Behavioral Science and the Law, 3*(2), 195–225.

Gorski, T., & Miller, M. (1986). *Staying sober.* Independence, MO: Independence Press.

Greenland, C. (1985). Dangerousness, mental disorder, and politics. In C. D. Webster, M. H. Ben-Aron, & S. J. Hucker (Eds.), *Dangerousness*. New York: Cambridge University Press.

Grisso, T. (1986). *Evaluating competencies: Forensic assessments and instruments*. New York: Plenum.

Grisso, T., & Vierling, L. (1978). Minors' consent to treatment. *Professional Psychology, 9,* 412–427.

Griswold v. Connecticut, 381 U.S. 479 (1965).

Grob, C. (1985). Single case study: Female exhibitionism. *The Journal of Nervous and Mental Disease, 173,* 252–256.

Grote, C., Kaler, D., & Meyer, R. (1986). Personal injury law and psychology. In M. Kurke & R. Meyer (Eds.), *Psychology in product liability and personal injury law*. New York: Hemisphere.

Gruenewald, D. (1978). Analogues of multiple personality in psychosis. *International Journal of Clinical and Experimental Hypnosis, 26,* 1–8.

Gutheil, T. (1986). Forensic assessment. In D. Weisstub (Ed.), *Law and mental health: International perspectives, vol. 1,* New York: Pergamon.

Gutheil, T., & Applebaum, P. S. (1982). *Clinical handbook of psychiatry and the law.* New York: McGraw-Hill.

Gutheil, T., & Bursztajn, H. (1986). Clinician's guidelines for assessing and presenting subtle forms of patient incompetence in legal settings. *American Journal of Psychiatry, 143*(8), 1020–1023.

Halleck, S. (1969). The psychiatrist and the legal process. *Psychology Today, 2,* 25.

Halleck, S. (1986). Responsibility in psychiatry and law. In D. Weisstub (Ed.), *Law and mental health: International perspectives, vol. 1.* New York: Pergamon.

Halleck, S. (1987). Personal communication.

Hammer v. Rosen, 198N.Y. 2d 65 (1960).

Hare, R., & Jutai, J. (1986). Psychopathy, stimulation-seeking, and stress. In J. Strelau, F. Farley, & A. Gale (Eds.), *The biological bases of personality and behavior* (vol. 2). New York: Hemisphere.

Hare, R. D. (1985). Comparison of procedures for the assessment of psychopathy. *Journal of Consulting and Clinical Psychology, 53,* 7–16.

Harlow, L., Newcomb, M., & Bentler, P. (1986). Depression, self-derogation, substance abuse, and suicide ideation. *Journal of Clinical Psychology, 42,* 5–20.

Hawton, K., & Catalan, J. (1987). *Attempted suicide.* New York: Oxford.

Hays, J., & Solway, K. (1972). The role of psychological evaluation in certification of juveniles for trial as adults. *Houston Law Review, 9*(4), 709.

Heath, D. (1986). Drinking and drunkenness in transcultural perspective. *Transcultural Psychiatric Research, 23,* 7–42.

Hedlund v. Superior Court of Orange County, 34 Cal. 3d 695 (1983).

Heins, M. (1984). The 'Battered Child' revisited. *Journal of the American Medical Association, 251,* 3295–3300.

Helman, C. (1981). "Tonic," "Fuel," and "Food": Social and symbolic aspects of the longterm use of psychotropic drugs. *Social Science and Medicine, 15B,* 521–533.

Henden, H., & Haas, A. (1987). Post-traumatic stress disorder. In C. Last & M. Hersen (Eds.), *Handbook of anxiety disorders.* Elmsford, NY: Plenum.

Herbert, M. (1987). *Conduct disorders of childhood and adolescence.* New York: John Wiley.

Herman, M. (1983). Assault on the insanity defense: Limitations on the effectiveness and effect of the defense of insanity. *Rutgers Law Journal, 14,* 241.

Herr, S., Aarons, S., & Wallace, R. (1983). *Legal Rights and Mental Health Care,* Lexington, MA: Lexington Books.

Herrenkohl, R., Herrenkohl, E., & Egolf, B. (1983). Circumstances surrounding the occurrence of child maltreatment. *Journal of Consulting and Clinical Psychology, 51,* 424–430.

Hersen, M., & Bellack, A. (1987). *Dictionary of behavioral assessment techniques.* Elmsford, NY: Plenum.

Hiday, V. A. (1982). The attorney's role in involuntary civil commitment. *North Carolina Law Review, 60*, 1027.

Hinton, J. W. (1983). The need for a multi-disciplinary approach to the study of dangerousness. In J. W. Hinton (Ed.), *Dangerousness: Problems of assessment and predictions*. Boston: George Allen & Unwin.

Hodges, W. F. (1986). *Interventions for children of divorce: Custody, access, and psychotherapy*. New York: John Wiley.

Hodges, W. F., Wechsler, R. C., & Ballantine, C. (1979). Divorce and the preschool child. *Journal of Divorce, 3*, 55–69.

Hoffman, K., & Browning, C. (1980). Mental health professionals in the legal process: A plea for rational application of clinical methods. *Law and Psychology Review, 6*, 21.

Hogan, D. (1979). *The regulation of psychotherapists: A review of malpractice suits in the United States, (vol. 3)*. New York: Academic Press.

Holmes, T. H., & Rahe, R. H. (1967). Social readjustment scale. *Journal of Psychosomatic Research, 11*, 213–218.

Holroyd, J., & Brodsky, A. M. (1977). Psychologist's attitudes and practices regarding erotic and non-erotic physical contact with patients. *American Psychologist, 32*, 843–849.

Horne v. Goodson (1987). *APA Practitioner, 11*(1), 6–7.

Horne v. Goodson Logging Co., 349 S.E. 2d 293 (1987).

Houston v. Alaska, No. 3339, Alaska Supreme Court (1979).

Howell, R. J., & Toepke, K. E. (1984). Summary of the child custody laws for the fifty states. *The American Journal of Family Therapy, 12*(2), 56–60.

Howells, K. (1982). Mental disorder and violent behavior. In P. Feldman (Ed.), *Developments in the study of criminal behavior, Vol. 2*. New York: John Wiley.

Howells, K. (1983). Social construing and violent behavior in mentally abnormal offenders. In J. W. Hinton (Ed.), *Dangerousness: Problems of assessment and predictions*. Boston: George Allen & Unwin.

Ifeld, F., Ifeld, H., & Alexander, J. (1982). Does joint custody work?: A first local look at outcome data of relitigation. *American Journal of Psychiatry, 62*, 139–142.

In re Gault, 367 U.S. 1 (1967).

In re Hemingway's Estate, 95 Pa. 291, 45 A.2d 726 (1900).

In re Lifschutz, 2 Cal.3d. 415 (1970).

In re Oakes, 8 Monthly Law Reporter (Mass. 1845).

In re William Wilson, MH no. 1124-82 (D.C. Superior Court, 1983).

In re Zuniga, 714 F.2d.632 (6th Cir. 1983).

Irving, H. H., Benjamin, M., & Trocme, N. (1984). Shared parenting: An experimental analysis using a large data base. *Family Process, 23*, 561–569.

Jablonski v. United States, 712 F.2d 391 (1983).

Jackson v. Indiana, 406 U.S. 715 (1972).

Jeffrey, R. W., & Pasewark, R. A. (1983). Altering opinions about the insanity plea. *Journal of Psychiatry and Law, 11*(1), 29–40.

Jellinek, E. (1960). *The disease concept of alcoholism*. New Haven: Hillhouse Press.

Jenkins v. United States, 307 F. 2d 637 (D.C. Circuit, 1962).

Jenkins, C., & Zyzanski, S. (1980). Behavioral risk factors and coronary heart disease. *Psychotherapy and Psychosomatics, 34*, 149–177.

Jones v. Brooklyn Heights Railroad, 23 App. Dib. 141.

Jordan, S. M. (1985). *Decision making for incompetent persons: The law and morality of who decides*. Springfield, Ill: C. C. Thomas.

Judd, J. S., Judd, F. K., & Burrows, G. D. (1986). The psychiatrist and negligence. *Australian and New Zealand Journal of Psychiatry, 20*(2), 233–236.

Kapp, M. B., & Bigot, G. (1985). *Geriatrics and the law: Patient rights and professional responsibilities*. New York: Springer Publishing Co.

Kardiner, A. (1941). *The traumatic neuroses of war*. New York: Paul Hoeber.

Kargon, R. (1986). Expert testimony in historical perspective. *Law and Human Behavior, 10*, 15.

Karon, B. (1976). The psychoanalysis of schizophrenia. In P. Magero (Ed.), *The construction of madness.* New York: Pergamon.

Kasl, S., & Cooper, C. (1987). (Eds.). *Stress and health.* New York: John Wiley.

Katz, J. (1967). *Psychoanalysis, psychiatry and law.* New York: John Wiley.

Kay, S., & Lindenmayer, J. (1987). Outcome predictors in acute schizophrenia. *Journal of Nervous and Mental Disease, 175,* 152–160.

Keefe, F., & Gil, K. (1987). Chronic Pain. In V. Hasselt, P. Strain, & M. Hersen (Eds.), *Handbook of developmental and physical disabilities.* Elmsford, NY: Plenum.

Keeton, M., & Gower, B. (1935). Freedom of testation in English law, *Iowa Law Review, 20,* 326.

Kegan, R. G. (1986). The child behind the mask: Psychopathy as developmental delay. In W. H. Reid, D. Door, J. I. Walker, & J. W. Bonner (Eds.), *Unmasking the psychopath.* New York: W. W. Norton.

Keilitz, I., Conn, N., & Giampetro, A. (1985). Least restrictive treatment of involuntary patients: Translating concepts into practice. *Saint Louis University Law Journal, 29,* 691.

Keith-Spiegel, P., & Koocher, G. (1985). *Ethics in psychology.* New York: Random House.

Kellam, A. (1969). Shoplifting treated by aversion to a film. *Behavior Research and Therapy, 7,* 125–127.

Kellner, R. (1986). *Somatization and hypochondriasis.* London: Praeger.

Kennedy, W. (1986). The psychologist as expert witness. In W. Curran, A. L. McGarry, & S. Shah (Eds.), *Forensic psychiatry and psychology.* Philadelphia: F. A. Davis.

Kentucky v. Stincer, 107 S.Ct. 989, 55 L. W. 4901 (1987).

Kerns, R., & Turk, D. (1984). Depression and chronic pain: The mediating role of the spouse. *Journal of Marriage and the Family, 46,* 845–852.

Kestenbaum, C. (1979). Children at risk for manic-depressive illness. *American Journal of Psychiatry, 136,* 1206–1208.

Killenbeck, M. (1986). We have met the imbeciles and they are us: The courts and citizens with mental retardation. *Nebraska Law Review, 65,* 768.

Kirman, W. (1980). The modern psychoanalytic treatment of depression. In G. Belkin (Ed.), *Contemporary psychotherapies.* Chicago: Rand McNally.

Klein, D., Depue, R., & Slater, J. (1985). Cyclothymia in the adolescent offspring of parents with bipolar affective disorder. *Journal of Abnormal Psychology, 94,* 115–127.

Kluft, R. (1987). An update on multiple personality disorder. *Hospital and Community Psychiatry, 38,* 363–373.

Knetch v. Gillman, 488 F.2d 1136 (9th Cir. 1973).

Kolevzon, M., & Green, R. (1985). *Family therapy models.* New York: Springer.

Kopelmon, M. (1987). Amnesia: Organic and psychogenic. *British Journal of Psychiatry, 150,* 428–442.

Kozak, M., Foa, E., & McCarthy, P. (1987). Obsessive-compulsive disorder. In C. Last & M. Hersen (Eds.), *Handbook of anxiety disorders.* Elmsford, NY: Plenum.

Kozol, H. L., Boucher, R. J., & Garofalo, R. F. (1972). The diagnosis and treatment of dangerousness. *Crime and Delinquency, 18,* 371–392.

Krupnick, J., & Horowitz, M. (1981). Stress response syndromes: Recurrent themes. *Archives of General Psychiatry, 38,* 428–435.

Kuhnley, E., Hendren, R. & Quinlan, D. (1982). Firesetting by children. *Journal of the American Academy of Child Psychiatry, 21,* 560–563.

Laboratory of Community Psychiatry, Harvard Medical School. (1973). *Competency to Stand Trial and Mental Illness.* (DHEW Pub. #ADM77-103). Rockville, MD: Department of Health, Education, and Welfare.

Landis, E., & Meyer, R. (1988). *Detecting deception.* Chicago, IL: Dorsey.

Lazarus, A. A. (1971). *Behavior therapy and beyond.* New York: McGraw-Hill.

Lehmkul, V. (1982). Choice of symptoms and loss of the father. *Zeitscrift fur Kinderund Jugendpsychiatrie, 10,* 262–273, (From *Psychological Abstracts,* 1983, *69,* Abstract No. 10733).

Leong v. Takasaki, 55 Hawaii 398, 520 P.2d 758, 94 ALR 3d 471 (1974).

Leupnitz, D. A. (1982). *Child custody: A study of families after divorce.* Lexington, MA: Lexington Books.

Levin, S., & Stava, L. (1987). Personality characteristics of sex offenders. *Archives of Sexual Behavior, 16*, 57–79.

Levy, A. M. (1985). Father custody. In D. H. Schetky & E. P. Benedek (Eds.), *Emerging issues in child psychiatry and the law.* New York: Brunner/Mazel.

Liebowitz, M., Goreman, J., Fryer, A., Levitt, M., et al. (1985). Lactate provocation of panic attacks. *Archives of General Psychiatry, 42*, 709–714.

Lipper v. Weston, 369 S.W.2d 698 (Tex. Civ. App., 1963).

Lipsitt, P. (1986). Beyond competency to stand trial. In Everstine, L. & Everstine, D. (Eds.), *Psychotherapy and the law.* Orlando, FL: Grune & Stratton.

Lipsitt, P., Lelos, D., & McGarry, A. (1971). Competency for trial: A screening instrument. *American Journal of Psychiatry, 128*, 105.

Loftus, E. (1986). Experimental psychologist as advocate or impartial educator. *Law and Human Behavior, 10*, 63.

LoPiccolo, J., & Stock, W. (1986). Treatment of sexual dysfunction. *Journal of Consulting and Clinical Psychology, 54*, 158–167.

Loving v. Virginia, 388 U.S. 1 (1967).

Lowery, C. R. (1981). Child custody decisions in divorce proceedings: A survey of judges. *Professional Psychology, 12*, 492–498.

Lowery, C. R. (1985). Child custody evaluations: Criteria and clinical implications. *Journal of Clinical Child Psychology, 14*(4), 35–41.

Lunde, D. (1976). *Murder and madness.* San Francisco: San Francisco Book Co.

Luria, Z., Friedman, S., & Rose, M. (1986). *Human sexuality.* New York: John Wiley.

Lykken, D. (1957). A study of anxiety in the sociopathic personality. *Journal of Abnormal and Social Psychology, 55*, 6–10.

Lynch v. Knight, 9 H.L.Ca. 577, 598 (1861).

MacAndrew, C. (1965). The differentiation of male alcoholic outpatients from nonalcoholic psychiatric patients by means of the MMPI. *Quarterly Journal of Studies on Alcohol, 26*, 238–246.

Malamuth, N. (1986). Predictors of naturalistic sexual aggression. *Journal of Personality and Social Psychology, 50*, 953–962.

Malkin, D., & Syme, G. (1985). Wagering preferences of problem gamblers. *Journal of Abnormal Psychology, 94*, 86–91.

Maloney, M. (1985). *A Clinician's Guide to Forensic Psychological Assessment.* New York: Free Press.

Marafiote, R. A. (1985). *The custody of children.* New York: Plenum.

Margulis, S. (1977). Introductory remarks. *Journal of Social Issues, 33*(3), 1–4.

Marmor, J. (1978). Psychological roots of violence. In R. Sadoff (Ed.), *Violence and responsibility.* New York: Spectrum.

Matson, J. (1987). Mental retardation – adults. In V. Van Hasselt, P. Strain, & M. Hersen (Eds.), *Handbook of developmental and physical disabilities.* Elmsford, NY: Plenum.

Mavromatis, M. & Lion, J. (1977). A primer in pyromania. *Diseases of the Nervous System, 38*, 954–955.

Mavroudis V. Superior Court, 162 Cal. Rptr. 724 (Ct.App. 1980).

McGarry, A., Curran, W., Lipsitt, P., Lelos, D., Schwitzgebel, R., & Rosenburg, A. (1983). *Competency to stand trial and mental illness.* Rockville, MD: NIMH, Center for Studies of Crime and Delinquency.

McGarry, A., Schwitzgebel, R., Lipsitt, P., & Lelos, D. (1981). *Civil commitment and social policy: An evaluation of the Massachusetts Mental Health Reform Act of 1970.* Rockville, MD: National Institute of Mental Health.

McIntosh v. Milano, 403 A.2d.500 (1979).

Meddin, B. J., & Hansen, I. (1985). The services provided during a child abuse and or neglect case investigation and the barriers that exist to service providers. *Child Abuse and Neglect, 9*, 175–182.

Megargee, E., and Bohn, M. (1979). *Classifying criminal offenders*. Beverly Hills, CA: Sage.

Megargee, E. I. (1976). The prediction of dangerous behavior. *Criminal Justice and Behavior, 3*, 1–23.

Megargee, E. I. (1981). Methodological problems in the prediction of violence. In J. R. Hays, T. K. Roberts, & K. S. Solway (Eds.), *Violence and the violent individual*. New York: Spectrum.

Megargee, E., & Cook, P. (1975). Negative response bias and the MMPI O–H scale: A response to Deiker. *Journal of Consulting and Clinical Psychology, 43*, 725–729.

Mehrabian, A., & Weinstein, L. (1985). Temperament characteristics of suicide attempters. *Journal of Consulting and Clinical Psychology, 53*, 544–546.

Meier, M., Benton, A., & Diller, L. (Eds.), (1987). *Neuropsychological rehabilitation*. New York: Guilford.

Meier v. Ross General Hospital, 69 Cal.2d.420 (1968).

Meissner, W. (1978). *The paranoid process*. New York: Jason Aronson.

Meister, R. (1980). *Hypochondria*. New York: Taplinger.

Melton, G. (1981). Effects of a state law permitting minors to consent to psychotherapy. *Professional Psychology, 12*, 647–654.

Melton, G. (1987). The clashing of symbols: Prelude to child and family policy. *American Psychologist, 42*, 345–354.

Menzies, R. J., Webster, C. D., & Sepejak, D. S. (1985). Hitting the forensic sound barrier: Predictions of dangerousness in a pretrial psychiatric clinic. In C. D. Webster, M. H. Ben-Aron, & S. J. Hucker (Eds.), *Dangerousness*. New York: Cambridge University Press.

Meriwether, M. (1986). Child abuse reporting laws: Time for a change. *Family Law Quarterly, 20*, 141–172.

Mester, R. (1986). The psychotherapy of mania. *The British Journal of Medical Psychology, 39*, 13–20.

Mestrovic, S. (1982). Admission patterns at South Carolina's state psychiatric hospitals following legislative reform. *Journal of Psychiatry and Law, 10*, 457.

Meyer, R. (1983). *The clinician's handbook*. Boston: Allyn & Bacon.

Meyer, R., & Salmon, P. (1988). *Abnormal psychology*. Boston: Allyn & Bacon.

Meyer, R., & Willage, D. (1980). Confidentiality and privileged communication in psychotherapy. In P. Lipsitt & B. Sales (Eds.), *New Directions in Psycholegal Research*. New York: Van Nostrand, Reinhold.

Meyers, C. (1986). The legal perils of psychotherapeutic practice: The farther reaches of duty to warn. In Everstine, L. & Everstine, D. (Eds.), *Psychotherapy and the law*. Orlando, FL: Grune & Stratton.

Mezer, N., & Rheingold, H. (1962). Medical capacity and incompetency: A psycho-legal problem. *American Journal of Psychiatry, 118*, 827.

Miller, B., & Welte, J. (1986). Comparisons of incarcerated offenders according to use of alcohol and/or drugs prior toffense. *Criminal Justice and Behavior, 13*, 366–392.

Miller, D. J. & Thelen, M. H. (1986). Knowledge and beliefs about confidentiality in psychotherapy. *Professional Psychology, 17*, 12–19.

Miller, R., & Fiddleman, P. (1982). Involuntary civil commitment in North Carolina: The results of the 1979 statutory changes. *North Carolina Law Review, 60*, 985–1026.

Millon, T. (1981). *Disorders of personality, DSM-III: Axis II*. New York: John Wiley.

Minchin, L. (1982). Violence between couples. In P. Feldman (Ed.), *Developments in the study of criminal behavior, vol. 2*. New York: John Wiley.

Minnesota v. Andring 342 N.W.2d 128 (1984).

Mischel, W. (1968). *Personality and assessment*. New York: John Wiley.

Mitchell, K. (1978). Involuntary guardianship for incompetents: A strategy for legal service advocates. *Clearinghouse Review, 12*, 451.

Molien v. Kaiser Foundation Hospital, 616 P.2d 813 (Cal. 1980).

Monahan, J. (1981). *Predicting violent behavior*. Beverly Hills, CA: Sage.

Monahan, J. (1982). The prediction of violent behavior: Developments in law and psychology. In C. Scheirer & B. Hammonds (Eds.), *Psychology and the law: The master lecture series, vol. 2.* New York: American Psychological Association.

Monahan, J., & Steadman, H. (1983). Crime and mental disorder: An epidemiological approach. In N. Morris & M. Tonry (Eds.), *Crime and justice: An annual review of research.* Chicago: University of Chicago Press.

Monahan, J., & Walker, L. (1985). *Social science in law.* Mineola, NY: Foundation Press.

Money, J. (1987). Sin, sickness, or status: Homosexual gender identity and psychoneuroendocrinology. *American Psychologist, 42,* 384–399.

Monroe, R. (1981). Brain dysfunction in prisoners. In J. Hays, T. Roberts, & K. Solway (Eds.), *Violence and the violent individual.* New York: SP Books.

Morissette v. U.S. 342 U.S. 246, 250 (1950).

Morris, G. (1987). *The kids next door.* New York: William Morrow.

Muehleisen, R. (1987). The high price of sexual impropriety. *Ohio Psychologist, 33*(8), 3–5.

Mueller, C. W. (1983). Environmental stressors and aggressive behavior. In R. G. Green & E. I. Donnerstein (Eds.), *Aggression: Theoretical and empirical reviews, vol. 2.* New York: Academic Press.

Mulvey, E. P., & Lidz, C. W. (1984). Clinical considerations in the prediction of dangerousness in mental patients. *Clinical Psychology Review, 4,* 399–401.

Murphy, V., Sobol, A., Neff, R., Olivier, D., & Leighton, A. (1985). Stability of presence: Depression and anxiety disorders. *Archives of General Psychiatry, 41,* 990–1100.

Nasrallah, H., & Weinberger, D. (Eds.), (1986). *Handbook of schizophrenia vol. 1: The neurology of schizophrenia.* Amsterdam: Elsevier.

National Association of Social Workers. (Oct., 1980). Professional ethics code adopted. *NASW News.*

National Center for State Courts (NCSC) (1982). *Provisional, substantive, and procedural guidelines for involuntary civil commitment.*

National Conference of Commissioners on Uniform State Laws. (1971). Uniform Marriage and Divorce Act. *Family Law Quarterly, 5,* 205–251.

Nelson, B. (1984). *Making child abuse an issue.* Chicago: University of Chicago Press.

Newberger, A. (1983). The helping hand strikes again: Unintended consequences of child abuse reporting. *Journal of Clinical Child Psychology, 12,* 307–312.

Newsweek. (July 13, 1987) p. 55.

Norris, C. (1987). Offenders with mental disease or defect: Implications of recent federal law. *American Journal of Forensic Psychology, 5*(3), 21–32.

O'Connell, J., & Carpenter, K. (1983). Payment for pain and suffering through history. *Insurance Counsel Journal, 50,* 411–417.

O'Connor v. Donaldson, 422 U.S. 563 (1975).

Olweus, D. (1980). The consistency issue in personality psychology revisited: With special reference to aggression. *British Journal of Social and Clinical Psychology, 19,* 377–390.

Orne, M. (1979). The use and misuse of hypnosis in court. *International Journal of Clinical and Experimental Hypnosis, 27,* 328–329.

Osborne, K. (1982). Sexual violence. In P. Feldman (Ed.), *Developments in the study of criminal behavior, vol. 2.* New York: John Wiley.

Padover, S. (1943). *The complete Jefferson.* New York: Duell, Sloan, & Pearce.

Pallis, C., & Bamji, A. (1979). McIlroy was here. Or was he? *British Medical Journal, 6169,* 973–975.

Palsgraf v. Long Island Railroad, 248 N.Y. 339, 162 N.E. 99 (1928).

Pankratz, L. (1981). A review of the Munchausen Syndrome. *Clinical Psychology Review, 1,* 65–78.

Pantle, M., Pasewark, R., & Steadman, H. (1980). Comparing institutional periods and subsequent arrest of insanity acquittees and convicted felons. *Journal of Psychiatry and Law, 8,* 305.

Pard v. U.S., 589 F. Supp. 518 (D. Ore 1984).

Parham v. J.R., 442 U.S. 584, 604 (1979).

Parsons, O., Butters, N., & Nathan, P. (Eds.) (1987). *Neuropsychology of alcoholism.* New York: Guilford.

Pasewark, R., Pantle, M., & Steadman, H. (1978). Characteristics and disposition of persons found not guilty by reason of insanity. *American Journal of Psychiatry, 136,* 655.

Pasewark, R., Randolph, J., & Bieber, D. (1984). Insanity plea: Statutory language and trial procedures. *Journal of Psychiatry and Law, 12,* 399.

Pasewark, R., & Seidenzahl, S. (1979). Opinions about the insanity plea and criminality among mental patients. *Bulletin of the American Academy of Psychiatry and Law, 7,* 199.

Pate v. Robinson, 383 U.S. 375 (1966).

Patterson, G. R. (1982). *A social learning approach, volume 3: Coercive family patterns.* Eugene, OR: Castalia.

Peele, S. (1984). The cultural context of psychological approaches to alcoholism. *American Psychologist, 39,* 1337–1351.

Pennsylvania v. Richie, 107 S.Ct. 989, 55 L.W. 4180 (1987).

Pennsylvania v. Walzack, 468 Pa. 210, 360 A.2d 914, 929 (1976).

People v. Lang, 26 Ill. App. 3d 648 (1975).

People v. McQuillan, 392 Mich. 511, 221 N.W.2d 569 (1974).

People v. Poddar, 16 C.3d 750, 518 P.2d 342 (1974).

Peters, R., Miller, K., Schmidt, W., & Meeter, D. (1987). The effects of statutory change on the civil commitment of the mentally ill. *Law and Human Behavior, 11*(2), 73–99.

Petersilia, J. (1980). Criminal career research: A review of recent evidence. In N. Morris & M. Tonry (Eds.), *Crime and justice: An annual review of research, vol. 2.* Chicago: University of Chicago Press.

Petrila, J. (1982). The insanity defense and other mental dispositions in Missouri. *International Journal of Law and Psychiatry, 5*(1), 81.

Pfeiffer, L., Eisenstein, J., & Dabbs, J. (1967). Mental competency evaluations for federal courts. *Journal of Nervous and Mental Disease, 144,* 320.

Pierce v. Georgia, 254 S.E. 2d 838 (1979).

Pisel v. Stamford Hospital, 180 Conn. 314, 430 A.2d 1 (1980).

Pleak, R. R., & Applebaum, P. S. (1985). The clinician's role in protecting patient's rights in guardianship proceedings. *Hospital & Community Psychiatry, 36,* 77–79.

Pogrebin, G., Regoli, I., & Perry, L. (1986). Not guilty by reason of insanity: A research note. *International Journal of Law and Psychiatry, 8,* 237–248.

Pope, K. S., Levenson, H., & Schover, L. R. (1979). Sexual intimacy in psychology training: Results and implications of a national survey. *American Psychologist, 34,* 682–689.

Psychiatric News. (Nov. 4, 1983). APA malpractice claim types remain constant but frequency, costs have doubled.

Poss, S., & Johnson, S. (1987). Use of the grade of membership (GOM) technique in review of federal pretrial forensic evaluations for competency to stand trial and criminal responsibility. (Unpublished manuscript).

Powell v. Texas, 392 U.S. 514 (1968).

Prasad, A., & Oswald, A. (1985). Munchausen's syndrome: An annotation. *Acta Psychiatrica Scandinavia, 72,* 319–322.

Prentky, R., & Knight, R. (1986). Impulsivity in the lifestyle and criminal behavior of sexual offenders. *Criminal Justice and Behavior, 13,* 141–164.

Quay, H. (Ed.) (1987). *Handbook of juvenile delinquency.* New York: John Wiley.

Quinsey, V., & Ambtman, R. (1978). Psychiatric assessment of the dangerousness of mentally ill offenders. *Criminal Justice, 6*(4), 249–257.

Rachlin, S. (1978). One right too many. *Bulletin of the American Academy of Psychiatry and Law, 3,* 99.

Rachman, S. (1980). *Obsessions and compulsions.* Englewood Cliffs, NJ: Prentice-Hall.

Rada, R., Laws, D., & Kellner, R. (1976). Plasma testosterone levels in the rapist. *Psychosomatic Medicine, 38,* 257–268.

Raymond v. Cotner, 120 N.W. 2d 892 (1963).

Reed, R. (1984). Personal communication.

Reid, W., Dorr, D., Walker, J., & Bonner, J. (Eds.) (1986) Unmasking the psychopath. New York: W. W. Norton.

Rennie v. Klein, 462 F. Supp. 1131 (D. N.J., 1978).

Rivers v. Katz, 504 N.Y.S. 2d 74 (1986).

Robinson v. California, 370 U.S. 660, 8L Ed.2d 758, 82 S.Ct. 1417 (1962).

Roche, J.P. (Feb. 6, 1956). A sane view of non-conformity. *New Republic*.

Rock v. Arkansas, 107 S.Ct. 989, 55 L.W. 4925 (1987).

Roe v. Doe, 429 U.S. 589 (1974).

Roesch, R. & Golding, S. (1980). *Competency to Stand Trial*. Urbana, IL: University of Illinois Press.

Roesch, R. et al. (1984). Fitness to stand interview test: How four professions rate videotaped fitness interviews. *International Journal of Law and Psychiatry, 7*, 115.

Rogers, R., Dolmetsch, R., & Cavanaugh, W. (1981). An empirical approach to insanity evaluations. *Journal of Clinical Psychology, 37*, 683.

Roman, M., & Haddad, W. (1978). *The Disposable Parent*. New York: Holt, Reinhart & Winston.

Rosen, A., Rekers, G., & Bentler, P. (1978). Ethical issues in the treatment of children. *Journal of Social Issues, 34*, 60–72.

Rosen, J. (1953). *Direct analysis*. New York: Grune & Stratton.

Rosenburg, A., & McGarry, A. (1972). Competency for trial: The making of an expert. *American Journal of Psychiatry, 128*, 82.

Roth, L. (1979). A commitment law for patients, doctors and lawyers. *American Journal of Psychiatry, 136*, 1121–1127.

Rouse v. Cameron, 373 F.2d 451 (D.C. Cir., 1966).

Roy, A. (1987). Five risk factors for depression. *British Journal of Psychiatry, 150*, 536–541.

Rubenstein, L. (1986). Making decisions about criminal responsibility: The more things change . . . In Everstine, L. & Everstine, D. (Eds.), *Psychotherapy and the law*. Orlando, FL: Grune & Stratton.

Ruman, M., & Lamm, M. G. (1985). Mediation: Its implications for children and divorce. In D. H. Schetky & E. P. Benedek (Eds.), *Emerging issues in child psychiatry and the law*. New York: Brunner/Mazel.

Rutter, M. (1987). Temperament, personality and personality disorder. *British Journal of Psychiatry, 150*, 443–458.

Sandler, J. (1985). Aversion methods. In F. Kanter & A. Goldstein (Eds.), *Helping people change*. New York: Pergamon.

Santosky v. Kramer, 50 U.S.L.W. 4333 (1982).

Sayre, A. (1932). Mens Rea, *Harvard Law Review, 45*, 974–1004.

Schachter, D. (1986). Amnesia and crime: How much do we really know? *American Psychologist, 43*, 286–295.

Schmidt, W. C. (1984). The evolution of a public guardianship program. *Journal of Psychiatry and Law, 12*, 349.

Schneidman, E. (1985). *Definition of suicide*. New York: John Wiley.

Schuckit, M. (1986). Genetic and clinical implications of alcoholism and affective disorder. *The American Journal of Psychiatry, 143*, 140–147.

Schulman, M. (1980). *A survey of spousal violence against women in Kentucky*. Washington: Law Enforcement Assistance Administration.

Schuman, D. C. (1986). False allegations of physical and sexual abuse. *Bulletin of the American Academy of Psychiatry and the Law, 14*(1), 5–21.

Schwartz, M. (1987). *Biofeedback*. New York: Guilford.

Schwitzgebel, R., & Schwitzgebel, R. (1980). *Law and psychological practice*. New York: John Wiley.

Scovern, A., & Kilmann, P. (1980). Status of electroconvulsive therapy: Review of the outcome literature. *Psychological Bulletin, 87*, 260–303.

Sgroi, S. M. (1982). *Handbook of clinical intervention in child sexual abuse*. Lexington, MA: Lexington Books.

Shah, S. A. (1978). Dangerousness: A paradigm for exploring some issues in law and psychology. *American Psychologist, 33*, 224–238.

Shannon, L. W. (1978). A longitudinal study of delinquency and crime. In C. Wellford (Ed.), *Quantitative studies in criminology*. Beverly Hills, CA: Sage.

Shapiro, D. L. (1984). *Psychological evaluation and expert testimony*. New York: Van Nostrand Reinhold.

Shapiro, D. L. (1986). Criminal responsibility: An integrative model. In Everstine, L. & Everstine, D. (Eds.), *Psychotherapy and the law*. Orlando, FL: Grune & Stratton.

Shaw v. Glickman, 415 a.2d.625 (Md. Spec. Ct. App. 1980).

Simon, R. (1967). *The jury and the defense of insanity*. Boston: Little Brown.

Simon, S. (1987). Personal communication.

Sinclair v. State, 116 Miss. 142, 132 So. 581 (1931).

Singer, J., & Kolligan, J. (1987). Personality: Developments in the study of private experience. *Annual Review of Psychology, 1987*. Palo Alto, CA: Annual Reviews Inc.

Skafte, D. (1985). *Child custody evaluations*. Beverly Hills, CA: Sage.

Skodol, A., & Karasu, T. (1978). Emergency psychiatry and the assaultive patient. *American Journal of Psychiatry, 135*, 202–205.

Slawson, P. F., & Guggenheim, F. G. (1984). Psychiatric malpractice: A review of the national loss experience. *American Journal of Psychiatry, 141*(8), 979–981.

Slobogin, C. (1985). The guilty but mentally ill verdict: An idea whose time should not have come. *George Washington Law Review, 53*, 494.

Slovenko, R. (1973). *Psychiatry and Law*. Boston: Little Brown.

Slovenko, R. (1987). The developing law on competency to stand trial. In Everstine, L. & Everstine, D. (Eds.), *Psychotherapy and the law*. Orlando, FL: Grune & Stratton.

Smith v. Estelle, 602 F.2d 694 (5th Cir. 1979).

Smith, R. (1979). *Privacy*. Garden City, NY: Anchor Press/Doubleday.

Smith, R., & Smith, C. (1981). Child rearing and single parent fathers. *Family Relations, 30*, 411–417.

Smith, S. R. (1987). Recent Supreme Court decision and psychology. *Bulletin of the American Academy of Forensic Psychology, 8*(1), 1–7.

Smith S. R., & Meyer, R. G. (1984). Child abuse reporting laws: A time for reconsideration. *International Journal of Law and Psychiatry, 7*, 351–360.

Smith, S. R., & Meyer, R. G. (1987). *Law, behavior and mental health: Policy and practice*. New York: New York University Press.

Solomon v. Solomon, 13 Ohio 517 (1903).

Sonne, J., Meyers, C. B., Borys, D., & Marshall, V. (1985). Client's reactions to sexual intimacy in therapy. *American Journal of Orthopsychiatry, 55*(2), 183–191.

Sparr, L., & Atkinson, R. (1986). Post-traumatic stress disorder as an insanity defense. *American Journal of Psychiatry, 143*, 608–613.

Spaulding, W. J. (1985). Testamentary competency: Reconciling doctrine with the role of the expert witness. *Law and Human Behavior, 9*, 113.

Squire, L., Slater, P., & Miller, P. (1981). Retrograde amnesia and bilateral ECT. *Archives of General Psychiatry, 38*, 89–95.

Stanford Law Review. (1978). Special project: Where the public peril begins: A survey of psychotherapists to determine the effects of *Tarasoff*. *Stanford Law Review, 31*, 165–190.

State of Wisconsin ex rel Jones and Galacia v. Gerhardstein, No. 85-1718 (Wis. Ct. App., Oct. 28, 1986).

State v. Carter, 641 S.W.2d 54 (Mo., 1982) *cert. denied*, 461 U.S. 932 (1983).

State v. Guatney, 207 Neb. 501, 299 N.W. 2d 538 (1980).

Steadman, H. J. (1977). A new look at recidivism among the Patuxent inmates. *The Bulletin of the American Academy of Psychiatry and the Law, 5* 200–209.

Steadman, H. J. (1981). Special problems in the prediction of violence among the mentally ill. In J. R. Hays, T. K. Roberts, & K. S. Solway (Eds.), *Violence and the violent individual*. New York: Spectrum.

Steadman, H. J., & Braff, J. (1974). Effects of incompetency determination on subsequent criminal processing: Implications for due process. *Catholic University Law Review, 23*, 754.

Steadman,. H. J., & Braff, J. (1975). Crimes of violence and incompetency diversion, *Journal of Criminal Law and Criminology, 66*, 73.

Steadman, H. J., & Cocozza, J. (1974). *Careers of the Criminally Insane.* Lexington, MA: Lexington Books.

Steadman, H. J., Keitner, L., Braff, J., & Arvanites, T. M. (1983). Factors associated with a successful insanity plea. *American Journal of Psychiatry, 140*, 401-405.

Steadman, H. J., Monahan, J., Hartstone, E., Davis, S., & Robbins, P. (1982). Mentally disordered offenders: A national survey of patients and facilities. *Law and Human Behavior, 6*, 31.

Steinkuehler v. Wempner, 169 Ind. 154, 81 N.E. 482 (1907).

Steinman, S. (1981). The experience of children in a joint custody arrangement: A report of a study. *American Journal of Orthopsychiatry, 51*(3), 403-414.

Steinman, S. (1985). Joint custody: The need for individual evaluation and service. In D. H. Schetky & E. P. Benedek (Eds.), *Emerging issues in child psychiatry and the law.* New York: Brunner/Mazel.

Steketee, G., & Foa, E. (1987). Rape victims: Post-traumatic stress responses and their treatment. *Journal of Anxiety Disorders, 1*, 69-86.

Stone, A. (1976a). *Mental health and the law: A system in transition.* New York: Aronson.

Stone, A. (1976b). The Tarasoff decisions: Suing psychotherapists to safeguard society. *Harvard Law Review, 90*, 358-378.

Stone, A. (1985). The new legal standard of dangerousness: Fair in theory, unfair in practice. In C. D. Webster, M. H. Ben-Aron, & S. J. Hucker (Eds.) *Dangerousness.* New York: Cambridge University Press.

Stone v. Proctor, 259 N.C. 633, 131 S.E. 2d 297 (1963).

Strauss, M., Gelles, R., & Steinmetz, S. (1980). *Behind closed doors: Violence in the American family.* Garden City, NY: Anchor Books/Doubleday.

Streiner, D., & Miller, H. (1981). Prorating incomplete Wiggins and MacAndrew Scales. *Journal of Personality Assessment, 45*, 427-429.

Stromberg, C. (1987). Psychic Harm, *Register Report, 13*(2), 3-5.

Stromberg, C., & Stone, A. (1983). A model state law on civil commitment of the mentally ill. *Harvard Journal of Legislation, 20*, 275-277.

Strupp, H. H., & Hadley, S. W. (1977, March). A tri-partite model of mental health and therapeutic outcomes. *American Psychologist, 32*, 187-196.

Szasz, T. (1977). *Psychiatric slavery.* New York: Free Press.

Szasz, T. (1986). *Insanity.* New York: Free Press.

Tarasoff v. Regents of the University of California, 551 P.2d.334 (1976).

Taub, S. (1986). Tardive dyskinesia: Medical facts and legal fictions. *Saint Louis University Law Journal, 30*, 833-874.

Taylor, P. J., & Gunn, J. (1984). Violence and psychosis I: Risk of violence among psychotic men. *British Medical Journal, 288*, 1945-1949.

Taylor, P. J. (1985). Motives for offending among violent and psychotic men. *British Journal of Psychiatry, 147*, 491-498.

Taylor, S. P., & Leonard, K. E. (1982). Alcohol and human physical aggression. In R. G. Green & E. I. Donnerstein (Eds.), *Aggression: Theoretical and empirical reviews.* New York: Academic Press.

Teplin, A. (1985). The criminality of the mentally ill: A dangerous misconception. *American Journal of Psychiatry, 142*, 593.

Thompson v. County of Alameda, 27 Cal.3d.741 (1980).

Thornberry, T., & Jacoby, J. (1979). *The Criminally Insane: A Community Follow-up of Mentally Ill Offenders.* Chicago: University of Chicago Press.

Thyer, B., & Himle, J. (1987). Phobic anxiety and panic anxiety. *Journal of Anxiety Disorders, 1*, 59-68.

Trepper, T., & Barrett, M. (1986). *Treating incest.* Nework: Haworth.

Turkat, I. (1985). Formulation of paranoid personality disorder. In I. Turkat (Ed.), *Behavioral case formulation.* New York: Plenum.

Turner v. Safley, 107 S.Ct. 2554, 55 L.W. 4719 (1987).
Tuter v. Tuter, 120 S.W. 2d. 203 (1938).
U.S. Department of Commerce. (1984). *Statistical abstract of the United States, 80.*
U.S. Study on Child Abuse and Neglect, (1981). *National study of the incidence and severity of child abuse and neglect.* Washington, D.C.: U.S. Government Printing Office.
United States v. Brawner, 471 F.2d 969 (D.C. Cir., 1972).
United States v. Freeman, 357 F.2d 619 (1954).
United States v. Salerno, 107 S.Ct., 55 L.W. 4663 (1987).
Underwager, R., Wakefield, H., Legrand, R., Bartz, C. S., & Erickson, J. (August, 1986). The role of the psychologist in the assessment of cases of alleged sexual abuse of children. Paper presented at convention of the American Psychological Association, Washington, DC.
United States Code, (1984) Title 18, Section 20 (a) Federal Rules of Evidence, 704(b). (as amended by public law 98-473).
University of Chicago Law Review (1985). Antipsychotic drugs and fitness to stand trial: The right of the unfit accused to refuse treatment (Editorial Comment) *Volume 52*, 773.
Vaillant, G. (1983). *The natural history of alcoholism: Causes, patterns, and paths to recovery.* Cambridge, MA: Harvard University Press.
Van Hasselt, V., Milliones, J., & Hersen, M. (1981). Behavioral assessment of drug addiction: Strategies and issues in research and treatment. *The International Journal of the Addictions, 16,* 43–68.
Victorian Railways Commission v. Coultas, 13 Acas. 222, 57 L.J.P.C. 69 (P.C. 1888).
Virkunen, M. (1975). Victim-precipitated pedophilia offenses. *British Journal of Criminology, 15,* 175–179.
Walker, L. (Ed.) (1987). *Handbook on sexual abuse of children.* New York: Springer.
Walker, N. D. (1983). Protecting people. In J. W. Hinton (Ed.), *Dangerousness: Problems of assessment and prediction.* Boston: George Allen & Unwin.
Walker, P. (1978). The role of antiandrogens in the treatment of sex offenders. In B. Qualls, J. Wincze, & D. Barlow (Eds.), *The prevention of seuxal disorders.* New York: Plenum.
Walker, P., & Meyer, W. (1981). Medroxyprogesterone acetate treatment for paraphiliac sex offenders. In J. Hays, T. Roberts, & K. Solway (Eds.), *Violence and the violent individual.* New York: SP Books.
Waller, J. (1987). Injury: Conceptual shifts and preventive implications. In L. Breslow (Ed.), *Annual review of public health, 1987.* Palo Alto, CA: Annual Reviews Inc.
Wallerstein, J. C., & Kelly, J. B. (1980). *Surviving the break-up: How parents and children cope with divorce.* New York: Basic Books.
Warshack, R. A., & Santrock, J. W. (1983). The impact of divorce in father custody and mother custody homes: The child's perspective. In L. A. Kurdek (Ed.), *Children and divorce: New directions for child development.* (No. 19) San Francisco: Josey-Bass.
Warshack, R. A., & Santrock, J. W. (March, 1979). The effects of father and mother custody on children's social development. Paper presented at the Society for Research in Child Development Meeting, San Francisco, CA.
Washington, v. United States, 129 U.S. App., D.C. 29 (1967).
Washton, A., & Gold, M. (1987). *Cocaine: A clinician's handbook*, New York: Guilford.
Waube v. Warrington (199 N.W. 2d 678 (M.D. 1972)).
Weiner, B. (1982). *American Medical News*, Aug. 6, 1982.
Weiner, B. A., Simons, V. A., & Cavanaugh, J. L. (1985). The child custody dispute. In D. H. Schetky & E. P. Benedek (Eds.), *Emerging issues in child psychiatry and the law.* New York: Brunner/Mazel.
Weiner, I., & Hess, A. (Eds.) (1987). *Handbook of forensic psychology.* New York: John Wiley.
Weisberg, R., & Wald, M. (1987). Confidentiality laws and state efforts to protect abused or neglected children: The need for statutory reform. In L. Everstine and D. S. Everstine (Eds.) *Psychotherapy and the law.* Orlando, FL: Grune and Stratton.
Weissman, H. (1985). Psycholegal standards and the role of psychological assessment in personal injury litigation. *Behavioral Sciences and the Law, 3,* 135–148.

Weitzman, L. J., & Dixon, R. B. (1979). Child custody awards. *University of California, Davis Law Review, 12*, 473-521.

Wells, G. (1986). Expert psychological testimony: Empirical and conceptual analyses of effects. *Law and Human Behavior, 10*, 83.

Wessel, M., & McCullough, W. (1982). Bereavement—An etiological factor in peptic ulcer in childhood and adolescence. *Journal of Adolescent Health Care, 2*, 287-288.

Whittington, H. (1982). Role of the psychiatrist in personal injury litigation. *Journal of Psychiatry and Law, 10*, 419-440.

Wicksramsekera, I. (1976). Aversive behavior rehearsal for sexual exhibitionism. In I. Wicksramsekera (Ed.), *Biofeedback, behavior therapy, and hypnosis*. Chicago: Nelson-Hall.

Widiger, T., Frances, A., Warner, L., & Bluhm, C. (1986). Diagnostic criteria for the borderline and schizotypal personality disorders. *Journal of Abnormal Psychology, 95*, 43-51.

Wigmore, J. (1970). *Evidence*. Boston: Little Brown.

Williams v. Mashburn. 602 P.2d. 1036 (1979).

Williams, J. (1983). Child abuse reconsidered: The urgency of authentic prevention. *Journal of Clinical Child Psychology, 12*, 312-315.

Wilson v. United States, 391 F.2d 460 (D.C. Cir. 1968).

Wilson, J. Q., & Herrnstein, R. J. (1985). *Crime and Human Nature*. New York: Simon & Schuster.

Winer, D. (1978). Anger and dissociation: A case study of multiple personality. *Journal of Abnormal Psychology, 87*, 368-372.

Winick, B. J. (1977). Psychotropic medication and competency to stand trial. *American Bar Foundation Research Journal*, 769.

Winick, B. J. (1985). Restructing competency to stand trial. *UCLA Law Review, 32*, 921.

Winslade, W. J. (1987). After *Tarasoff*: Therapist liability and patient confidentiality. In L. Everstine and D. S. Everstine (Eds.), *Psychotherapy and the law*. Orlando, FL: Grune and Stratton.

Wisconsin v. Yoder, 406 U.S. 205 (1972).

Wolfgang, M., & Ferracuti, F. (1967). *The subculture of violence*. Beverly Hills, CA: Sage.

Wolfgang, M., & Tracy, P. E. (1982). The 1945 and 1958 birth cohorts: A comparison of the prevalence, incidence, and severity of delinquent behvior. Paper presented to the Conference on Public Danger, Dangerous Offenders, and the Criminal Justice System, Kennedy School of Government, Harvard University.

Wolfgang, M., & Weiner, N. A. (1982). Patterns in injurious and violent delinquency in a birth cohort: A preliminary analysis. In J. Q. Wilson, & R. J. Herrnstein (1985) *Crime and human nature*. New York: Simon & Schuster.

Wolfgang, M., Figlio, R. F., & Sellin, T. (1972). *Delinquency in a birth cohort*. Chicago: University of Chicago Press.

Wolpe, J. (1987). Carbon dioxide inhalation treatments of neurotic anxiety. *The Journal of Nervous and Mental Disease, 175*, 129-133.

Woodman, D. D. (1983). Biological perspectives of 'dangerousness.' In J. W. Hinton (Ed.), *Dangerousness: Problems of assessment and prediction*. Boston: George Allen & Unwin.

Wormith, J. (1986). Assessing deviant sexual arousal. *Advance in Behavior Research, 8*, 101-109.

Wulach, J. S. (1980). The incompetency plea: Abuses and reforms. *Journal of Psychiatry and Law, 8*, 317-328.

Wyatt v. Stickney, 325 F. Supp. 781 (M.D. Ala., 1971).

Yochelson, S. & Samenow, S. (1976). *The criminal mind*. New York: Jason Aronson.

Zander, T. (1976). Civil commitment in Wisconsin: The impact of *Lessard v. Schmidt*. *University of Wisconsin Law Review*, 503-562.

Zeig, J. (Ed.) (1987). *The evolution of psychotherapy*. New York: Brunner/Mazel.

Zipkin v. Freeman, 436 S.W.2d.753 (Mo. 1968).

Ziskin, J. (1981). *Coping with psychiatric and psychological testimony*, 3rd edition. Venice, CA: Law and Psychology Press.

Zlotnick, A. (1981). First do no harm: Least restrictive alternative analysis and the right of mental patients to refuse treatment. *West Virginia Law Review, 83*, 376.

Zuckerman, M., Buchsbaum, M., & Murphy, D. (1980). Sensation seeking and its biological correlates. *Psychological Bulletin, 88*, 187–214.

Index